William Nicholson

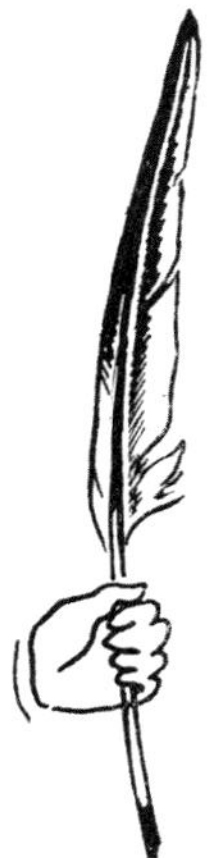

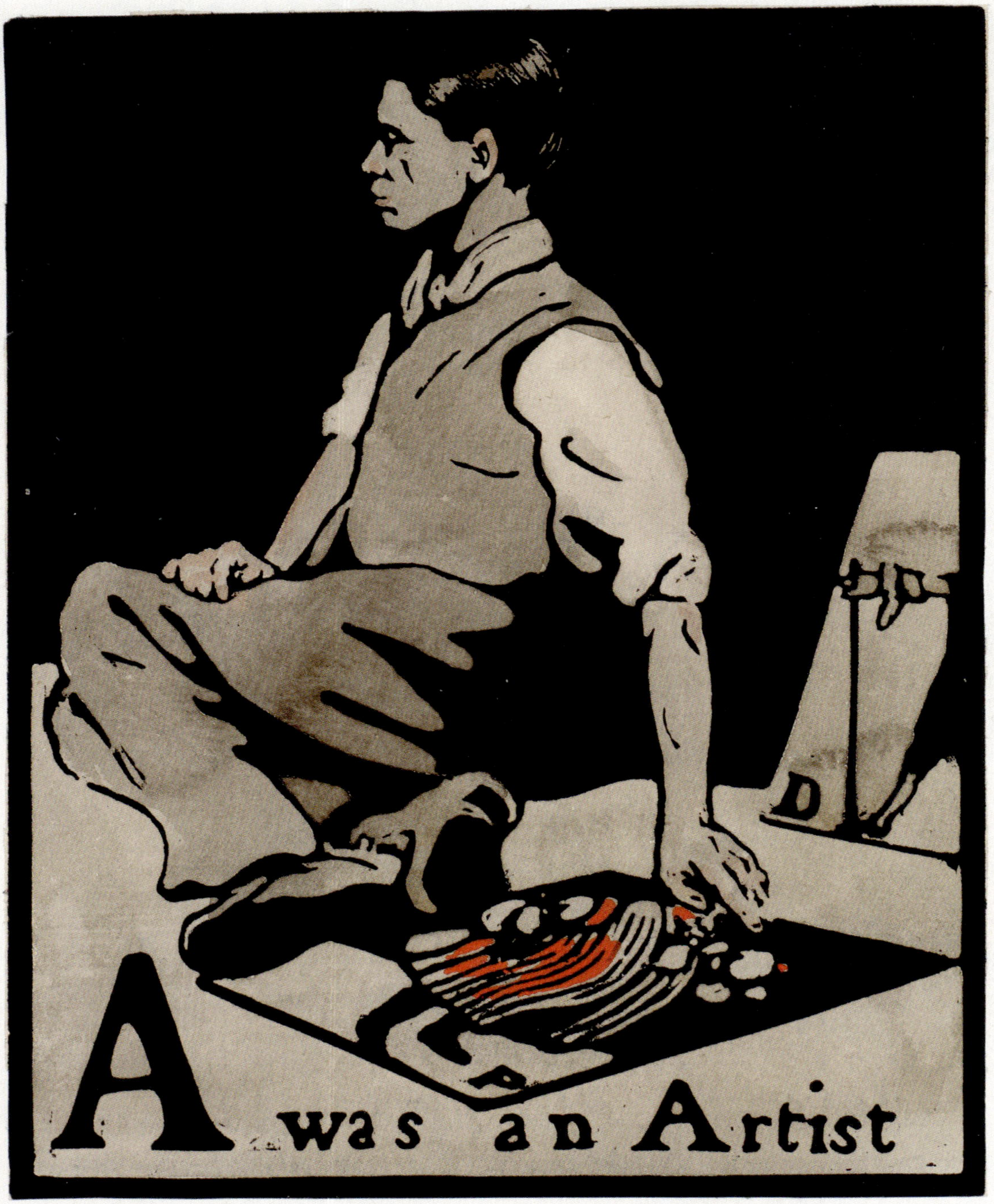

D
A was an Artist

William Nicholson

EDITED BY
Simon Martin &
Melanie Vandenbrouck

Pallant House Gallery

William Nicholson, Pallant House Gallery,
22 November 2025 – 10 May 2026

Pallant House Gallery
8–9 North Pallant
Chichester
West Sussex PO19 1TJ
United Kingdom
+44(0) 1243 774557
www.pallant.org.uk

British cataloguing in Publication Data
A catalogue record for this book is available
from the British Library

ISBN: 978-1-869827-64-9

Designed by Adrian Hunt
Set in Kepler
Printed in the UK by Gomer Press Ltd

Distributed for Pallant House Gallery by
Yale University Press, New Haven and London

Authorised Representative in the EU: Easy Access System Europe, Mustamäe tee 50, 10621 Tallinn, Estonia, gpsr.requests@easproject.com

p.2
1 *A was an Artist*
From *An Alphabet*, William Heinemann, London, 1897
Hand-coloured woodcut on paper, 24.6 x 19.8cm
Private collection

Pallant House Gallery's exhibitions are the keystone of the Gallery's activities: bringing the curious from far and wide, placing our collections into context, providing a showcase for new research supported by scholarly yet accessible high-quality publications, life-long learning opportunities for creative engagement, and enjoyment and inspiration for thousands of individuals from all backgrounds. This is all made possible with the generosity of our Partners, Patrons, Friends and benefactors. Thank you to the following supporters, who have been instrumental in making this season a reality.

EXHIBITION SUPPORTERS

Presenting Partner
evelyn PARTNERS

Foundations and Trusts
The Finnis Scott Foundation
The Michael Marks Charitable Trust

Gallery Partners
Piano Nobile Gallery, London
Patrick Bourne & Co.
Richard Green Gallery, London

Corporate Partner
Howden

GALLERY SUPPORTERS

Principal Partner
DREWEATTS EST. 1759

Civic Partner
Chichester District Council

Major Partner
SOFAS & STUFF

Exhibition Circle
Judy Addison Smith
John Austin
George and Jane Blunden
Edward and Victoria Bonham Carter
The John Booth Charitable Foundation
Vanessa Branson
Mark Burch
John and Susan Coldstream
Jolyon and Christine Drury
Derek and Christine Dunton
Jonathan and Jacqueline Gestetner
Marion Gibbs CBE
Jeremy Gould and Julia Prescot CBE
Jamie Korner OBE and Julia Korner
Gordon and Louise Lawson
Charles and Sarah Martin
Jillie and Peter Moss
Gareth Neame OBE DL
David and Deborah Stileman
Paul and Sandy Thornton
Hugh and Clare Twiss
Angela Wormald

And all those who wish to remain anonymous

CONTENTS

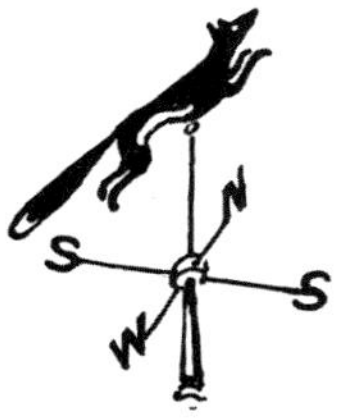

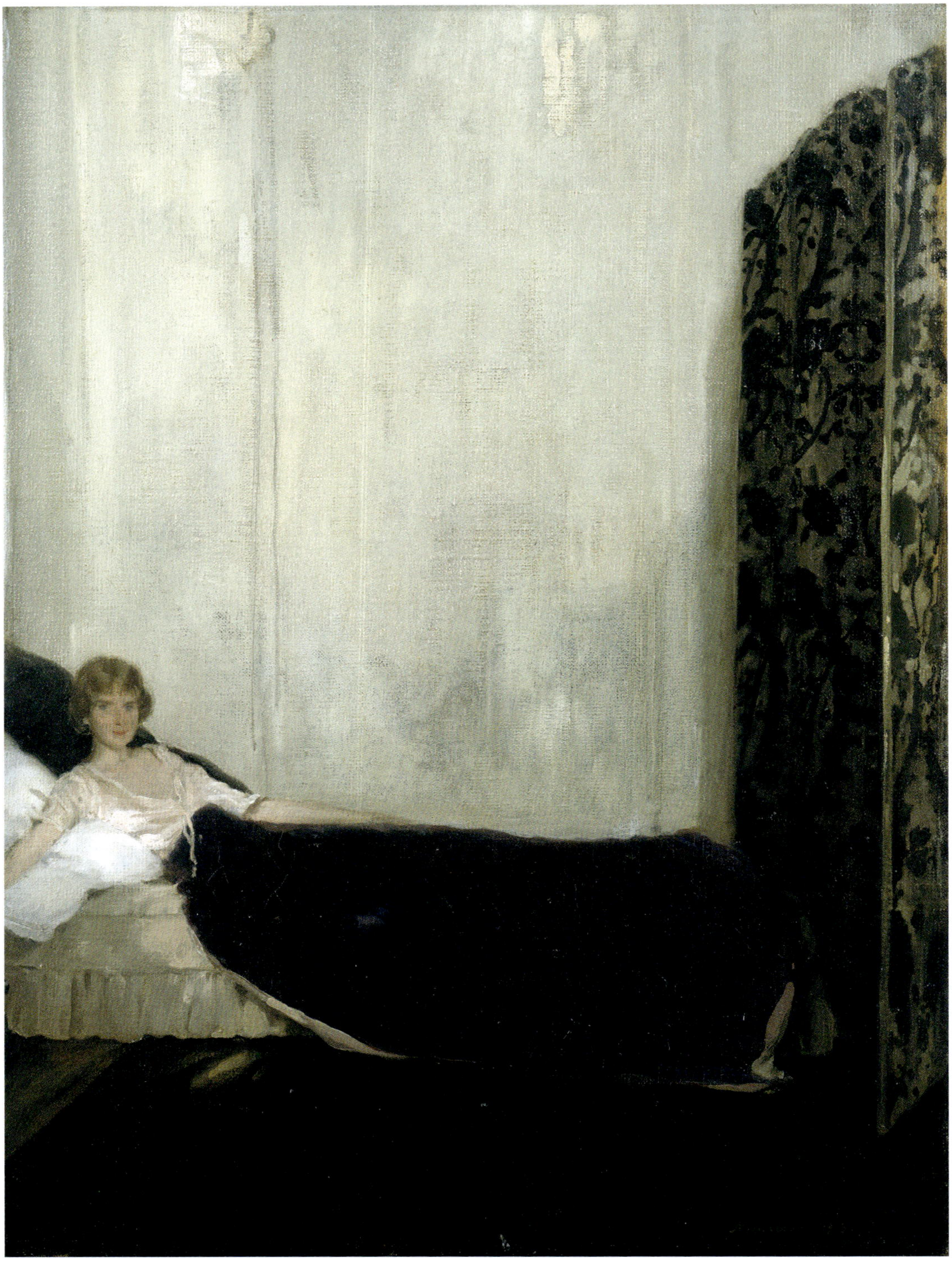

2 *Sybil Hart-Davis*, 1913
Oil on canvas, 86.5 x 63.5cm
Private collection

DIRECTOR'S FOREWORD

SIMON MARTIN

In an article in *Country Life* in 2017, Her Majesty Queen Camilla (then the Duchess of Cornwall) chose Sir William Nicholson's *Gold Jug* (1937; see p.8) from the Royal Collection as her favourite picture, commenting that, 'I can never pass it without stopping to marvel at the way the artist catches the play of light on the jug's lustrous surface.' Many of us would undoubtedly share that sense of wonder at Nicholson's bravura handling of paint. We are therefore hugely honoured that His Majesty The King agreed to lend his painting to the Pallant House Gallery exhibition, enabling it to be seen in the context of the artist's wider work, together with loans from national institutions, regional museums, private collections and the artist's family: we are grateful to each of them.

It is over 20 years since the last major museum exhibition dedicated to Nicholson, at the Royal Academy of Arts in 2004, coinciding with the publication of Sanford Schwartz's biography, which was followed by Patricia Reed's catalogue raisonné of the oil paintings in 2011. Whilst there have been exhibitions exploring other aspects of his life and art, such as *Beggarstaffs: William Nicholson & James Pryde* at the Fitzwilliam Museum, Cambridge, in 2019, and another at his former home in Rottingdean, Sussex, in 2022, the current exhibition aims to present Nicholson in the round, considering his extraordinary virtuosity across the different forms of artistic creativity to which he turned his hand: as poster artist, printmaker, book illustrator and theatre designer, not to mention as painter of sublime still lifes, landscapes and portraits, or indeed his distinctive self-presentation.

Through our exhibitions and activities Pallant House Gallery seeks to provide new perspectives on Modern British art. This book features several specially commissioned essays on different aspects of Nicholson's work, and I am grateful to my fellow authors for their contributions: Stephen Calloway, Miriam O'Connor Perks, Jane Pritchard, Patricia Reed and Melanie Vandenbrouck. Among these, Patricia Reed has provided invaluable expertise and was instrumental in securing key loans to the exhibition. This book could not have been realised without project manager Harriet Olsen, designer Adrian Hunt, copy editor and indexer Alexandra Pel and Mark Eastment and his colleagues at our distributors, Yale University Press.

A great many individuals and institutions have assisted with the research and logistics for the exhibition – these are each mentioned in the Acknowledgements. I would like to recognise the artist's family members, in particular Desmond and Di Banks, Lady Bowness and Dr Sophie Bowness and Tim and Catherine Nicholson.

We are appreciative of the financial support that has made such an ambitious exhibition possible: our Presenting Partner, Evelyn Partners; the members of the Exhibition Circle (listed on the imprint page); our Supporting Partners, The Finnis Scott Foundation and The Michael Marks Charitable Foundation; our Gallery Partners, Piano Nobile Gallery, Patrick Bourne & Co. and Richard Green Gallery; our Paint Partner, The Little Greene Paint Company; and the Friends, Patrons and Supporters of Pallant House Gallery. Finally, I extend my sincere gratitude to our dedicated Trustees and Volunteers and all my colleagues at Pallant House Gallery, who go the extra mile to realise ambitious exhibitions of consistently high quality.

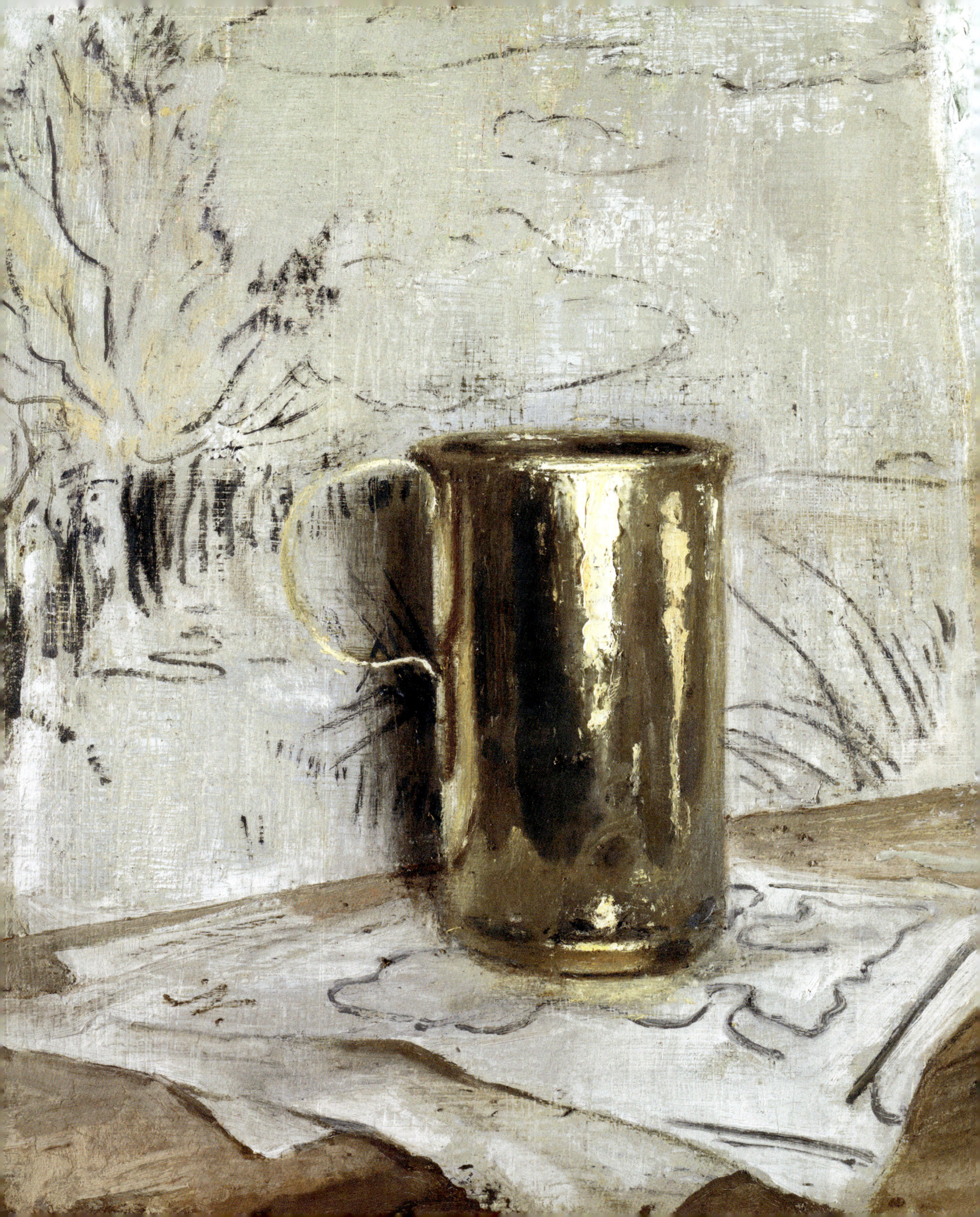

1 WILLIAM NICHOLSON: THE ILLUSIONIST

SIMON MARTIN

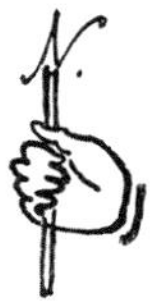

'"Must learn to observe."
This maxim is as perfect for a painter as for a scientist.'[1]

As an artist, Sir William Nicholson (1872–1949) was primarily concerned with the act of observation as something that could be both poetic and analytic. He was able to represent the gleam of a reflection in a lustrous vessel in the most understated, yet lyrical manner: capturing the momentary fall of light, but somehow also making it timeless. He was not interested in expounding avant-garde theories or working to a manifesto – he wrote none, claiming that, 'It is difficult to rebuild in words what one records in paint.'[2] If one is to look for a connecting thread across his long artistic career, which spanned from the Victorian period to the 1940s, it is perhaps in what the ancient Greeks called 'scopophilia': an aesthetic pleasure to be drawn from looking at an object or person;[3] that pleasure to be taken from looking at beautiful things, at the interplay of light and dark, shadows and shapes, patterns and forms. Just as laughter can be infectious, so too Nicholson's evident enjoyment in looking and painting can be felt and shared by the viewers of his works, which has made him one of the most singular and much-loved Modern British artists. Arguably, a sense of playfulness underpins much of his work, whether in the traditional genres of portraiture, still life or landscape or in poster design, book illustration, printmaking, stage and costume design and, not least, in his dandified sense of dress and self-presentation. Only an artist with an instinct for play could have spent hour upon hour drawing intricate ink designs over the entire surface of a cotton dress (fig.35) or creating a *Glove Letter* for his sweetheart (c.1920s; private collection). The artist's youngest daughter, Elizabeth [Liza], wrote of how he liked working, 'as if he were playing a game with the view, with the flowers in mugs and jugs, with the lights and shades, shapes and spaces, in the same way as he played tennis – as if the landscape

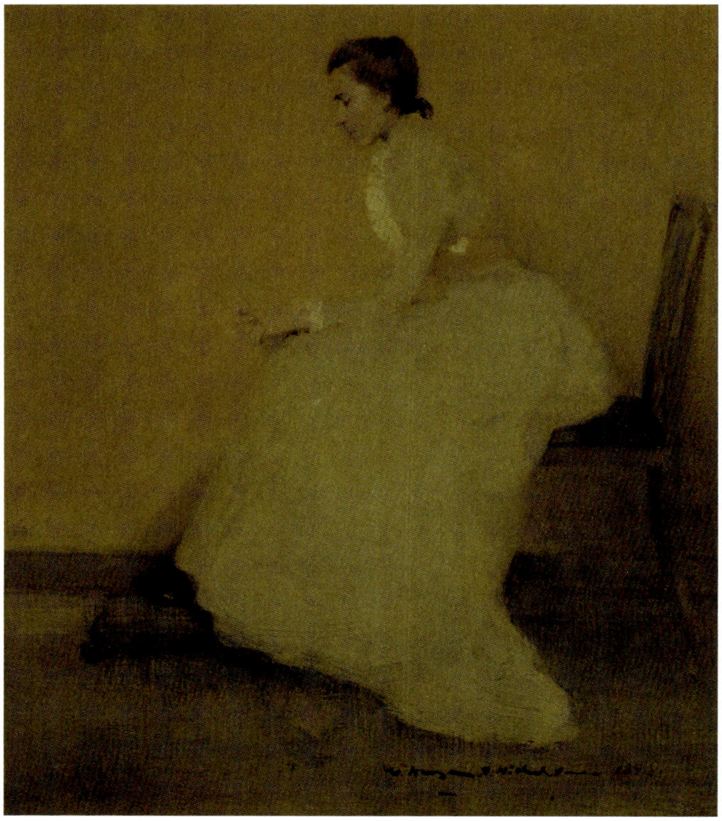

p.8 Detail of *Gold Jug*, lent by His Majesty The King, fig.113

3 *Lady in Yellow* (believed to be Mabel Pryde), 1893
Oil on canvas, 72.5 x 62cm
Private collection

or still life were bouncing back and playing ball with him'.[4] And yet despite this evident playfulness, his 'delicious whimsicality' and 'subtle humour', in the words of Stanley Kennedy North, at the same time Nicholson's painting could be 'uncommonly serious'.[5]

Although Nicholson was one of the most admired and technically assured painters of modern times, critics and art historians have often struggled to know how, and where, to place him in the history of art. In 1967 an article in *The Times* declared that: 'One of the unsolved problems of European art is the true status of William Nicholson',[6] whilst the artist's biographer Sanford Schwartz wrote of the 'beckoning challenge' created by the 'uncategorizable nature of his work, and the seeming anonymity of his voice, combined with Nicholson's undeniable mastery',[7] suggesting that for international audiences, in particular, he may represent 'one of the Sleeping Beauties of English art'.[8]

Nicholson was an independent voice who stood apart from joining groups or artist organisations, and his work appears largely untouched by the sweep of successive movements, such as post-impressionism, cubism, vorticism, futurism, surrealism and so on. At times, Nicholson could be viewed as closer to the continent in approach, with *The Daily Telegraph* noting in 1903 that he was 'not wholly an English artistic personality'.[9] Yet, after his death his daughter-in-law, the artist Winifred Nicholson (née Roberts; 1893–1981), was to recall how, 'He became as English as Hogarth and reaches as high a point of excellence. The doors are shut on Cubism, on Guernica, on Post-Impressionism even. He is painting still lifes at the same time as that other still-life painter across the Channel, Braque – and the doors are closed between them.'[10]

On occasion he was described as a *petit maître* – which if understood to mean a 'dandy' might have some currency, but Nicholson was never a 'minor talent'.[11] The journalist and photographer Bruce Bernard (1928–2000), for example, thought this label demeaning.[12] In truth, Nicholson had a feeling for the intensity of small-scale works, just as James Abbott McNeill Whistler (1834–1903) called for small sketch-like oils to be taken seriously as artworks. Although he accepted a knighthood in 1936, he had declined an invitation to be considered for election to the Royal Academy a decade before, writing to Alfred Munnings (1878–1959) that, 'The idea of a label of any sort scares away from me all desire to paint.'[13] Nicholson's uniqueness and individuality has meant that he has been left out of many textbook accounts of Modern British art. Nicholson's works 'stand apart from the main channels through which modern art developed, and they offer no alternative direction, but the most interesting of them (which are typically the most informal) are among the most literally attractive English paintings of the period,' wrote Charles Harrison in 1981 in his study *English Art and Modernism*, noting how the artist 'fell from the view of modernist observers while many lesser painters became celebrated for their incompetent attempts to ape a modern manner.'[14] On top of this, Nicholson's work is both absolutely of its time, but, arguably, can also have a timeless quality that makes him harder to pin to a particular moment. His woodcuts are often seen as a manifestation of the Edwardian period, but in fact they date from the decade before King Edward VII came to the throne in 1901. His paintings have far more in common stylistically with the bravura handling of his forebear Édouard Manet (1832–1883) and of Diego Velázquez (1599–1660), whose works he copied in the Louvre Museum whilst a student at the Académie Julian in Paris, than they do with Piet Mondrian (1872–1944), who was born in the same year as Nicholson and was a friend of his son, the modern artist Ben Nicholson (1894–1982).

Perhaps more than anything else, Nicholson has been defined by his position at the head of an artistic dynasty and, in particular, as a yardstick of sorts against which to measure the comparative modernity of his son Ben (who was a 'joiner upper' of groups including 7 & 5, Unit One and Abstraction-Création and a key figure in the St Ives group). Sometimes the apple falls far from the tree, and sometimes it falls closer. His own father, William Newzam Nicholson, was not known for his aesthetic concerns, but rather as a solid pillar of the community: the one-time MP for Newark who had made his fortune as an iron-goods manufacturer of farm tools, engines and boilers that were shipped all over the world. Yet Nicholson was permitted by his father to attend the art school founded and directed by Hubert von Herkomer (1849–1914), even though he was later expelled, apparently either, in his own words, 'chucked out for bad work and poor attendance' or for 'dressing as a female student dressed in black and holding an open umbrella', or perhaps both.[15] There, he met a fellow student, the talented painter Mabel Pryde (1871–1918), and in turn her brother, the artist James Pryde (1866–1941); their uncles were the Scottish artists Robert Scott Lauder (1803–1869) and James Eckford Lauder (1811–1869). Nicholson and Mabel Pryde eloped and were to have four children together. In addition to Ben Nicholson and their second son, Anthony Nicholson (1897–1918), who was killed whilst serving in the First World War, their daughter, Nancy Nicholson (1899–1977), was an artist and textile designer who married the poet Robert Graves, and their son Christopher 'Kit' Nicholson (1904–1948) was a modernist architect who married the textile designer E.Q. Myers (1908–1992).[16] Their children were to be the subjects of numerous tender portraits by both parents, as in *Ben Nicholson as a Child of Six or Seven Years* (1901; fig.5) and *Nancy in a Feather Hat* (1910; fig.60).

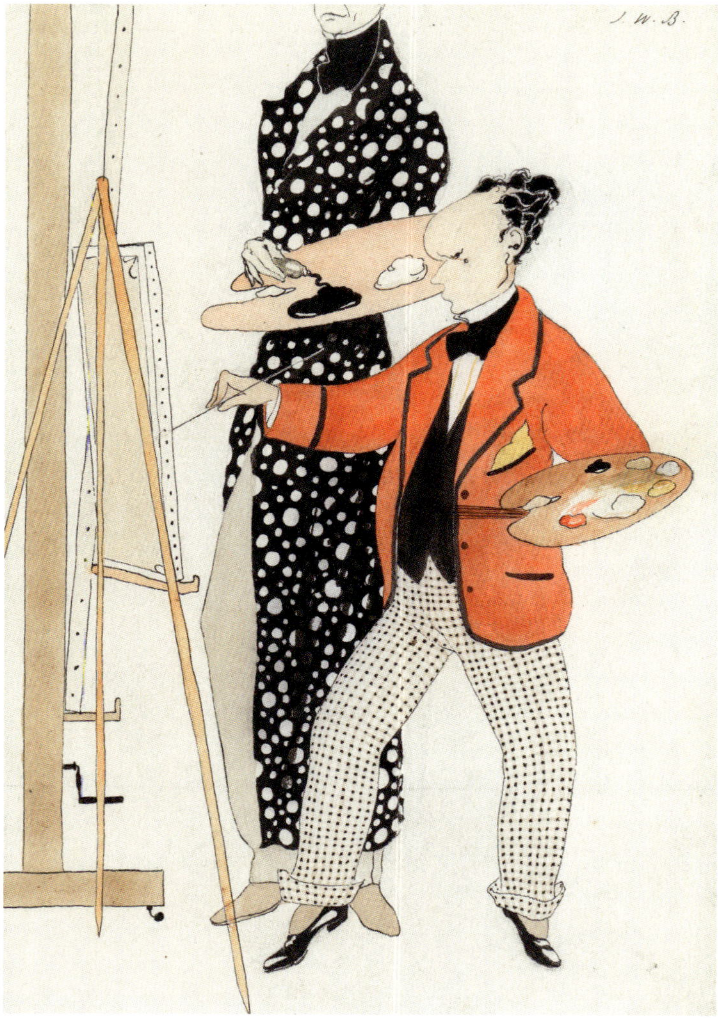

The artist Max Beerbohm (1872–1956) once wrote to the painter and printmaker William Rothenstein (1872–1945) that the Nicholsons were 'more like a troupe than a family',[17] a quality that William Orpen (1878–1931) captured in his memorable 1907 painting *A Bloomsbury Family* (fig.50), which articulates the complex dynamics: Nicholson in profile in a flamboyant spotted dressing gown, ever-the-dandy, whilst his wife stands behind him in the shadows, and their children sit around the tea table together with Staffordshire figures that appear like additional characters in the family drama.[18]

Writing about his father, Ben Nicholson noted that he had 'merely wanted to paint'.[19] Ben began his career close to the metaphorical tree, painting still lifes that at first glance are similar to the elder Nicholson's and even feature the same striped jugs, passed from father to son, such as *1914 (The Striped Jug)* (private collection). But rapidly, as his work became increasingly abstract in outlook, his father was led to ask, 'I don't know what has happened to Ben, he used to paint so nicely.'[20] A caricature (c.1916; fig.4) believed to be by Ivan Wilkie Brooks (1891–1952) shows Nicholson in an elegant black and white spotted dressing gown towering above his son painting at the easel in his favourite school 1st XI cricket blazer. Father and son had a complicated relationship and suffered periods of estrangement in the 1920s, particularly following Mabel Pryde's death from the Spanish influenza in 1918 and William's speedy remarriage the following year to Edith 'Edie' Stuart Wortley (née Phillips, also known as the painter Elizabeth Drury; 1890–1958), a war widow with whom Ben had previously had his own romantic interests. However, throughout the 1920s and 1930s, Nicholson sent his son an allowance supporting him and his family during his marriages to Winifred Nicholson and Barbara Hepworth (1903–1975), when Ben's

4 IVAN WILKIE BROOKS (?) (1891–1952)
William Nicholson and Ben Nicholson, c.1916
Ink and wash on paper, 30.8 x 20.3cm
Lent by the National Portrait Gallery, London. Given by an anonymous donor, 1996

5 *Ben Nicholson as a Child of Six or Seven Years*, 1901
Oil on canvas, 89 x 71.3cm
Private collection

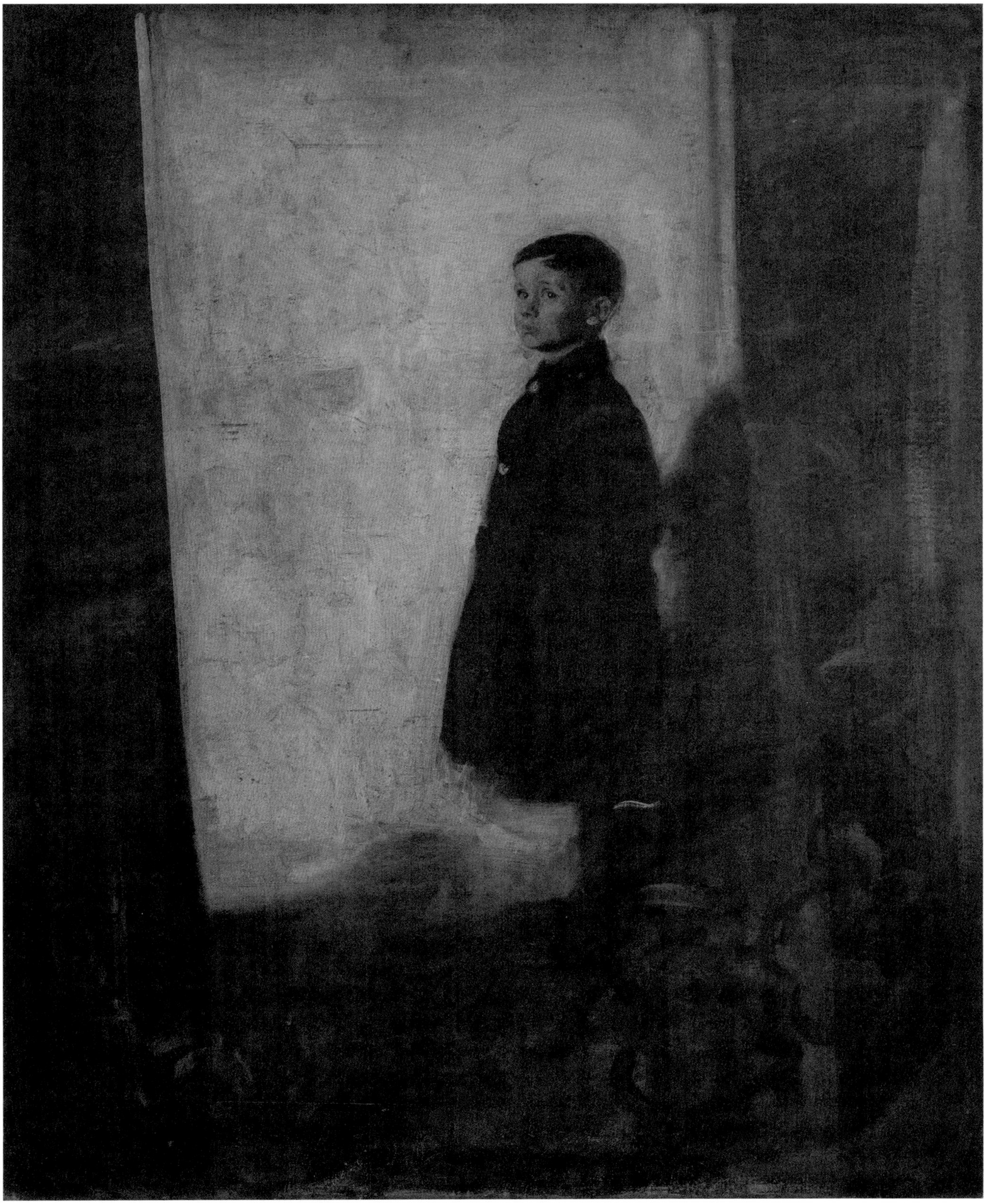

6 J. & W. BEGGARSTAFF
Reproduction of a poster advertising
Harper's Magazine, 1895
Colour lithograph on paper
Private collection

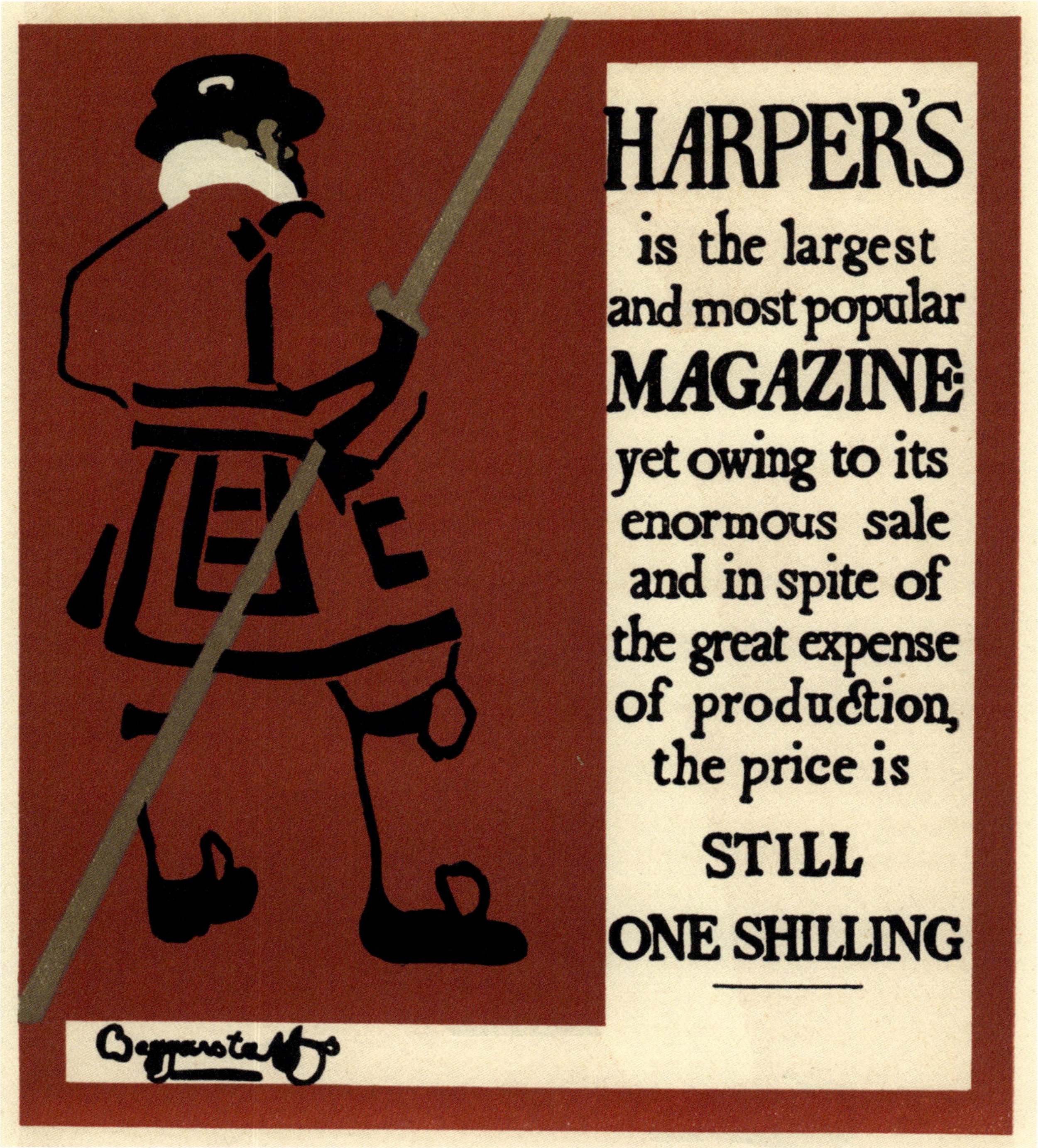

avant-garde work was selling for relatively little. Many years later Ben was to observe, 'Of course I owe a lot to my father – especially to his poetic idea and to his still life theme. That didn't come from Cubism … but from my father.'[21] There seems to have been an element of competition, or a desire to transcend his father, even if William Nicholson's painterly style became looser in the 1930s. Ultimately, William Nicholson was fundamentally a realist painter, but undoubtedly his approach always required abstract thinking. Ben's wish to position himself as an 'advanced' artist of international standing does seem to colour some of his remarks about his father's work. However, he was to note:

> In my opinion, Father's work reputation will increase year by year on the basis
> 1. of his still lifes
> 2. of his poetic landscapes
> … the character studies come into the scheme of things certainly but they are 'local' – and the portraits are even more 'local' – whereas the finest of 1. and 2. above are, in my opinion, universal, and it is this universality which endures and it is this which makes him a finer painter than any other British painter of his generation, except perhaps [Walter] Sickert. [Augustus] John's work lacks this universality and his chart will fall with time.[22]

Alan Bowness (himself the son-in-law of Ben Nicholson and Barbara Hepworth and the future Director of the Tate Gallery) noted that William Nicholson 'made and abandoned several reputations'.[23] This comment encapsulates the challenge for art historians when it comes to his 'place' within the history of art and design, for arguably Nicholson could be assigned not one, but several places for quite separate bodies of work, encompassing not only painting, but also graphic design, printmaking and book illustration. Nicholson's flexibility across different media led one critic to describe him as 'a veritable master of evasion, a sort of illusionist. You think you have him pigeon-holed here, you shut the door tight, and lo! you open another pigeon-hole to find him there, and sitting quite comfortably, too. This versatility is full of surprises.'[24]

In chronological order, the first of these 'places' would be as one half of 'J. & W. Beggarstaff', the pseudonym that he and his brother-in-law, James Pryde, used for their collaborative partnership in the design of posters and other graphic work between 1894 and 1899. They have been described as 'England's most artistically radical poster-makers',[25] who, in the words of Dennis Farr, 'revolutionized certain aspects of poster design in Europe'.[26] The second 'place' might be as the maker of around 200 woodcuts and the designer of distinctive books between 1896 and 1900, and the third 'place' – although arguably the most significant – as the painter of almost 900 paintings during the 20th century; this is not to forget that for some people he might deserve a 'place' simply for the reason of being the illustrator of some of the most-loved modern children's books, such as *The Velveteen Rabbit* (1922) and *Clever Bill* (1926). There are substantial books devoted to these separate aspects of Nicholson's work, but a key question might be to ask how they relate to each other, for fundamentally his approach to each required not only skill, but an abstract conception of light and space, whether in print or paint. The artist's one-time friend, the actor Edward Gordon Craig, noted how:[27]

> Nicholson being so old and wise, 'decided clever', someone called him, could turn from one process to another and master each in about three-quarters of an hour. So to etch, to paint in oils, to paint in watercolour,

7 J. & W. BEGGARSTAFF
Reproduction of a poster advertising Kassama Corn Flour, 1894
Colour lithograph on paper
Private collection

8 J. & W. BEGGARSTAFF
Reproduction of a poster advertising Rowntree's Elect Cocoa, 1896
Colour lithograph on paper
Private collection

> to paint in tempera, fresco painting, lithography, wood-engraving, to invent new ways of making posters and invent better ways day after day, was as easy for him as for an all-round sportsman to turn from hockey to tennis, from tennis to polo, from polo to billiards, excelling in each, to everyone's delight and despair – Nicholson was like that. Besides excelling in every branch of the technique of his art, he was skilful beyond words in handling anything where eye and hand and brain have to be under perfect control, and in perfect harmony.[28]

Nicholson and Pryde were often referred to as the 'Beggarstaff Brothers' (despite not using the label themselves), having taken the name 'Beggarstaff' from a sack of fodder that they came across in an old stable, which appealed as it was 'a good, hearty, old English name'.[29] Together, they designed 22 posters for theatre productions and such products as *Harper's Magazine* (fig.6), Kassama Corn Flour (fig.7) and Rowntree's Elect Cocoa (fig.8), although many were speculative designs that were never published. Their posters were striking in their bold simplicity, so that all unnecessary detail was stripped out in order to focus on the silhouette of the form, which the eye and mind could complete. Their technical approach was radical for the time: essentially, they would make cut-paper collages to create a stencil that could be photolithographed and distributed in large quantities. Their designs were shown in 1894 and 1896 at the International Artistic Pictorial Poster Exhibitions at the Westminster Royal Aquarium in London, where they were seen as English alternatives to continental poster artists, such as Henri de Toulouse-Lautrec (1864–1901), an undoubted influence. As Sanford Schwartz wrote: 'They had an audacious way of using shape and line to infer forms that aren't actually drawn in, and, operating in the heyday of the poster, they made what were by common consent the only English examples that could stand comparison, as works of art, with any then being produced on the continent.'[30]

The first of the Beggarstaff commissions was a theatre poster for a production of *Hamlet* (1894; fig.70) which was starring their friend Edward Gordon Craig (who was the son of Ellen Terry, a leading actress of the late 19th and early 20th centuries, and E.W. Godwin (1833–1886), the radical Victorian architect), who with his wife, May, had moved in with the Nicholsons at The Eight Bells, a former public house in Denham in Buckinghamshire. Other designs followed for *The School for Scandal* and *Cinderella* (fig.75), but the striking poster for a production of *Don Quixote* at the Lyceum Theatre (fig.71) was rejected by its star, Henry Irving (declaring 'no more mills!'), who also refused a later, final Beggarstaff design for *Robespierre* in 1899. Although the Beggarstaff venture was ultimately a commercial flop, the critical response in some quarters was very positive. The reviewer of *The Art Journal* asked:

> What will the average man in the street say when he sees the great poster designed by 'The Beggarstaff Brothers' (Messrs. Pryde & Simpson [*sic*]) to advertise Harper's Magazine? It would be charming to hear his frank criticism. Nothing so strong and so amazingly defiant of accepted convention has yet invaded the hoarding. It is a *tour de force;* the great beefeater, in solid scarlet on a scarlet background, with his brown spear, balanced by a huge white panel, most admirably lettered, is a triumph of decorative arrangement. It is only fair that such a plucky attempt should receive lavish appreciation. In simplifying drawing and pattern to the last degree, Messrs. Beggarstaff have struck a new

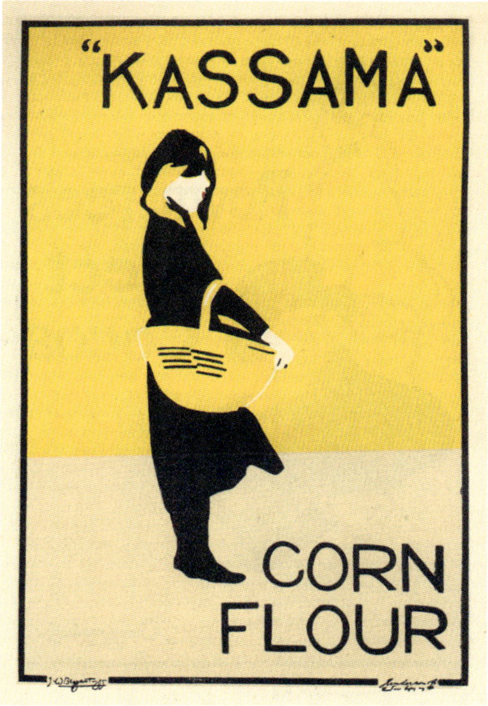

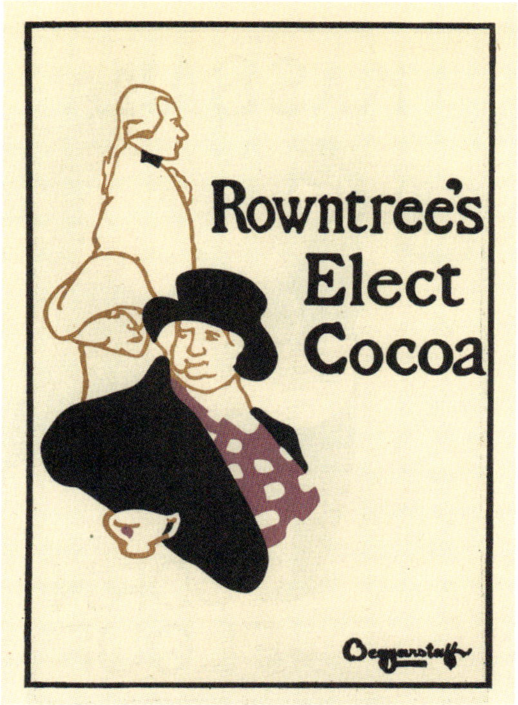

note, which might be fitly echoed in mural decoration of more permanent sort. It is English, it is modern, and it is good — *very good.*[31]

Aside from his work with Pryde, Nicholson quickly established a reputation in his own right for his work as a printmaker after his hand-coloured woodcut *Persimmon*, depicting the Prince of Wales's Derby-winning horse, was shown at the Fine Art Society in London in 1896. There, it was noticed by Whistler, who introduced Nicholson to the publisher William Heinemann. The following year, Nicholson created one of his most iconic images, a woodcut of Queen Victoria walking with a cane and accompanied by a Sky terrier (fig.9). Although Heinemann initially refused to handle it, describing it as being like 'an animated tea-cosy',[32] it was published by William Ernest Henley (1849–1903) in his *New Review* (owned by Heinemann) in a double-page supplement to celebrate the Queen's Diamond Jubilee, and it could also be bought as an original hand-coloured woodcut. It was a hugely popular success. Oscar Wilde wrote that it was wonderful and that he would hang it in his chalet as 'Every poet should gaze at the portrait of his Queen, all day long.'[33] Whereas Aubrey Beardsley (1872–1898) had caricatured the Queen as a Degas ballerina and Beerbohm had shown her looking distinctly unamused, in the words of Frances Spalding, who opened her book *British Art Since 1900* with the image: 'Nicholson's reduction of the fierce and dumpy Queen to a black pyramid, alleviated by the attention to her head, hands and dog, was gently humorous: *risqué* but affectionate. Like much Edwardian art, it broke with former conventions but had sufficient restraint to make its challenge acceptable.'[34] When Whistler praised his print, Nicholson modestly observed that, 'The Queen was a wonderful subject.' 'You know,' Whistler replied, 'Her Majesty might well say the same of *you*!'[35] Henley commissioned Nicholson to follow up Queen Victoria with a series of portrait prints for the magazine, which included such actors and writers as Sarah Bernhardt (fig.77) and Rudyard Kipling, with political figures including William Gladstone (former prime minister), Frederick Roberts, 1st Earl Roberts (a general in the British army who was then commander-in-chief in Ireland,

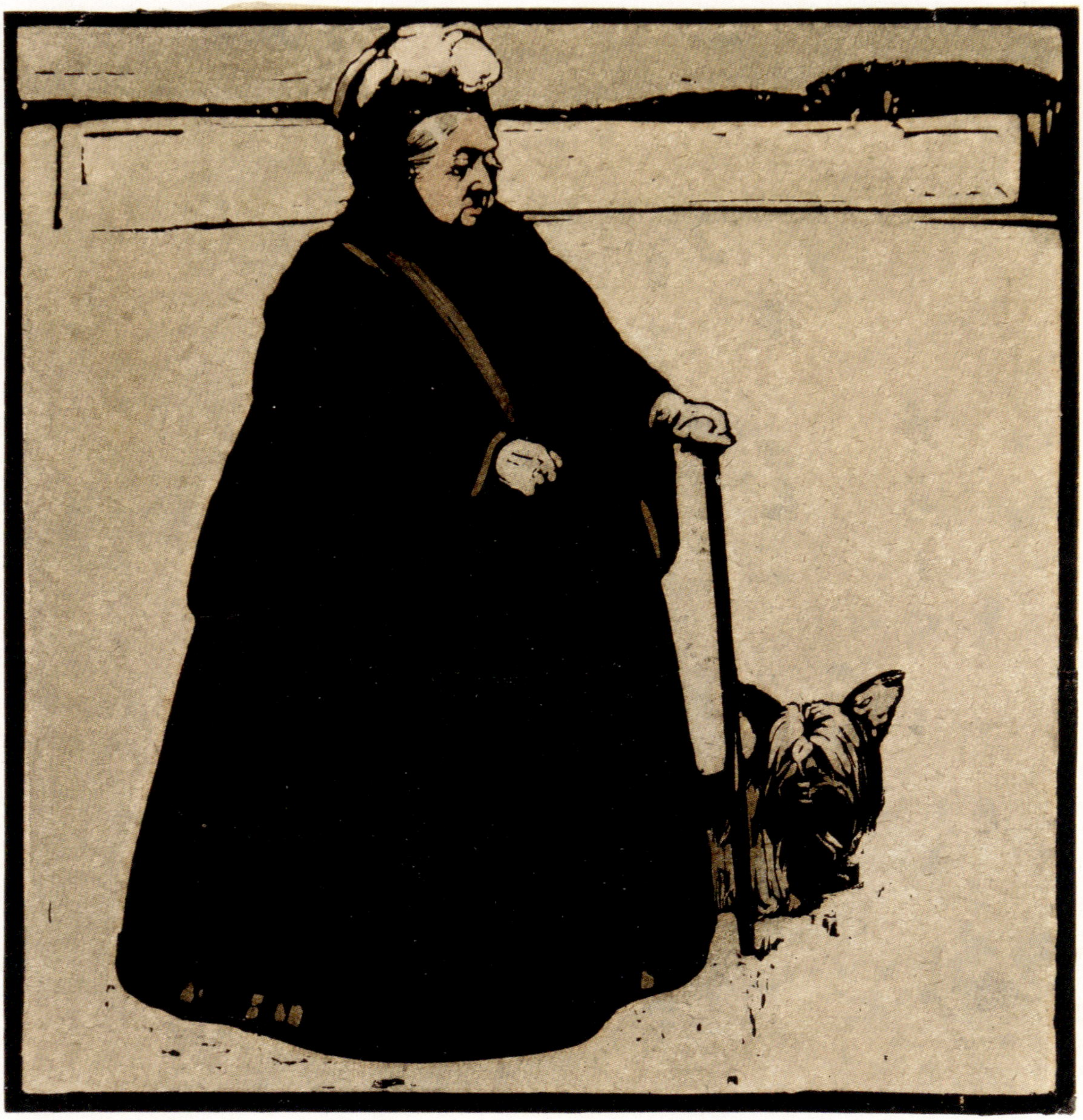

9 *H.M. The Queen* (Queen Victoria)
From *Twelve Portraits*,
William Heinemann, London, 1899
Colour woodcut on paper, 24.2 x 23cm
Private collection

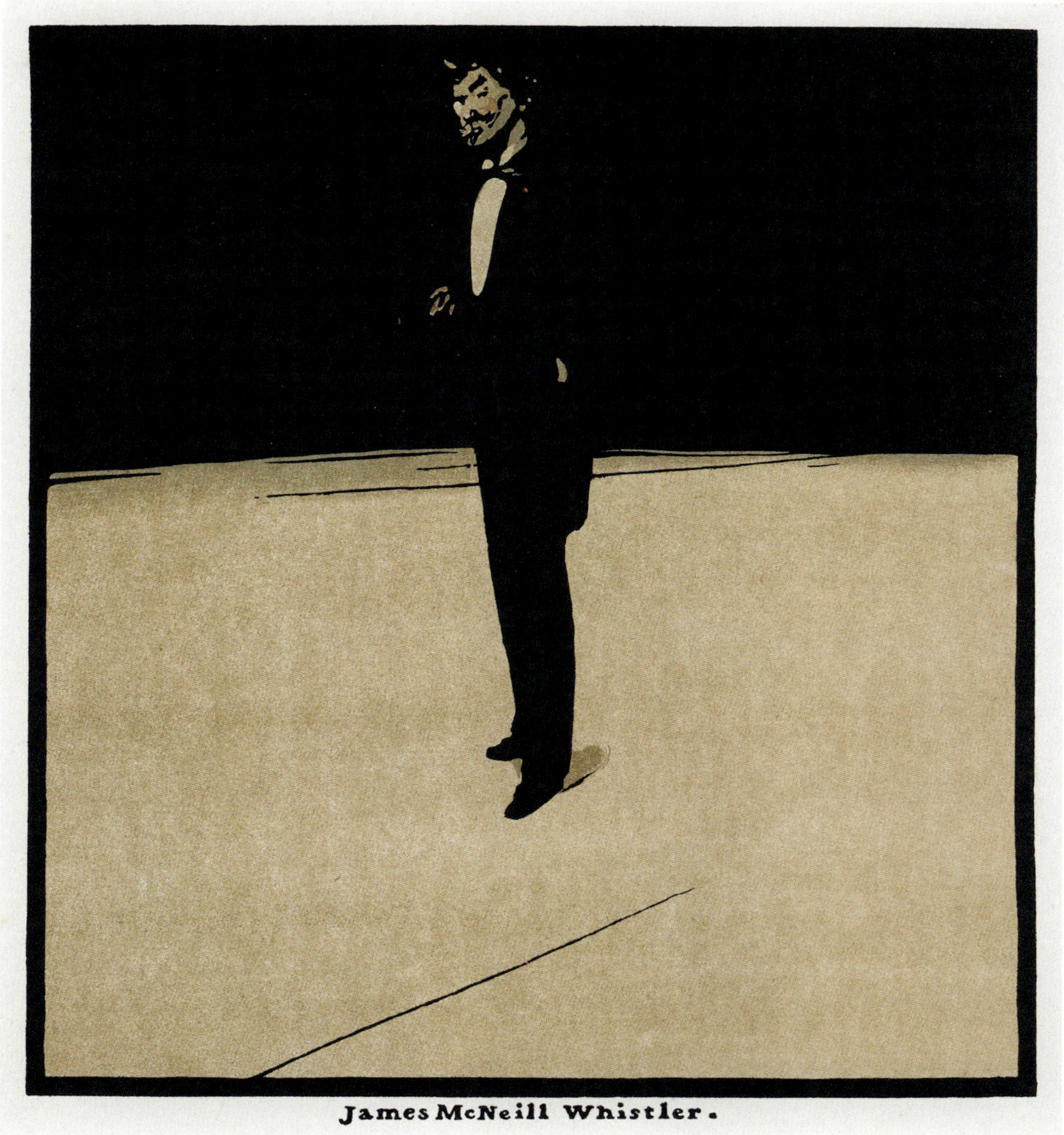

10 *James McNeill Whistler*, 1897
Lithograph on paper from the original woodblock, 24.5 x 22.5cm
Pallant House Gallery
(Muriel Wilson Bequest, 2019)

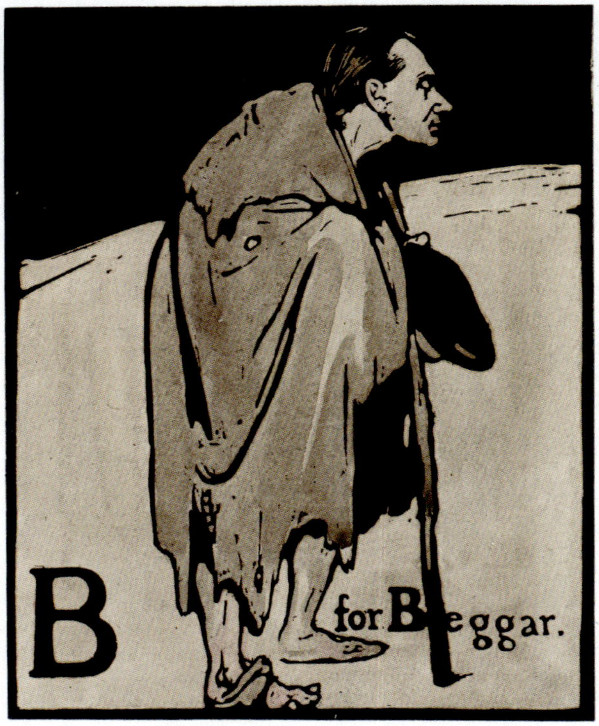
B for Beggar.

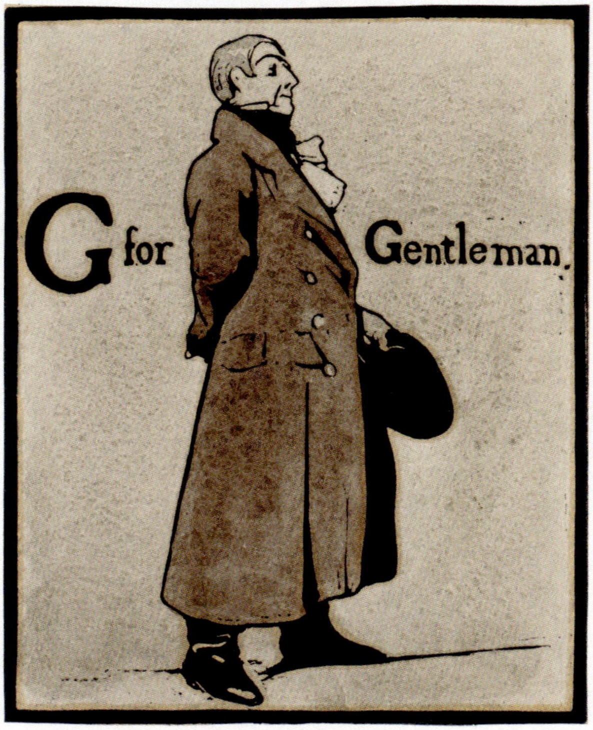
G for Gentleman.

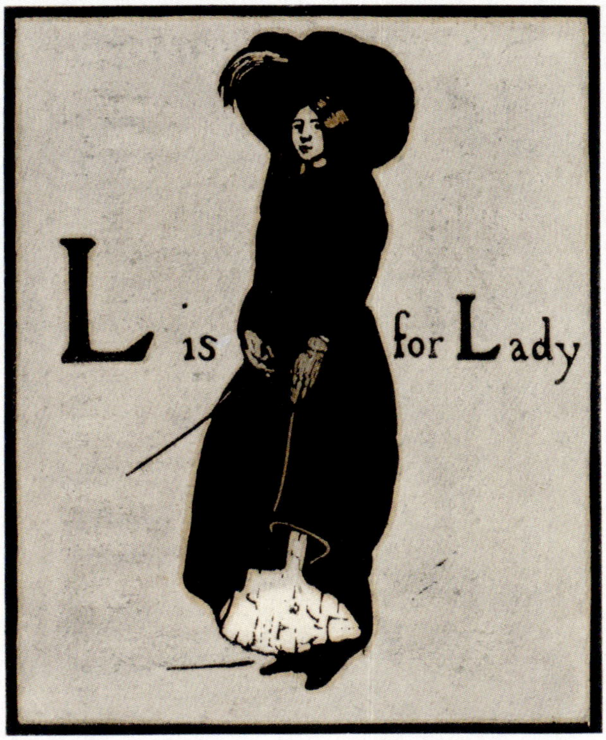
L is for Lady

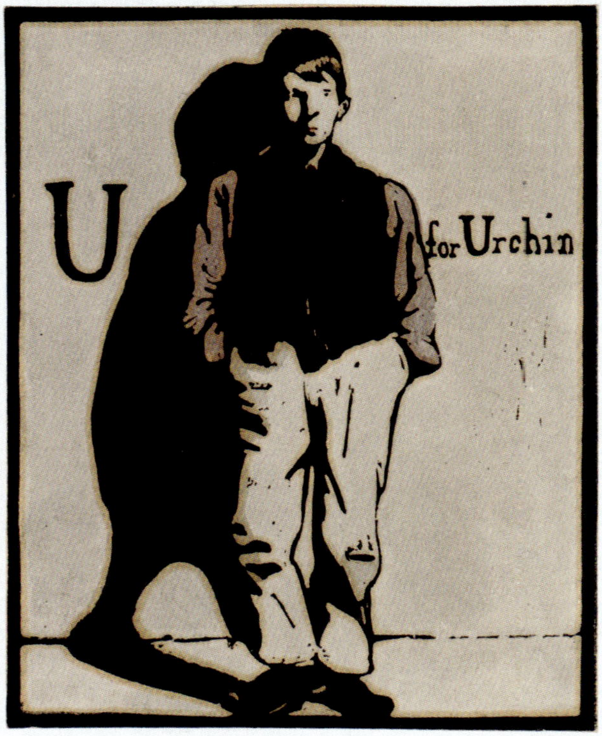
U for Urchin

11 *B for Beggar*, *G for Gentleman*, *L is for Lady* and *U for Urchin*
From *An Alphabet*, William Heinemann, London, 1897
Hand-coloured woodcuts on paper, 24.6 x 19.8cm each
Private collection

having previously served in India and Afghanistan), the colonialist Cecil Rhodes and the German prince and politician Otto von Bismarck. Each of these, including the Queen, was ultimately published by Heinemann as *Twelve Portraits* in 1899. The selection of these contemporary subjects was undoubtedly very much of its time: some of these were hugely popular figures, such as Rhodes, who was celebrated as a hero of the British Empire, but whose policies are now condemned for their role in colonialism and racism.

Whistler featured as the subject of one of the portraits in this portfolio, as an 'arrangement in black': his face and white shirt emerging from the dark background, whilst his black trousers stand out against the lighter foreground. Whistler commented, 'The art of leaving out is proof of the perfect acquaintance with the art of putting in. Mr. Nicholson states the few essential facts, and makes all else merely accessory.'[36] The understated drama implicit in this relationship of foreground to background, like a spot-lit actor on a stage, is a principle that Nicholson employed later in such portraits as *The Viceroy's Orderly (Duffadar Valayat Shah)* (1915; fig.29) and *Lady in Grey* (1918; fig.36), depicting his second wife, Edie, and in such still-life paintings as *The Lustre Bowl with Green Peas* (1911; fig.30). Nicholson understood that when wood is cut from the block it registers as light or space and he applied the principle in paint with reflected light, whether on a face, shirt or bowl, to achieve similar effects. As Robert Nichols was to note, 'Pattern is to him, roughly speaking, black and white content, and "the value of the pattern depends on the interestingness of the shape and relative placings of the darks to the light".'[37]

William Heinemann's first official commission from Nicholson was *An Alphabet* (1897; fig.11), having seen two sample woodcuts, *A was an Artist* (a self-portrait of Nicholson as a pavement artist; fig.1) and *D is for Dandy* (arguably also a self-portrait of sorts; fig.74). The subjects of the subsequent 24 letters presented a broad social stratum: ranging from *B for Beggar* (a nod to the Beggarstaffs), *F is for Flower Girl*, *U for Urchin* and *W for Waitress* to the upper echelons of society, with *C is for Countess*, *G for Gentleman*, *L is for Lady* and *N for Nobleman*. Heinemann wrote in the prospectus:

> The simplicity of [Nicholson's] method will appeal especially to the artist, but the picturesquement of treatment must be appreciated by all, while the wholesomeness and truth to nature of these designs will ensure for them a welcome in every English home. The parent will pleasantly conjure up reminiscences of quaint customs of the past, and the child will be fascinated alike by the bizarre attraction of colour and by the impressive types selected.[38]

The blocky and simplified style of Nicholson's prints with chunky hand-cut lettering was reminiscent of 18th-century broadsheets and 'chapbooks' by the mid-19th-century artist Joseph Crawhall (1821–1896), and, in the words of Robert Nichols, 'for lack of a press Nicholson used to print by treading the block'.[39] *An Alphabet* provided the prototype for several other print series by Nicholson, including his second portfolio, *An Almanac of Twelve Sports* (1897; fig.12), with a different sport for every month, and *London Types* (1898; fig.13). As with paintings of music halls by Walter Sickert (1860–1942), the realism of his subject matter was rooted in the lives of ordinary men and women on the streets of London and tied to very specific locations across the metropolis, from the bus driver (Knightsbridge Road) on the cover, to the guardsman (The Horse Guards), the hawker (Kensington), the Beefeater (The Tower), the sandwich man (Trafalgar Square),

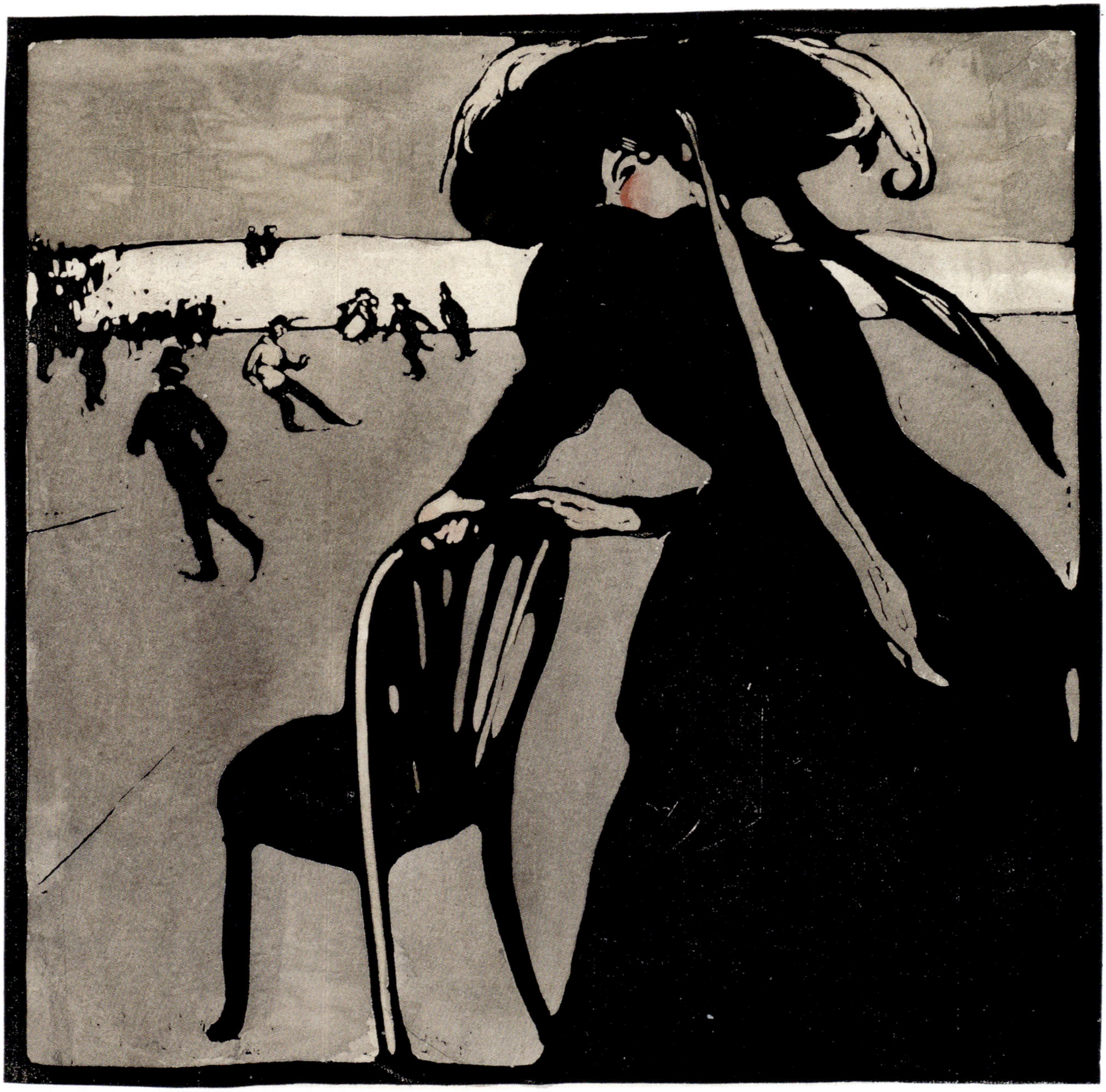

12 *Skating*
From *An Almanac of Twelve Sports*,
William Heinemann, London, 1897
Colour woodcut on paper, 20 x 20cm
Private collection

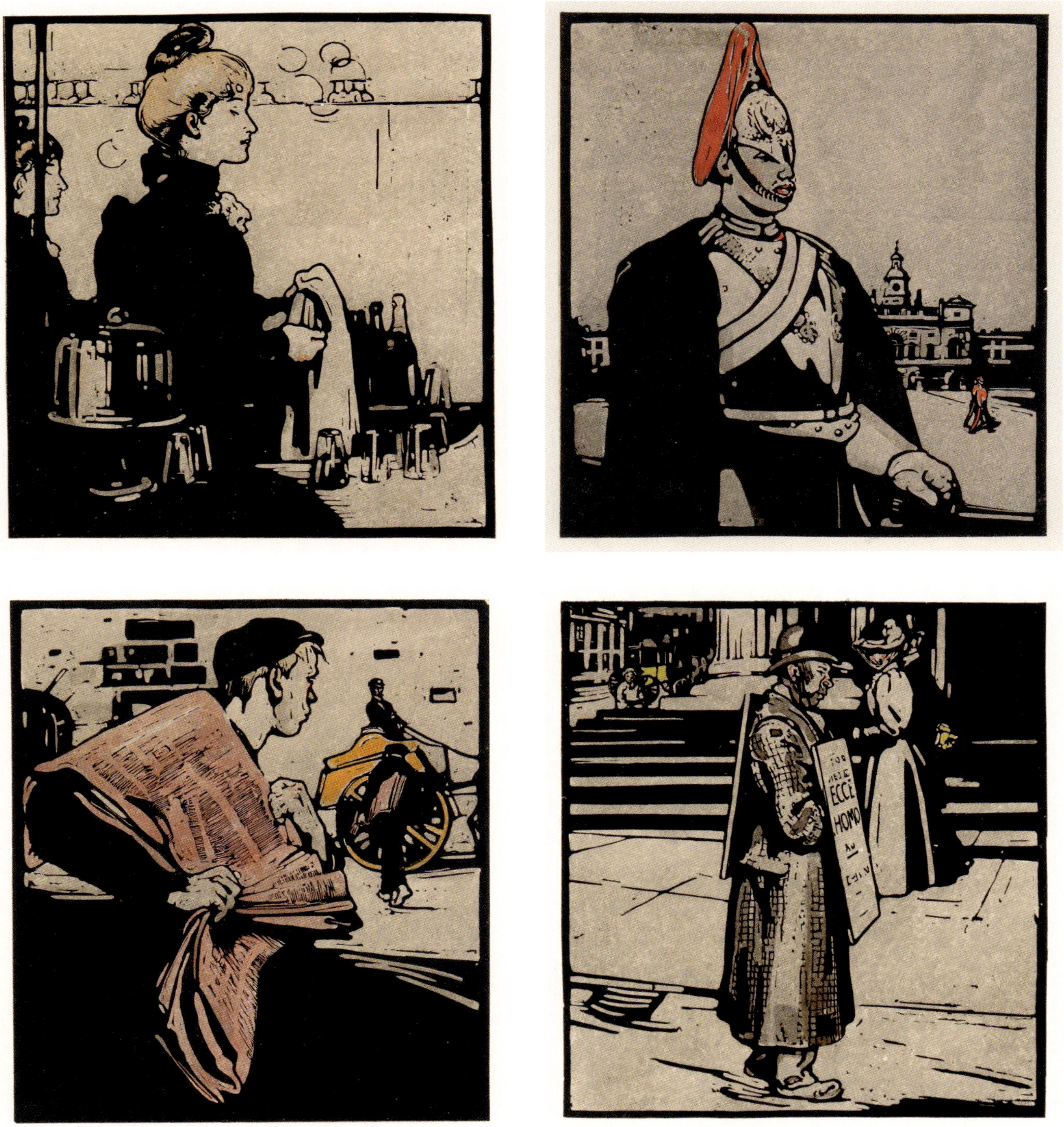

13 Clockwise from top left: *Barmaid*, *Guardsman*, *Sandwich Man* and *Newsboy*
From *London Types*, William Heinemann, London, 1898
Colour woodcuts on paper, 25.5 x 23cm each
Private collection

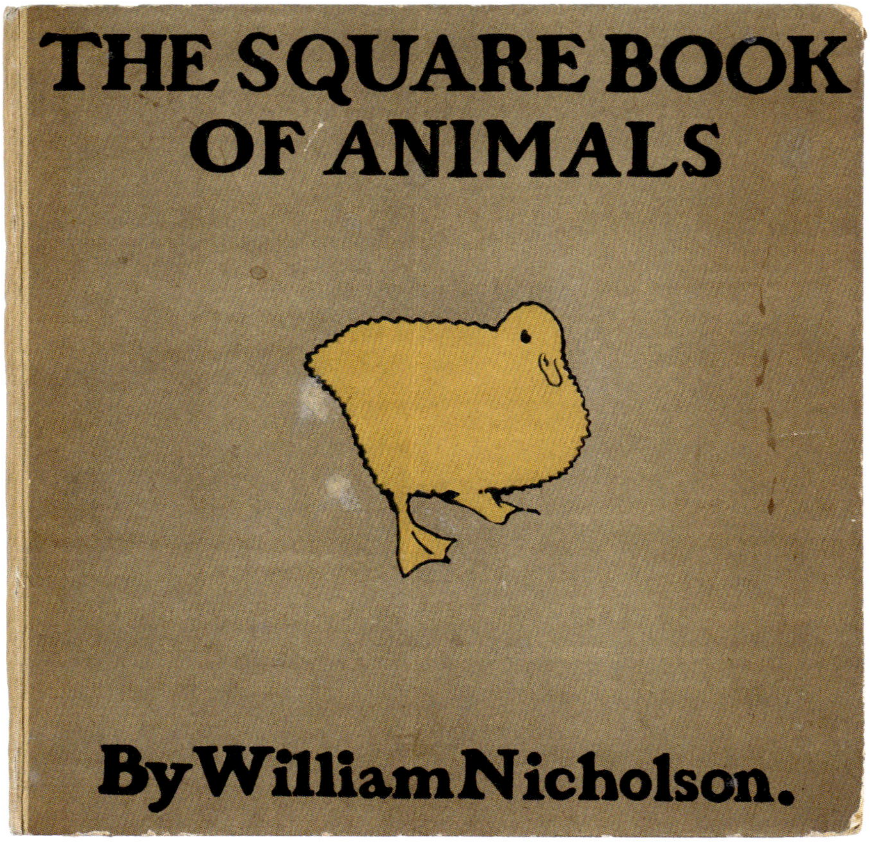

14 William Nicholson and Arthur Waugh,
The Square Book of Animals,
William Heinemann, London, 1899
[but dated 1900]
Book, 28 x 29cm
Private collection

15 Woodcut and woodblock for *Cockerel*
From William Nicholson and Arthur
Waugh, *The Square Book of Animals*,
William Heinemann, London, 1899
[but dated 1900]
Woodblock, 12.5 x 12.5cm
Private collection

Opposite:
16 Bookplate for William Heinemann, 1897
Woodcut on paper, 7 x 7cm
Private collection

17 Bookplate for William Ernest Henley, 1900
Woodcut on paper, 7.5 x 7.5cm
Private collection

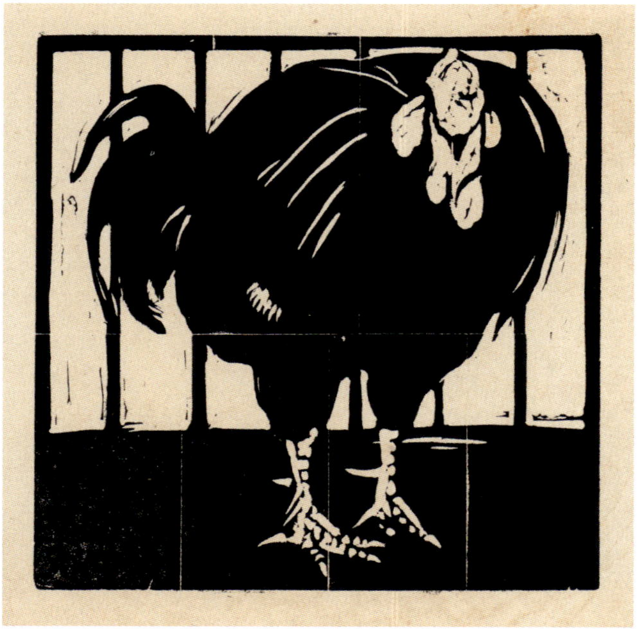

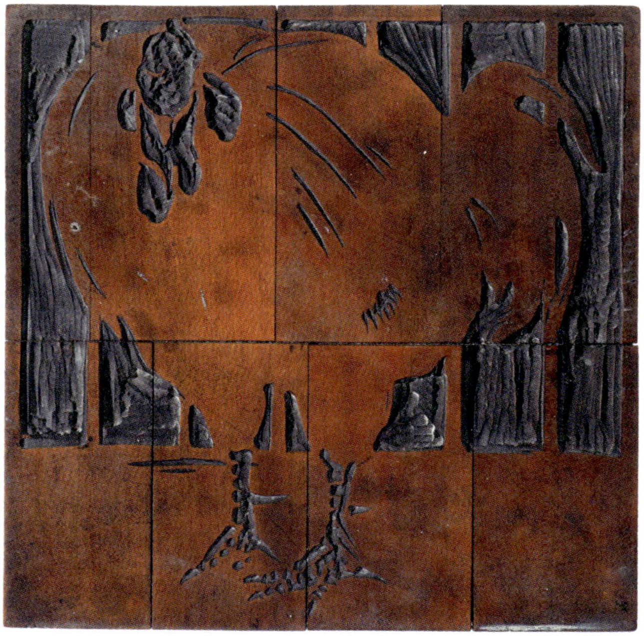

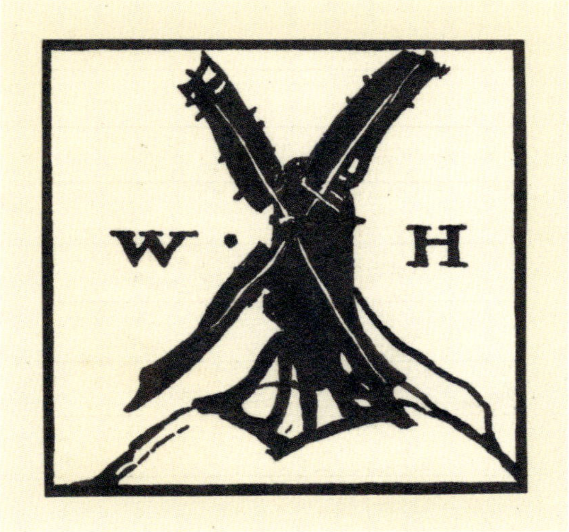

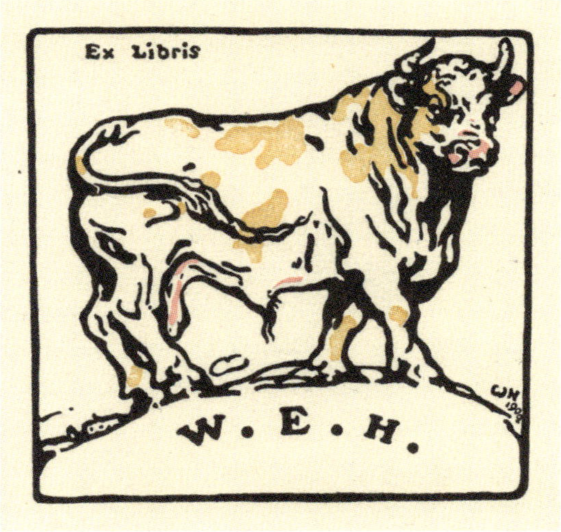

the coster (Hammersmith), the lady (Rotten Row), the bluecoat boy (Newgate Street), the policeman (Constitution Hill), the newsboy (The City), the drum major (Wimbledon Common), the flower girl (Any Corner) and the barmaid (Any Bar). Heinemann published the portfolios in hand-printed and coloured deluxe editions, as well as mass-produced editions of lithographic reproductions of Nicholson's woodcuts, which were also issued in French and American versions. Nicholson designed a personal *Ex Libris* for Heinemann (fig.16) featuring a windmill adapted from an engraving by Jacques Callot (1592–1635) of the Siege of Breda, which came to be adopted as the colophon for all of Heinemann's books. For Henley he created a bookplate depicting a bull (fig.17), reflecting the poet's love of old London and based on a sculpture of a bull on the inn sign of the Bull and Mouth Inn at Aldersgate Street in London. He also designed another for the caricaturist Phil May (1864–1903), featuring a coster girl, a subject for which May was known.

Whilst Nicholson's dandified personal dress, alignment with the notion of 'art for art's sake' and friendships with the likes of Whistler and Beerbohm might orient him more to the aesthetic movement and the 'decadents' associated with *The Yellow Book*, published by the Bodley Head between 1894 and 1897 and featuring distinctive covers by Beardsley, his portfolios for Heinemann created an association with the 'Hearties', a group around Henley and his *National Observer* that was known for its strong, masculine and imperialistic worldview. Yet, after Beardsley died in 1898, Nicholson – then aged just 26 years and known as 'The Kid' – was regarded as his successor as the leading graphic printmaker in England. However, within a couple of years his concentrated period of work as a printmaker came to an end. *The Square Book of Animals*, published in 1899 (with a date of 1900) by William Heinemann (fig.14) and featuring 12 lithographed illustrations of animals and birds together with rhymes by Arthur Waugh, was actually based on some of Nicholson's earliest woodcuts, such as *Cockerel* (fig.15). In fact it features a note at the front declaring that the book was designed in 1896, so a work featuring one of his earliest woodcuts of swans was quite literally his swansong as a printmaker. He did, however, continue to illustrate and design covers for numerous publications in the subsequent decades, including covers for such books as David Dwight Wells's *Her Ladyship's Elephant* (1898; fig.22), several volumes of poetry by his son-in-law Robert Graves (*On English Poetry*, 1922; fig.21), *The Owl: A Miscellany* (fig.41) and *The Winter Owl* (an anthology of poetry, prose and drawing that Nicholson and Graves launched in 1919; fig.42) and notably Siegfried Sassoon's *Memoirs of a Fox-Hunting Man* (1929; fig.24) and his own *The Book of Blokes* (1929; fig.20).

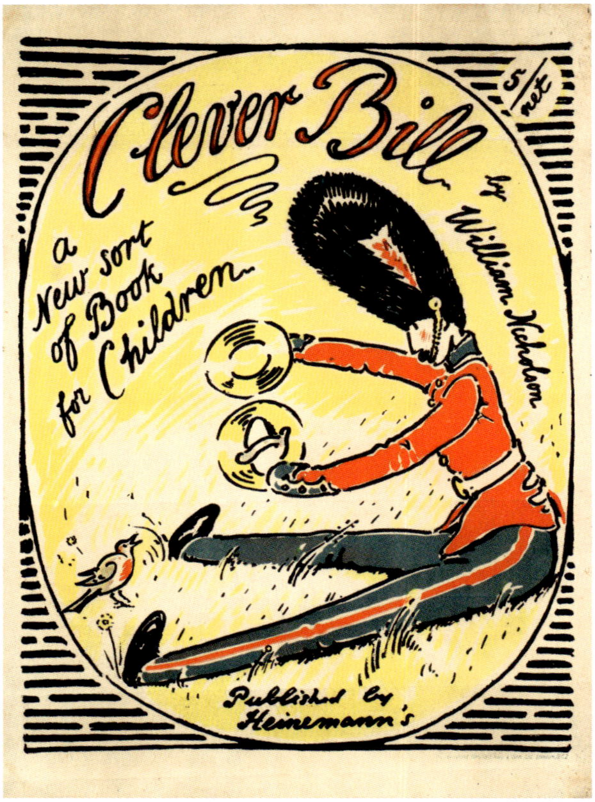

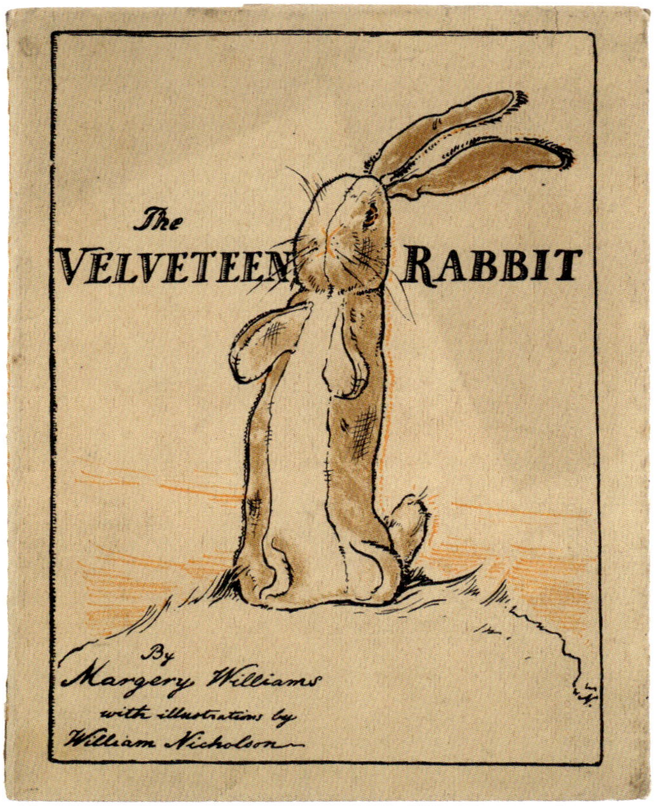

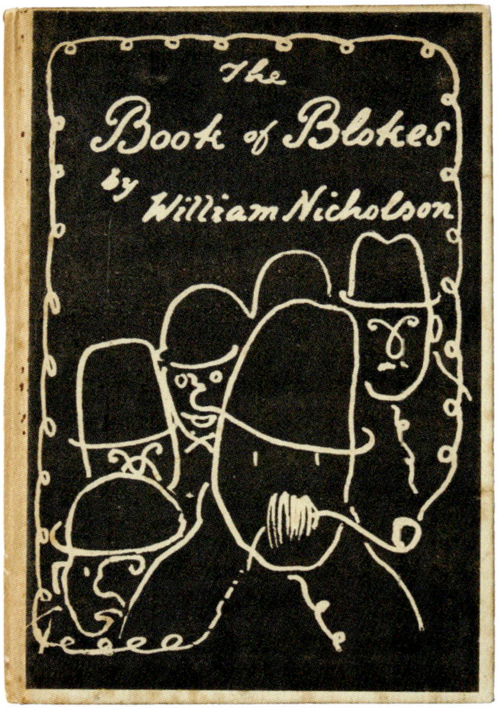

18 *Clever Bill*, 1926
Poster, 58 x 43.5cm
Private collection

19 Cover design for Margery Williams, *The Velveteen Rabbit*, first edition, William Heinemann, London, 1922, inscribed by William Nicholson: *For Penny Nicholson from The Velveteen Rabbit and from Father who drew him*, 1922
Book, 24 x 19cm
Private collection

20 *The Book of Blokes*, first edition, [Faber & Faber, London, 1929]
Book, 18.8 x 13cm
Private collection

21 Cover design for *On English Poetry* by Robert Graves, William Heinemann, London, 1922
Book, 20 x 13cm
Private collection

22 Cover design for *Her Ladyship's Elephant* by David Dwight Wells, William Heinemann, London, 1898
Book, 19.7 x 12.7cm
Private collection

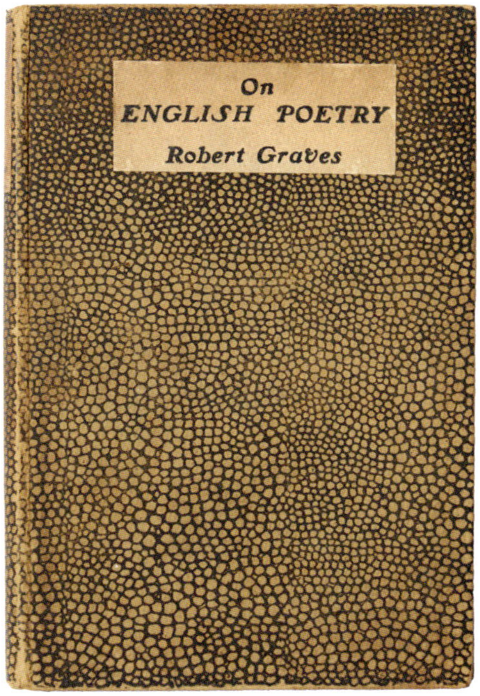

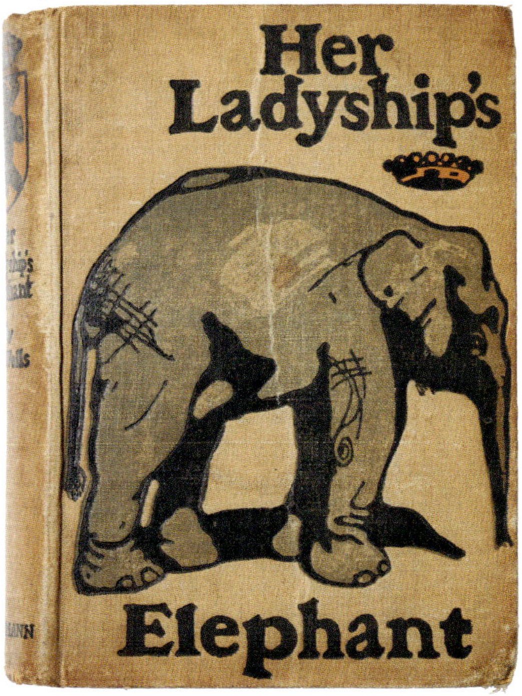

23 Cover design for *The Hour of Magic and Other Poems by W.H. Davies*, Jonathan Cape, London, 1922
Book, 23 x 15cm
Private collection

24 Cover design for *Memoirs of a Fox-Hunting Man* by Siegfried Sassoon, Faber and Gwyer, London, 1929
Book, 23 x 16cm
Private collection

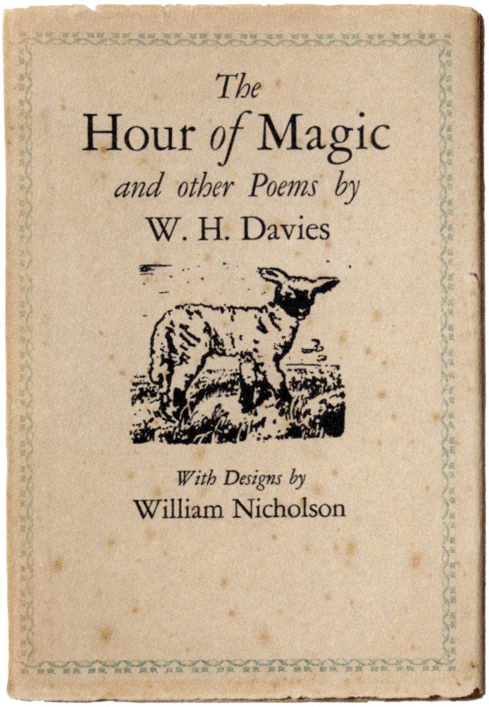

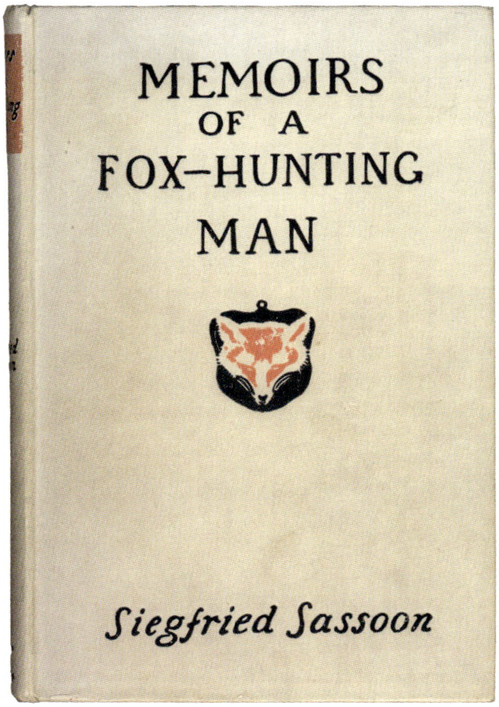

25 *Portrait of a Man of Letters: W.E. Henley*, 1901
Oil on canvas, 37.5 x 29.8cm
Tate: Bequeathed by Mrs W.E. Henley 1925

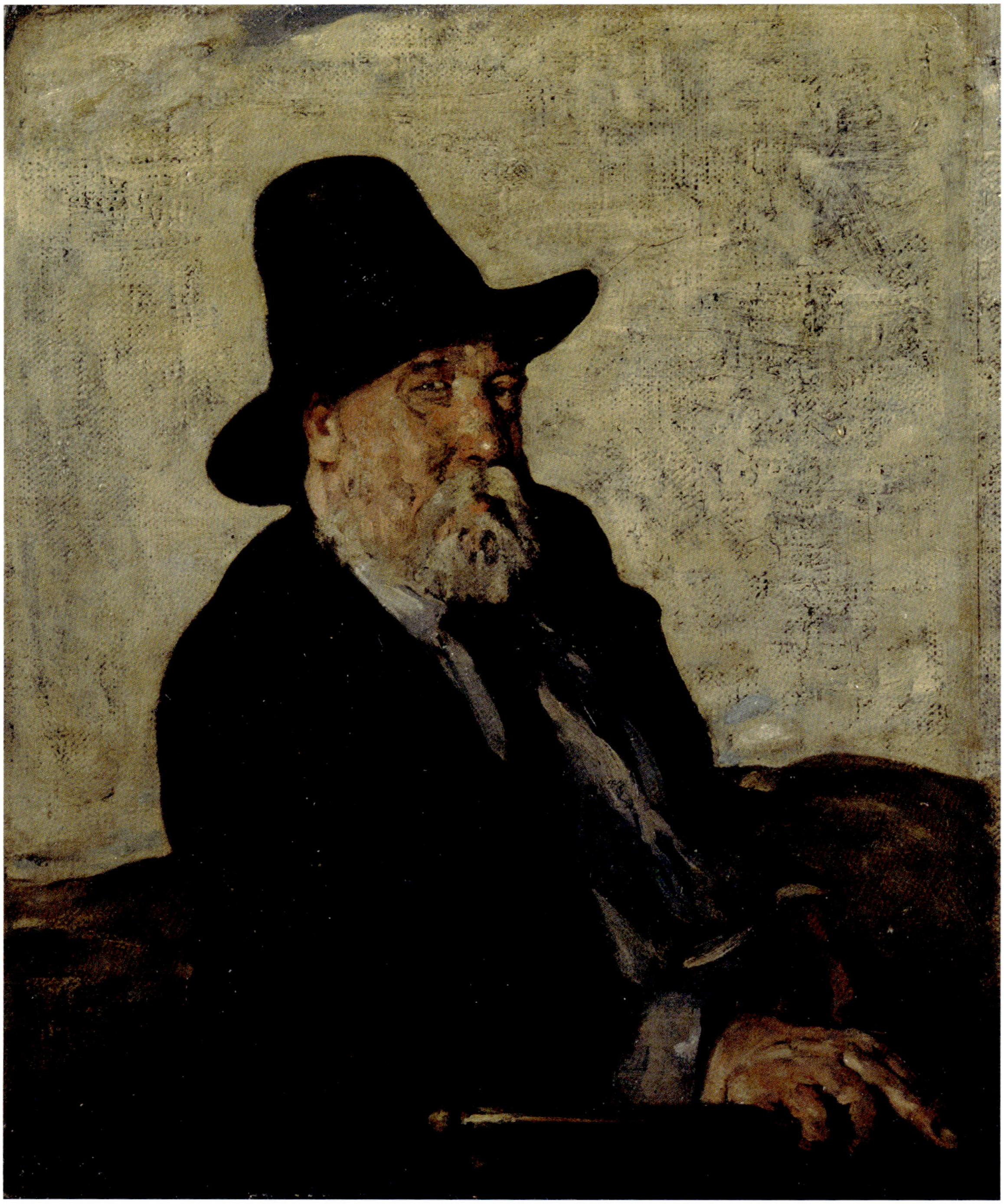

Encouraged by Whistler and with a sense of freedom resulting from an arrangement with the Stafford Gallery, which offered him a retaining fee in return for his entire output, in 1901 Nicholson comprehensively shifted his attention from printmaking to painting.[40] His initial focus was portraiture: both a pragmatic financial decision and also a logical development from his emphasis on 'character and types' in prints and his last portfolio, *Characters of Romance* (1900), which features imaginary portraits of 16 literary figures including Miss Haversham, Don Quixote, Baron Munchausen and Long John Silver – the last was apparently based on Nicholson's collaborator on *London Types*, W.E. Henley, whose wooden leg and irascible character had been an inspiration to Robert Lewis Stevenson when writing *Treasure Island*. Henley was to be the subject of Nicholson's first formally commissioned portrait in oil, *Portrait of a Man of Letters: W.E. Henley* (1901; fig.25). Significantly, Nicholson executed the image in both oil and woodcut, the only occasion that he did this, and it provides a striking insight into how his understanding of light and dark in printmaking could lead to his pared down painterly works. He took a similar approach in his portraits of two other literary friends, *Sir Max Beerbohm* (c.1902; fig.66) and *Sir James Matthew Barrie* (1904; fig.67), in which the figure is placed in profile before a simplified buff-coloured background. After Henley's death, the distinctive hat he wore for his portrait was given to Nicholson, who later painted a still life entitled *Henley's Hat* (1917; untraced). It is a reminder that his still lifes can sometimes also act as proxy portraits, most memorably with *Miss Jekyll's Gardening Boots* (1920; fig.26): the gardening boots that he had painted whilst awaiting evening sittings with their owner, the garden designer Gertrude Jekyll (1843–1932). Somehow the boots are more evocative of what she represented than the portrait of the gardener herself, *Gertrude Jekyll* (1920; fig.27).

Amongst the numerous formal commissioned portraits of aristocrats and noteworthy individuals, it is perhaps to be expected that the most engaging and successful of Nicholson's portraits are also the most informal, particularly those depicting his own children, in which his paternal affection is palpable. Being able to get small children to hold still and pose, for even the shortest time, is an art in itself. There is evidence that at least some of these paintings were based on photographs, such as the aforementioned *Ben Nicholson as a Child of Six or Seven*. A portrait of Ben in a mandarin paper cap and holding a puppet of Mr Punch from the English seaside entertainment Punch and Judy, entitled *The Paper Cap* (1906; private collection), illustrates the artist's interest in folk art and the playful qualities of dressing up. This interest is also palpable in a group of portraits of a Morris dancer in his feathered hat and bells that was begun whilst Nicholson was living in the Oxfordshire village of Woodstock in 1901 (figs.28 and 64), which are almost unique in Modern British art. Whilst, on the one hand, they form a continuation of the sort of English 'characters' in his *London Types*, each painting depicts one particular individual, Edward 'Feathers' Russell, the 'Fool' of the Eynsham Morris, who would not historically have been accorded the status of a portrait. In a similar way, his portrait of *The Viceroy's Orderly* (1915; fig.29), Duffadar Valayat Shah, which was painted in India in 1915, is far more striking and impressive than his rather unsympathetic official portrait of the Viceroy, Lord Hardinge (The President's Secretariat, Rashtrapati Bhavan, New Delhi), the commission that was the reason for the six-month trip to the sub-continent, then at the heart of the British Empire. Elizabeth Lutyens, the daughter of the architect Edwin Lutyens (1869–1944), with whom

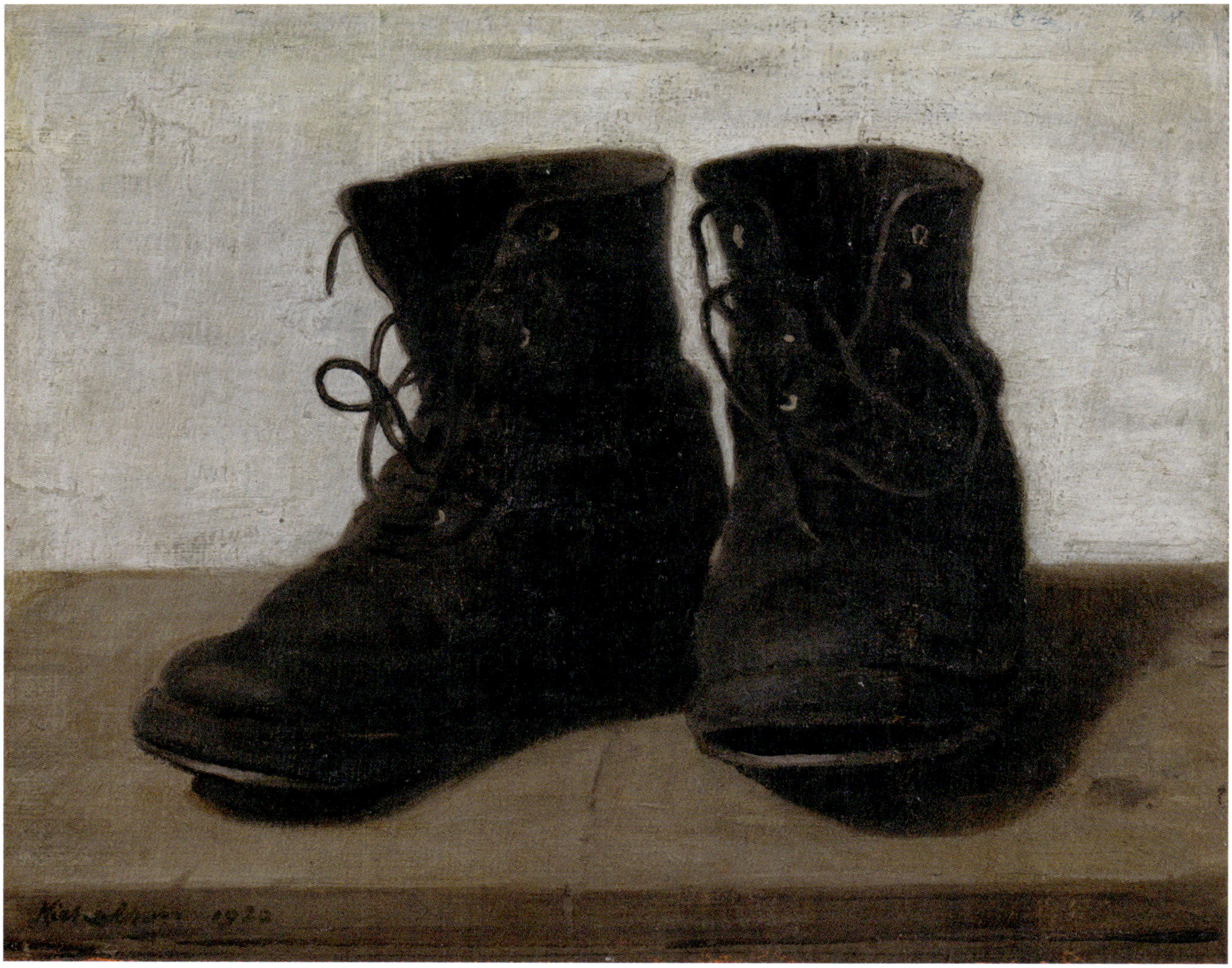

26 *Miss Jekyll's Gardening Boots*, 1920
Oil on wood, 32.4 x 40cm
Tate: Presented by
Lady Emily Lutyens 1944

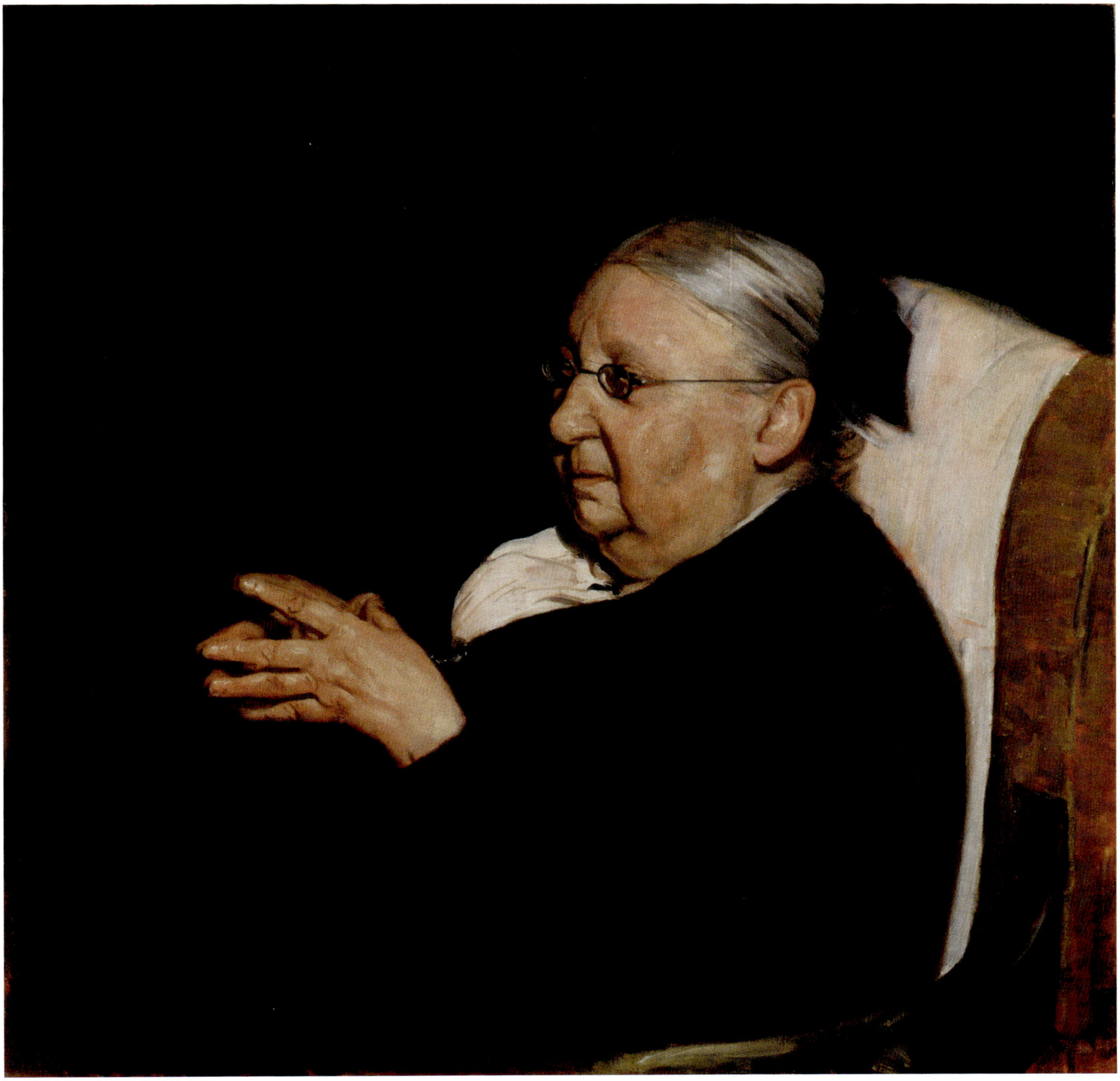

27 *Gertrude Jekyll*, 1920
Oil on canvas, 76.5 x 77.5cm
Lent by the National Portrait
Gallery, London. Given by wish
of Sir Edwin Lutyens, 1947

28 *Chairing the Feathers: The Eynsham Morris at the Gates of Blenheim Palace*, 1902
Oil on canvas, 114 x 92cm
English Folk Dance and Song Society

Nicholson had travelled to India, recalled another (lost) work featuring 'Spectacular Sikhs in red and gold tunics, huge black beards and white turbans occupied the foreground and the Viceroy could be seen as a tiny, insignificant figure standing on top of a stairway at the back'.[41] Shah's beautiful clothing and elaborate headdress would have appealed to Nicholson, providing the opportunity to render the effect of light and shade on various white fabrics, and yet the portrait is so much more than this, for it presents a colonial servant as dignified and imposing, and it seems to make a subtle point about Nicholson's feelings about the Raj and reflects his view that servants should be treated with respect whoever they are. The artist's biographer Sanford Schwartz wrote of how: 'The little information we have about his six months in India says that he was unimpressed with the British Raj and the system he [the Viceroy] symbolized. And when he diddled the white Raj, he did so with the strength of someone who felt free to be cavalier with figures of authority.'[42] Nicholson was never an explicit social or political commentator, but it is striking that his painting *Sport on the SS* Cedric (1921; fig.37) employed a vertiginous vertical perspective to depict the distinction between figures on the first-class upper decks (possibly a depiction of himself) observing the crowds gathered to watch and participate in sports on the lower decks, which appears to be where all the fun is happening. It is a very different type of image to many of the glamorised depictions of transatlantic travel in the 1920s. Similarly, in a later and more loosely handled painting, *Waiting for the* Heraclea (1937; fig.38), Nicholson depicted a nocturnal scene overlooking the Venetian lagoon in which the shabby characters depicted awaiting the ship's arrival do not quite match the grandeur of the setting.

Nicholson's contribution to a series of prints commissioned by the British Government's War Propaganda Bureau for a series entitled 'The Great War: Britain's Efforts and Ideals' was an image entitled *The End of War* (1917; fig.39), depicting a soldier decisively nailing shut the door on war, surrounded by blood and devastation. It has none of the bravado or patriotism of other artists' commissions. Bloodshed was also powerfully evoked in his painting *Ballroom in an Air Raid* (1918; untraced), which depicts civilians taking refuge in the basement of the Piccadilly Hotel in London, with a red carpet rolled up in the centre of the room, stretching to the far distance. Aside from an official commission from the Canadian War Memorials Committee, *The Canadian Headquarters Staff* (1918; Canadian War Museum, Ottawa), he painted only one work depicting an active soldier, *A Soldier of the 1914–18 War* (1917; fig.62). Although not a specific portrait, it is possible that the model was his son Tony, who completed his military training in February 1917 and was sent to France two months later, whom he had depicted the previous year in *A View of the Shop from Chelsea* (1916; fig.61). Nicholson received a telegram informing him of Tony's death on active service in October 1918, less than a month before the Armistice. This makes his painting of *Armistice Night* (11 November 1918; fig.40) a particularly bittersweet painting: whilst on one level an accomplished study in *contre-jour* with celebrating figures placed in silhouette before the nightlights and exploding fireworks, it also has an unsettling quality with injured soldiers limping on crutches in the foreground: a reminder of the human impact of war. In the context of Tony's death, Nicholson's painting of *The Cenotaph, Morning of the Peace Procession* (1919; Annabel's, Berkeley Square, London) must have been especially poignant.

Neither still life nor landscape were to emerge as significant themes in Nicholson's oeuvre until after 1906, once he was well established as a

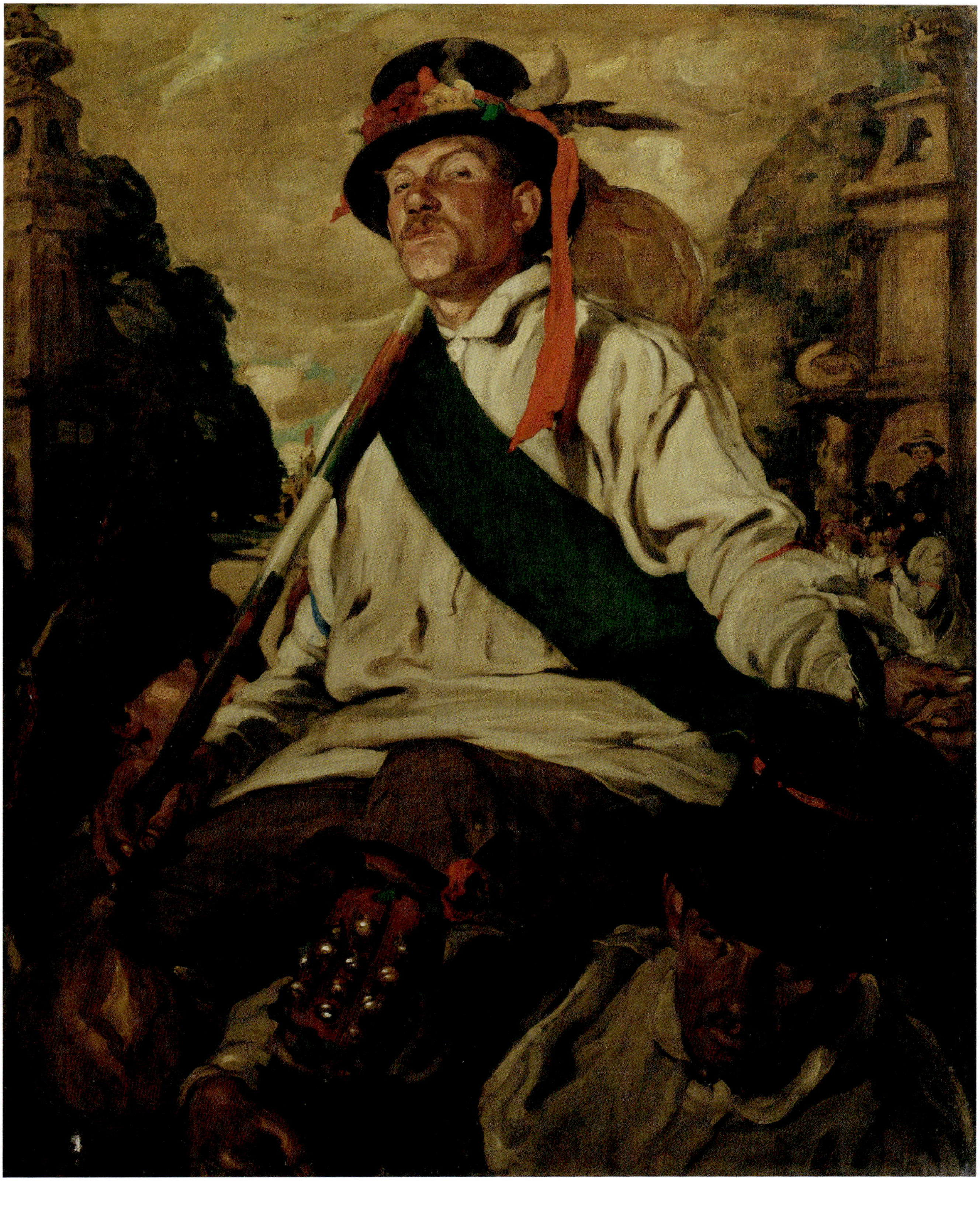

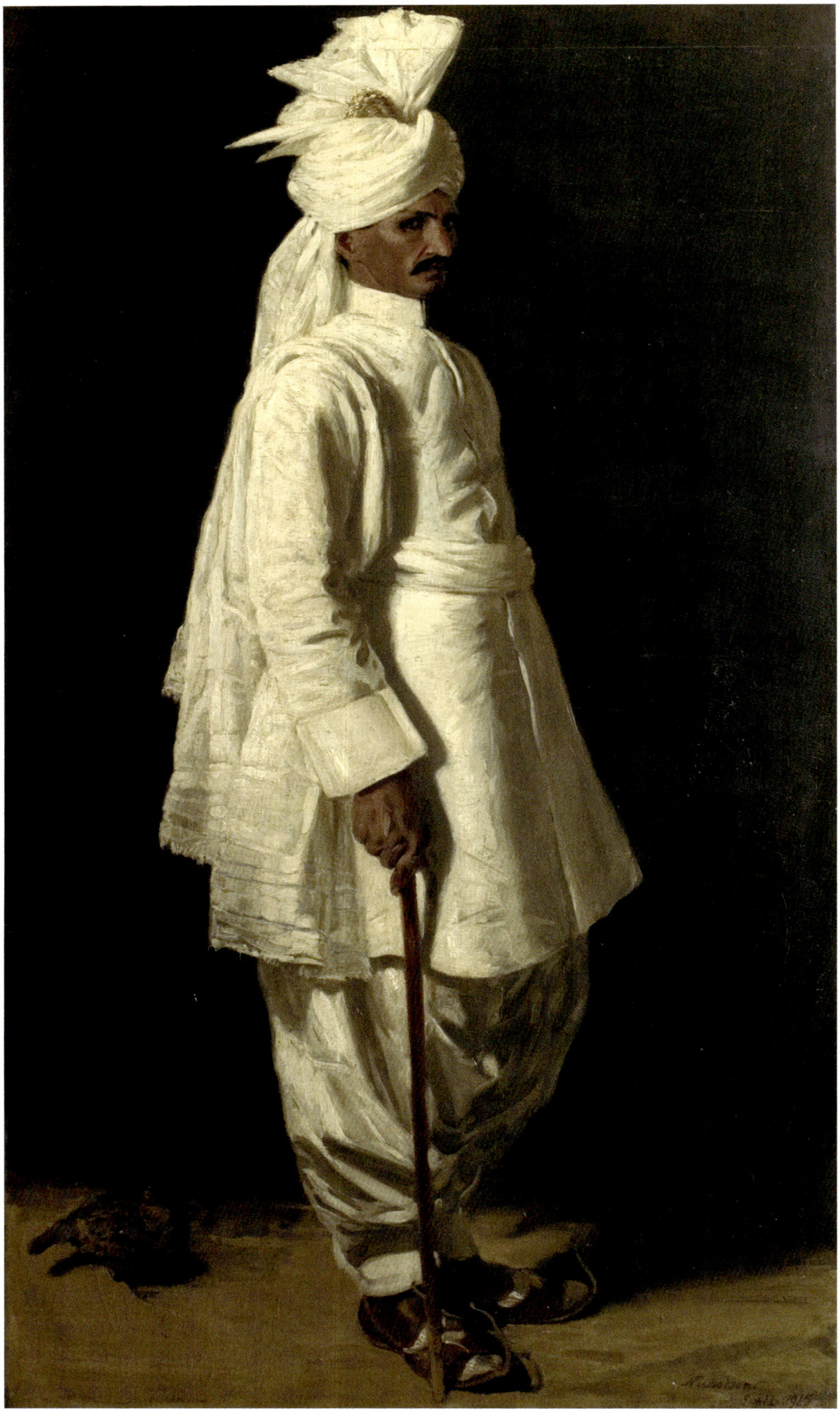

29 *The Viceroy's Orderly (Duffadar Valayat Shah)*, 1915
Oil on canvas, 198.1 x 99.1cm
Nottingham City Museums and Galleries (Nottingham Castle)

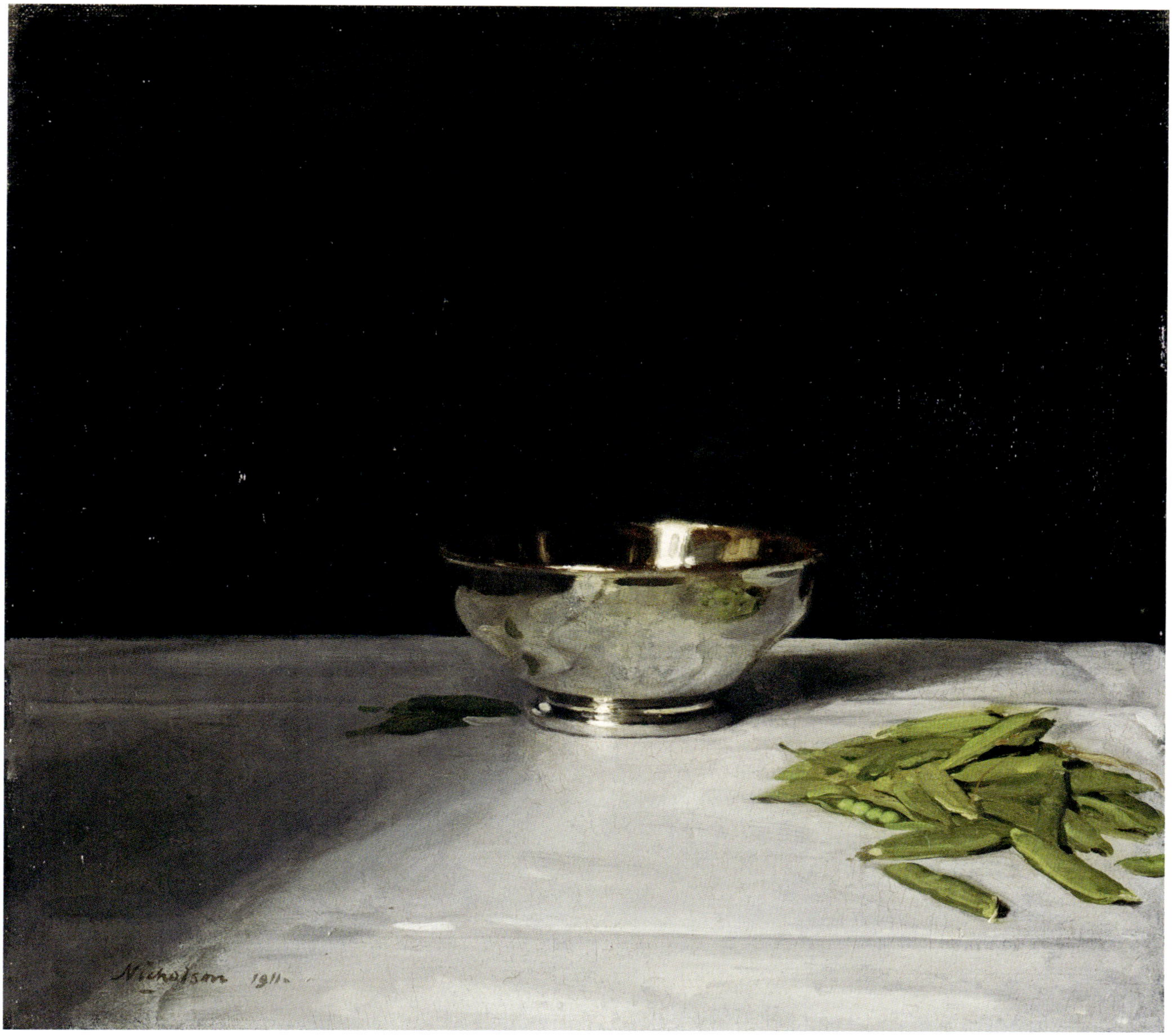

30 *The Lustre Bowl with Green Peas*, 1911
Oil on canvas, 55 x 60cm
National Galleries of Scotland.
Bequeathed by Sir Alexander Maitland
with life interest to Colonel Peter Dunphie.
Presented by Colonel Dunphie 1997

portrait painter. This is reflective of the fact that initially, at least, it was portraiture that gave him the financial freedom to paint other things. With a few exceptions, such as *The Vale of Health, Hampstead* (1912; fig.31), most of the landscapes Nicholson painted depict the English downlands, initially in Sussex and later in Wiltshire. His earliest landscapes were painted during a holiday near Littlehampton in 1906, but in 1909 he and Mabel Pryde took a house in Rottingdean, along the coast eastwards from Brighton. From then on Nicholson became the self-professed 'Painter of the Downs' – walking from the village up past the windmill onto the Sussex Downs or along the chalk coastal cliffs. His evocative views are like no other, largely because they are so pared down, spare and almost abstract, often with vast skies with subtly changing qualities of light conveyed through tonal harmonies. Part of the surprise of these works is their scale, for they convey the monumentality of the landscape before the artist and yet were painted *en plein air* on the size of a canvas that could fit into his painter's box and be carried. Frederick Wedmore wrote in 1909 of how, 'Every figure in his great, little landscape-pictures is still "a person of the drama" and so lives with an intensity that is foreign absolutely to the pure landscape painter's figures.'[43] At times, his approach seems so spare as to be almost abstract, with stark contrasts of light and shade creating a dramatic sense of scale and distance. There were occasional forays further afield, to more remote landscapes, such as Brittany or even India; in the 1920s to the Wiltshire Downs around his home at Sutton Veny; and in the mid-1930s to southern Spain, where he met his final partner, the writer Marguerite Steen (1894–1975). These works, such as *Spanish Hills* (1935; fig.139), are as loose as Nicholson was ever to be and perhaps show how he responded to wider movements in art. Occasionally, Nicholson also painted buildings in such works as *The First Communion* (1907; private collection) or *La Place des Papes, Avignon* (1925; fig.122), but these are almost closer to the intensity and informality of the views of walls in southern Italy by the 18th-century Welsh artist Thomas Jones (1742–1803) than they are to most modern artists.

Arguably, Nicholson was best at his most informal, which is also when he was most playful. This is when the boundaries between landscape and portraiture or landscape and still life dissolve. At first glance his *A Young Nobleman Surveys the City* (1910; fig.34) looks exactly as the title given it by Lillian Browse suggests: a portrait of a figure in a landscape, but in fact on closer glance we see that it is a painting of a wooden figure, placed before a landscape painting. It employs the same three-quarter view of the spectator surveying as his earlier portrait *Rosy of Winchelsea* (1901; fig.33), depicting the daughter of Edward Gordon Craig and May Gibson. What looks to be a windowsill with a view of a city beyond in *Studio Still Life* (1914; fig.90) turns out to be an arrangement of objects before a painting of a townscape: it is impossible to discern a line between what is real and what is art. It seems that Nicholson liked to play games with space and perception, so that nothing is as it first seems. Despite their small scale, his still-life arrangements can seem monumental, and through his exquisite technical execution and mastery at depicting reflected light in glass and lustrous metals, he somehow created the feeling that we, the viewer, are contingent with the space and moment he was depicting. Whether in his still lifes or indeed his landscapes, portraits or prints, he engages us, the viewer, in the act of looking. He makes it feel as if we are there with him, that we might see our own shadow in the foreground. Nicholson's favourite word was apparently 'magic'.[44] This is highly appropriate, because in so many ways he was the consummate illusionist.

31 *The Vale of Health, Hampstead*, 1912
Oil on canvas, 60.5 x 55cm
Estate of Mirabel Cecil

32 *The Windmill, Brighton Downs (Brighton Downs, Rottingdean)*, 1910
Oil on canvas, 33 x 40.6cm
Nottingham City Museums and Galleries (Nottingham Castle)

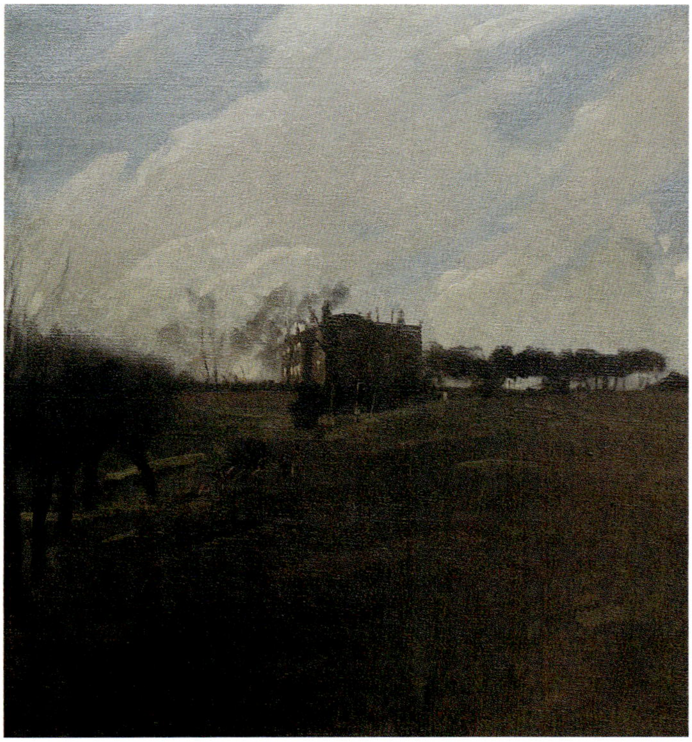

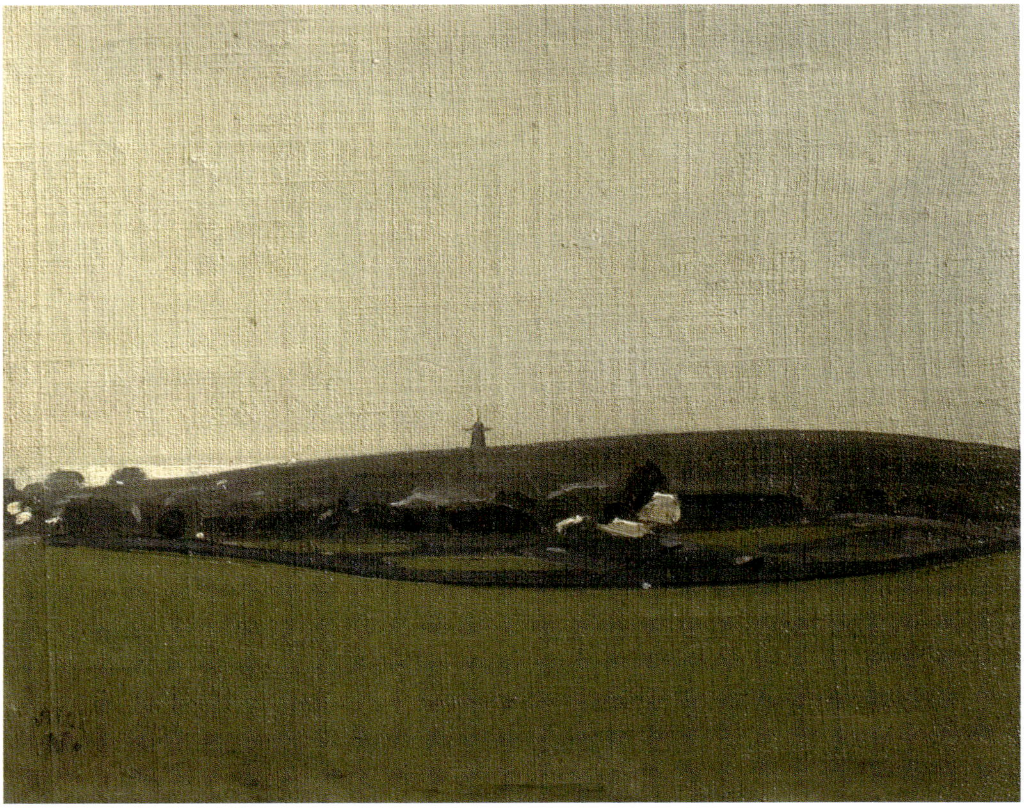

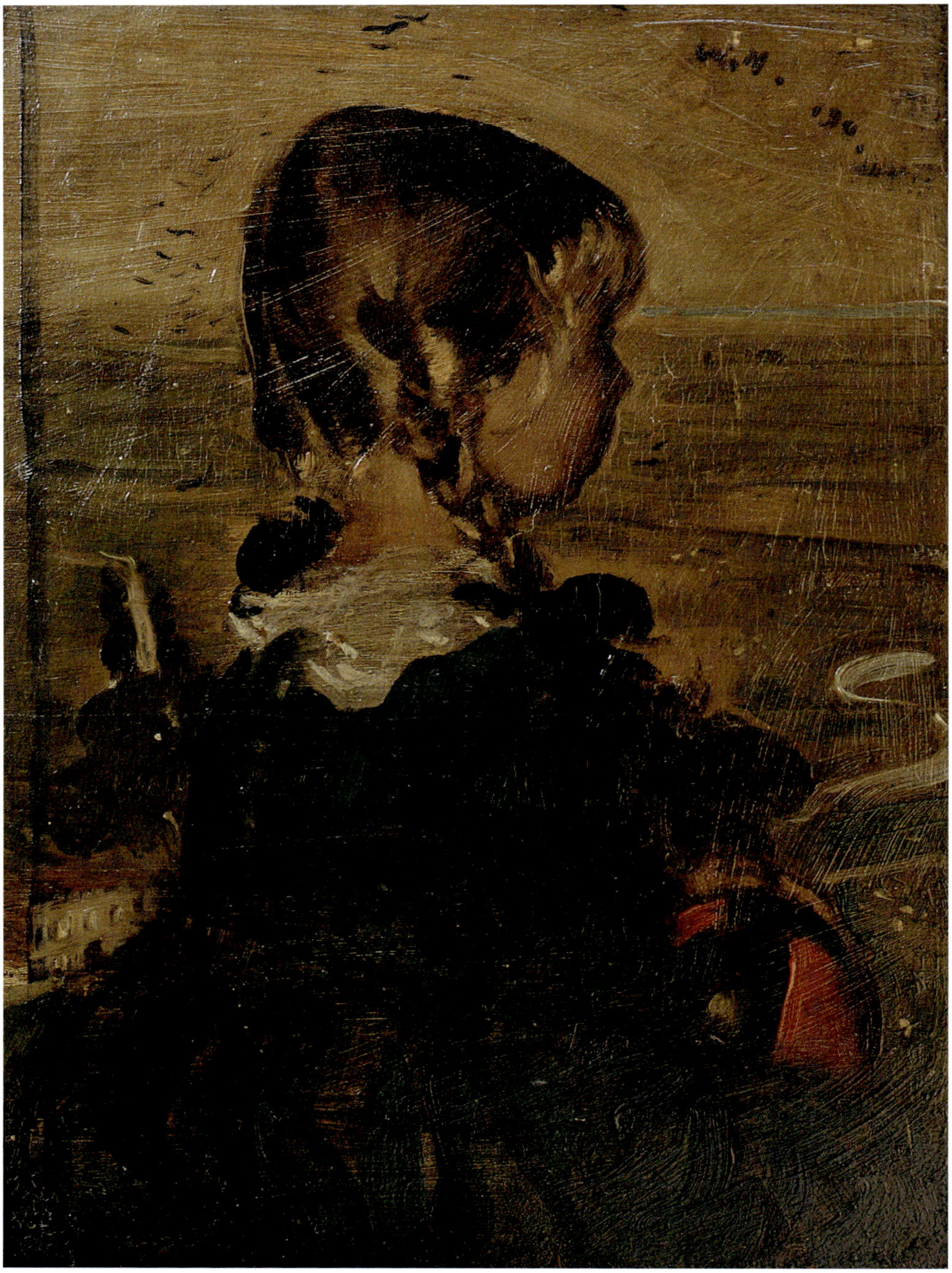

33 *Rosy of Winchelsea*, 1901
Oil on panel, 26.5 x 20.5cm
Estate of Mirabel Cecil

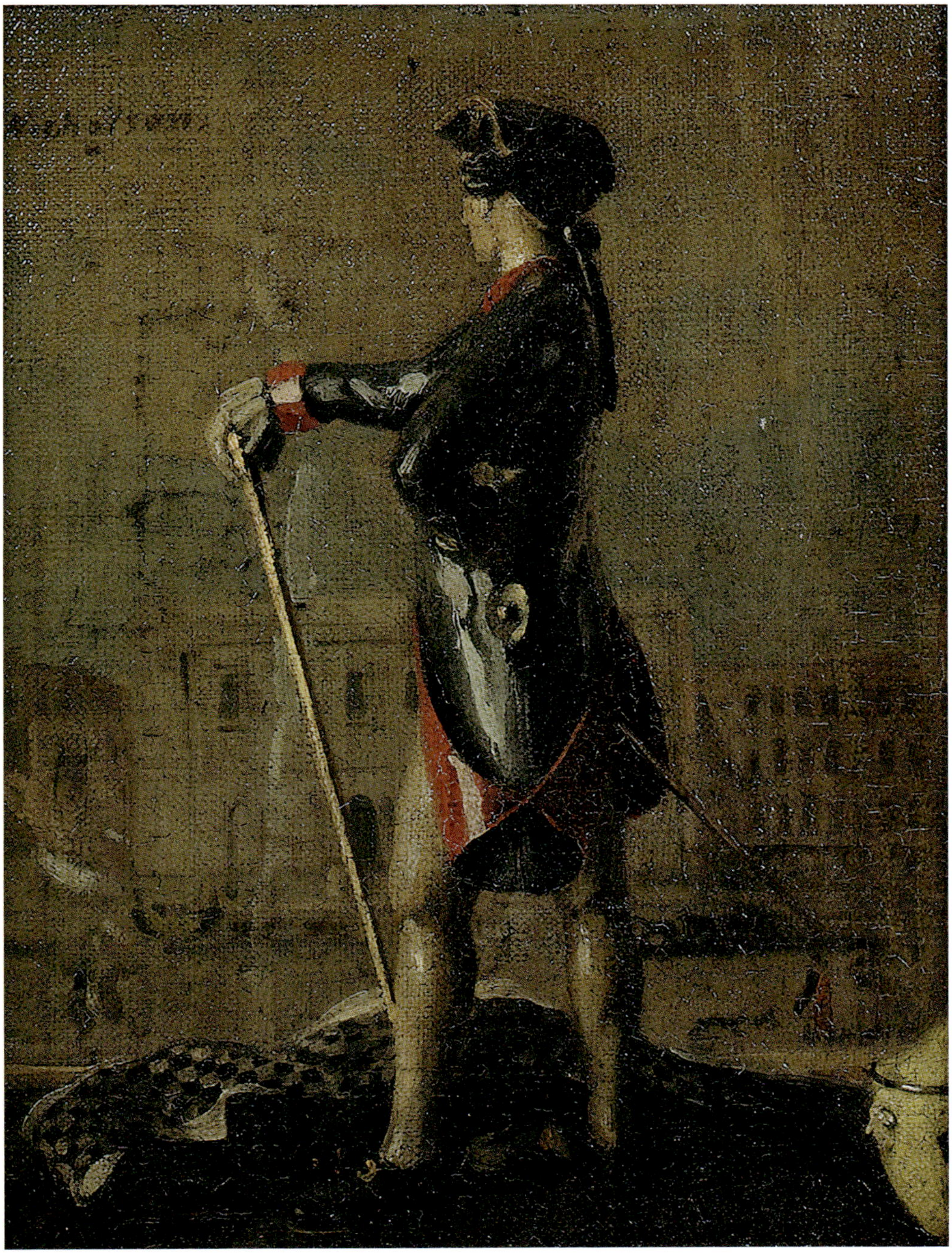

34 *A Young Nobleman Surveys the City*, 1910
Oil on canvas board, 34 x 27.6cm
Private collection

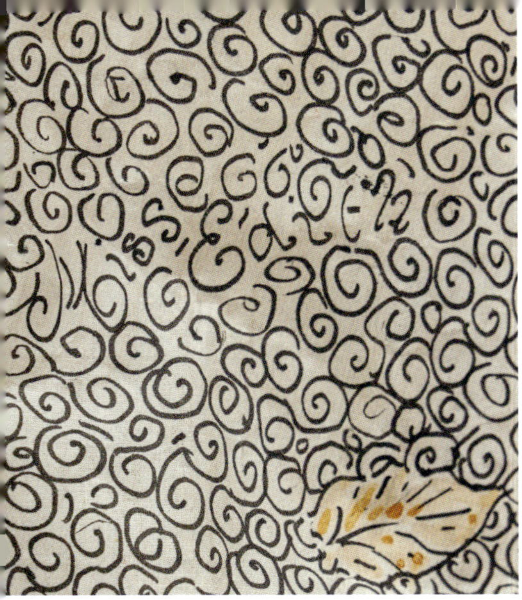

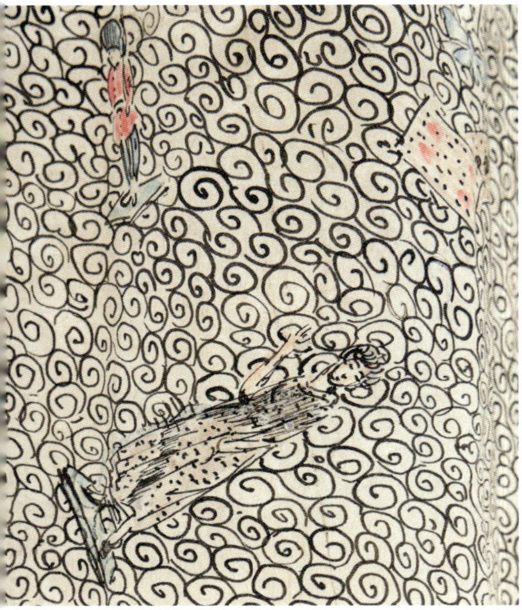

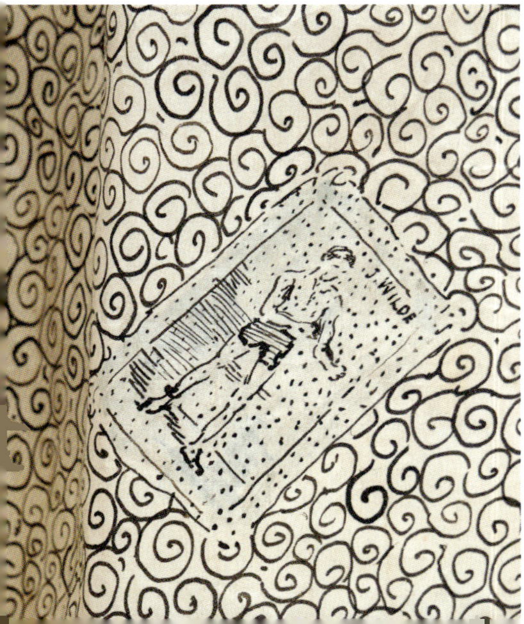

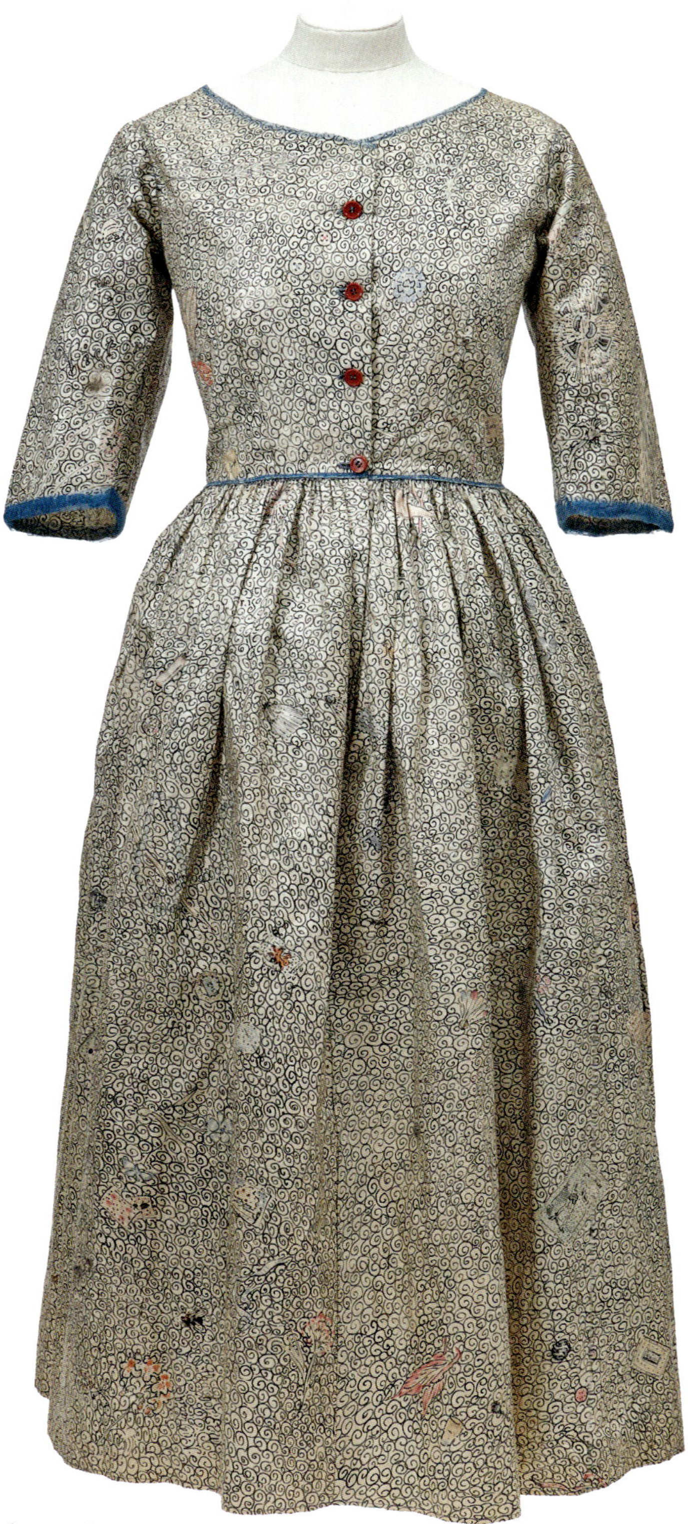

35 Edie Nicholson's dress, 1918
Ink on glazed cotton with
blue silk trim
Private collection

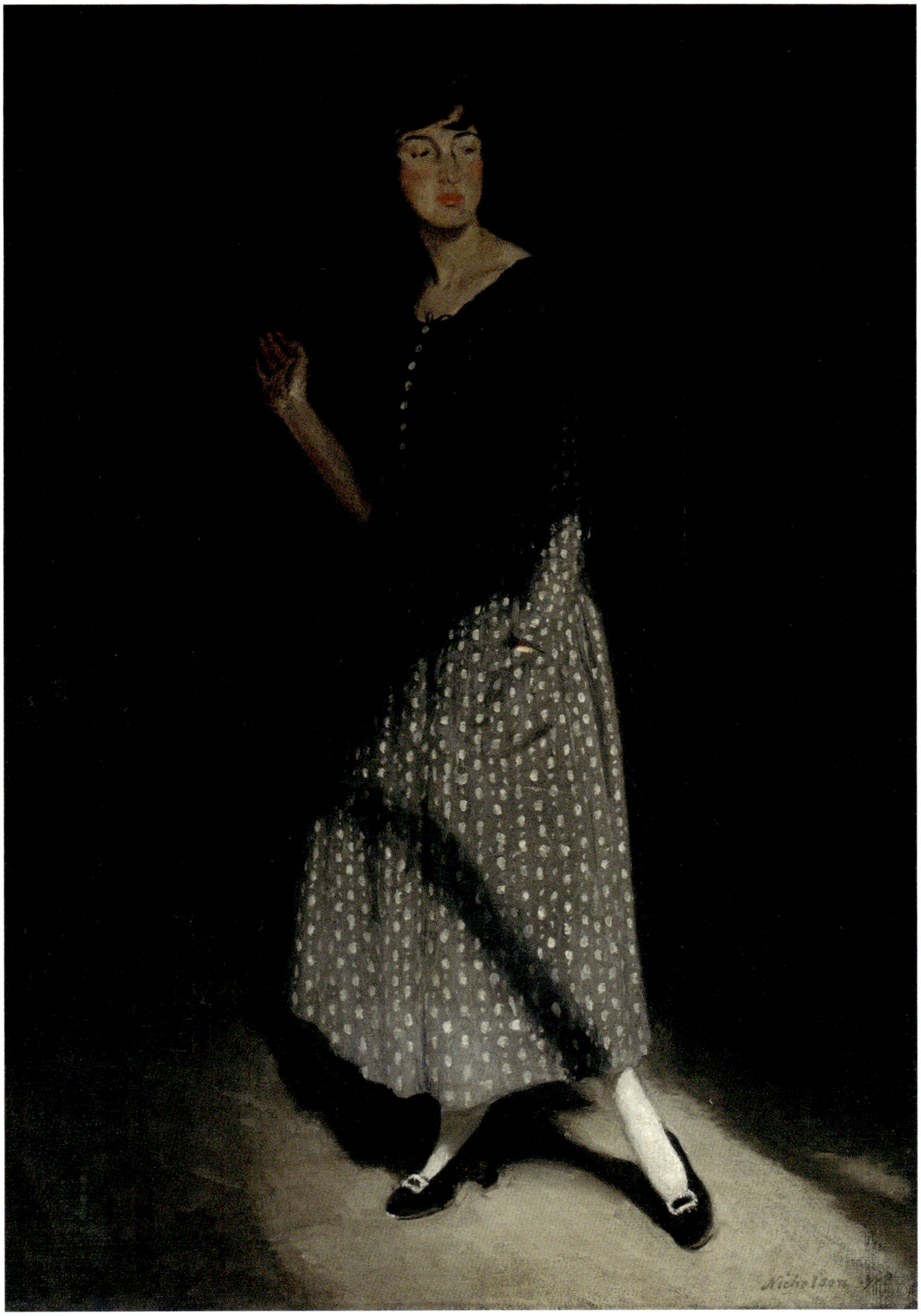

36 *Lady in Grey* (Edie Nicholson), 1918
Oil on canvas laid on board, 100.5 x 66.5cm
Private collection, courtesy Osborne
Samuel Gallery, London

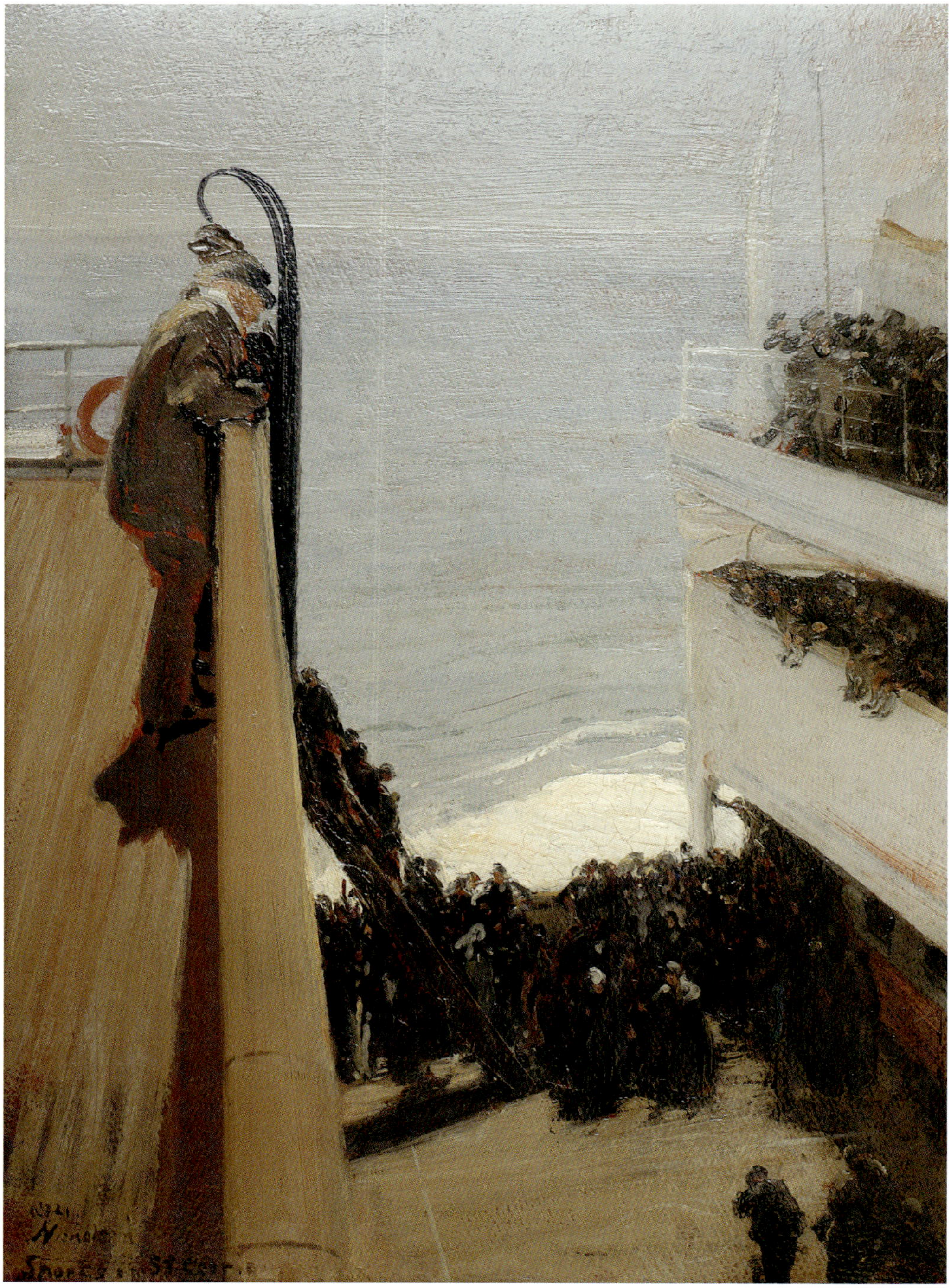

37 *Sport on the SS* Cedric, 1921
Oil on canvas board, 58.5 x 40.5cm
Estate of Mirabel Cecil

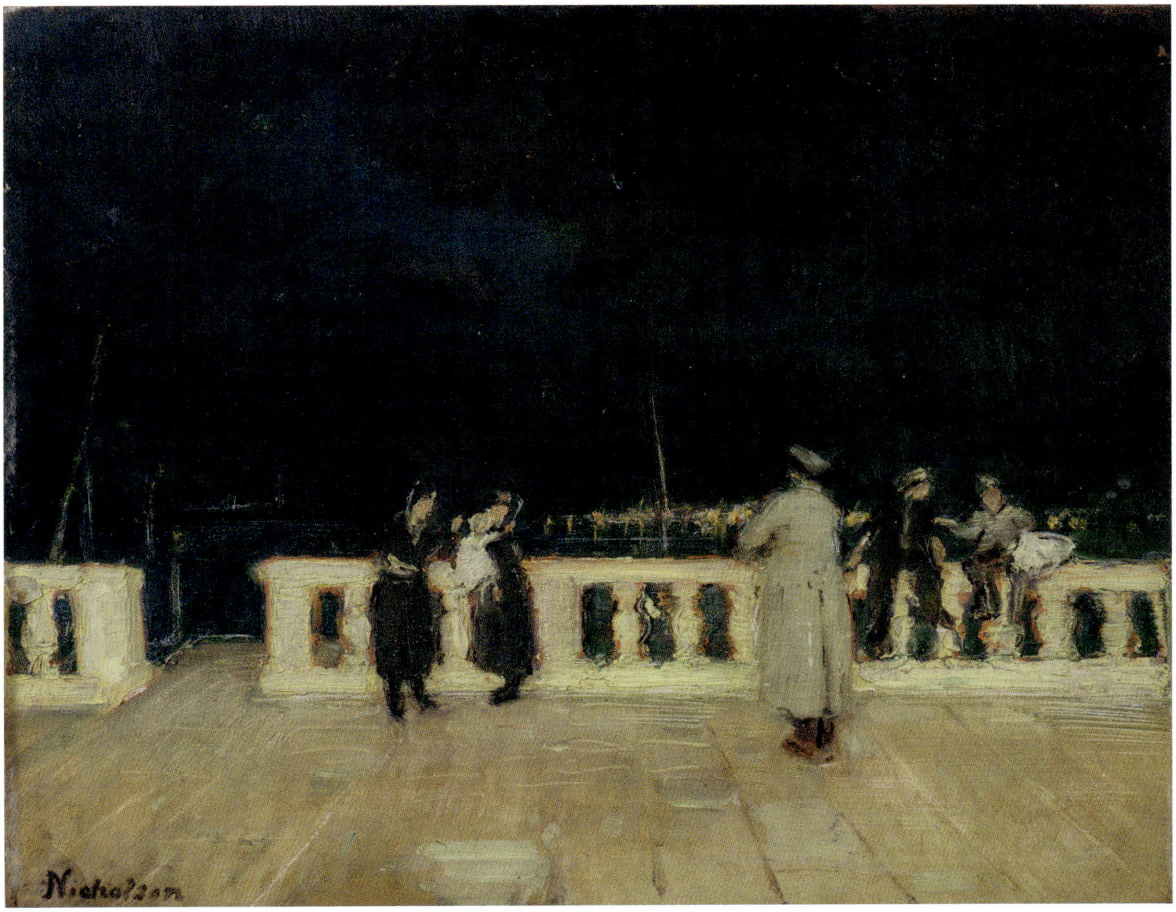

38 *Waiting for the* Heraclea, 1937
Oil on panel, 33 x 40cm
Private collection. On long term loan to The Courtauld Gallery, London

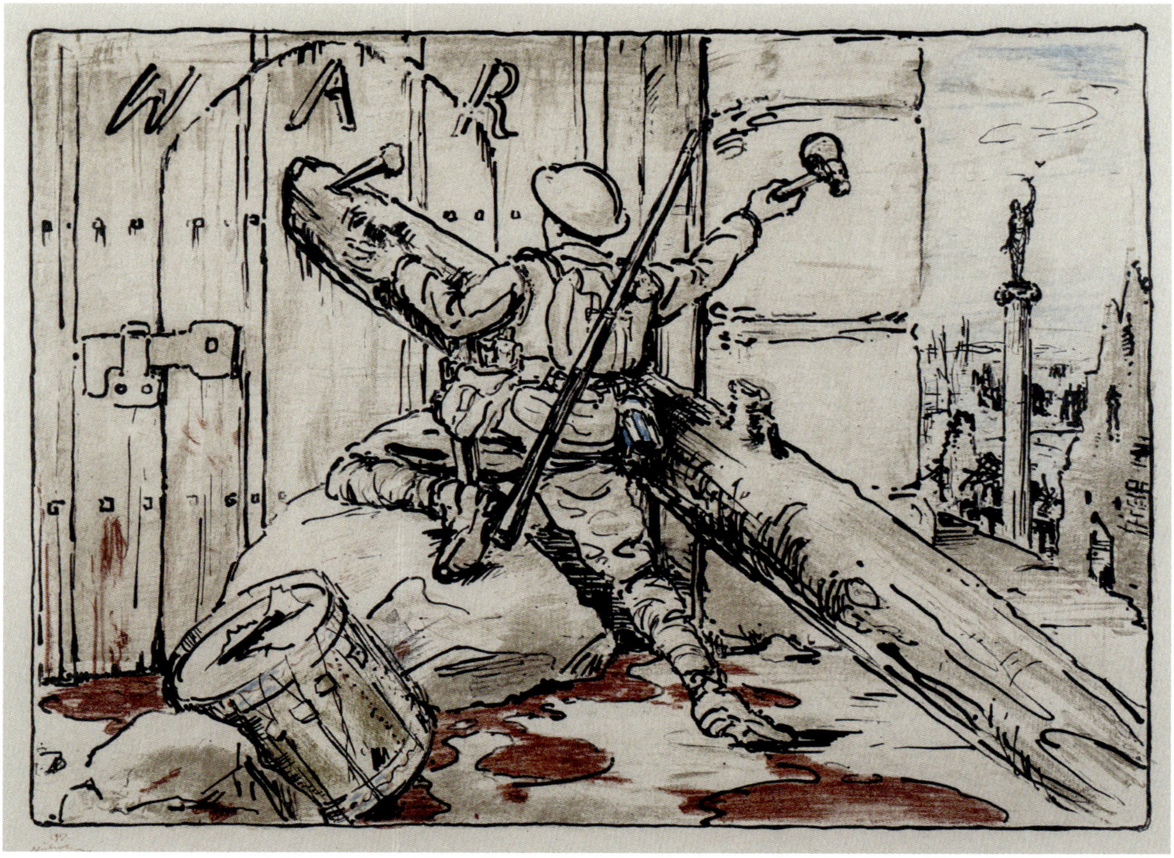

39 *The End of War*, 1917
Lithograph on paper, 43 x 58cm
Pallant House Gallery
(Purchased 2024)

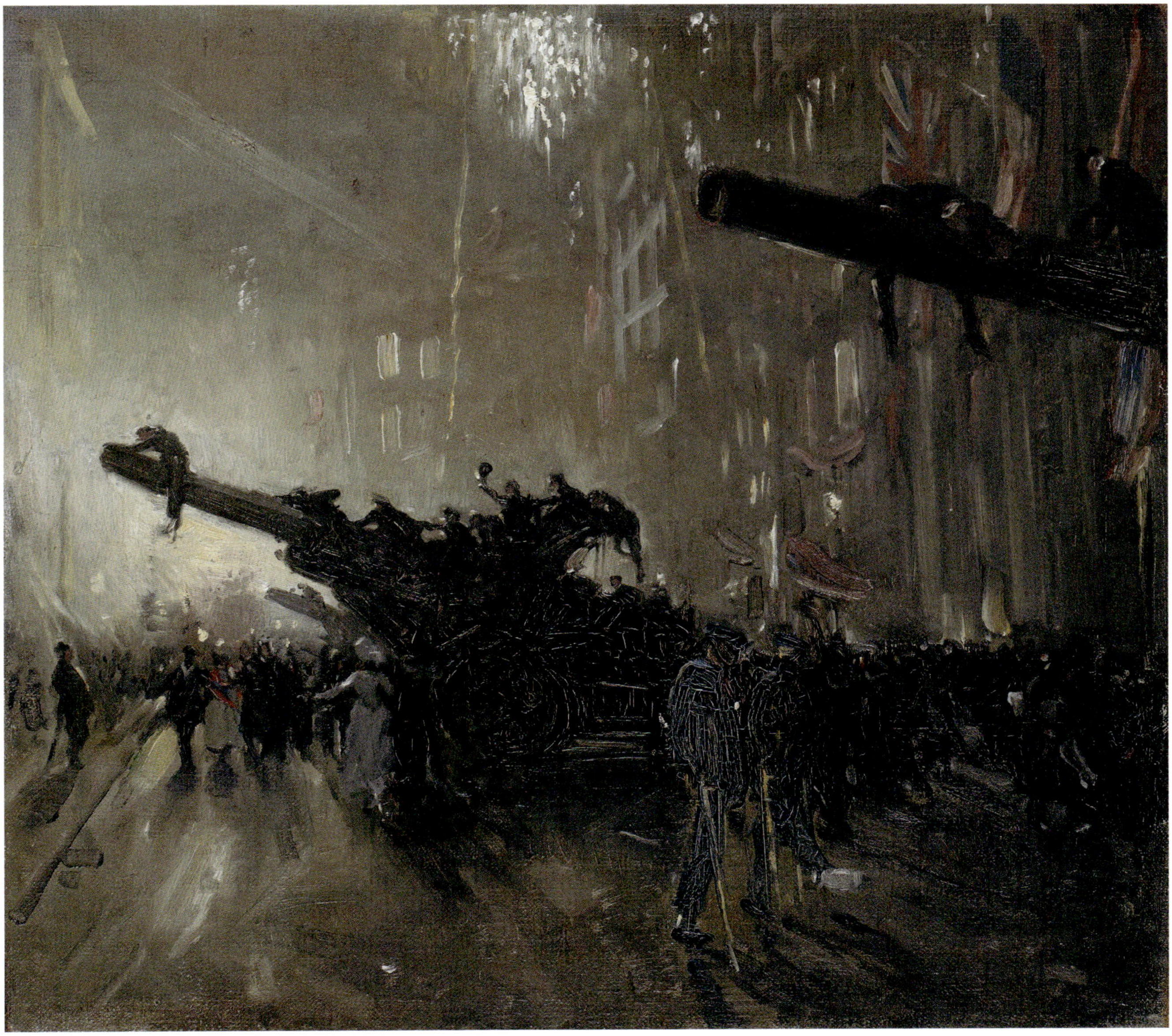

40 *Armistice Night*, 1918
Oil on canvas, 54 x 59.1cm
The Fitzwilliam Museum,
University of Cambridge

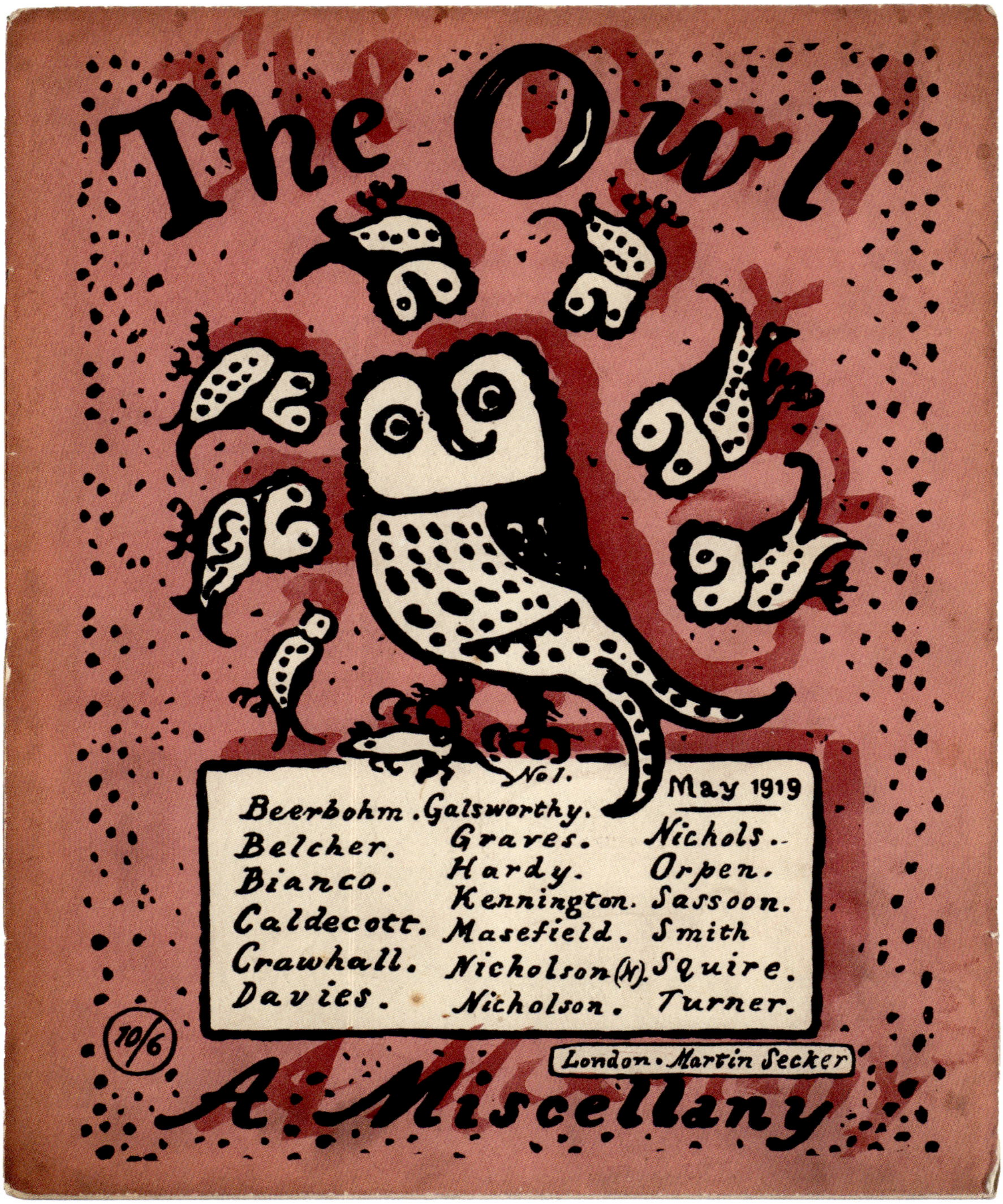

41 Cover design for *The Owl: A Miscellany*, no.1, edited by Robert Graves and William Nicholson, Martin Secker, London, May 1919
Journal, 32 x 26cm
Private collection

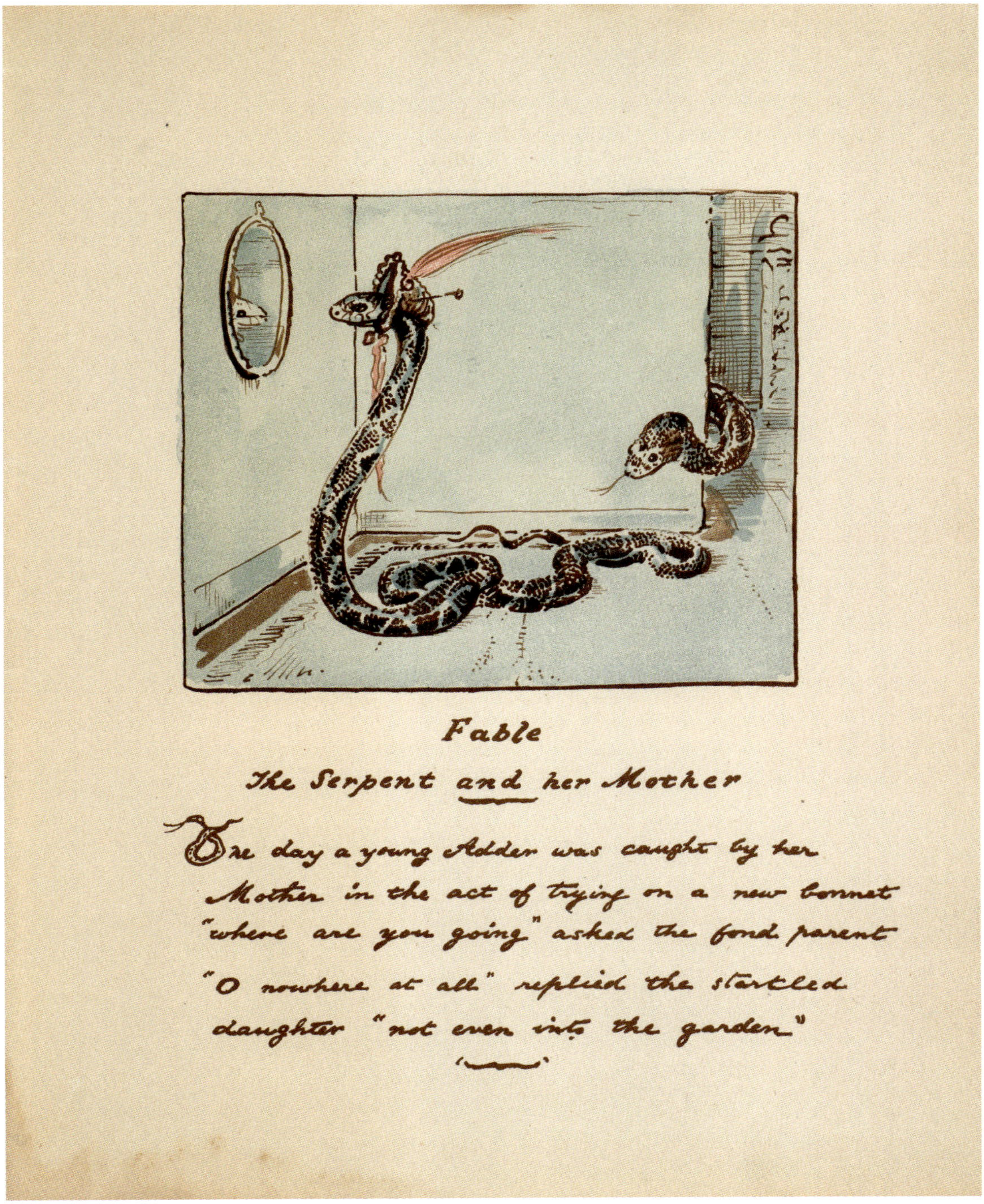
Fable

The Serpent and her Mother

One day a young Adder was caught by her
Mother in the act of trying on a new bonnet
"where are you going" asked the fond parent
"O nowhere at all" replied the startled
daughter "not even into the garden"

42 *The Serpent and her Mother*
From Robert Graves and William Nicholson (eds), *The Winter Owl*, Cecil Palmer, London, 1923
Journal, 32 x 26cm
Private collection

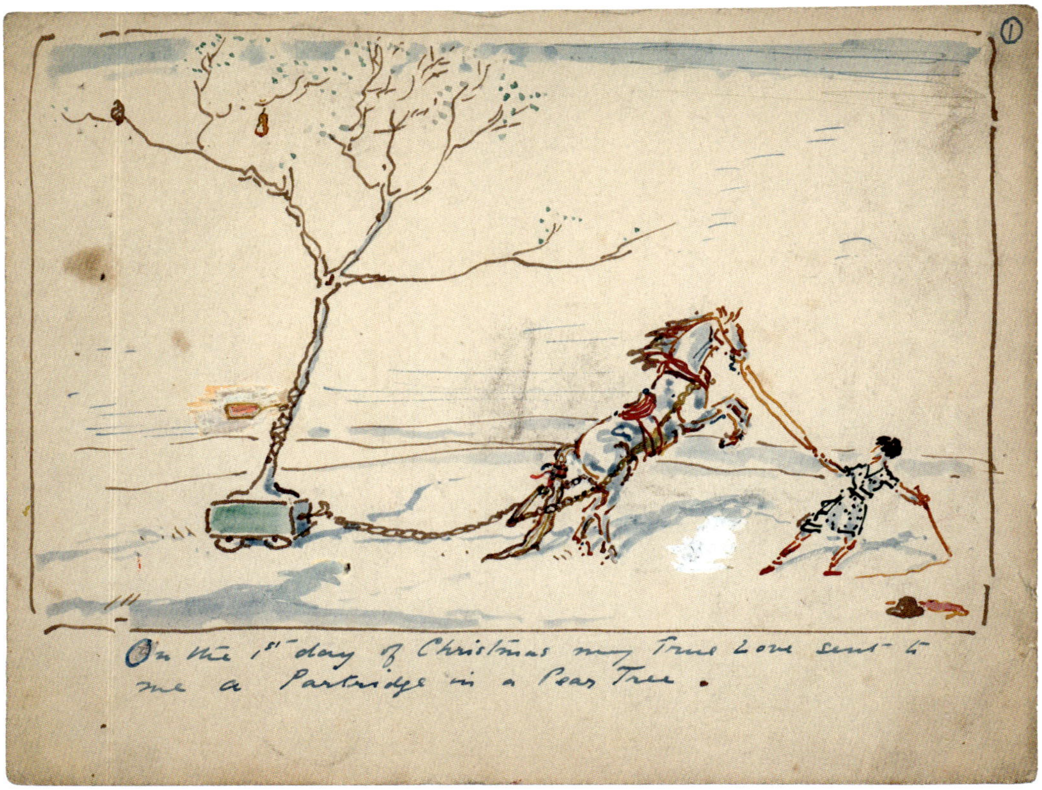

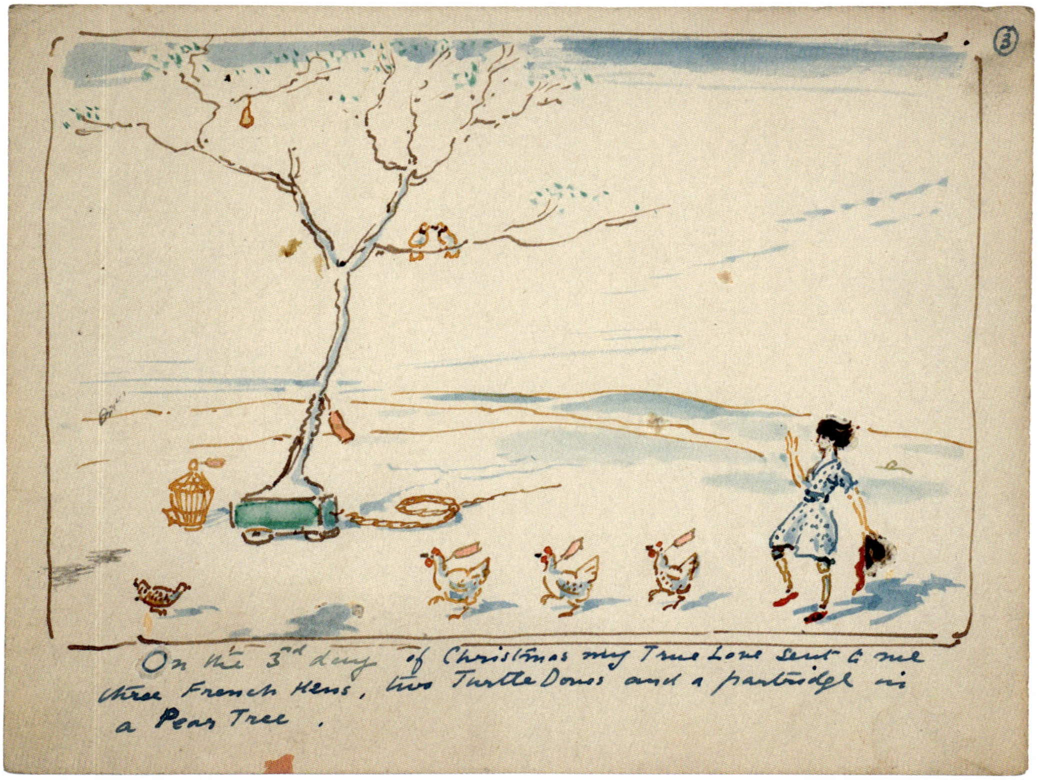

43 *The Twelve Days of Christmas* (days 1, 3, 6 and 7), c.1920s
Pen and watercolour on paper, 14 x 22cm each
Private collection

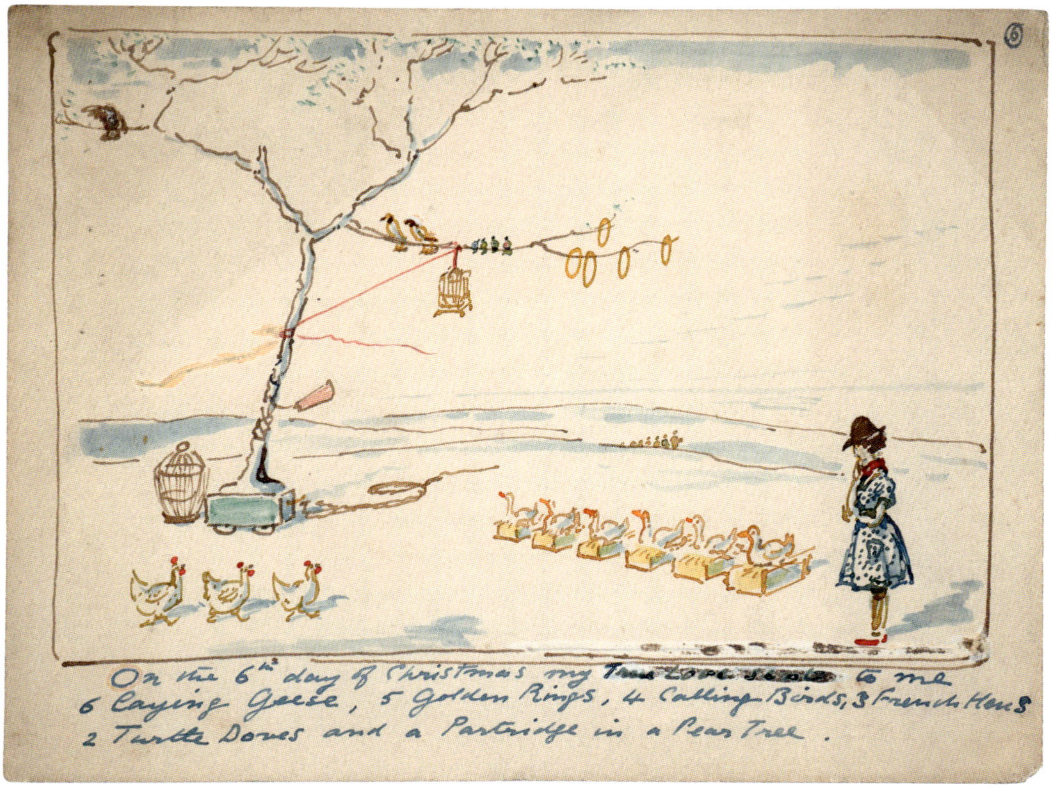
6
On the 6th day of Christmas my True Love sent to me
6 Laying Geese, 5 Golden Rings, 4 Calling Birds, 3 French Hens
2 Turtle Doves and a Partridge in a Pear Tree.

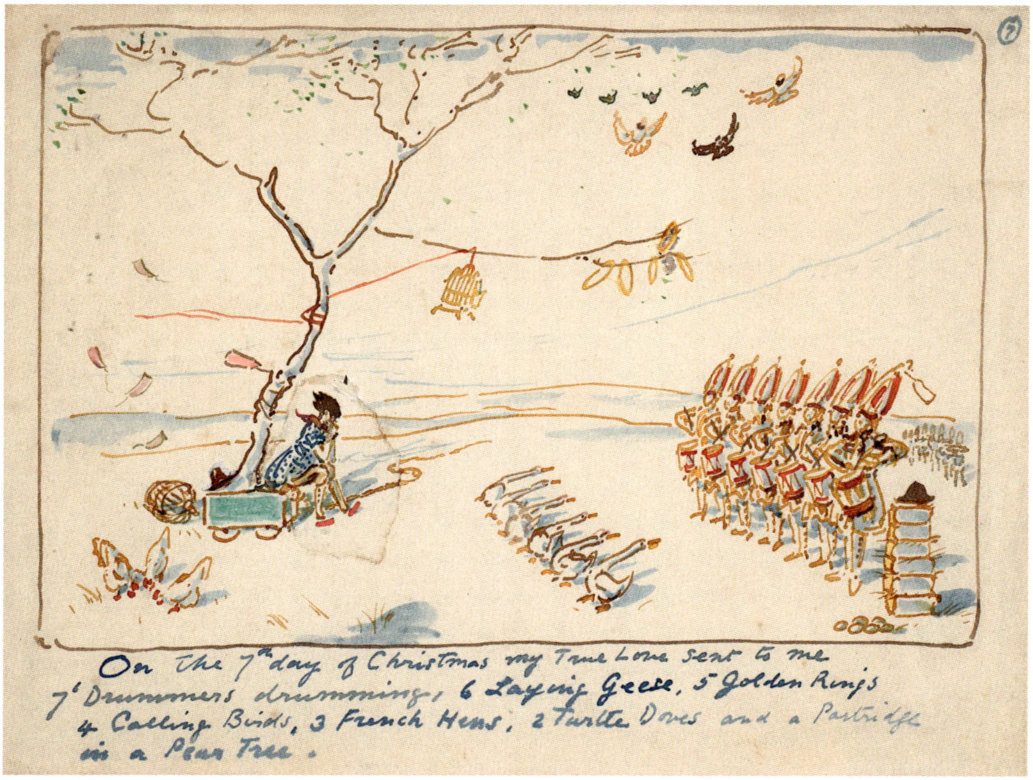
7
On the 7th day of Christmas my True Love sent to me
7 Drummers drumming, 6 Laying Geese, 5 Golden Rings
4 Calling Birds, 3 French Hens, 2 Turtle Doves and a Partridge
in a Pear Tree.

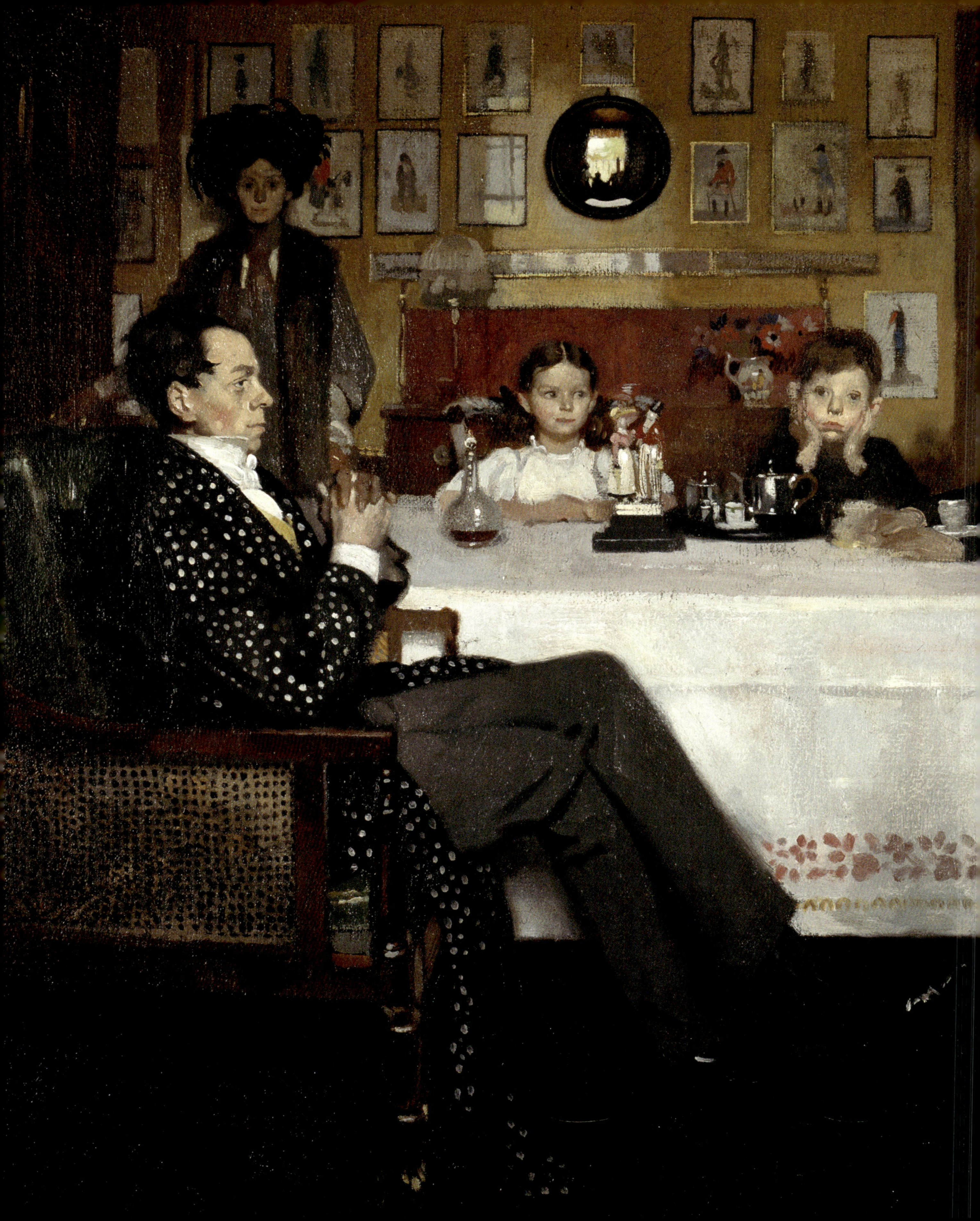

2 'CERTAIN CONGRUITIES OF DARK CLOTH, THE RIGID PERFECTION OF HIS LINEN': THE SELF-FASHIONING OF AN ARTIST

STEPHEN CALLOWAY

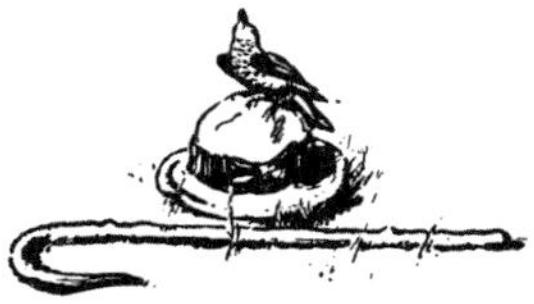

In his magisterial, if quirkily opinionated, 1908 two-volume study *Modern Art* the German art historian Julius Meier-Graefe (1867–1935) attempted to characterise the young artists who, first coming to prominence in the 1890s, made that decade so extraordinary and distinctive. Full of admiration for their impatience with convention, daring innovation and powers of self-invention, Meier-Graefe described them – with an obvious nod to Friedrich Nietzsche's *Zarathustra* – as 'superboys'.[1] They were, as he saw it, 'a generation which [...] at the age of twenty is more educated than we are now, and a hundred times more imaginative than we can ever hope to become. [...] They are more distinguished and refined than we.'[2] Widely travelled himself, Meier-Graefe observed that 'The members of this generation are to be found everywhere, in London, in Paris, and in Germany.'[3]

That this was indeed a generational phenomenon seems to be borne out by the fact that much of the mythology of the avant-garde and decadent 'nineties' in London grew up around one exceptional cohort of young artists and writers all born in the year 1872 and mostly friends, collaborators or, at times, cordial rivals. Among the central figures of this group, which included Max Beerbohm, William Rothenstein, Edward Gordon Craig and others now largely forgotten, the reputations of two, Aubrey Beardsley and William Nicholson, have stood every test of time. Both created remarkable bodies of work, but both in their ways also exemplify the Nietzschean ideal of the artist as genius and self-inventing personality.

Of course, the notion of the artist or writer creating a highly recognisable persona through the way they dress, act and present themselves – what we might define (without any derogatory implication) as the invention of a 'pose' – was not entirely new in the 1890s. Lord Byron (1788–1824), creator of the compellingly dangerous Romantic

p.50 Detail of fig.50

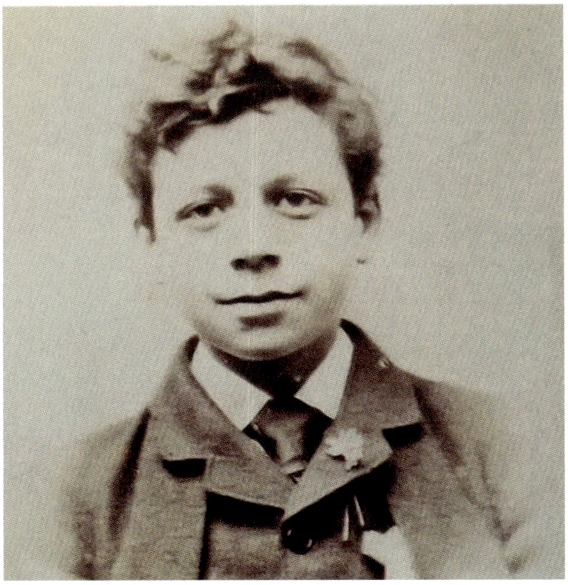

44 William Nicholson aged about 13, c.1885 Private collection

pose, and George 'Beau' Brummell (1778–1840), the insouciant dandy and social arbiter, both achieved in the early years of the century what we now refer to as celebrity status; and in the decade preceding the 'nineties' both James McNeill Whistler and Oscar Wilde realised how the power of personal image and idiosyncratic style could be enlisted as a means of relentless self-promotion. Although essentially a more reticent figure than any of these high-profile precursors, from the time of his initial emergence in the London art world and even through to his later years of rather more retired life, Nicholson seems to have possessed something of their mercurial character and desire for public attention when it came to the creation and nurturing of his own image.

Nicholson came from a traditional, conservative background in the Midlands, where his father, also William, in addition to being a successful ironwork manufacturer of such items as tractor seats, served for some years as MP for Newark. Though he would have wished otherwise, William senior, to his credit, allowed his son to follow his ambition to become a painter. A handful of surviving early photographs (fig.44) show William junior to have been an unremarkable youth of the period, who dressed in ordinary clothes and looked rather young for his age. Escaping this conventional upbringing, at Hubert von Herkomer's art school in Bushey he gained his first real introduction to the world of artists, an experience later extended by several months at the famous Académie Julian in Paris. At Herkomer's he met as a fellow student Mabel Pryde, who, in spite of initial parental misgivings on both sides, would become his wife in 1893. 'Prydie', as she was generally known, was an independently minded young woman from a somewhat more interesting family milieu in Edinburgh. Her brother, James Pryde, also a painter, was just a few years older, but already seemed a more established figure.

That summer of 1893 James Pryde visited the young couple in their first home, The Eight Bells, the former inn in the tiny village of Denham in Buckinghamshire. Endlessly extending his stay as he and his brother-in-law explored the possibilities of working collaboratively, it was he who would play the first major role in Nicholson's development both artistically and also in terms of personal style. A frequently reproduced photograph (fig.45) taken probably by Mabel Nicholson in 1898 at Chaucer's House, Woodstock, shows her husband outside standing in profile, whilst through the window we can discern the substantial figure of Pryde, holding up William and Mabel's first child, Ben. Nicholson, with his close-cropped and oiled hair and fresh face, still looks very much younger than his years, which seems to explain why to Mabel and her brother he was always known as 'The Kid'. He sports a bold tweed suit – the coat with high lapels and broad sleeves, the trousers cut long over the boots – and the same style of high, 'stand-up' starched collar

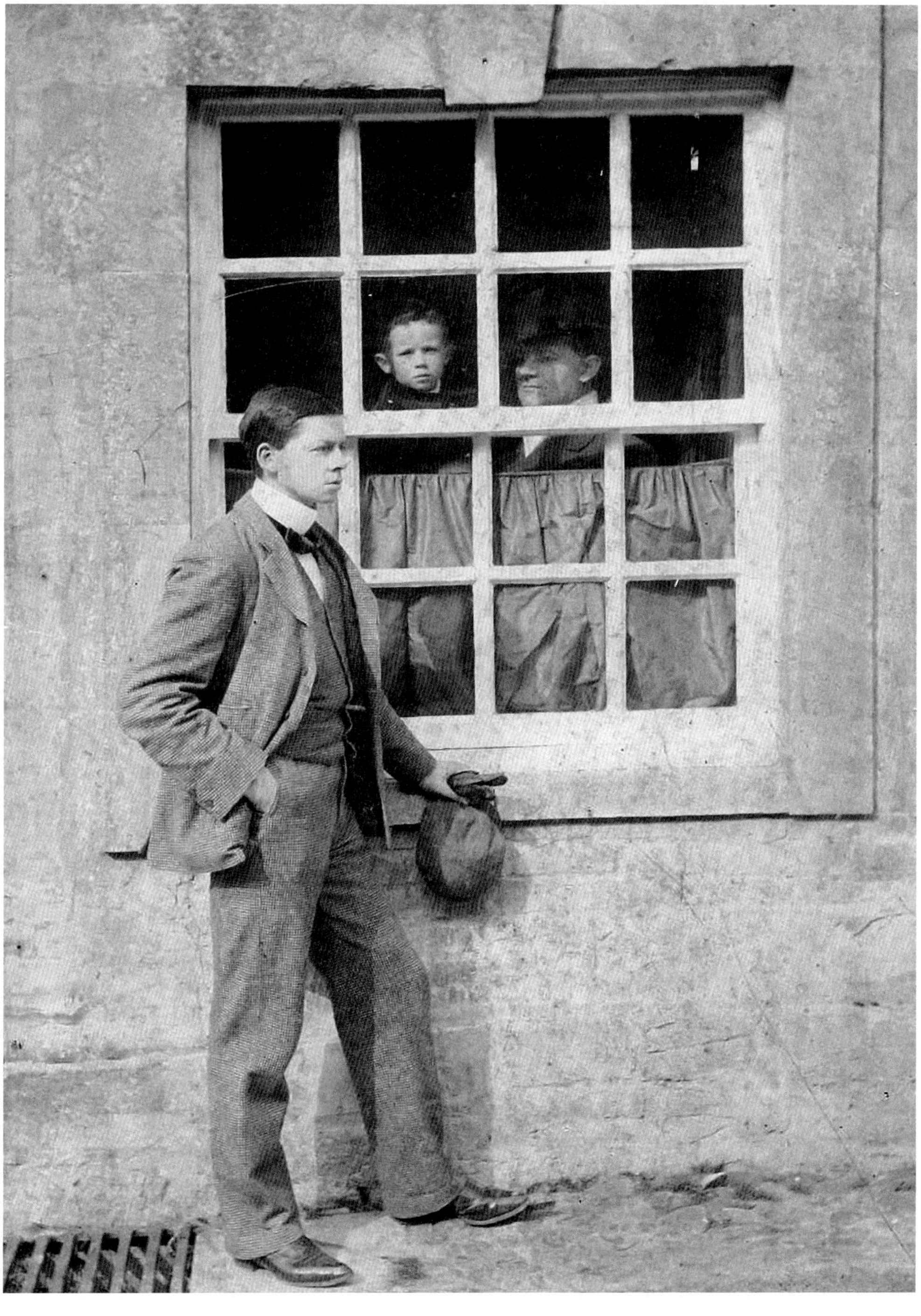

45 William Nicholson standing on the pavement outside a window at Chaucer's House, Woodstock, with James Pryde inside holding up Ben, c.1898, probably taken by Mabel Nicholson
Private collection

and dark, formal and, most likely, ready-made bow tie to which Pryde had introduced him.

This was the look of a 'Masher', or more precisely that of a 'Nut' (sometimes spelled 'Knut'), a style adopted in the 1890s and early Edwardian years by many young men-about-town. These ranged in background from dapper shop assistants and ambitious clerks through to some rather richer and more leisured would-be dandies; they aimed to be thought fashionable in dress and socially smart, but were generally considered to fall into the category of 'not-quite-gentlemen'. A famous devotee of the Nut style was the popular illustrator and caricaturist Phil May.[4] He became a friend and helpful supporter of Pryde and Nicholson during the time when, under their invented joint name 'J. & W. Beggarstaff' (also known as the 'Beggarstaff Brothers'), they were trying to establish themselves in the novel area of pictorial poster design. Winning considerable acclaim in artistic circles for the striking inventiveness of their large, boldly collaged images, they also – probably in part through May's good connections in the world of illustrated magazines – began to attract attention in the press. May himself drew them for *The Studio* magazine in 1895 wearing matching versions of the classic wide, tent-like cabmens' coats with oversize pearl buttons and the low-crowned bowler hats favoured by the Nuts.[5] Similarly, another magazine artist of the day, Will True (b.1866, fl.1890s), made them the subject of the first of his 'Posterdom Caricatures' in the specialist publication *The Poster*, adding to the amusing aspect of their choice of matching clothes by emphasising the contrast between Pryde's considerable height and bulk and the diminutive figure of Nicholson.[6] Ben Nicholson, always somewhat doubtful about his father's dandyism, remarked a little uncharitably 'Together they would have made a very good comic turn in the Edwardian music hall.'[7]

46 JAMES PRYDE (1866–1941)
Portrait of William Nicholson, 1901
Lithographic reproduction on paper of a hand-coloured woodcut published in *The Studio*, 21 x 14cm
Private collection

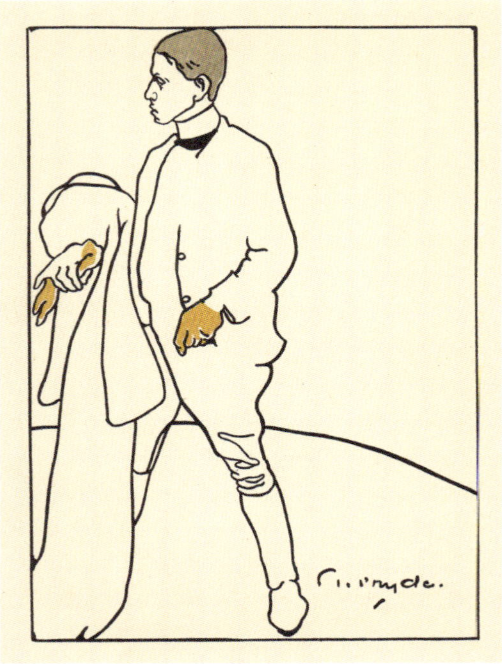

With the almost complete failure – financially speaking – of the Beggarstaff enterprise, Nicholson and Pryde began to drift apart both in terms of artistic aims and sartorial style. Pryde continued to dress conspicuously, but, as an aficionado of the boxing ring and the theatre and a stalwart of the Savile Club, increasingly in the style of the sporting gent, with huge top coat, silk hat, gloves, spats and gold monocle. By contrast, Nicholson began to dress in a distinctly more theatrical style, greatly influenced by his growing interest in the Regency period, an enthusiasm which he shared with Beerbohm and a group of new friends, the American playwright Edward Knoblock (1874–1945), the interior decorator Victoria Sackville-West (1862–1936) and her ambitious young architect, Edwin Lutyens. Keenly observant, Prydie, in one of her more ambitious portraits (fig.47), painted in 1911, portrayed her husband in a sort of fancy-dress

47 MABEL PRYDE NICHOLSON (1871–1918)
Portrait of William Nicholson, 1911
Oil on canvas, 91.5 x 81.5cm
Private collection

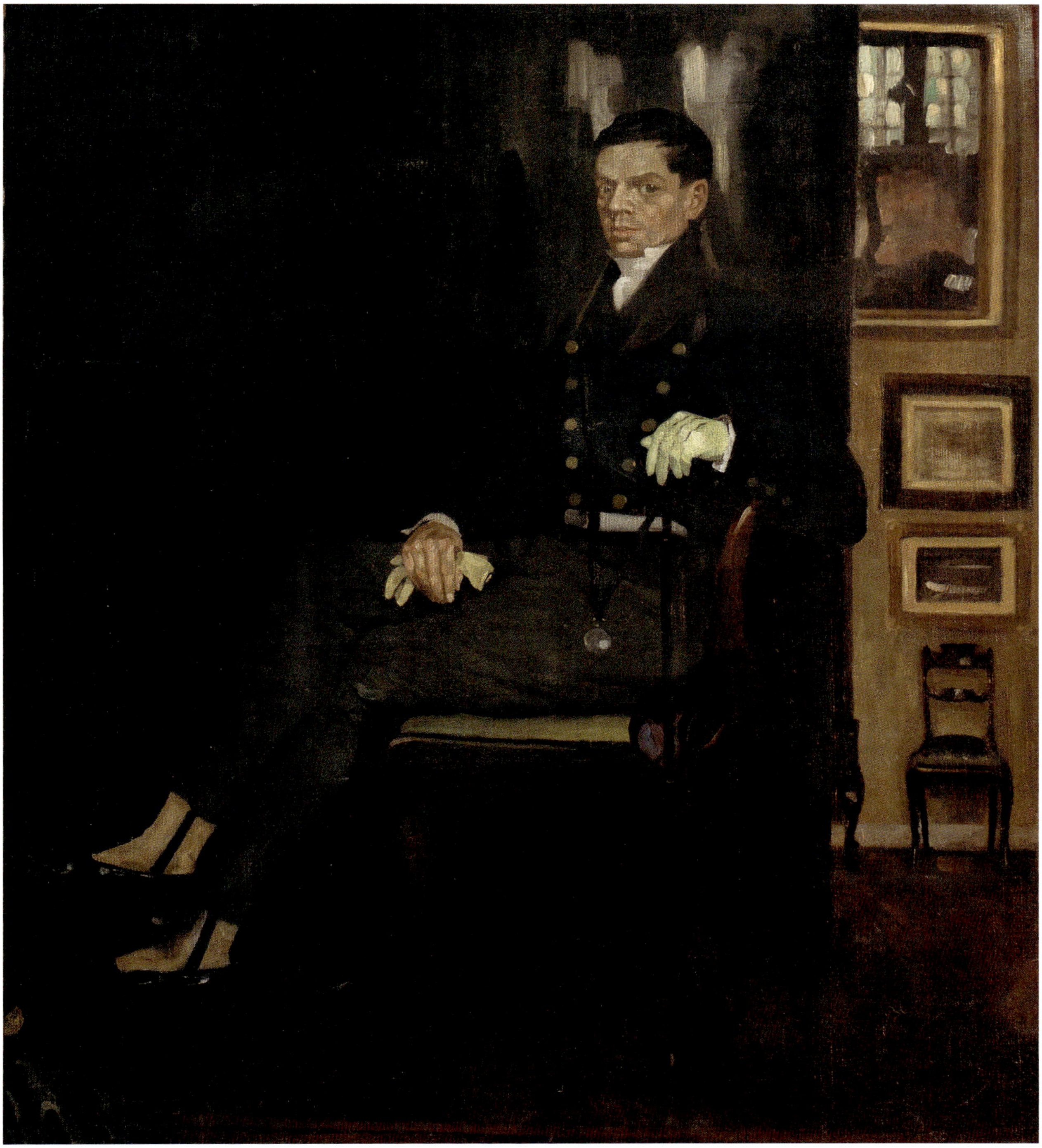

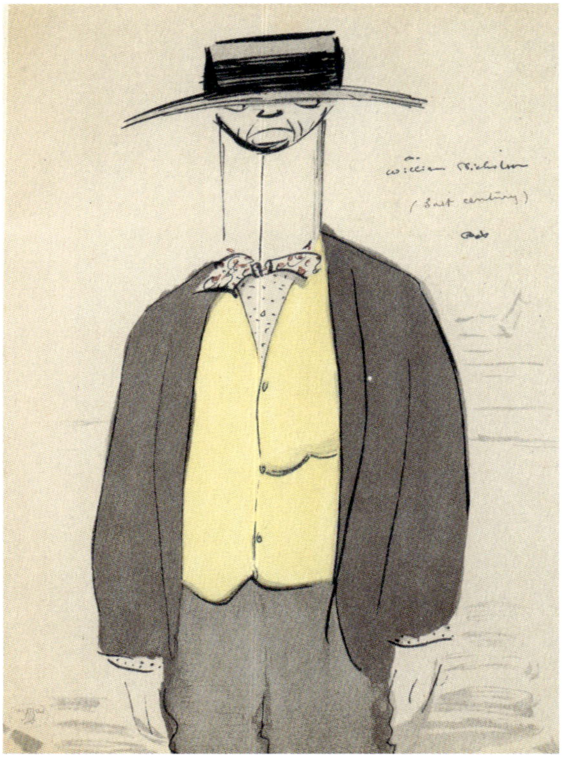

48 MAX BEERBOHM (1872–1956)
Caricature of William Nicholson in Robert Graves and William Nicholson (eds), *The Owl: A Miscellany*, no.2, Martin Secker, London, October 1919
Journal, 32 x 26cm
Private collection

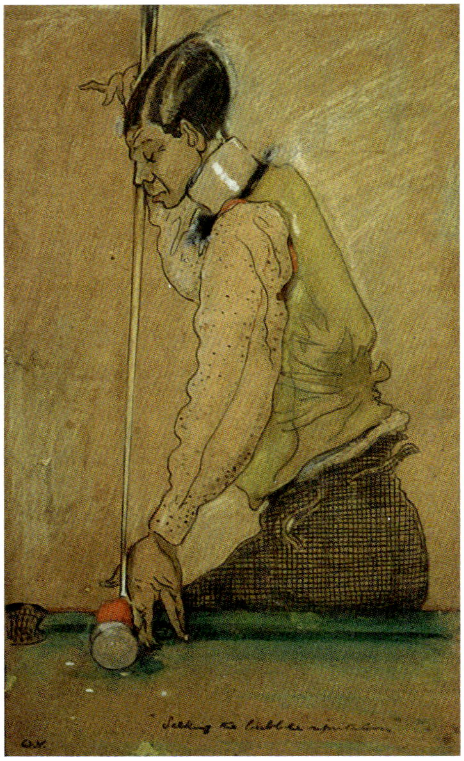

49 *Seeking the Bubble Reputation (in the Cannon's Mouth)*, a self-portrait playing snooker, c.1916
Pen, ink and watercolour, 42 x 22cm
Private collection

version of that period: dark blue-green cut-away coat with velvet collar, high white collar and stock, strapped pantaloons and patent pumps, a quizzing glass dangling on a silk ribbon. Closely modelled on the style advocated by Beau Brummell, this stiffly mannered and tightly buttoned look is instantly recognisable in the celebrated series of caricatures of the dandies of 1816–18 drawn by Richard Dighton (1795–1880); Nicholson had acquired an impressive group of these rare prints and, when the Nicholson family moved to Mecklenburgh Square in Bloomsbury, he hung them in their smart Neo-Regency drawing room.[8] It was not long before Nicholson was to be seen parading a version of this look as his usual day wear.

Beerbohm had made Brummell and the dandy style the subject of one of his earliest and most brilliant essays, first published in 1895; he was now clearly fascinated by Nicholson's adoption of the Beau's precepts. In several of the caricatures (fig.48) he made of his friend, Beerbohm revelled in the way in which Nicholson grasped Brummell's ideal of creating 'the supreme effect through means the least extravagant': his bullet head of dark and brilliantined hair contrasting with crisp white collar and stock; the extraordinary outline of his skin-tight, wasp-waisted frock coat adorned with a velvet collar; narrow trousers over sleekly polished leather boots and a curious Regency cane fashioned from some exotic wriggly wood. Nicholson seemed to be remaking the original dandy style, his 'supreme effect' no doubt recalling to Beerbohm another celebrated line from his essay: 'In certain congruities of dark cloth, in the rigid perfection of his linen, in the symmetry of his glove with his hand, lay the secret of Mr. Brummell's miracles.'[9]

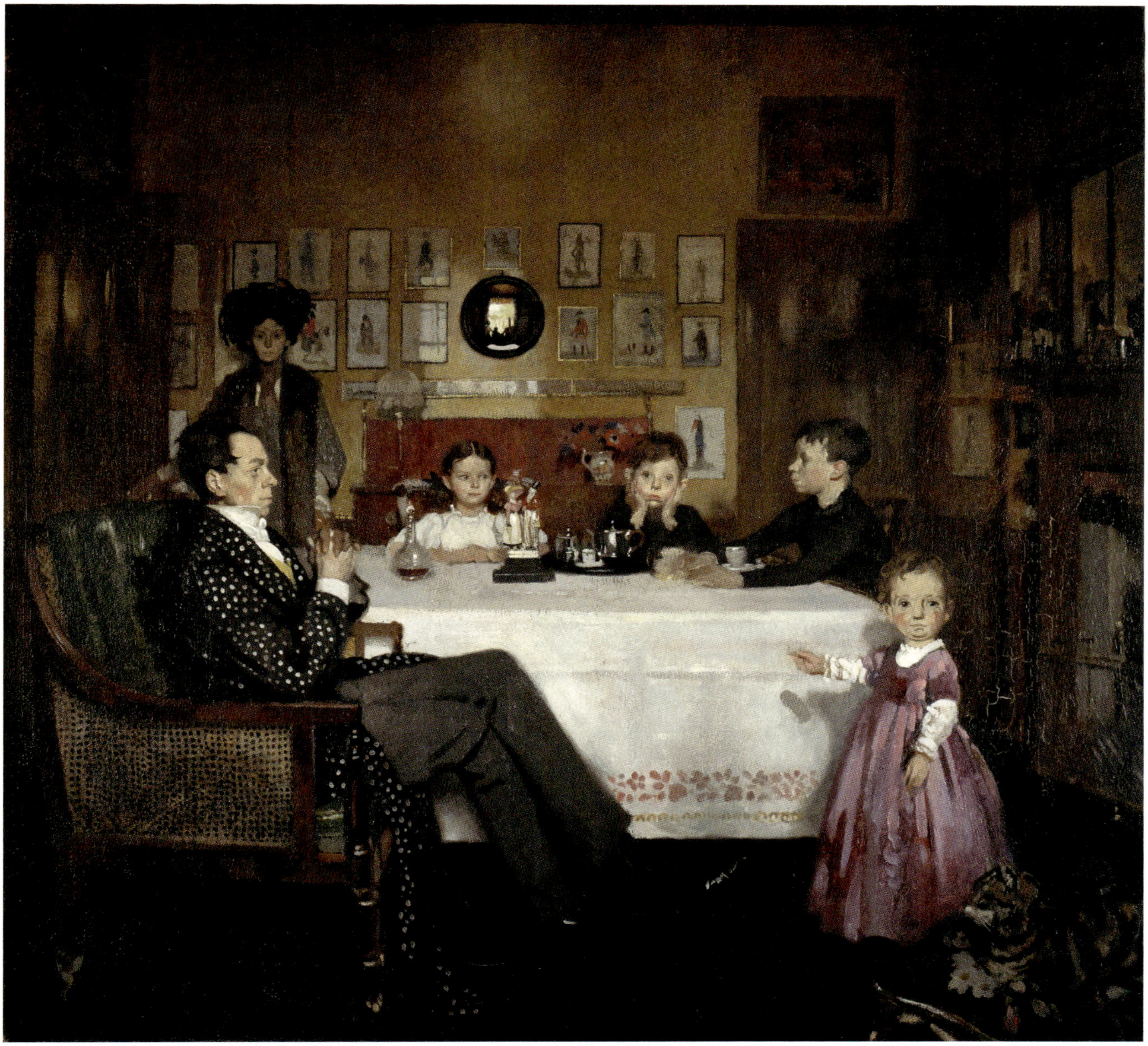

50 WILLIAM ORPEN (1878–1931)
A Bloomsbury Family, 1907
Oil on canvas, 86.5 x 91.5cm
National Galleries of Scotland.
Presented by the Scottish Modern
Arts Association 1964

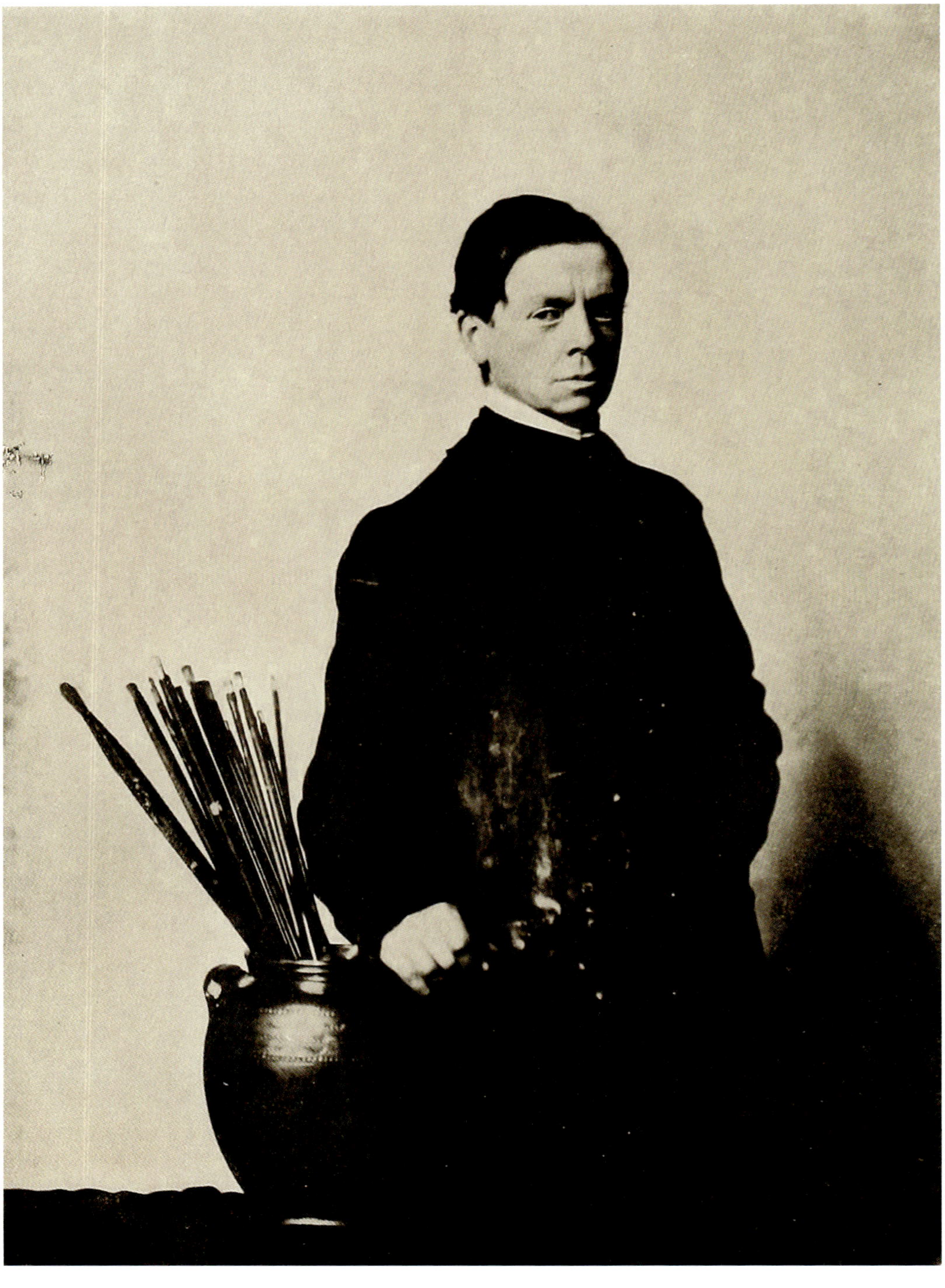

51 MALCOLM ARBUTHNOT
(1877–1967)
William Nicholson,
aged 40
Private collection

William Orpen, in his celebrated family portrait of the Nicholsons, *A Bloomsbury Family* (1907; fig.50), seems in his depiction of his friend to have played upon the rigid profile pose employed to such effect by Dighton in his caricatures. Nicholson, seated to the left in a Regency library bergère chair, is in his own version of 1820s 'at home' dress: his starched collar and yellow waistcoat 'the colour of newborn ducklings' contrasting with a much-loved and long-cherished black and white polka-dot dressing gown. Like a lounging figure from one of the illustrations to *Tom and Jerry, or Life in London* (a favourite Regency period popular novel), one shiny black slipper dangles from his foot. But there is nothing nonchalant about the image; Orpen's 'informal portrait' seems so buttoned-up as to verge on caricature. It hints too at some domestic drama. The children gathered round the table are conventionally dressed, but look bored and resigned. By contrast, Prydie, dressed fashionably in Edwardian style with an extravagantly feathered hat, stands by the door; reaching for the doorknob, she seems on the point of leaving.

In a second painting, *The Café Royal, London* (1911–12; Musée d'Orsay, Paris), Orpen again depicted Nicholson, this time walking into the famous, lavishly gilded and mirrored Grill Room, a favoured gathering place of artists and writers. Again he is shown in rigid profile, and again the image seems almost cruelly to caricature the way his tight clothes emphasise the extreme angularity of his pose, suggesting perhaps more the character of a military martinet than that of an artist. Cleverly, Orpen created a powerful contrast between the small, lean and dapper Nicholson and two sprawling, expansive figures in the foreground. One is James Pryde in his usual costume of dark overcoat and billycock hat; the other, Augustus John (1872–1949), bearded and with untidy hair, wears a shabby, brown velvet-collared suit, but no collar and tie:

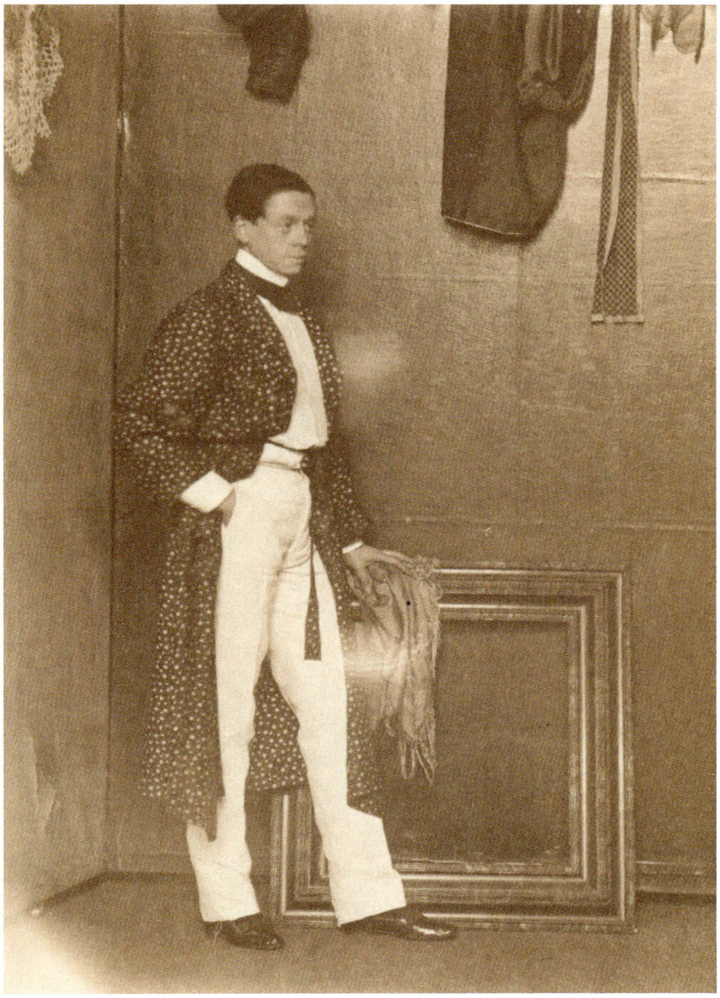

52 E.O. HOPPÉ (1878–1972)
William Nicholson in 1911
Private collection

the very picture of louche bohemianism. Although Nicholson and Orpen and their respective wives were close in these years, it is known that Nicholson did not greatly appreciate either of these depictions by his friend and fellow portraitist. Oddly, three photographs all taken at about the same time (by the photographers Alvin Langdon [1882–1966], Malcolm Arbuthnot [1877–1967] and E.O. Hoppé [1878–1972]; figs.51 and 52) and showing him in very similar poses were among his favourite images of himself.

In seeking to chart the evolution of Nicholson's style of dress as an expression of his wish not merely to create a 'look', but also to project an image of his artistic personality, we are fortunate that we have so helpful a sequence of surviving portraits, drawings and photographs to document his appearance at almost every stage of his life. This is in no small part a result of the fact that he was a popular figure, welcome everywhere, it seems, and on good terms with all manner of people with whom he came into contact. This is not to say that he struck an easy or enjoyable relationship with every sitter of whom he painted a portrait; some he found difficult and a few, such as the Viceroy of India, Lord Hardinge, quite impossible.

It is also clear that not everyone Nicholson encountered understood or appreciated his carefully cultivated pose; indeed some entirely misread his character from his dress and studied manner. Sybil Waller formed a somewhat less than favourable impression during the months in 1910 when Nicholson was painting a double portrait of her and her father, the designer and collector Pickford Waller (1849–1930). The picture became known as *The Conder Room* from its setting in the salon of Waller's house filled with painted silk panels by the Australian artist Charles Conder (1868–1909).[10] She thought it turned out 'not such a complete success as most of his previous work', whilst of the artist himself she wrote: 'Nicholson was a strange man, he had a decidedly artificial manner, which rather debarred one from intimacy, though he was a very amusing and witty companion. He was a complete "Masher" [...] his costume was so eccentric as almost to verge on fancy dress.'[11] This last observation is not so wide of the mark; Nicholson did greatly love fancy dress and throughout his life kept in his various studios a well-stocked dressing-up box, full of both men's and women's clothes, hats, shoes and other accessories of all kinds and dates. A description by Marguerite Steen (Nicholson's companion in his later years) gives an idea of his brilliance at improvising outfits. Staying in Paris in Knoblock's apartment, where he was painting a roomful of decorative glass panels, he was seized with the desire to take his then mistress, Marie, to a masquerade ball. Pulling together various items found in his host's rooms – fortunately including a Venetian mask, to which he added a black eye patch – he created a brilliant costume topped off with plumes from the cleaner's feather duster.[12] 'He looked,' wrote Steen, 'like some sinister creation of Aubrey Beardsley's. So macabre in fact, that when they went into the Café de Paris at about four in the morning a woman who came in with two Americans shrieked off into hysterics and had to be carried out by her companions.'[13]

There were other unfavourable reactions to Nicholson's customary dressing up and habitual striking of a pose. Among his own circle he had perfected a party piece of singing and dancing in the style of the 'black-face minstrels' popular in the music halls of the day. This imitation was, because of his angular figure, jerky movements and tight clothes, held to be successful and highly amusing. However, in a story recounted by his friend, the poet and self-styled 'man-of-the-road' W.H. Davies (1871–1940), an episode occurred in which Nicholson encountered an actual troupe of street entertainers: 'When these men saw Nicholson coming – dressed exactly like themselves, in a black coat and white trousers – they looked considerably angry and whispered together. All of them then set their eyes on Nicholson and waited until he had gone, thinking he had a tin whistle in his pocket or a banjo under his coat, and was a rival!'[14]

Augustus John, who painted a portrait of Nicholson (1909; fig.53), life-size, seated in his studio, but wearing a dark, heavy and almost all-enveloping topcoat of the kind favoured by Pryde, sensed the degree to which Nicholson in these years was striking a very specific artistic pose that did not necessarily reflect his amiable nature.[15] Many years later in his ragbag of memoirs, *Chiaroscuro*, John recalled his impression that: 'William Nicholson, whose pernickety mannerisms first repelled me, on further acquaintance revealed the sensitive mind and warm heart he had taken so much trouble to conceal under a too elaborate mask.'[16] John's equally astute characterisation of Pryde seems telling here, too, as the influence he had once had over Nicholson still hovered in the background, even though they were no longer close: '"Jimmy" had been an actor and still appeared to be playing an important role in some out-of-date melodrama: the performance was non-stop and must have put a strain on even his constitution.'[17]

Even when working in his studio, Nicholson wore his formal and precisely ordered clothes, including his high collars and stocks or bow ties and, almost invariably, the white duck trousers mentioned in W.H. Davies's story. Elegantly cut and always most carefully laundered, these came to form one of the most noticeable and idiosyncratic elements of his wardrobe. In his choice of painting clothes he cut a figure rather at odds with most other artists in the 20th century and more akin to the grandees of the Victorian art world such as Frederic Leighton (1830–1896) and John Everett Millais (1829–1896), who liked to cultivate a public image of being

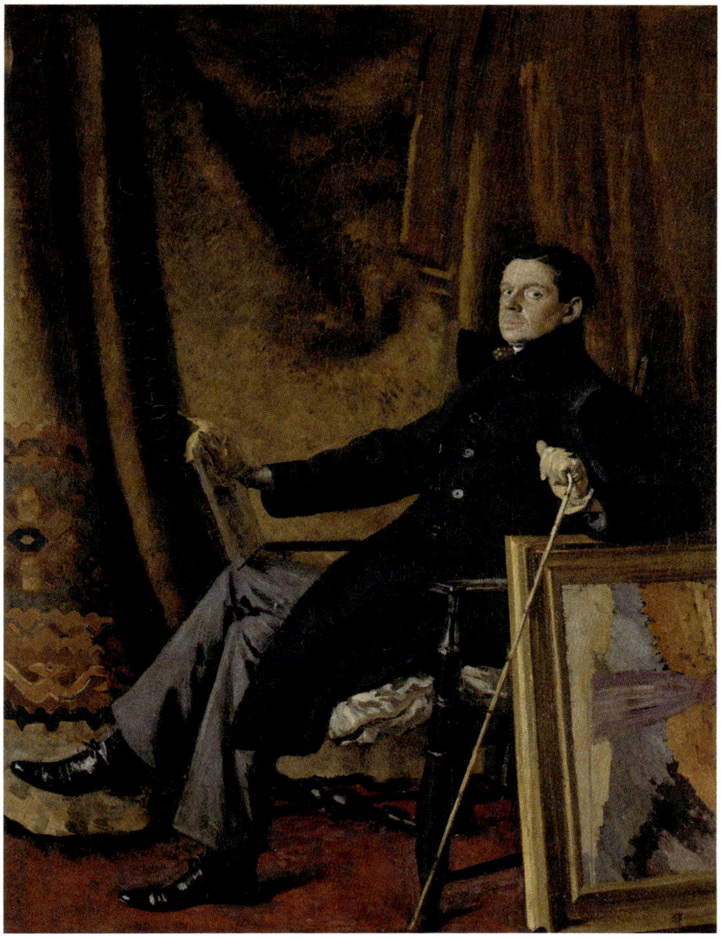

53 AUGUSTUS JOHN (1872–1949)
William Nicholson, 1909
Oil on canvas, 190.2 x 143.8cm
The Fitzwilliam Museum, University of Cambridge

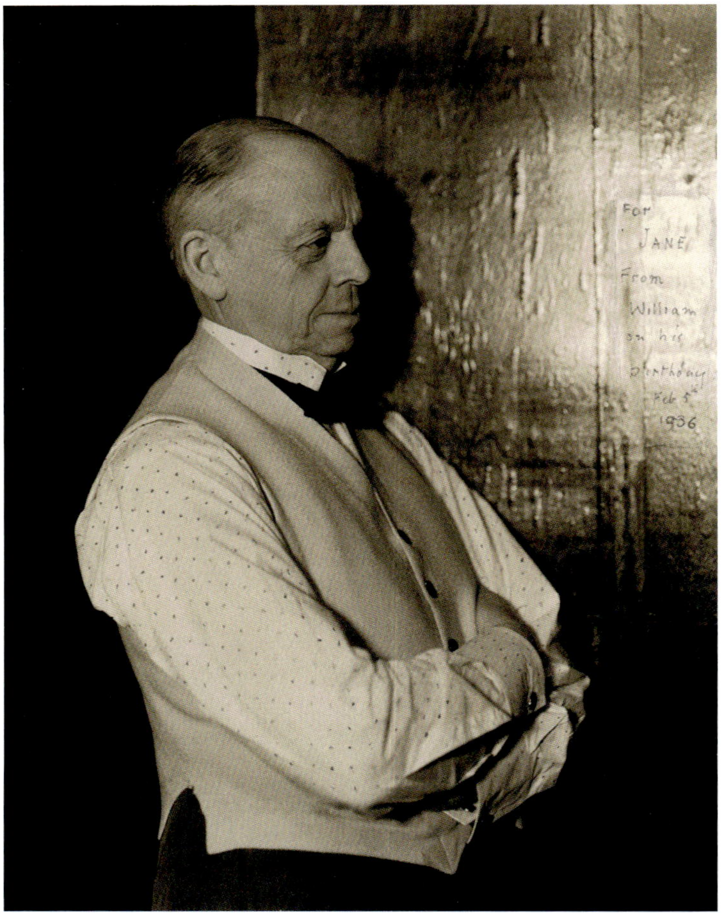

54 ANONYMOUS
William Nicholson, c.1935
Private collection

well-dressed gentlemen, not scruffy artists, when photographed in their immaculate and artistically arranged painting rooms. Over the following years Nicholson would rigorously maintain this look and, even as he aged, he never really softened it. Winifred Nicholson recalled a conversation in 1926 when she had observed the parallel between her father-in-law's work and his dress, which uncannily echoed Beerbohm's lines of almost 30 years before: 'This art of his was typically English, the expression of his date and place in it. His immaculate white shirts with their pinpoint black spots pinpointed that [...] His art was about tone, light and shade in the sense of gradation of white to black, never of rainbow gradation [...] his mastery of black, and black to grey, created masterpieces.'[18]

Even in his later years Nicholson made little change in his manner or to what had become a well-honed sartorial image. An oft-reproduced black-and-white photograph of about 1935 (fig.54), by which time he was in his early sixties, shows him standing in clothes much the same as those he had worn in 1910: crisp, patterned shirt, high starched collar and dark stock and a plain – no doubt canary-yellow – waistcoat. Perhaps aware of his deliberate echoing of earlier years, Nicholson inscribed the mount with the words 'This was Me!' He did not dwell in the past, however, and, notwithstanding a complicated relationship with his son Ben (the result of inevitable artistic rivalries as much as stylistic differences, half-grudgingly softened by mutual respect), he was generally at ease with and enjoyed the company of young people. One such happy encounter came when he was commissioned to do a portrait (1933; fig.57) of Diana Low (1911–1975), a thoroughly modern young woman and herself an aspiring painter. With the painting progressing well – it was to prove one of his very finest and most vivacious works – she proposed that *she* should now paint a picture of *him*. The result was a delightful small canvas (c.1933; fig.56) recording an image of Nicholson, lying full-length on a day bed, wearing his yellow waistcoat, white ducks and black slippers. He is smoking his customary Balkan Sobranie with an extravagant gesture and blowing a plume of smoke. He looks rather old and tired. It is an affectionate testament to an unlikely friendship, but it also serves to reveal the way in which in the mid-1930s Nicholson still held to his old look precisely, clearly feeling neither need nor desire to 'update' himself.

One unforeseen difficulty in maintaining his wardrobe arose, however, when after the Second World War and close to the end of his life, Nicholson's preferred Edwardian-style shirts made from patterned or his particular favourite spotted cloth were no longer to be found. In previous times such things had been so popular as to be available from any gentlemen's outfitters. In order to maintain his look, Nicholson now had to resort to artistic ingenuity, employing his young granddaughter Jane to embellish plain white shirts with the required 'pinpoint black spots' painstakingly by hand.[19] It is a fitting detail on which to conclude, a demonstration of the artist's determination to hold to the look and persona he had created and perfected over a lifetime. In this we might see Nicholson as the truest heir of those masters of self-creation – Byron, Brummell and Wilde – but also as the great forerunner of more recent artists, such as Andy Warhol (1928–1987), David Hockney (b.1937) and Gilbert & George (Gilbert Prousch, b.1943, and George Passmore, b.1942), who have realised the power of image and styled themselves as much as their work.

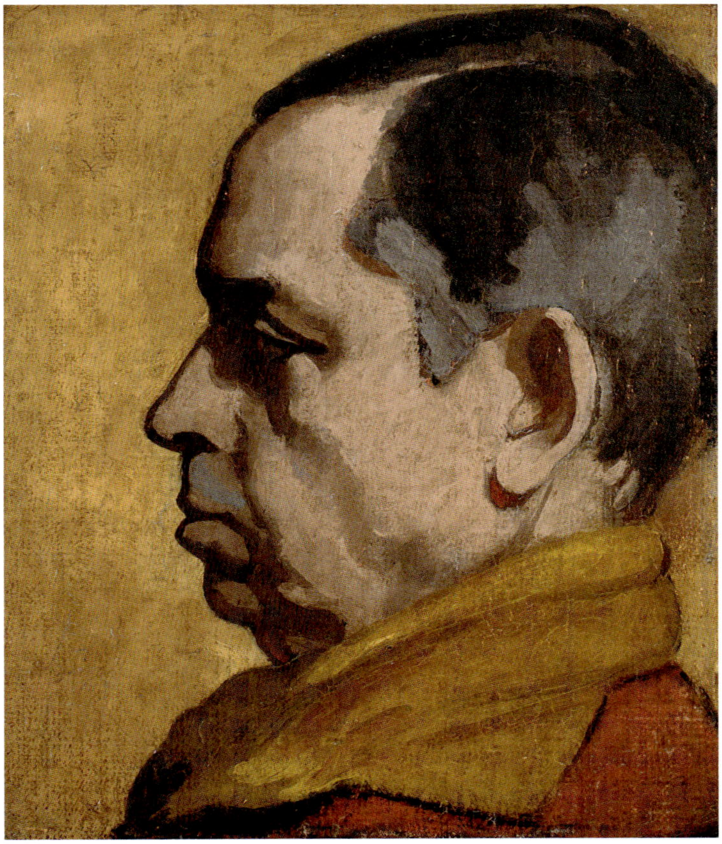

55 ELIZABETH DRURY [EDIE NICHOLSON] (1890–1958)
William Nicholson, 1921
Oil on board, 46 x 37.5cm
Private collection

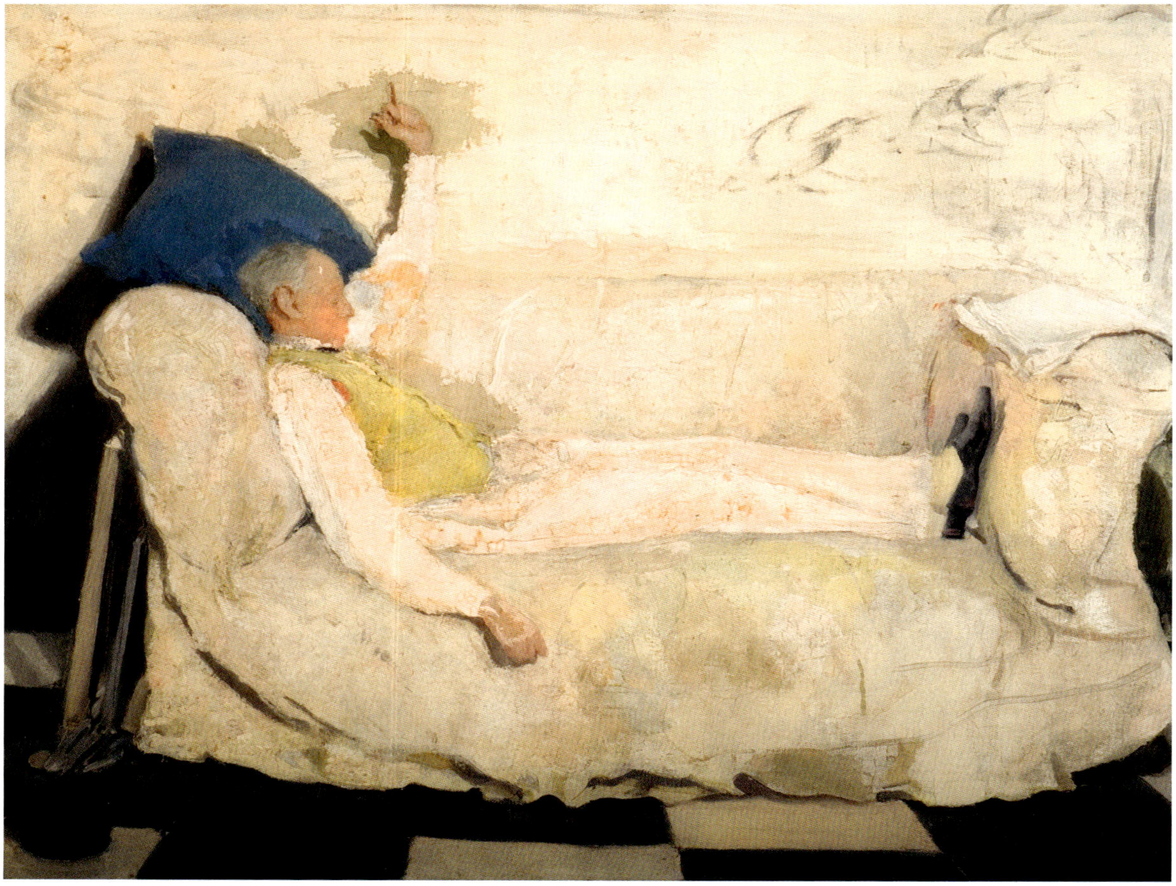

56 DIANA LOW (1911–1975)
William Nicholson, c.1933
Oil on canvas, 52 x 67.5cm
Wolverhampton Art Gallery

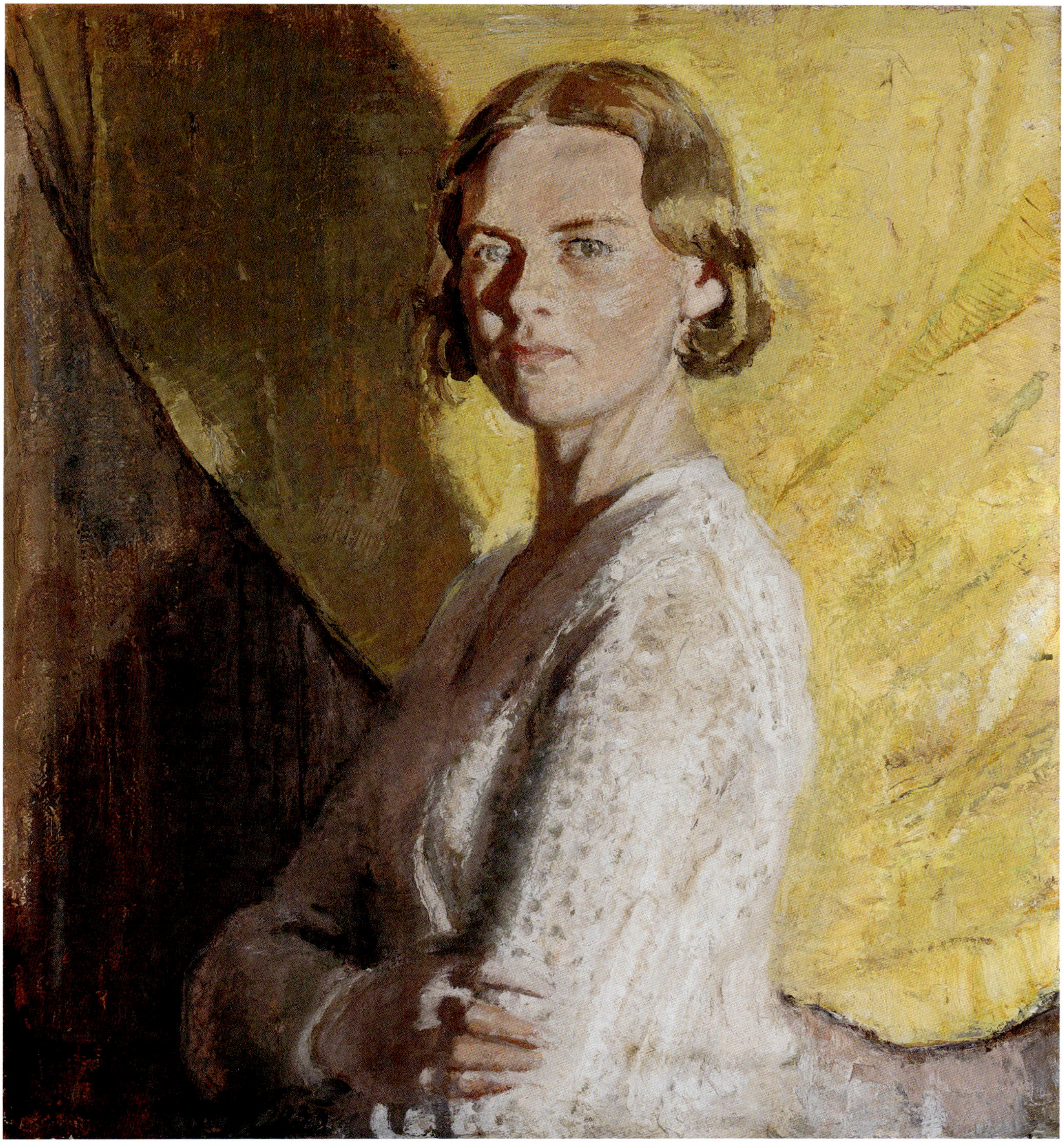

57 *Diana Low*, 1933
Oil on canvas, 61 x 56cm
Private collection

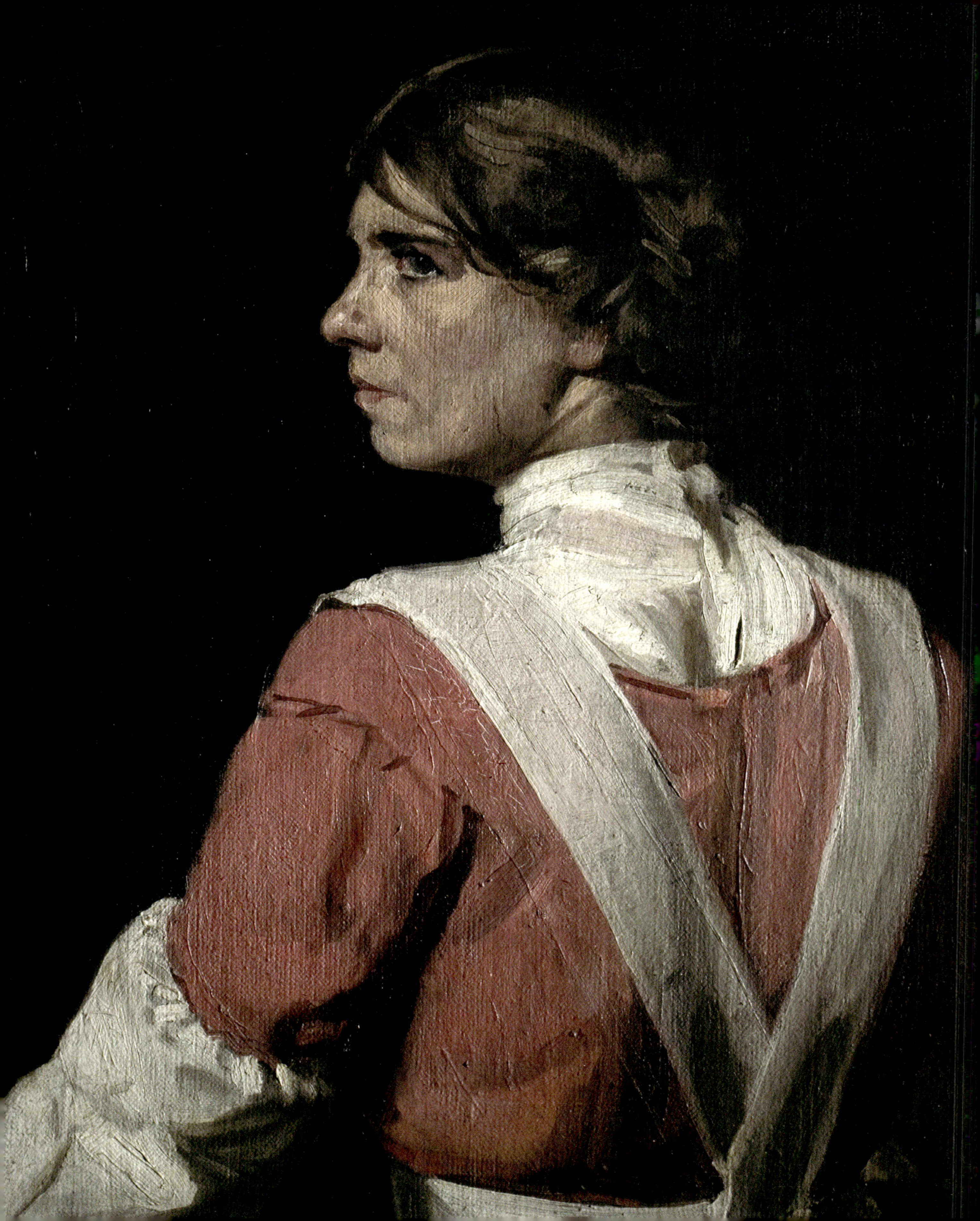

3 NICHOLSON AND PORTRAITURE

PATRICIA REED

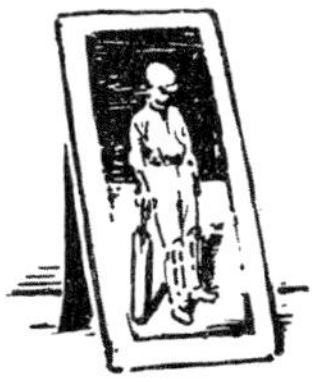

'Nothing frightens me more than a possible queue of sitters,' wrote William Nicholson to a prospective client who wanted two portraits, but at the beginning of the 20th century undoubtedly the best way for an artist to obtain an assured income was to become a portrait painter.[1] There was no shortage of work, and the most successful could name their fees. Nicholson's own teacher, Hubert von Herkomer, largely financed his art school at Bushey from his portraiture. Students were able to follow the progress of the professor's portraits from preliminary sketches to 'Varnishing Day' at the Royal Academy as part of the curriculum, and some were employed to make copies. This combination of studio assistants, copyists, private views and preparatory studies all in a grand studio did not appeal to Nicholson. He hoped to become a painter of not only portraits, but landscapes and still lifes too. Working in other media attracted him, including the theatre – a positive result of his time at Herkomer's Art School.

With his *Characters of Romance* (1900), a portfolio of portraits of well-loved fictional characters, Nicholson made the transition from woodcuts to drawings for reproduction by lithographic printers. In the autumn of 1900 he travelled to New York to make portrait drawings of notable Americans for reproduction in *Harper's Weekly*. The main drawback of the relationship with his publisher, William Heinemann, was that Nicholson had begun to feel more like an employee than an artist: there was the physical labour of cutting the blocks and hand colouring the deluxe edition prints at so much a print, not having complete freedom to choose his subjects, the demands of the printer, time constraints and payment methods which frequently found him in debt, having spent his advance. However, he gained a good friend in Heinemann with his p.66

58 *Miss Wish Wynne, Actress, in the Character of Janet Cannot for the Play* The Great Adventure, 1913
Oil on canvas, 59.1 x 54.3cm
Nottingham City Museums and Galleries (Nottingham Castle)

59 *Portrait of Nancy Nicholson beside a Table*, 1902
Pencil and ink on paper, 30.5 x 21.6cm
Estate of Mirabel Cecil

60 *Nancy in a Feather Hat (The Artist's Daughter)*, 1910
Oil on canvas, 75 x 62.2cm
Richard Green Gallery, London

many contacts both in London and abroad, and through him he met many poets and writers whose company he found more congenial than that of artists. As a result of his publishing experience, Nicholson was very keen to keep the copyright of his paintings, having received only £10 10 shillings for Queen Victoria (fig.9), with which he declared Heinemann had 'papered the world'.[2]

Within a very short space of time, the three years from 1897 to 1900, Nicholson's name had become known to thousands of people through his printmaking, while the popularity of his *An Alphabet* (1897) also secured him the attention of the next generation. Thus he began his career as portrait painter with a unique advantage. Nicholson had already demonstrated the first requirement of a portraitist: he could 'capture' a likeness. While avoiding caricature and sentimentality, there was often humour in his work, which was primarily based on observation. He was a 'realist' in the sense that he painted what he saw. The honesty of this approach is the key component of some of his finest portraits, such as *Nancy in a Feather Hat* (1910; fig.60), *Gertrude Jekyll* (1920; fig.27) and *Diana Low* (1933; fig.57) – observation and then simplification, or 'the art of leaving out', as James McNeill Whistler had described it.[3] On the other hand, Nicholson was unable to flatter his sitters, nor could he take them as seriously as they did themselves, which could be a disadvantage. In Nicholson's early portraits the influence of his graphic work can be seen in his preference for a limited palette with notes of colour and also in the use of photography for visual and tonal purposes.[4] Once he was no longer bound by the constraints of colour block printing, he found the freedom to experiment with the infinite possibilities of oil paint. Colour, tone and surface texture were a constant source of interest and enjoyment to Nicholson throughout his career.

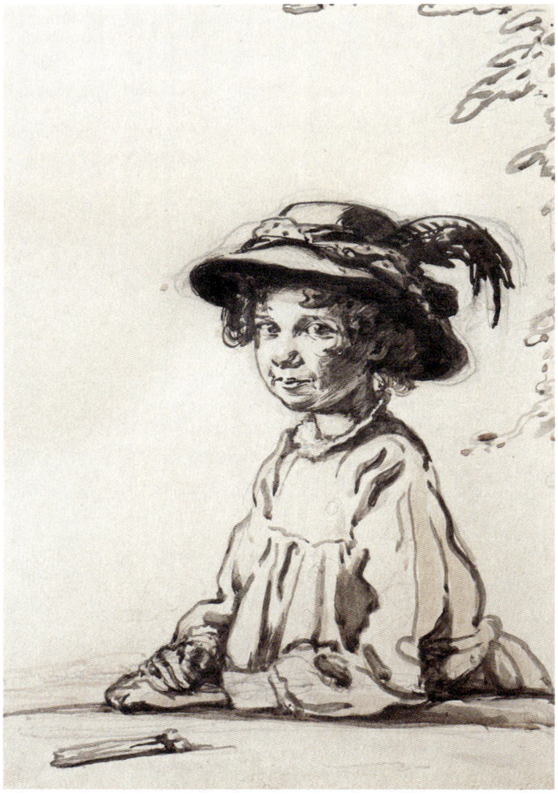

In two early portraits of friends their differing personalities are distinguished by Nicholson's handling of paint. In *Portrait of a Man of Letters: W.E. Henley* (1901; fig.25) the poet and editor of the *New Review* confronts the viewer, leaning on the edge of the picture frame as if ready to engage in conversation. He is wearing his famous hat, his walking stick placed prominently in the foreground, a reference to many years of ill health. (Having contracted tuberculosis as a young man he had one leg amputated and began writing poetry when in hospital.) The low horizon line opens up the picture space behind him, possibly suggesting the countryside around Worthing, West Sussex, where Nicholson visited him for sittings. A coarse

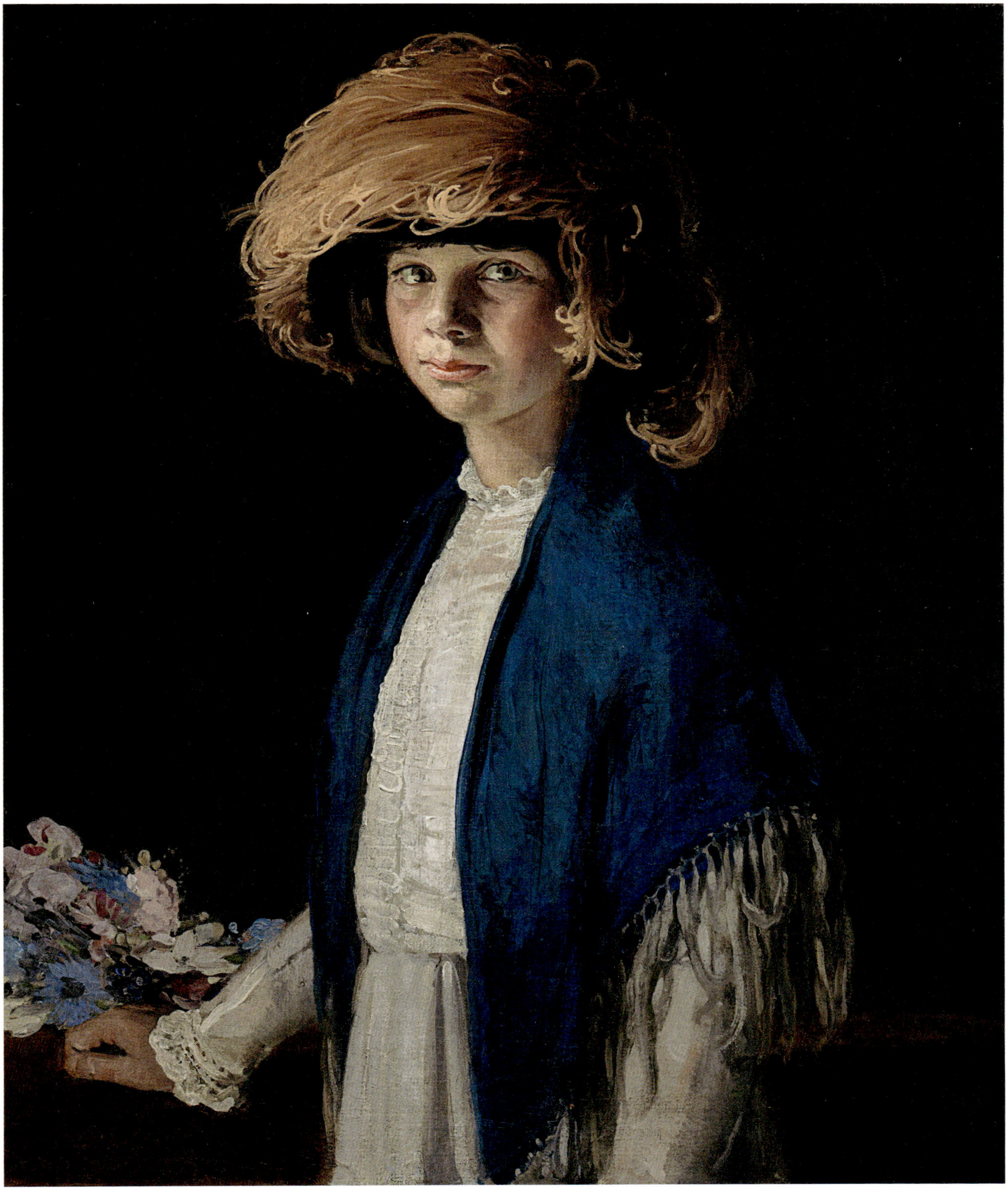

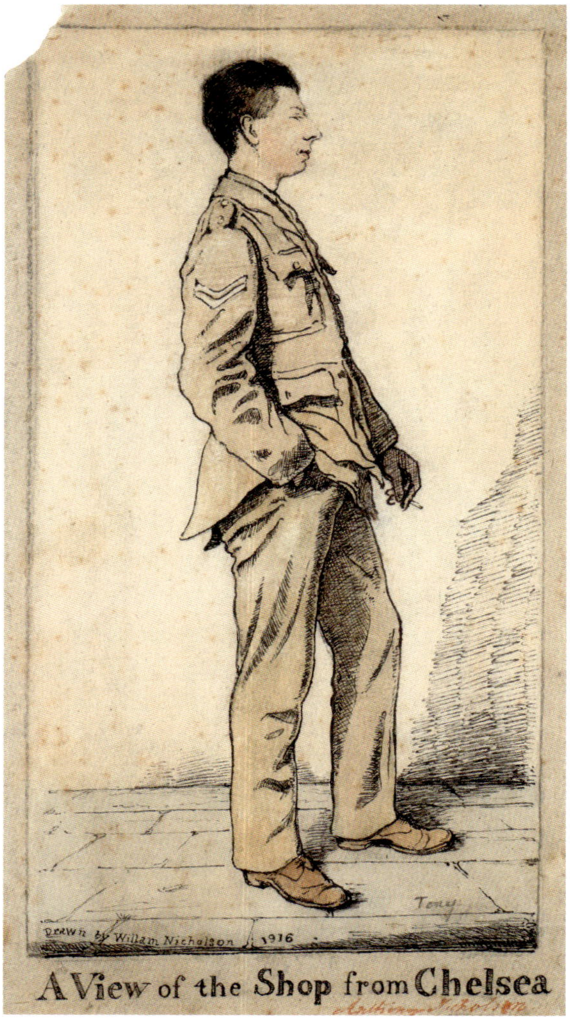

61 *A View of the Shop from Chelsea*
(portrait of Tony Nicholson), 1916
Pencil on paper, 47 x 29cm
Private collection

canvas and freely applied paint are used to convey the sitter's robust and controversial personality. This was Nicholson's first commissioned portrait, paid for by a subscription from Henley's many friends and admirers. For his friend Max Beerbohm Nicholson portrayed the humourist full-length, standing in a shallow picture space against a light background articulated by a few shadows (c.1902; fig.66). He is shown in profile, detached from the viewer, his gaze lowered with ironic modesty. Highlighted details from top hat to patent leather shoes recall the hand-coloured woodcut of Whistler (1897; fig.10), in which white was added to certain areas and a note of red provided by his *Légion d'honneur* ribbon. (Beerbohm would probably have considered the latter excessively colourful.) Nicholson's subtle use of varnish on certain areas of the fine-weave canvas creates a suitably elegant arrangement. Critics complained of the 'tobacco-coloured' backgrounds used in this and other early portraits, but when gilt-framed and hanging on the wallpaper-patterned walls of large Edwardian houses, figures stood out to advantage.

A great admirer of Whistler, Nicholson had used the profile portrait in his very early works and then to great effect in his woodcut portraits, including himself in profile in *An Alphabet*: *A was an Artist* (his only self-portrait; fig.1). He continued to use profiles in his paintings: *Edward Russell Dancing the Morris* (1901; fig.64, see also fig.28), *The Boy with the Caroline Mug* (1901; Newark College, Lincoln), *Miss Wish Wynne* (1913; fig.58), *A Soldier of the 1914–18 War* (1917; fig.62) and Beatrice Webb in the portrait with her husband (1928; fig.65). There were practical advantages too, especially for young sitters, as profiles were easier and less distracting for both sitter and artist.

Nicholson's first solo exhibition, at the newly opened Stafford Gallery in London in June 1903, immediately demonstrated his mastery of painting and his innovative technique. Among the 23 works shown were the portraits of Henley (the only commissioned work), Beerbohm, Marie Tempest (1903; National Portrait Gallery, London) and three of Edward Russell (1872–1942), the Morris dancer.[5] An untraced portrait of his brother-in-law, James Pryde, in the costume of Jingle, the confidence trickster from Charles Dickens's *Pickwick Papers*,

62 *A Soldier of the 1914–18 War*, 1917
Oil on canvas, 89 x 85cm
Private collection

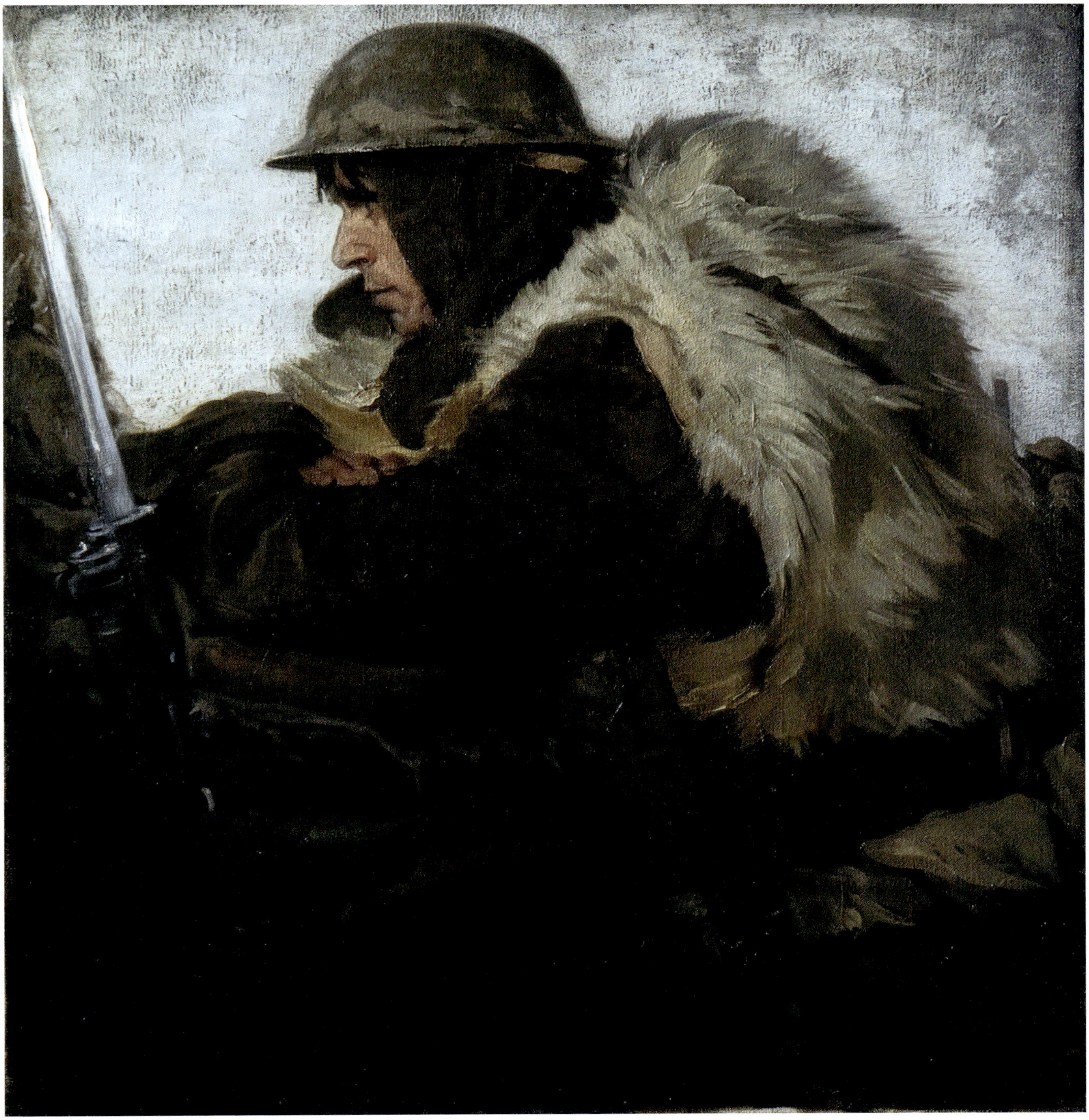

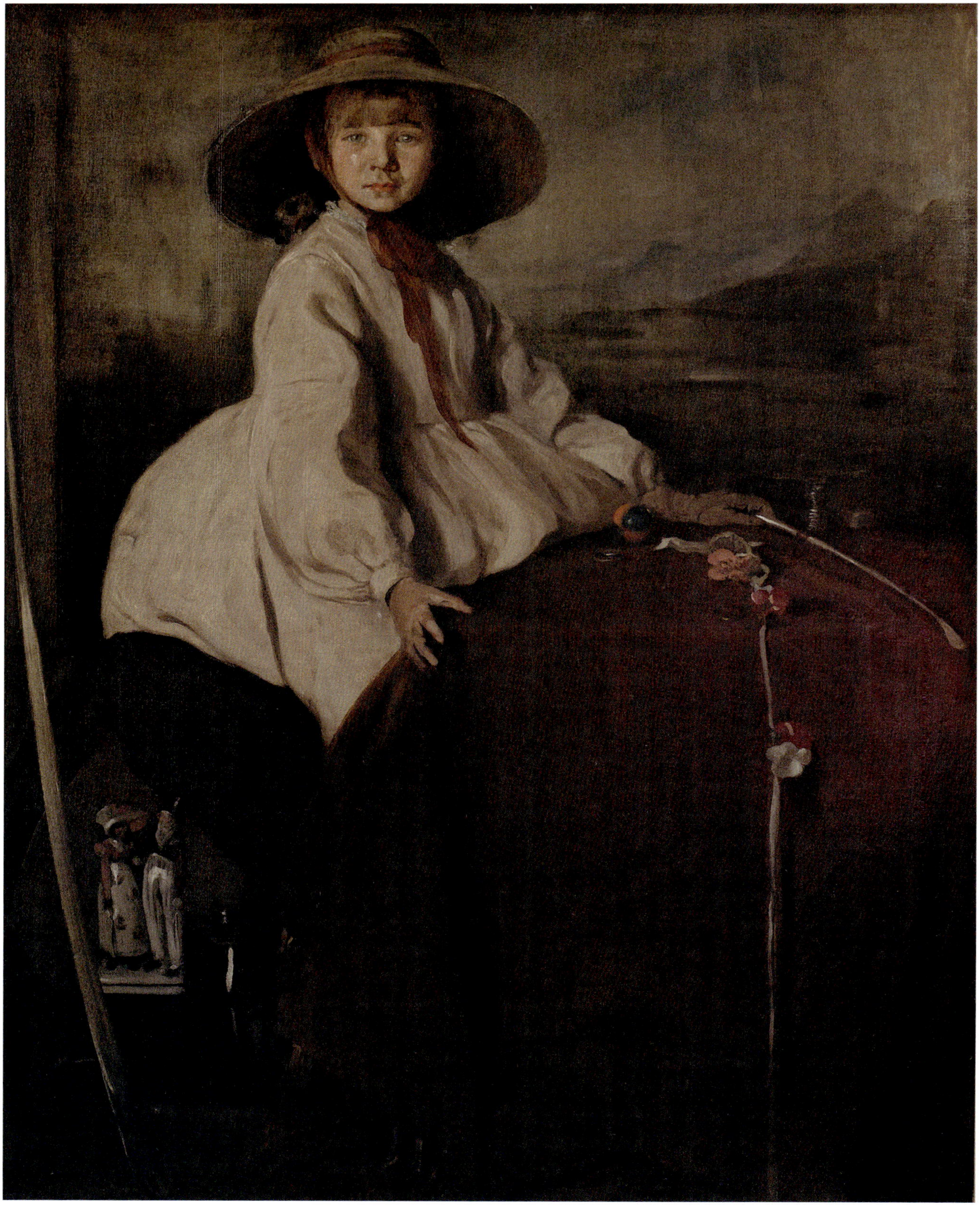

63 *La Petite Marchande (The Little Shopkeeper)*, 1902
Oil on canvas, 114.5 x 90cm
Estate of Mirabel Cecil

might be linked to a discarded subject from the *Characters of Romance*. Some visitors would have recognised Pryde from *An Alphabet* under *B for Beggar* (fig.11), where he is depicted holding a staff. Portraits of children were also exhibited: two of Nicholson's son Ben, including *The Boy with the Caroline Mug*, two of his daughter Nancy and two of Rosemary Craig (1894–1976), the daughter of Edward Gordon Craig: *Rosy of Winchelsea* (1901; fig.33) and *La Petite Marchande (The Little Shopkeeper)* (1902; fig.63).[6] There were also a seascape, a landscape, two townscapes and designs for playing cards, but no still life. Nicholson's first appeared in the foreground of the portrait of Mrs Curle at the dinner table in 1905.[7] (Many of Nicholson's later portrait commissions that took him away from his studio also produced landscapes and still lifes.) One visitor to the Stafford Gallery exhibition was to become Nicholson's most important patron, T.W. Bacon of Ramsden Hall, Billericay, Essex. The commission for a portrait of his three-year-old son Anthony[8] inaugurated what would be the largest collection of Nicholson's work.

It was fortunate that Nicholson enjoyed the company of children, as they became his first subjects. His friend Harrington Mann (1864–1937) made a good living by specialising in this field, though some artists declined to paint children.[9] From 1894 to the early 1930s Nicholson lived with children and grandchildren around, which may explain in part why he never sentimentalised them. He had a sense of fun, evidenced by his work on children's books, and excelled at puns and jokes, as well as sports and games. To entertain young sitters sometimes a member of the family would be on hand to read. The teenage Ursula Lutyens, daughter of the artist's friend, the architect Edwin Lutyens, recalled with pleasure sitting for a first portrait by Nicholson in 1916 as her mother was there to read Father Brown stories to her.[10]

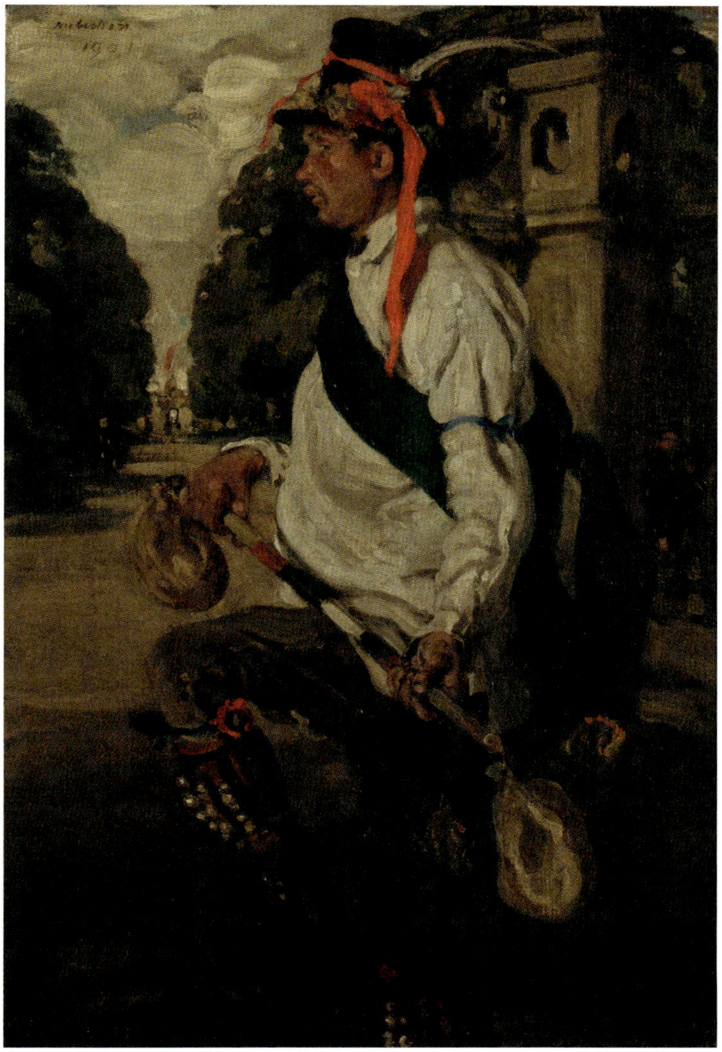

64 *Edward Russell Dancing the Morris*, 1901
Oil on canvas, 52 x 24.3cm
ING UK Art Collection

Reviewing Nicholson's contribution to the National Portrait Society's 'Inaugural Exhibition' in 1911, the *Morning Post* declared: 'Parents who want their children immortalised can always depend on this delightful painter. He does not paint someone else's child by mistake.'[11] In *Rosy of Winchelsea* Rosy is depicted looking down over Winchelsea from her grandmother Ellen Terry's home at Tower Cottage. For once the horizon lines in Nicholson's prints and his early paintings occur in real life. With her back to the viewer Rosy gives the impression that she is tired of posing and would like to go and play with the ball she is holding. (She is the sitter in several paintings.) The silky texture of her fine, blonde hair becomes the subject of the painting, also celebrated in *Jennie as Infanta* (1913; fig.68).

For portrait commissions, the normal procedure for payment was a third on commission, a third when the work was well underway and the remainder on completion. On 26 April 1905 Nicholson quoted his future patron T.W. Bacon £220 for the 30 x 25 inch canvas of his eldest son, Anthony, and the work was completed to mutual satisfaction, seemingly within two weeks.[12] In 1907 Nicholson painted a double portrait of Francis Bacon and his baby brother Kit for the price of 'Anthony and a half', which was £367 for a 45 x 35 inch canvas.[13] Unlike most portrait painters he did not keep records, but an illustrated letter (in draft) to a prospective client survives giving his prices for a portrait around 1921: '17 x 19 £250; 22 x 24 £350; 27 x 37 £450; 34 x 39 £600 and a full length £1,000'; for an extra figure, half as much again as the other figure, as in 'Anthony and a half'.[14] These were substantial sums given that his small landscapes and still lifes of 13 x 16 inches were sold through galleries before the First World War for £50 – for example *The Ruby Glass* (fig.112) in 1910. In 1920 *The Silver Casket and Red Leather Box* (fig.99), a work of similar dimensions, cost £175. The pricing for non-commissioned portraits, such as *Nancy in the Feather Hat*, were discretionary. When this work was first shown at the Goupil Gallery Salon in London in 1910, the price was £315. It was snapped up by the Duke of Marlborough, who, it would appear, later tried to negotiate a reduction in the price. He was unsuccessful, and the work was returned to the gallery.[15]

If the client had come via his current dealer, then Nicholson had to pay the dealer's commission, which varied. This could cause problems if a work was abandoned, for instance the Spencer family portrait,[16] but it did provide encouragement for him to complete a painting. Portrait frames were always chosen and paid for by the sitter, though Nicholson was happy to give an opinion, as it was a subject he considered important.

A necessary expense for a portrait painter was a suitable studio in which to receive sitters. In the early days Nicholson and Pryde had the use of the studio of the Scottish artist E.A. Walton (1860–1922). For three years Nicholson shared the studio of his friend William Orpen, who painted the artist and his family in their home at Mecklenburgh Square: *A Bloomsbury Family* (1907; fig.50). Between 1909 and 1916 Nicholson leased the first-floor studio at The Pheasantry, 152 King's Road, Chelsea. It was a large space; the next occupant, Madame Astafieva, was able to hold ballet classes there.[17] A visitor in 1913 recalled a high-ceilinged room with a black mirror glass on the wall, Victorian dresses lying around, a parrot, a large collection of pottery, Augustus John's portrait of Nicholson (1909; fig.53) and Nicholson himself: 'A slight figure, clad in white ducks, walking to and fro as he worked, with his light nervous step, making witty comments in abrupt staccato sentences.'[18] His next studio was more conveniently placed for sitters just off Piccadilly at 11 Apple Tree Yard, tucked away in the mews behind Stafford House on the north side of St James's Square. The interior was even more picturesque.[19]

One of the disadvantages of painting in central London in the first half of the 20th century was the occurrence of fog, together with the smoke from coal fires that dirtied windows and spoilt the light. Nicholson had addressed this problem in 1910 with the installation of 'daylighting' in his Chelsea studio. This was the invention of his friend, the mathematician Mark Barr (1871–1950), and involved 'a costly and highly scientific combination of various lights. By means of this painting is rendered independent of the weather and the time.'[20] Nicholson wrote to his patron T.W. Bacon: 'My new light has nearly ruined me again isn't it dreadful to live in a city where one has to make and pay for one's own daylight? – but it is *good* and most successful. I shall never stop working now.'[21] There was also a portable version which Nicholson used when painting the author and garden designer Gertrude Jekyll in late October 1920. Wishing to make the most of shortening days, the 77-year-old Miss Jekyll would only agree to sit for her portrait in the evenings. She found Nicholson an entertaining conversationalist – they spoke about Whistler, and she later thanked him for his 'capital good fellowship' when returning a small screw which had come detached from his lighting apparatus.[22]

Nicholson's female sitters in commissioned portraits were often society women for whom having their portrait painted was a pleasant way to pass the time. Nicholson was an amusing conversationalist and generally enjoyed company while he was working. It was exciting to be involved in the creation of a work of art – 'our work', as Nicholson always called it, one that would be exhibited publicly. Then there were the visits to the studio, with its intoxicating smell of oil paint and turpentine, mixed with Balkan Sobranie cigarettes, which could involve going to an out-of-the-way place like Chelsea.[23] Friends of the sitter, or the artist, might drop by – who knew what might happen.

However, for male sitters it was the opposite. They often resented the time spent sitting for what were usually presentation portraits. It was difficult to arrange sittings, and there was little to talk about. Nicholson's working method did not endear him to such busy sitters as Lord Hardinge, Viceroy of India (1915; The President's Secretariat, Rashtrapati Bhavan, New Delhi).[24] He did not do preparatory studies, but worked directly on the canvas, scraping out and starting again when dissatisfied. Consequently, the sitter had little opportunity to comment on the proposed composition. This process could go on for months, or even years, especially with female sitters, yet when necessary a work could be completed in a day or two. On occasion a portrait had already been exhibited when Nicholson took it back to 'correct' some faults which could result in its destruction. An extreme case was the fate of *Breakfast at Chartwell* (1934–6; destroyed) in December 1941. The portrait of Winston Churchill and his wife, Clementine, at breakfast was already hanging in the National Gallery, London, prior to the opening on New Year's Day of the Nicholson and Jack B. Yeats (1871–1957) exhibition, when the artist began a few minor but ultimately ruinous improvements.[25]

In the 1920s Nicholson was fortunate to have a number of agreeable elderly academic sitters, whose conversation helped create some very fine portraits. One his academic sitters, A.C. Benson, the Master of Magdalene College, Cambridge, made a note of his conversation with Nicholson in his diary, dated 23 June 1917: 'He said many interesting things about the problems of real painters: the reduction of accessories to a minimum – the constant simplification of all redundance – the concentration on the real subject – the choice of the subject; a picture isn't a real thing – it's an illusion, a grouped thing – it's as definite a thing as a violet or a rose … These things are not intelligible to me, but I have the agreeable sense in being in the presence of a mystery.'[26] This sitting was the beginning of the first of four attempts at Benson's portrait; the work was finally completed seven years later, in May 1924, in three days.[27]

Another diarist described the evolution of the commissioned portrait of the social reformers Sidney Webb (1859–1947) and his wife, Beatrice Potter (1858–1943), which was to hang in the Founders' Room of the London School of Economics (fig.65).[28] Beginning in March 1928 Nicholson paid several visits to their Hampshire home, Passfield Corner, where Beatrice Webb found him: 'an attractive person, sincere, intelligent and artistically wide-awake with whom we were quickly friends'.[29] Contrary to his normal working method, Nicholson made a number of preparatory studies, about ten days work in all. 'I doubt the result,' she wrote, 'It may be a clever picture ("especially of the brickwork" G.B.S. [George Bernard Shaw] suggests) but it will be an insignificant portrait – the figures being too small relatively to the background and too insignificant for the Founders' Room.'[30] Nicholson was now hard at work, and by 15 June she noted that: 'He has taken an incredible time over me owing to the wrong scheming of the painting.[31] I have been painted in and painted out half a dozen times – now at least the figure satisfies him and is quite good enough for me – rather too young and good-looking – but that fault is inevitable in a woman's portrait.'[32] Nicholson was away for the summer, but he was back at the end of September requesting more sittings. While still finding him 'a most agreeable and sympathetic person … If only he would leave it alone and be gone!' wrote Beatrice, continuing: 'Portraits are usually disappointing: pictures of persons should be regarded as symbols not as representations.'[33] The completed work was hung in the Founder's Room and unveiled to friends and subscribers on 14 January 1929.

Nicholson's composition of the seated Beatrice and the standing Sidney conceals the fact, apparent in the many press photographs of the well-known couple, that Beatrice was noticeably taller and slimmer than her husband and with a striking profile. Sidney has also gained a couple of extra inches by standing on the metal hearth surround. Like Beatrice, he is holding long strips of paper – the galley proofs for their latest volume on English local government, which form a visual link between them – running across the floor and then via Peter, the light-haired Sealyham terrier, who is looking up at Sidney. For the first time Nicholson included several objects that tell us something about a sitter: there is Sidney's briefcase, a blue book lying on his chair, perhaps a parliamentary report, and on the shelf above him the statuette of a beaver. This could be a *jeu d'esprit* by the artist, as the couple were known to be industrious in the extreme, and a later photograph of the room shows a piece of Chinese porcelain in this location. Although the fire seems to provide little heat (why did Beatrice not move her chair nearer?), light reflects off an array of brass items: among them a trivet, a poker, fire tongs and the studs on Sidney's chair. Another light source is the large bay window outside the shallow picture space. In the foreground centre is a mysterious object – is it a piece of wood for the fire, brought in by Peter? Perhaps another joke by 'this delightful painter'.

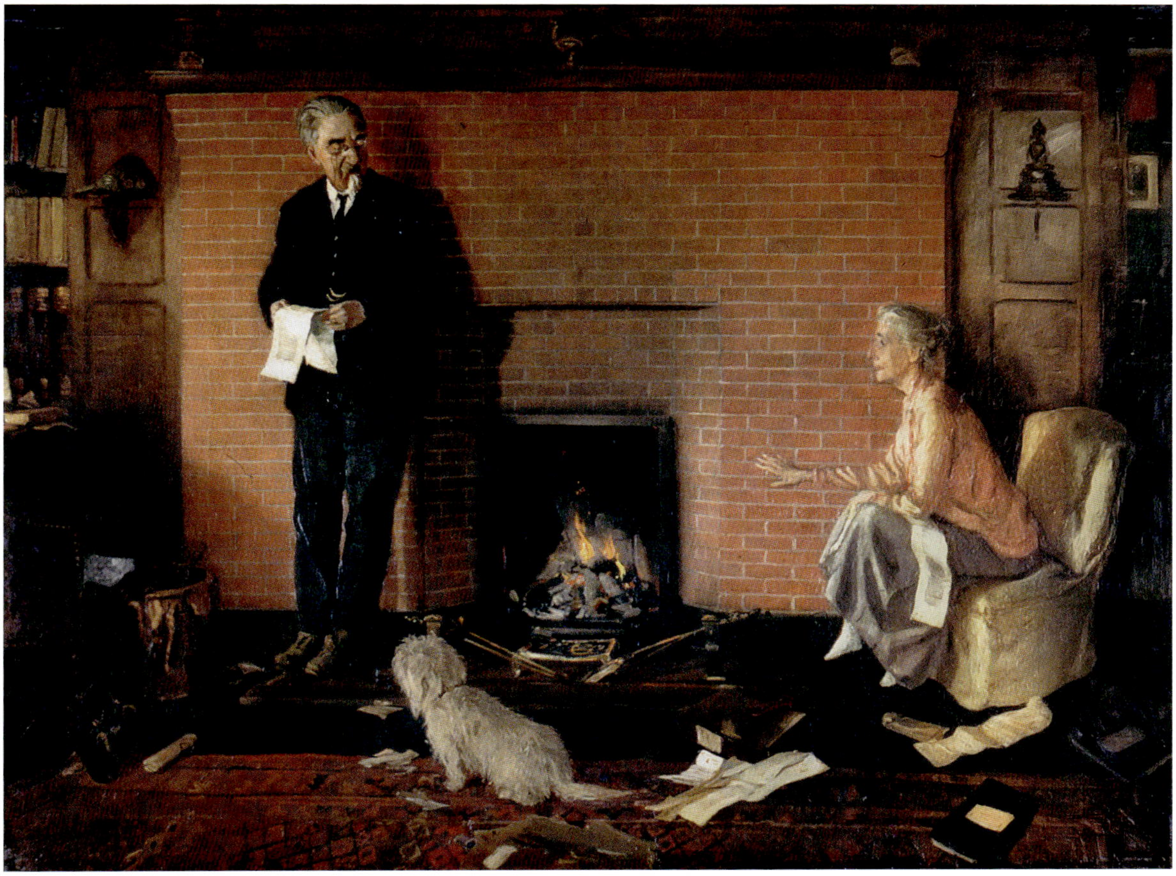

65 *Sidney and Beatrice Webb*, 1928
Oil on canvas, 134.5 x 174cm
London School of Economics
and Political Science

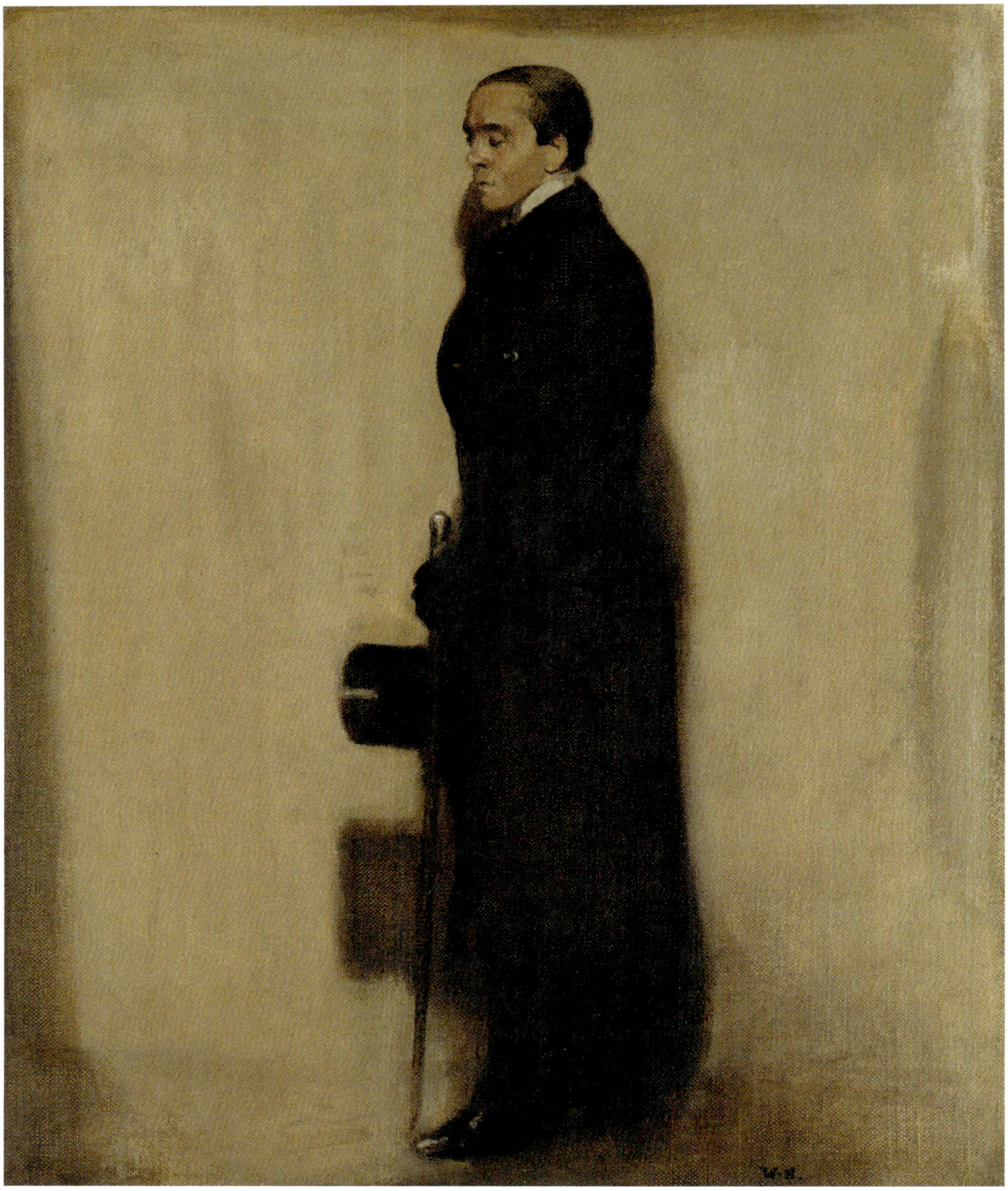

66 *Sir Max Beerbohm*, c.1902
Oil on canvas, 51 x 42.5cm
Lent by the National Portrait Gallery,
London. Bequeathed by
Gertrude Kinnell (née Cass), 1953

67 *Sir James Matthew Barrie*, 1904
Oil on canvas, 58.4 x 52.7cm
National Galleries of Scotland.
Purchased with Art Fund support 1943

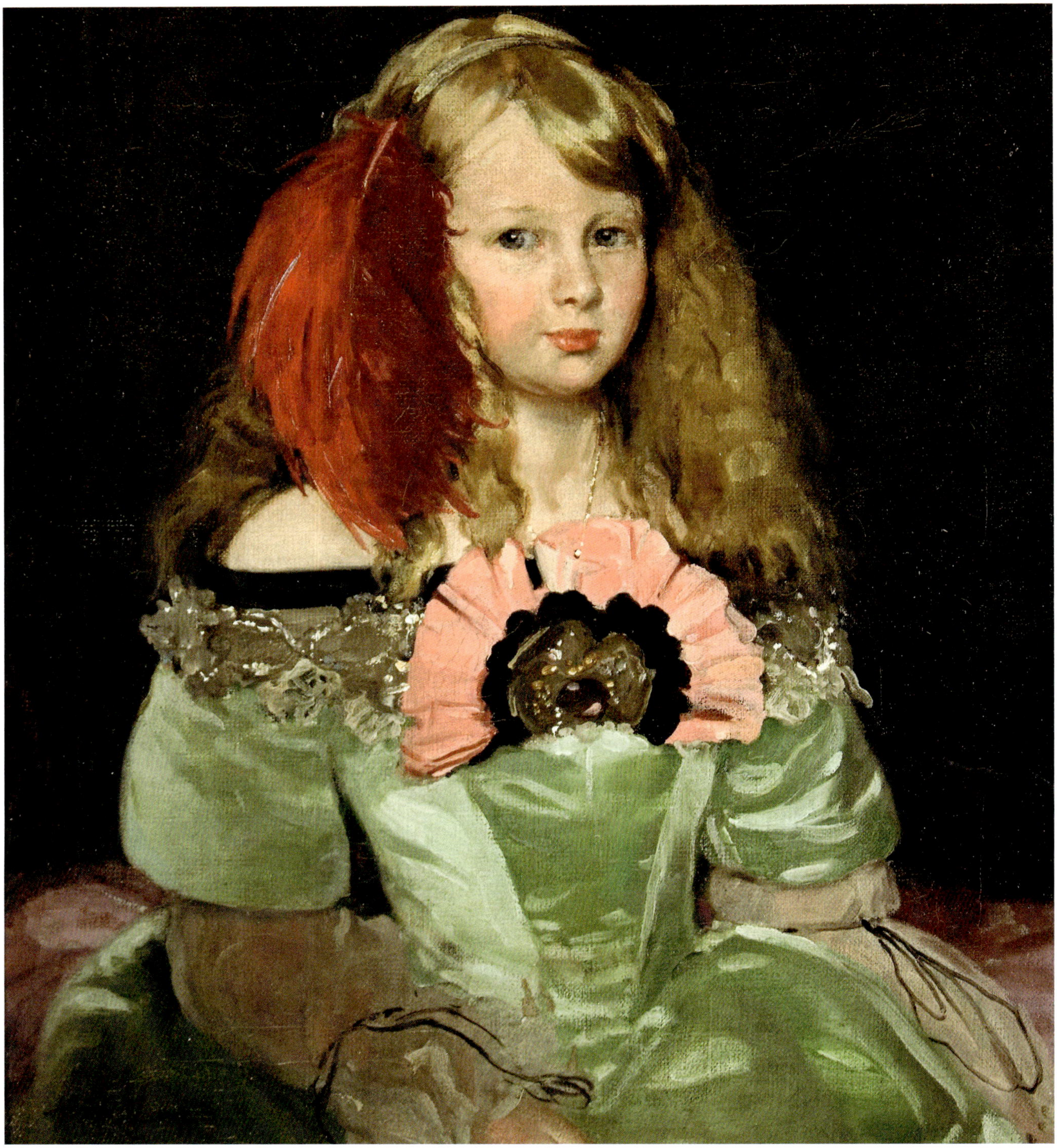

68 *Jennie as Infanta*, 1913
Oil on canvas, 58.5 x 55cm
Eric and Rosayn Anderson,
courtesy The Fine Art Society

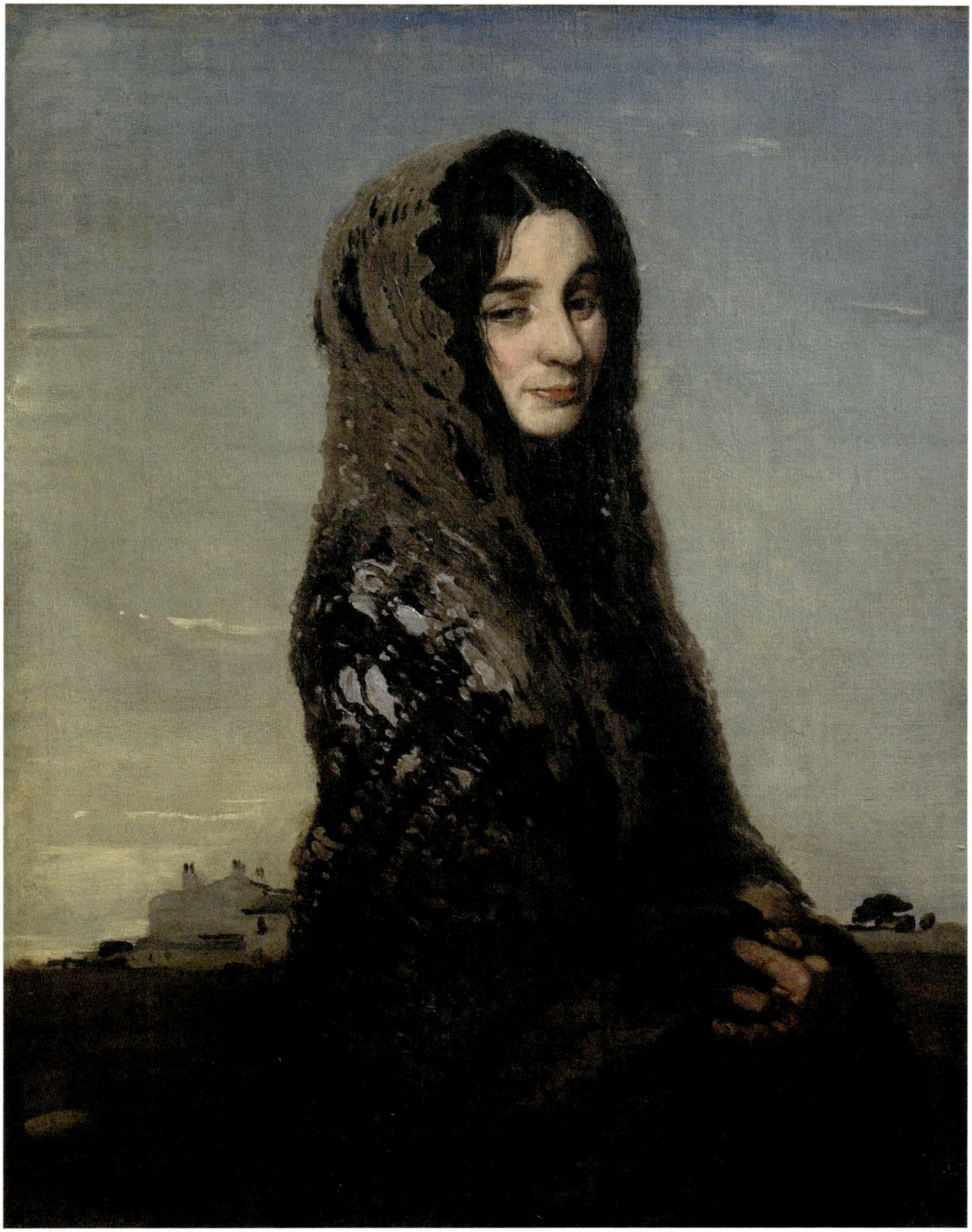

69 *The Grey Shawl*, 1910
Oil on canvas, 90 x 70cm
Private collection, courtesy
Piano Nobile, London

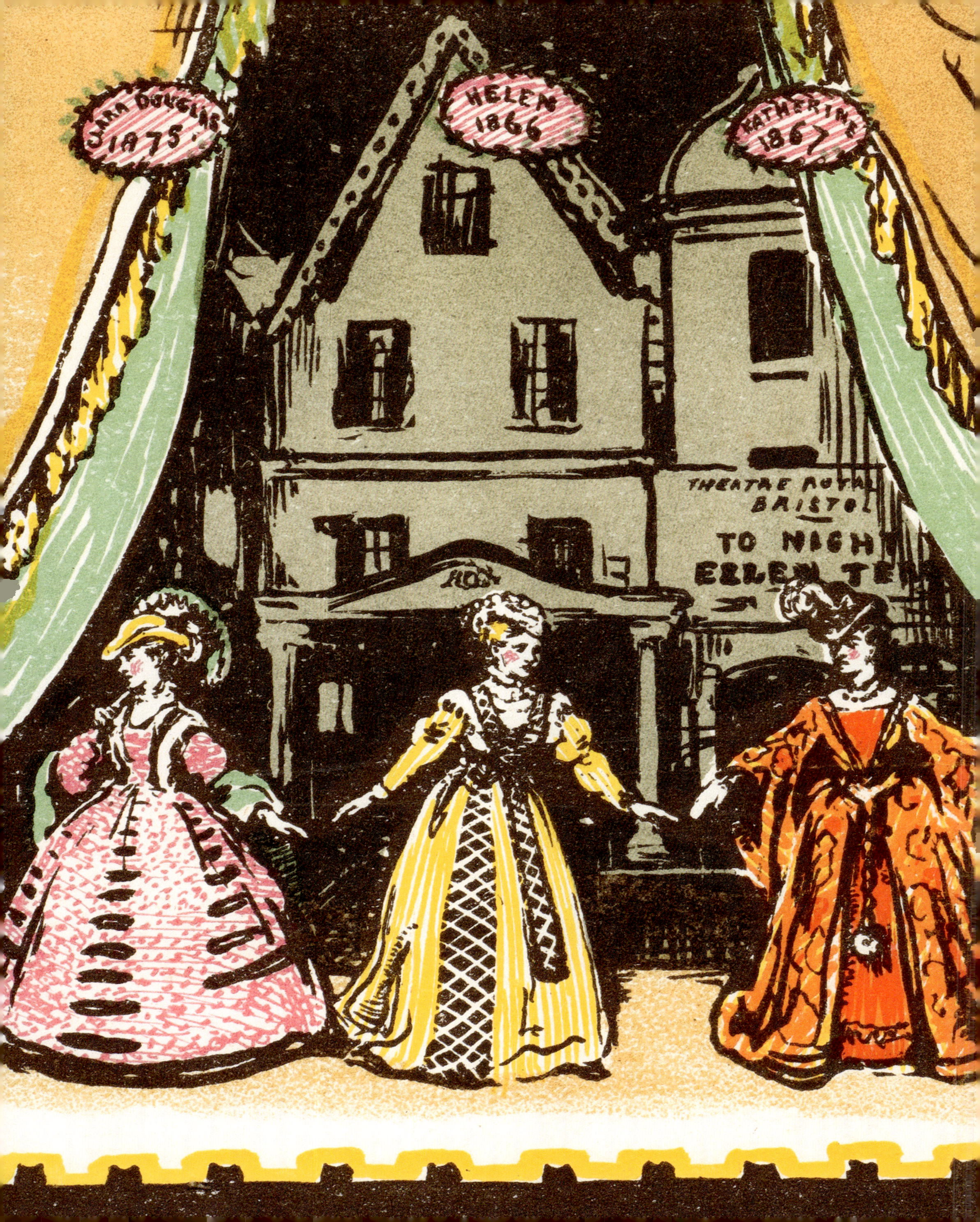
CLARA DOUGLAS 1875.
HELEN 1866
KATHERINE 1867
THEATRE ROYAL BRISTOL

4 WILLIAM NICHOLSON AND THE THEATRE

JANE PRITCHARD

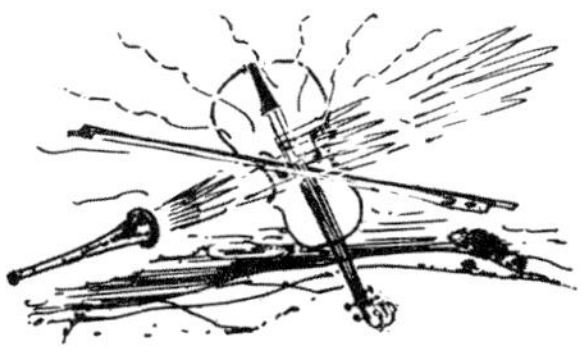

William Nicholson's professional involvement with the theatre came about as a result of a meeting in 1893 between the then actor Edward Gordon Craig and Nicholson's brother-in-law, James Pryde, on a train heading to Denham in Buckinghamshire, the area in which they were all living. The resulting friendship among the three of them made a significant impact. Craig learnt from Nicholson much about woodcuts and their ability to show light and shade, effects he would use in many of his images of theatre. Pryde's pictorial world, with its dramatic voids, would be echoed in Craig's designs for the stage, and under Craig's influence the collaboration between Pryde and Nicholson as the Beggarstaff Brothers began. Together they would produce striking and innovative graphic marketing material for the stage (1894–9).

In 1894 Craig, who had recently married and whose daughter was to be the subject of Nicholson's charming *Rosy of Winchelsea* (1901; fig.33), was encouraged by his mother, the actress Ellen Terry, to find work to support his growing family.[1] He secured a regional tour as an actor with W.S. Hardy's Company. Craig persuaded Hardy that the Beggarstaffs should create posters for *Hamlet* and *School for Scandal*, in both of which he starred, to advertise the tour. The bold simplicity of the posters was particularly eye-catching. The collaged and silkscreened poster for *Hamlet* (fig.70) showed the prince clad in black gazing at Yorick's skull. Terry appeared to have encouraged the Beggarstaffs to create posters for *Becket* (1894), the never-produced *Don Quixote* (1895) and *Robespierre* (1899) for Henry Irving at the Lyceum.[2] Nicholson included depictions of Irving (fig.76), along with Sarah Bernhardt (fig.77), in his 1899 portfolio *Twelve Portraits*, celebrating luminaries of the day. Another of their striking posters was for *Cinderella* (fig.75), apparently for the production at the Theatre Royal, Drury Lane, in 1895 and starring

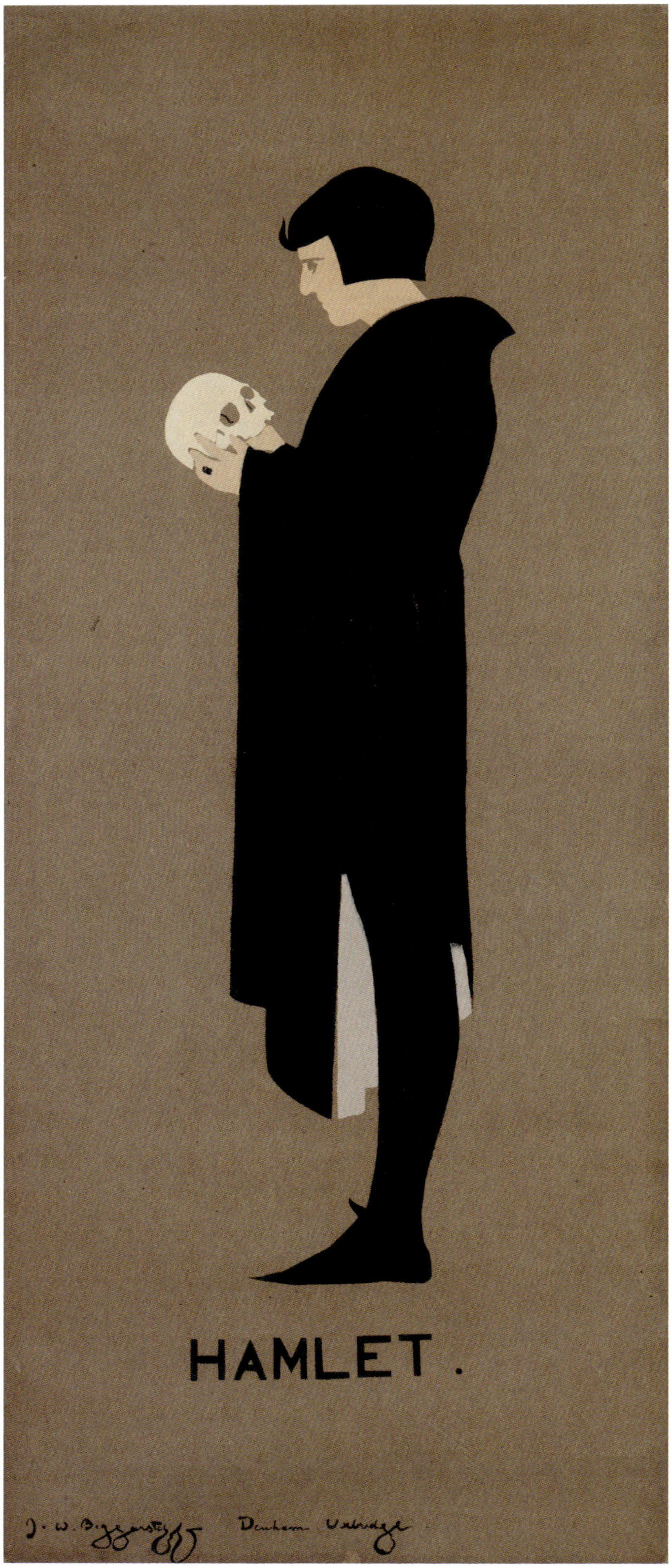

p.82 Detail of fig.78

70 J. & W. BEGGARSTAFF
Hamlet, 1894
Stencil on brown paper,
180 x 75cm
Victoria and Albert
Museum, London

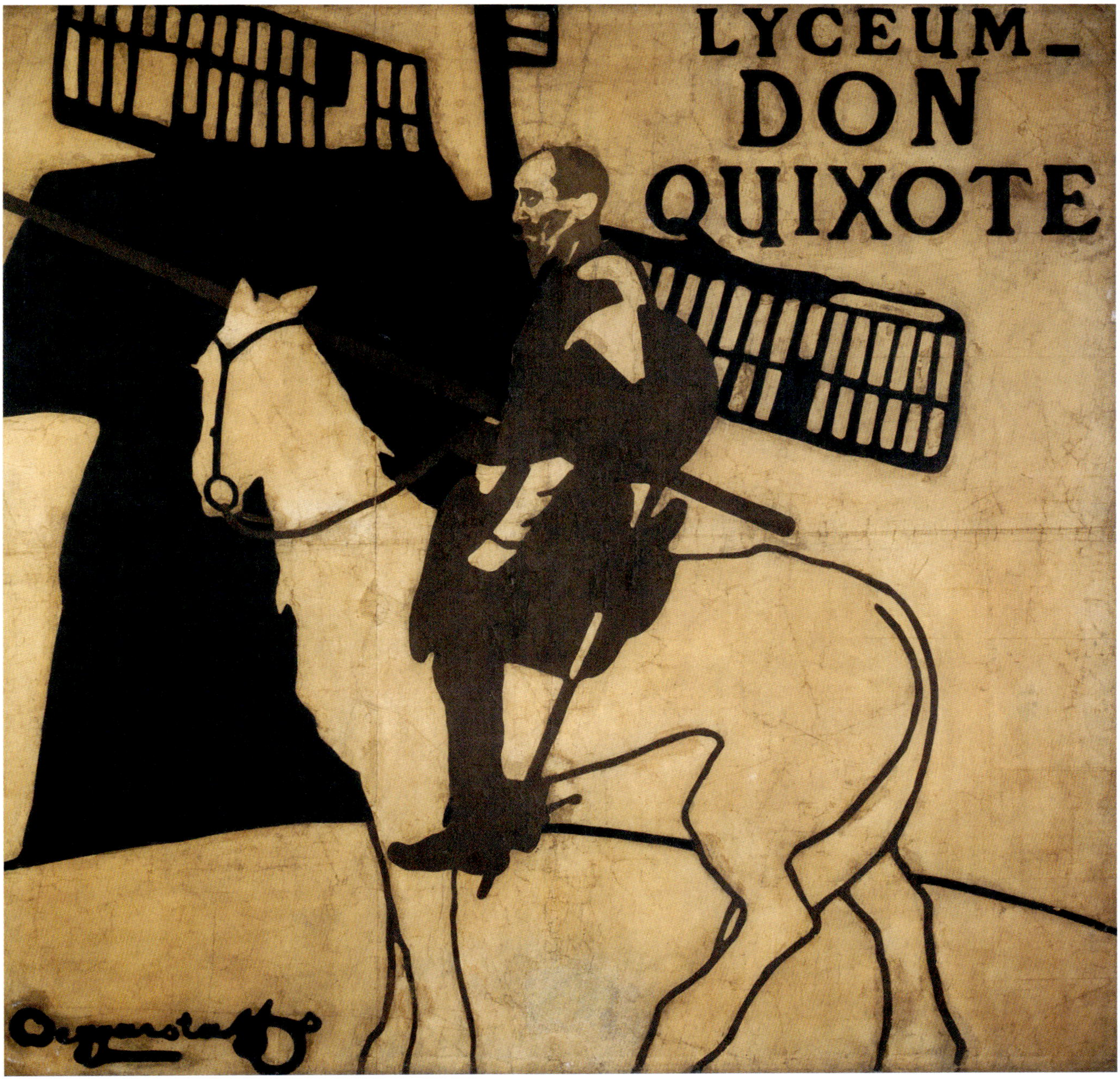

71 J. & W. BEGGARSTAFF
Don Quixote, 1895
Collage on paper, 193.3 x 196.5cm
Victoria and Albert Museum, London

72 *Miss Ellen Terry as Mamillius, 1856*
From the *Souvenir Programme Given by the Theatrical and Musical Professions as a Tribute to Miss Ellen Terry on the Occasion of Her Jubilee*, J. Miles & Co., London, 1906
Lithograph on paper, 35.5 x 28cm
Private collection

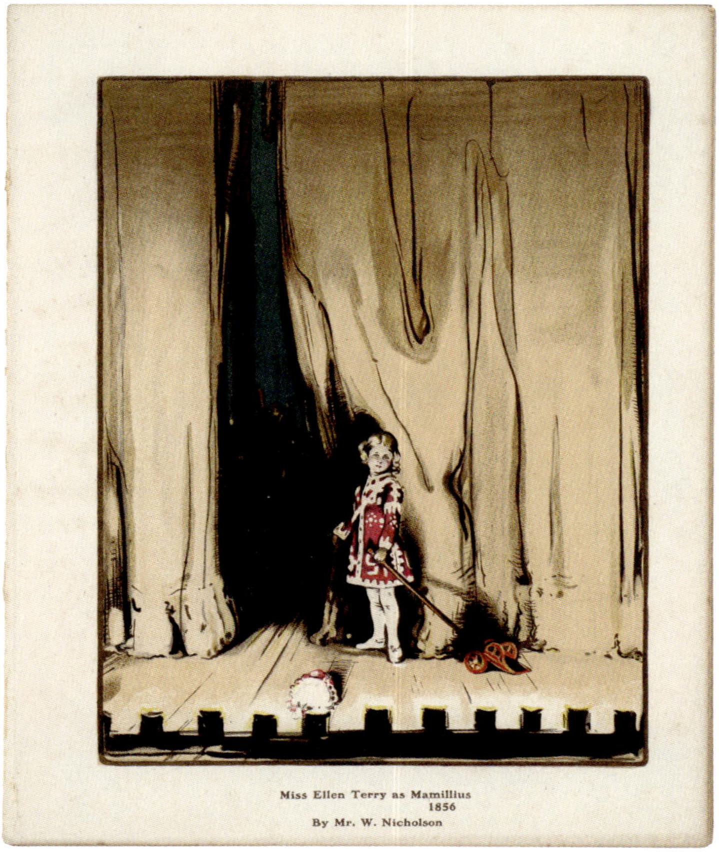

Dan Leno and Isa Bowman. This was strikingly different from the standard pictorial pantomime posters of the day, and the impresario Augustus Harris was nervous about accepting it, until Phil May, another illustrator, cartoonist and poster designer, also noted for his economy of line, praised Harris for his originality in commissioning it.

Links with Terry led to Nicholson illustrating a souvenir scroll and programme for her Jubilee in 1906, marking the 50th anniversary of her first appearance on stage. The 1.5 m long scroll (fig.78) depicts Terry in her most famous roles, from Mamillius in William Shakespeare's *The Winter's Tale* in 1856 to that as Lady Cecily Waynflete in George Bernard Shaw's *Captain Brassbound's Conversion*, staged in 1906. Illustrated with eight plates by as many artists (including Nicholson's friends William Orpen and James Pryde), the souvenir programme included another rendition of Terry as Mamillius by Nicholson (1906; fig.72) extracted from a studio photograph of 1856 by Martin Laroche (1814–1886).[3] Nicholson removed Charles Kean's Leontes from the image and placed the actress, wearing her red and silver tunic with tights, in front of a beige stage curtain with footlights in the foreground, with a toy go-cart, inspired by an image on a Greek vase, placed to her right.

Nicholson's work designing for the stage began with the first performances of J.M. Barrie's *Peter Pan* (1904) at the Duke of York's Theatre. The artist is credited in the theatre programme with the costumes for 'the Esquimaux [i.e. the Lost Boys], Pirates and Redskins'. A design by him for Peter exists, but this is crossed through, suggesting it was rejected.[4] The programme credits Henry Ford (1860–1941) as being responsible for the costume for the first Peter (Nina Boucicault), although his tunic and tights were not so dissimilar to Nicholson's suggestion. Overall, who designed what for the first season of *Peter Pan* is confusing, and the sets have been said to be designed, without credit, by Nicholson's neighbour, Edwin Lutyens.[5] For the second season, the following Christmas, Wilhelm (Charles Pitcher, creator of spectacles, ballets and pantomimes, 1858–1925) teamed with Nicholson and designed the costumes for Peter, Tiger Lily and the Mermaids – two designers whose work differed widely, but who together were able to work magic and helped to establish this play as a timeless experience for young audiences. Nicholson particularly enjoyed designing pirates, whom Barrie insisted should not be travesties of Gilbert and Sullivan, but have a ferocity.[6]

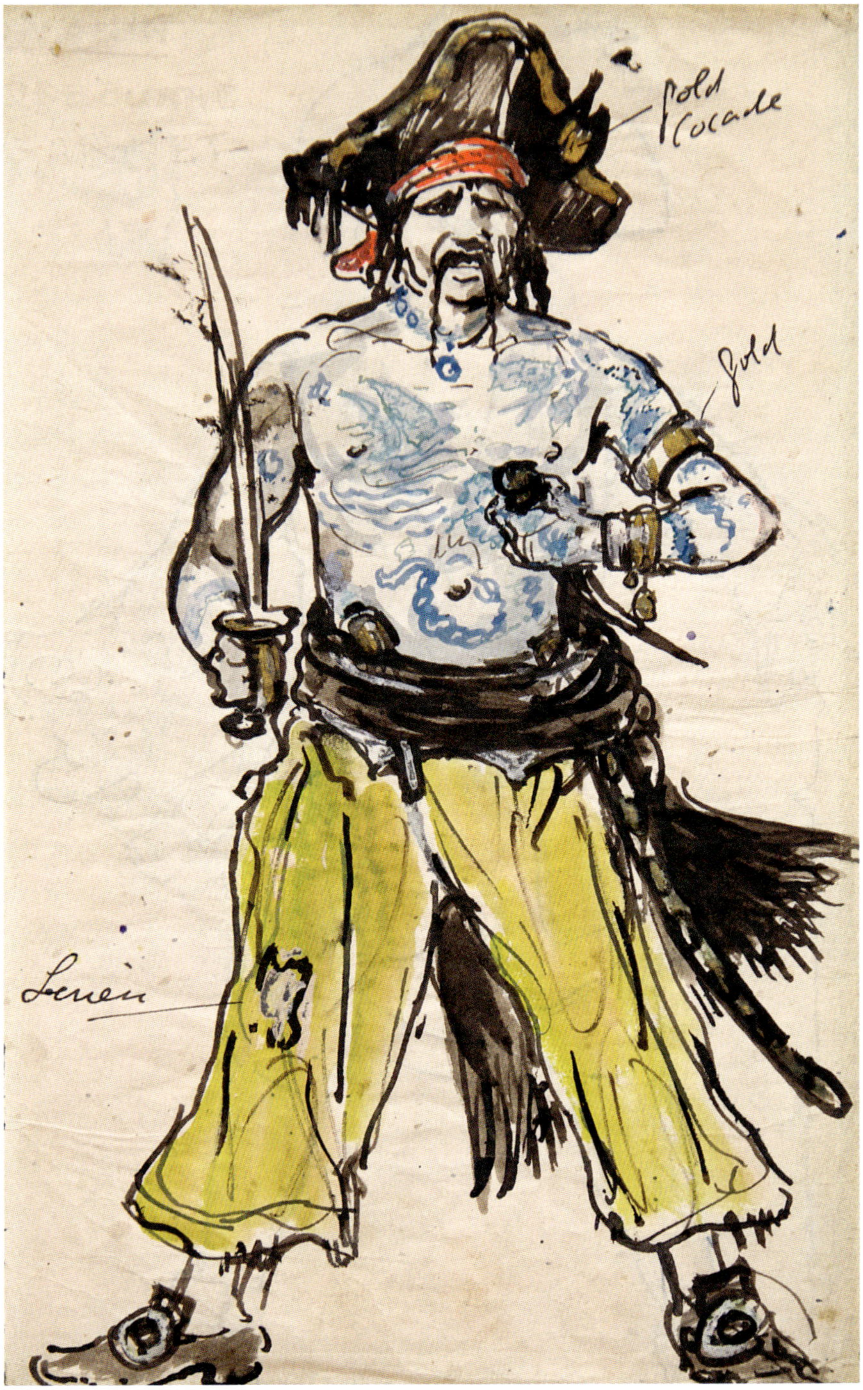

73 Costume design of a pirate
for *Polly* by John Gay, 1922
Watercolour on paper, 25.5 x 15cm
Pallant House Gallery
(On loan from a private collection, 2013)

Possibly it was his success with the pirates that suggested Nicholson as the designer for *Polly* (1922) at the Kingsway Theatre, the sequel to the phenomenally successful *The Beggar's Opera*, in which Macheath was transported to the West Indies and became a pirate (fig.73). Claud Lovat Fraser (1890–1921), designer of *The Beggar's Opera*, had died prematurely in June 1921. He was a pioneering, imaginative designer, who with Nigel Playfair, the manager of the Lyric Theatre, Hammersmith, did much to revitalise design on the postwar London stage. Emphasis was placed on the cut of the costumes and effective colour schemes. The shape of Nicholson's 18th-century dresses is strikingly like those designed by Fraser. The craft used by both artists was discussed by Amelia Defries and Maria Pitt Chatham:

> By instinct and experience; such artists as Lovat Fraser or William Nicholson knew how to use a bit of velvet for a low tone here, a bit of satin for a highlight there; to turn a piece of silk inside out for half tones; and, how to use the pure range of silks just where they were wanted in the picture, even as nature uses texture in flowers to get the lights and tones and the sensation needed for sheer beauty.[7]

These creative collaborations indicate that Nicholson was influenced and inspired by an artistic circle of friends. Fraser was a friend of Craig, who praised his *Beggar's Opera*, and when Fraser began as an artist, working on broadsides and chapbooks, he claimed to be inspired by Nicholson's prints and the work of the Beggarstaffs. In turn, for the stage Nicholson seems to have been inspired by Fraser.

In the early 1920s Nicholson was asked to assist with two fund-raising matinees, each receiving a single performance. In December 1921 he was credited with the sets for the comedy *Not So Bad as We Seem; or, Many Sides to a Character* at the Lyric Hammersmith in aid of the Hammersmith Infant Welfare Centre and in June 1923 for W.J. Turner's *The Man who Ate the Popomack* at the Savoy Theatre in aid of the library fund of the British Drama League. Perhaps surprisingly, Nicholson does not appear to have participated in the 1922 *International Theatre Exhibition: Designs and Models for the Modern Stage* at the Victoria and Albert Museum, which was sponsored by the League. His absence from the exhibition may have encouraged Lord Howard de Walden, President of the Drama League, to purchase nine designs for *Polly* in the summer of 1923 and present them to the V&A.[8]

Nicholson's next designs were for two ballets choreographed by Léonide Massine included in revues created by C.B. Cochran, who was proud of employing the best British designers. Surviving correspondence indicates how Nicholson and Massine collaborated particularly on *The Rake*, billed as 'A Hogarth Impression', for which Nicholson was responsible for the single set built by John Bull and costumes made by the well-established costumiers Alias. The set reflected the decline of society, conveying the atmosphere of Hogarth's eponymous series of prints. The critic G.E. Fussell wrote that the modern set was powerful:

> It is a blaze of sunshine yellow, almost as brilliant as a sunshine room at a colour clinic for nervous diseases. This gives additional excitement to the action. A window at the back lets in more light to accentuate the brilliance of the room still more. A mirror (painted on the back screen) hangs crookedly, and two candlesticks at its base hold unsnuffed candles with exaggeratedly flamboyant flames. The

entry of the grotesques on a note of blue colour (I think lighted from the lighting bridge …) was an extraordinarily fine conception.[9]

Again the women's dresses followed the Fraser pattern for the 18th century, but during the previews in Manchester and Liverpool Massine, concerned about the movement, requested they 'be two or three inches less each side & at least five inches shorter in length'. Massine, who danced as the Beau, also asked for changes in the costume worn by his partner, Eleanor Marra: 'As the corset woman now undresses really, perhaps you could make her dress in more attractive & rich colours will make better contrast when her knickers are shown.' In addition, Massine required 'drawings for the makeup of every important character'.[10]

The Rake was performed in Cochran's 1925 revues *On with the Dance* and *Still Dancing*, and for Cochran's revue of 1926 Massine and Nicholson collaborated on *The Tub*, a Florentine ballet based on the episode in *The Decameron* in which Peronella (Vera Nemchinova; fig.83) hides her lover, Giannello (Massine), in a large pot when her dim-witted husband, Piero (Nicolas Zvereff; fig.79), returns home unexpectedly. The amusing ballet was described as 'a very gay, exquisitely decorated little comedy' and as 'beautiful to the eye'. The set showed a hilly terrain glimpsed between two buildings. A wall between the buildings made it possible for the horses of the hunting party to be simply represented by heads. In this ballet Nicholson was assisted by his second wife, Edie, who painted under the name of Elizabeth Drury. From the designs and photographs it is possible to suggest that Nicholson's approach to Renaissance costumes was influenced by those for Fraser's controversial *As You Like It* (1919). Again, there was a simplicity of pattern: 'the brilliant costumes with their riotous colours giving the scene a sense of vivacious rhythms, the musical setting being taken from Haydn'.[11] However, comparing Nicholson's design for Peronella with Nemchinova's costume as realised by Alias shows that a straight, high-waisted gown was transformed into a tutu, keeping the same decorative pattern for the fabric.[12]

Nicholson designed two further productions: Noël Coward's *The Marquise* at the Criterion Theatre, which ran for 129 performances from 16 January 1927, and Arthur Sullivan's *Cox and Box*, which had two performances by the D'Oyly Carte Opera at Sadler's Wells in June 1935. *The Marquise* (figs.84 and 85) was a light romantic comedy described in the programme as set in the 18th-century 'Chateau de Vriaac not far from Paris'. It was created for Nicholson's long-standing friend (he had portrayed her in 1901; National Portrait Gallery, London) Marie Tempest, who co-starred with her husband, W. Graham Brown. Once again it appears to be Nicholson's preferred period for costumes. An unidentified reviewer noted that Nicholson was 'responsible for the lovely dresses and beautifully effective scene of the play. He should do more work for the stage, he has a real flair for it.'[13]

Theatrical elements can be found in Nicholson's wider work, and when a poster was needed for the National Theatre's 1983 production of *The Rivals* it was based around Nicholson's *D is for Dandy* from his 1897 *An Alphabet* (fig.74). Nicholson was a master of creating character through costume at a time when approaches to costume were changing. Like Fraser's, Nicholson's designs were true to the spirit of the period in which a production was set, but never copied its styles. Both would suppress or simplify details which would detract from the theatrical effect made by the costumes and learnt that further adaptation could be necessary for dance. Design for the stage was only a small part of Nicholson's output, but it deserves recognition along with his paintings, prints and illustrations.

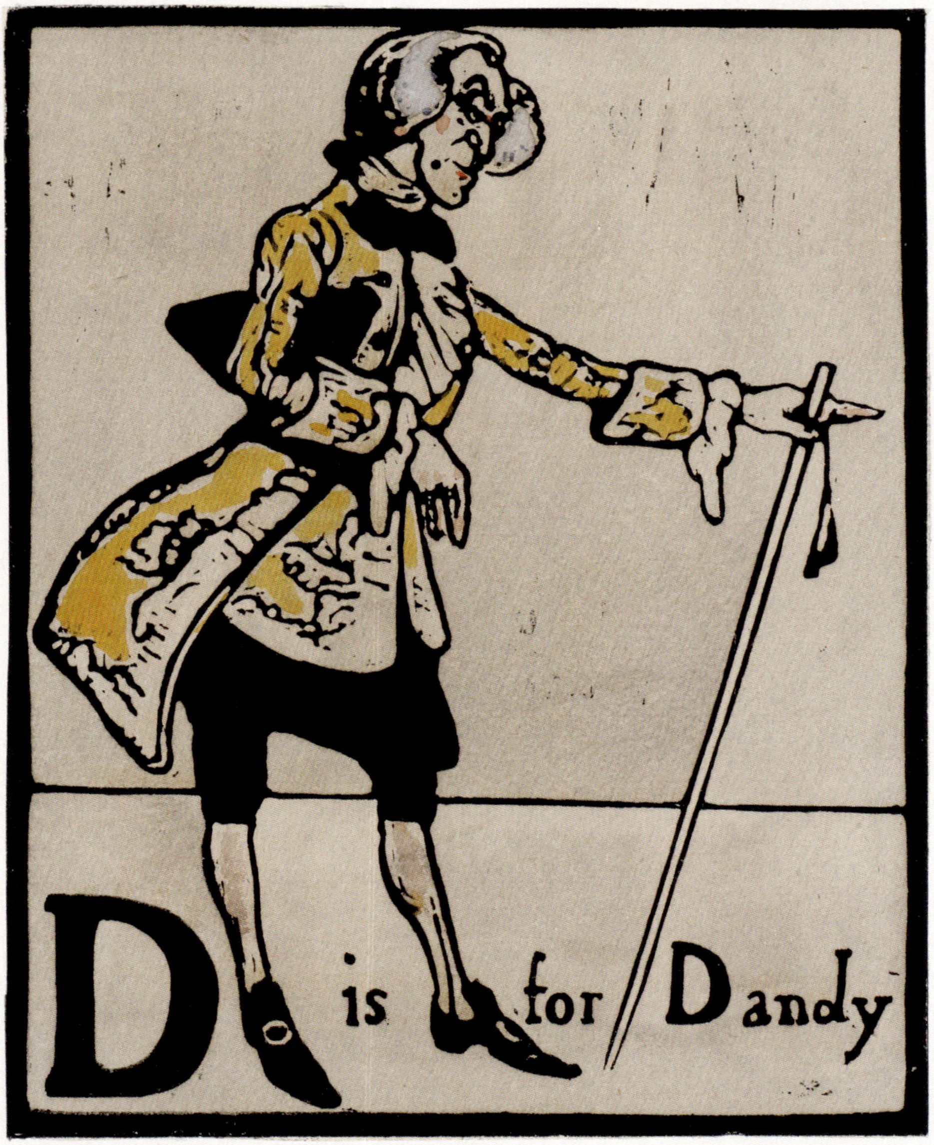

74 *D is for Dandy*
From *An Alphabet*, William Heinemann,
London, 1897
Hand-coloured woodcut on paper, 24.6 x 19.8cm
Private collection

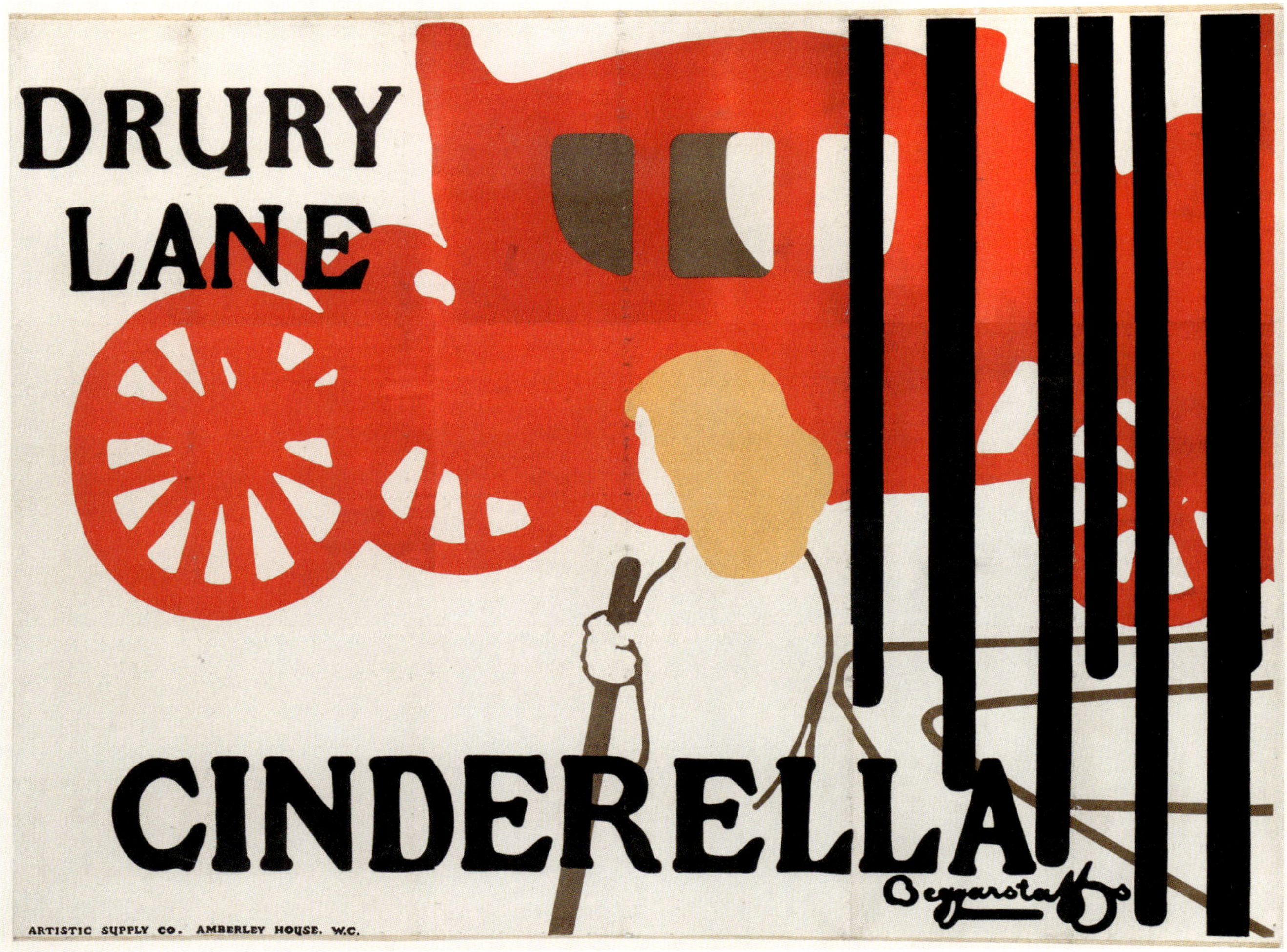

75 J. & W. BEGGARSTAFF
Poster advertising *Cinderella*, 1895
Lithograph on paper, 223.5 x 293cm
Victoria and Albert Museum, London

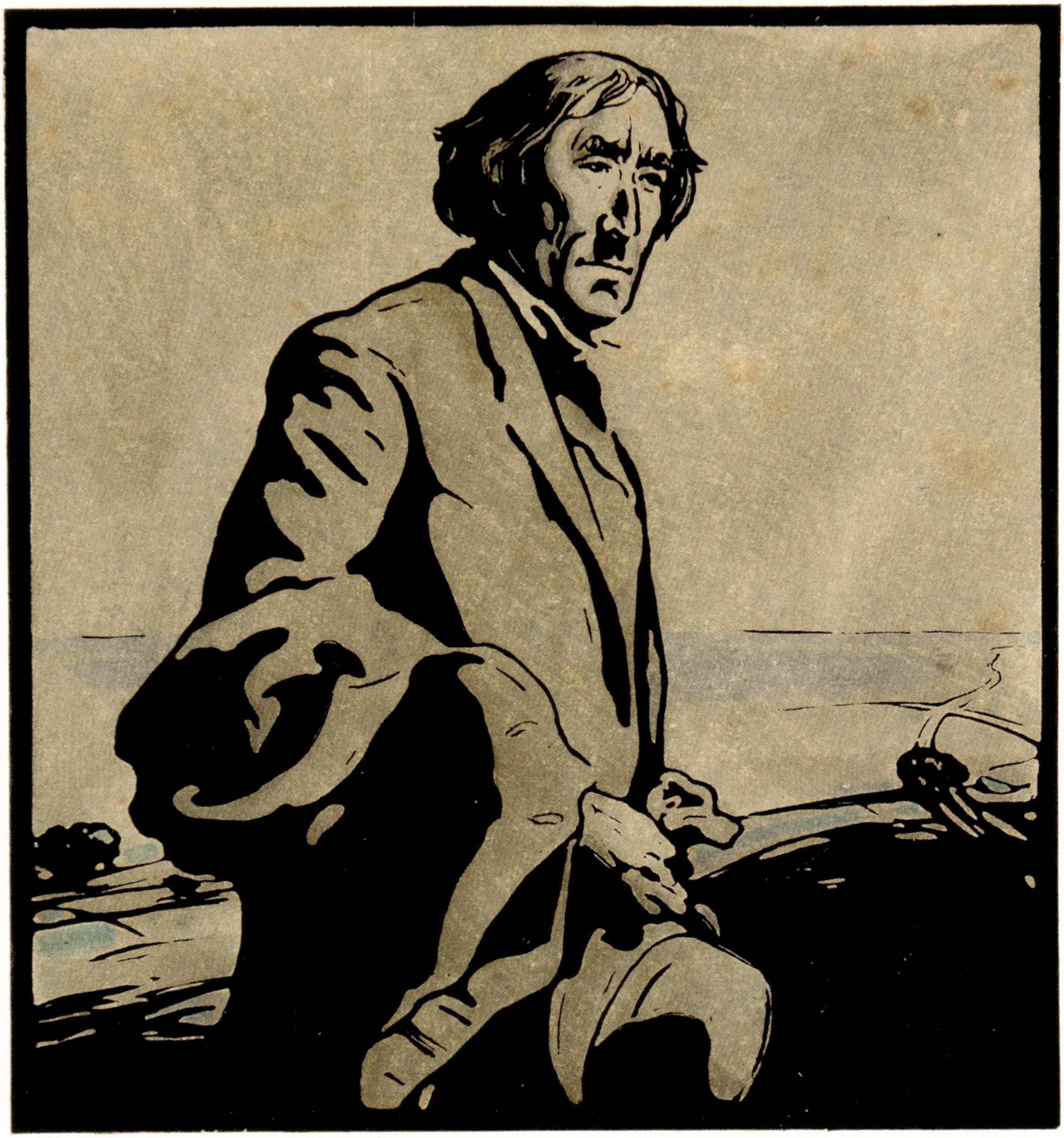

76 *Sir Henry Irving*
From *Twelve Portraits*,
William Heinemann, London, 1899
Colour woodcut on paper, 24.2 x 23cm
Private collection

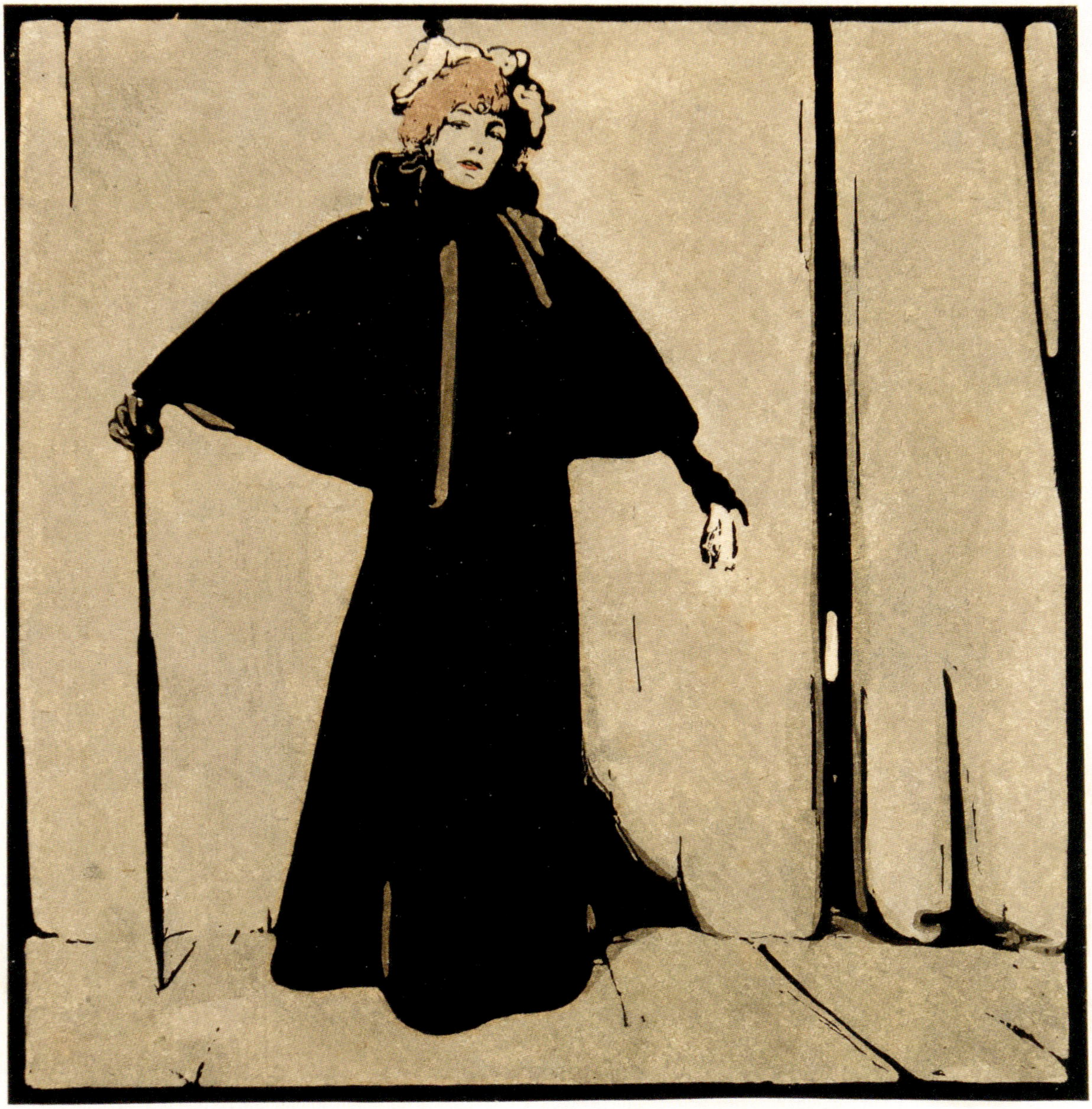

77 *Sarah Bernhardt*
From *Twelve Portraits*, William
Heinemann, London, 1899
Colour woodcut on paper, 24.2 x 23cm
Private collection

78 Ellen Terry Jubilee scroll, 1906
Lithograph on paper, 16.2 x 149.5cm
Private collection

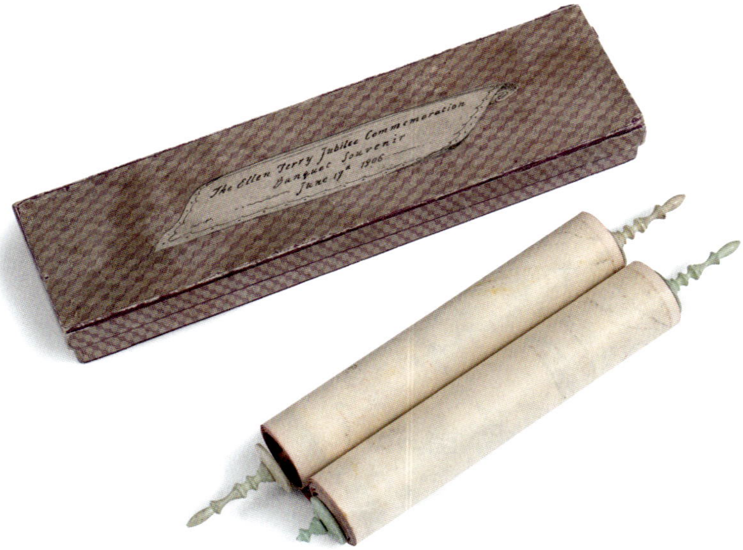

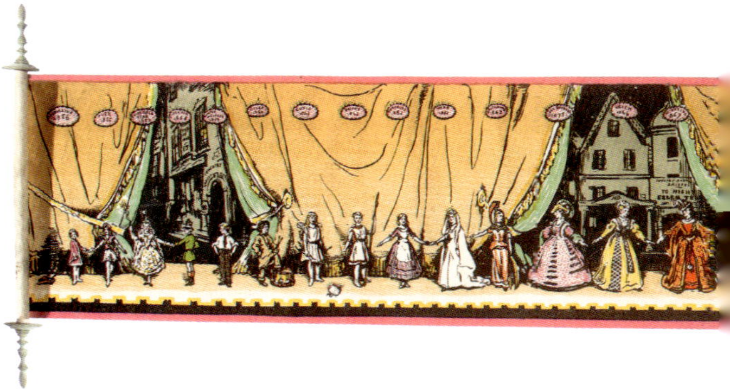

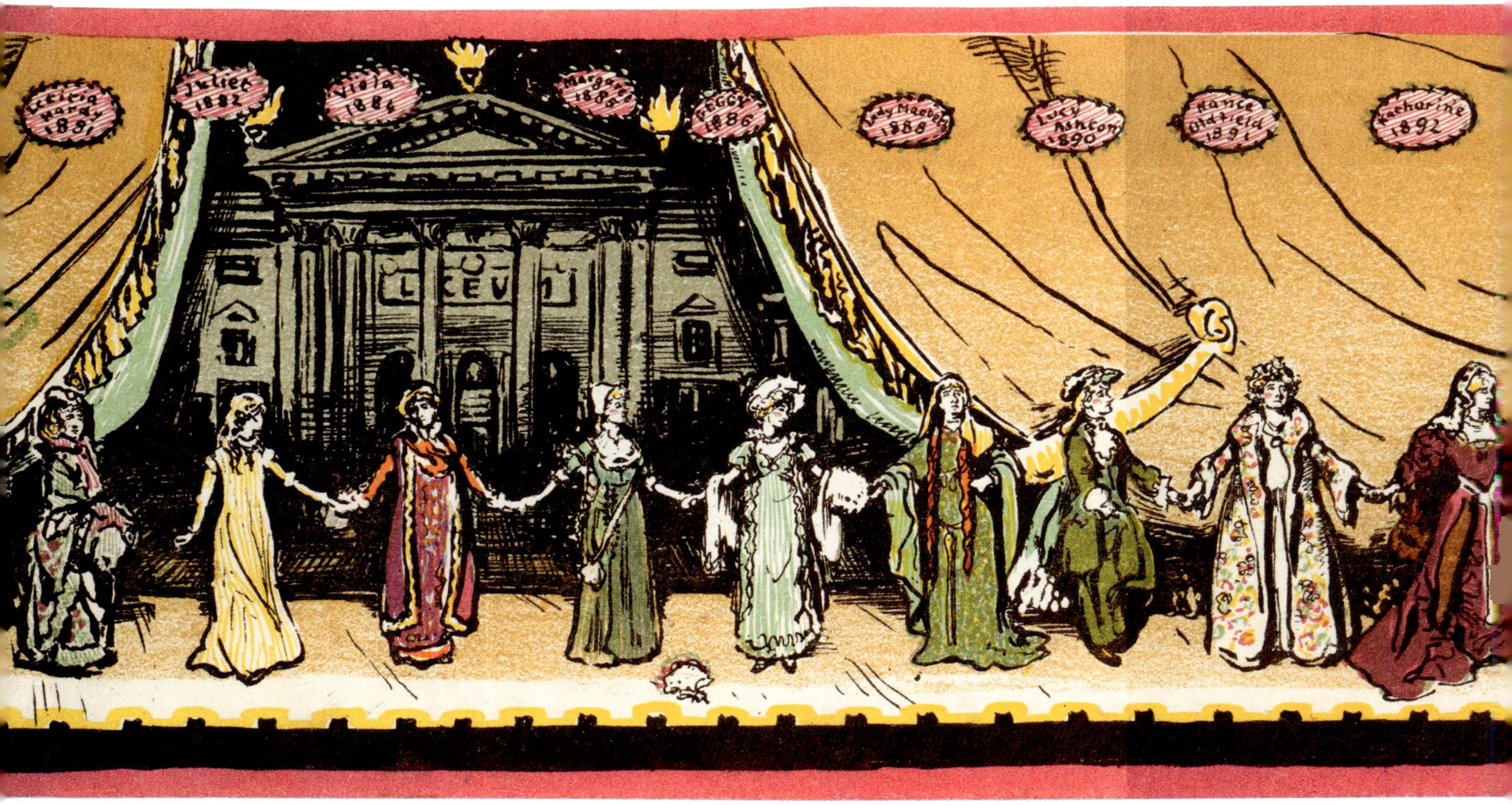

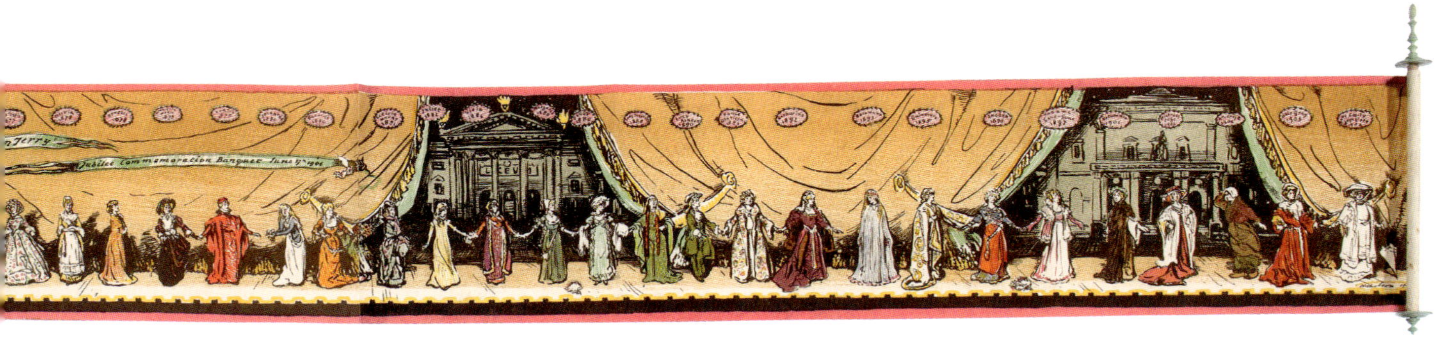

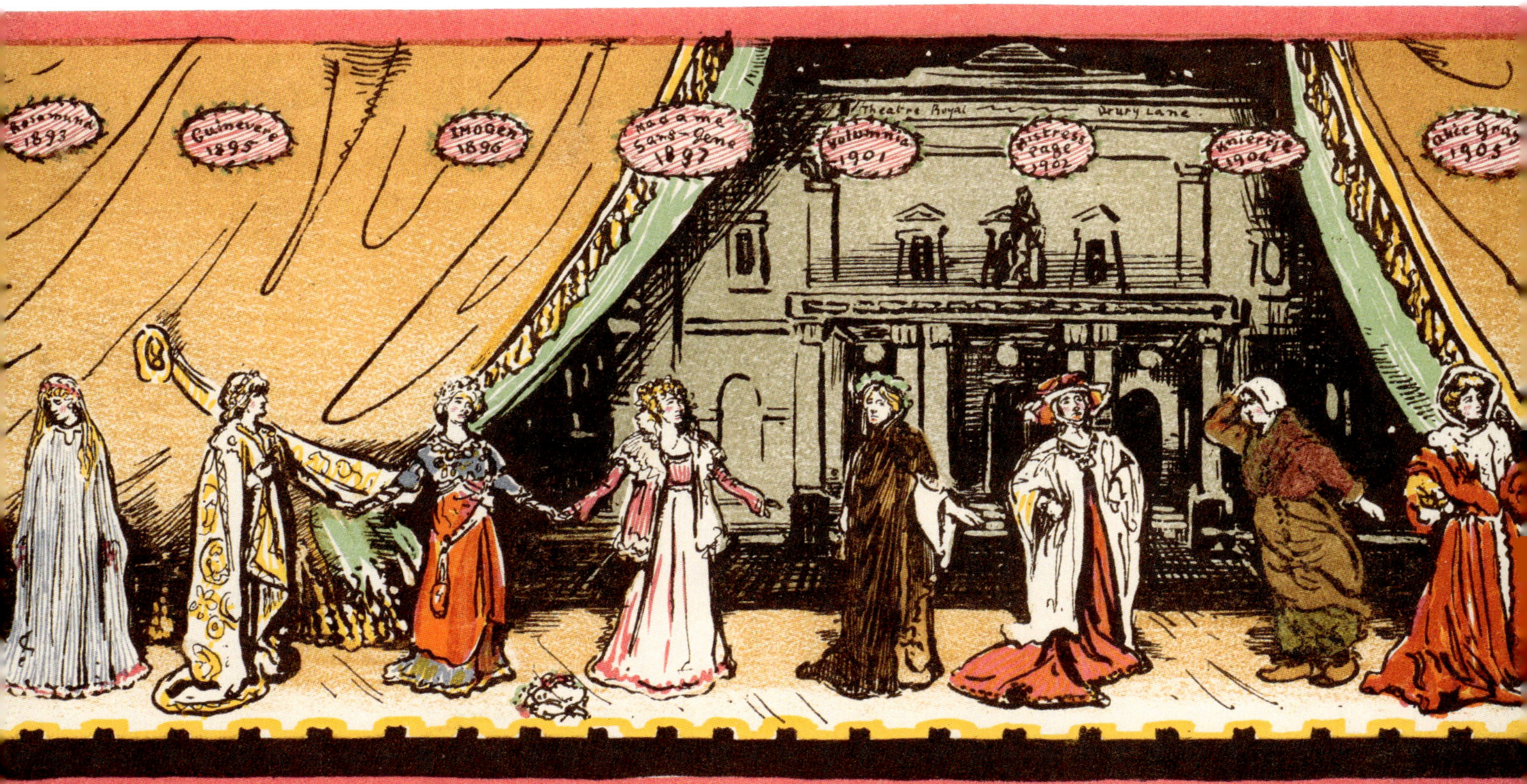
Rosamund 1893
Guinevere 1895
Imogen 1896
Madame Sans-Gene 1897
Theatre Royal Drury Lane
Volumnia 1901
Mistress Page 1902
1904
1905

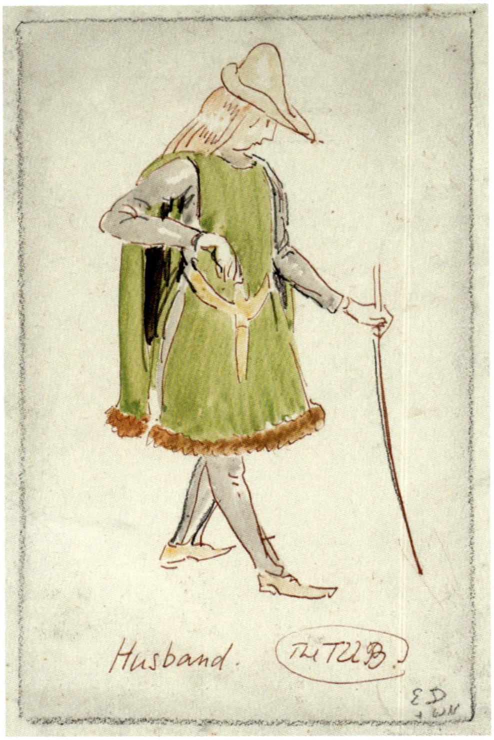

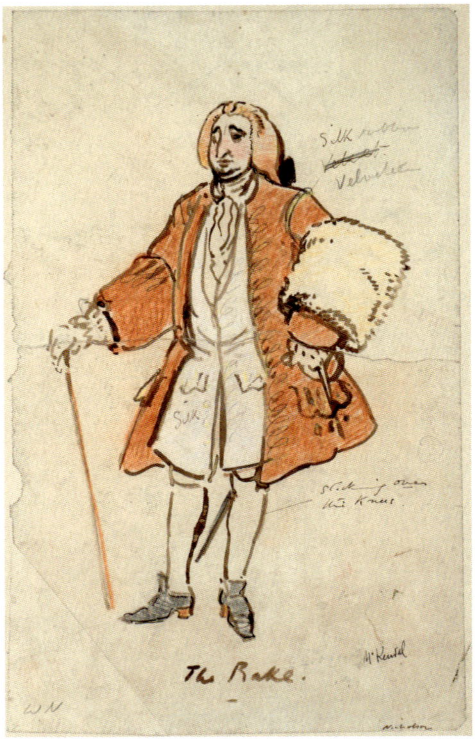

79 WILLIAM NICHOLSON (1872–1949) and ELIZABETH DRURY [EDIE NICHOLSON] (1890–1958)
Costume design of 'The Husband' for *The Tub*, 1926
Performed in C.B. Cochran's 1926 revue
Pen and watercolour on paper, 28.7 x 17.8cm
Private collection

80 Costume design of 'The Rake' for *The Rake*, 1925
Performed in C.B. Cochran's 1925 revues *On with the Dance* and *Still Dancing*
Pen and watercolour on paper, 40.8 x 24.8cm
Private collection

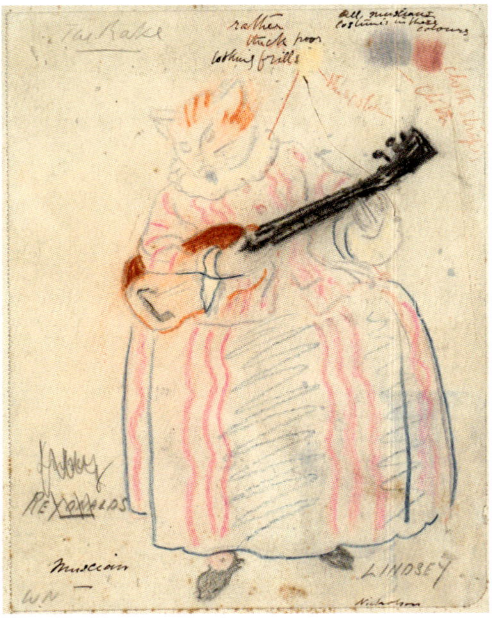

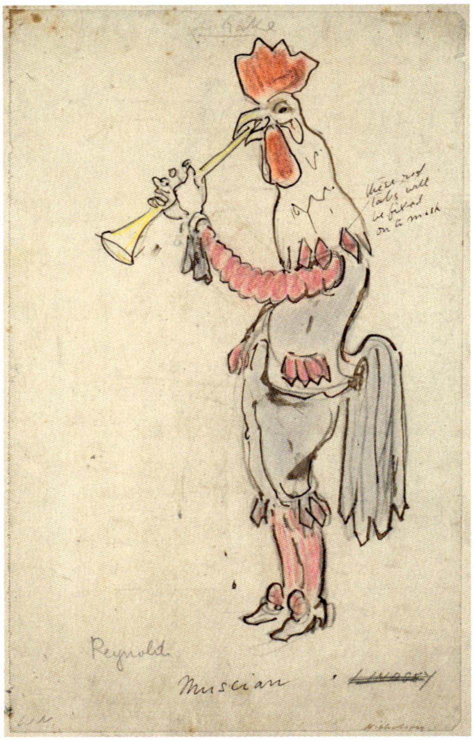

81 Costume design of 'The Cat' for *The Rake*, 1925
Performed in C.B. Cochran's 1925 revues *On with the Dance* and *Still Dancing*
Pencil and crayon on paper, 25.2 x 19.1cm
Private collection

82 Costume design of 'The Cock' for *The Rake*, 1925
Performed in C.B. Cochran's 1925 revues *On with the Dance* and *Still Dancing*
Pen and watercolour on paper, 41 x 25cm
Private collection

Opposite:
83 WILLIAM NICHOLSON (1872–1949) and ELIZABETH DRURY [EDIE NICHOLSON] (1890–1958)
Costume design of 'The Wife' for *The Tub*, 1926
Performed in C.B. Cochran's 1925 revue
Pen and watercolour on paper, 28.8 x 19cm
Private collection

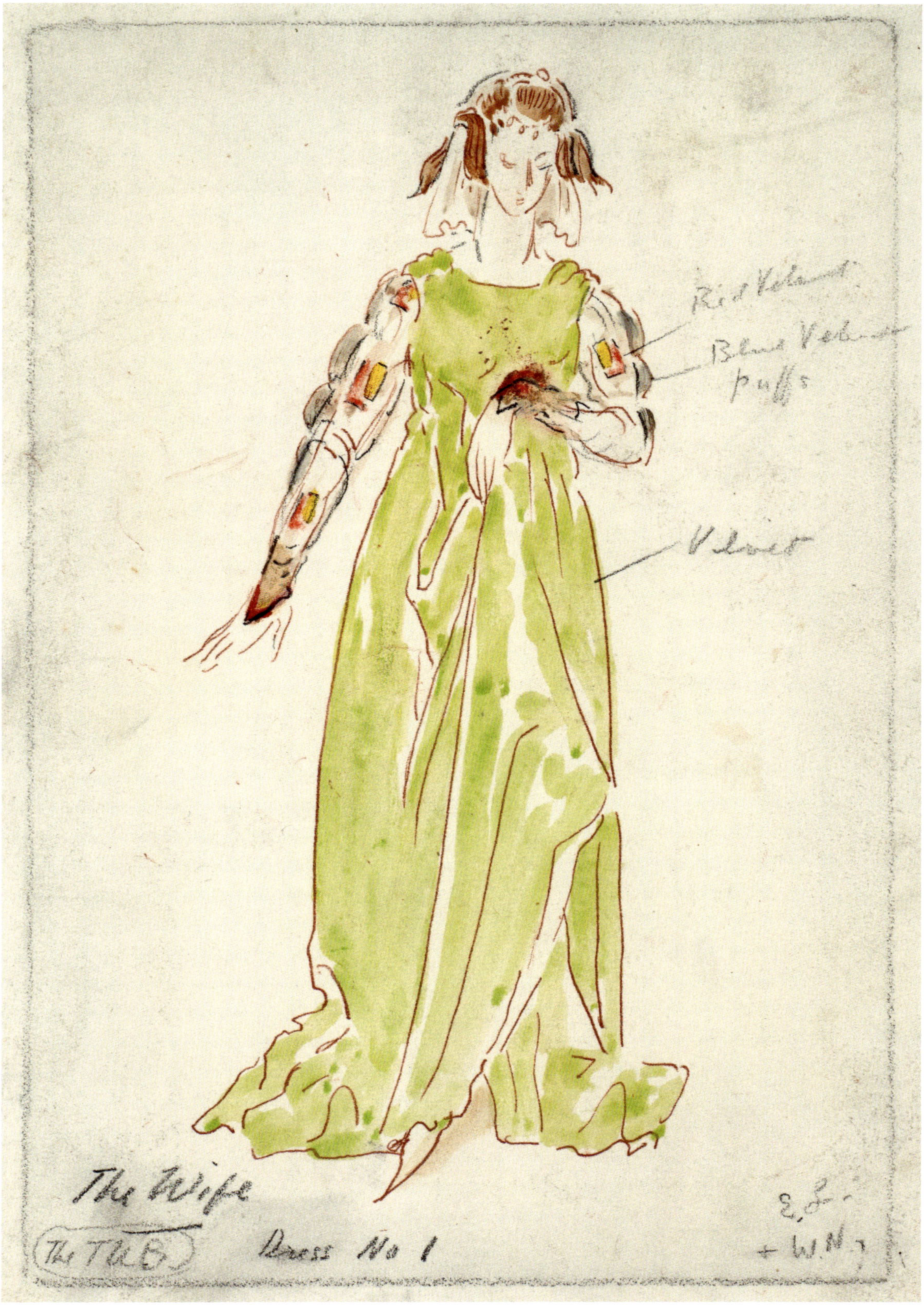
Red Velvet
Blue Velvet puffs
Velvet
The Wife
The Tub
Dress No 1

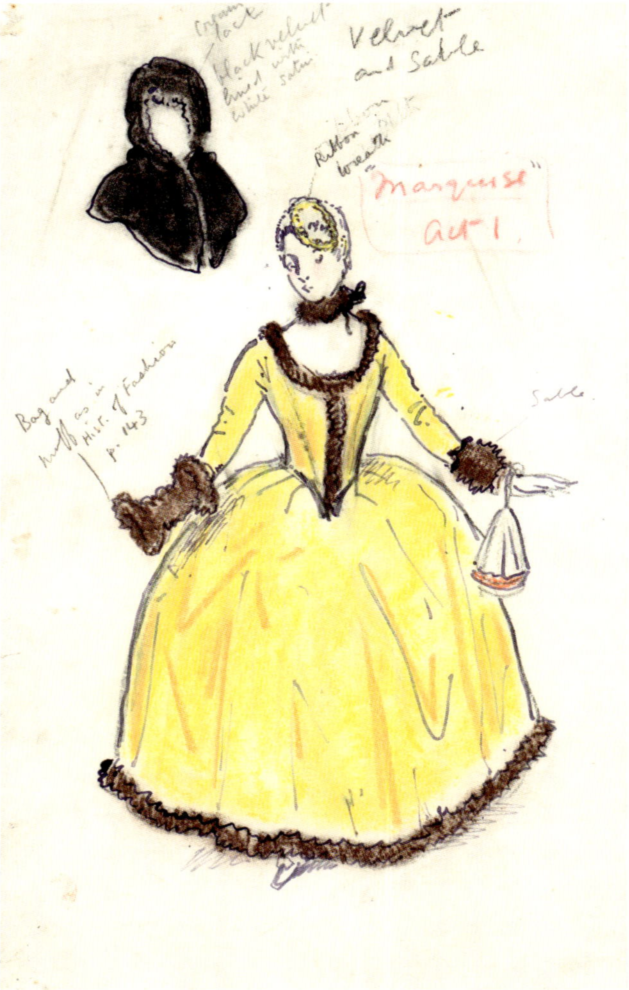

84 Costume design of 'The Marquise' for
The Marquise by Noël Coward, 1927
Pen and watercolour on paper,
40.8 x 24.8cm
Private collection

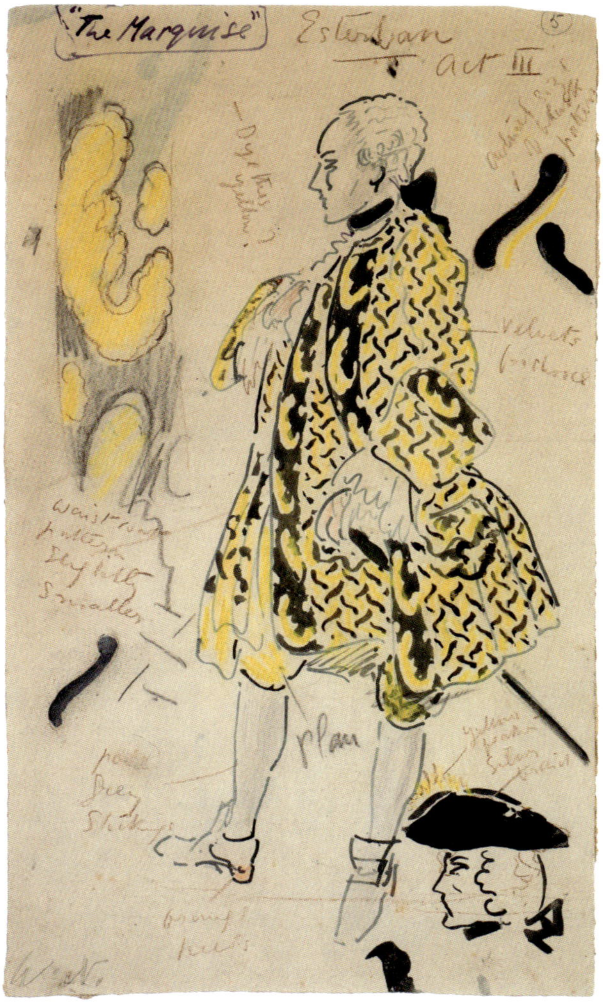

85 Costume design of 'Esteban' for
The Marquise by Noël Coward, 1927
Pen and watercolour on paper,
40.8 x 24.8cm
Private collection

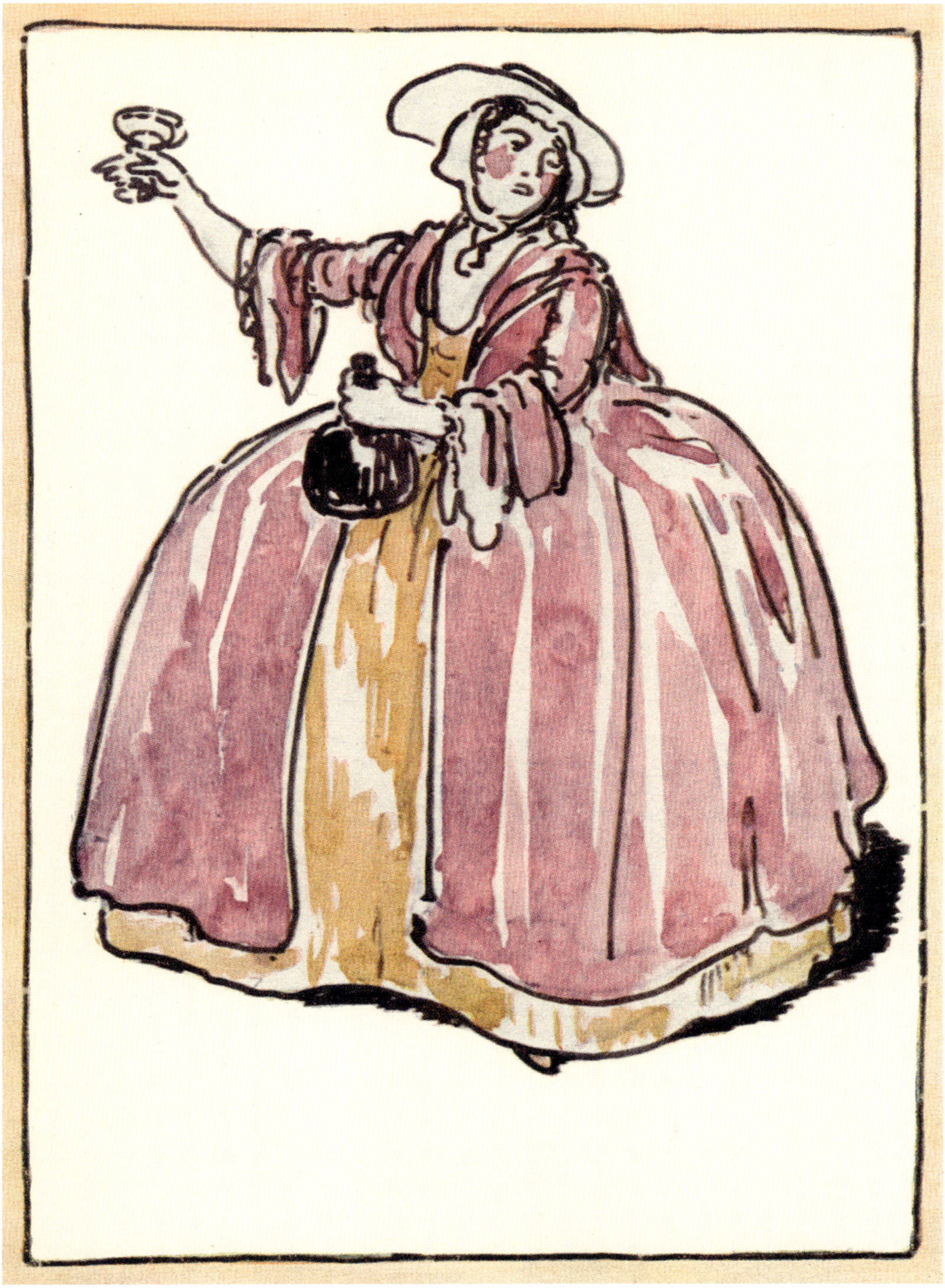

86 Illustration of 'Mrs Trapes'
for *Polly* by John Gay,
William Heinemann,
London, 1923
Colour plate, 26.7 x 20.3cm
Private collection

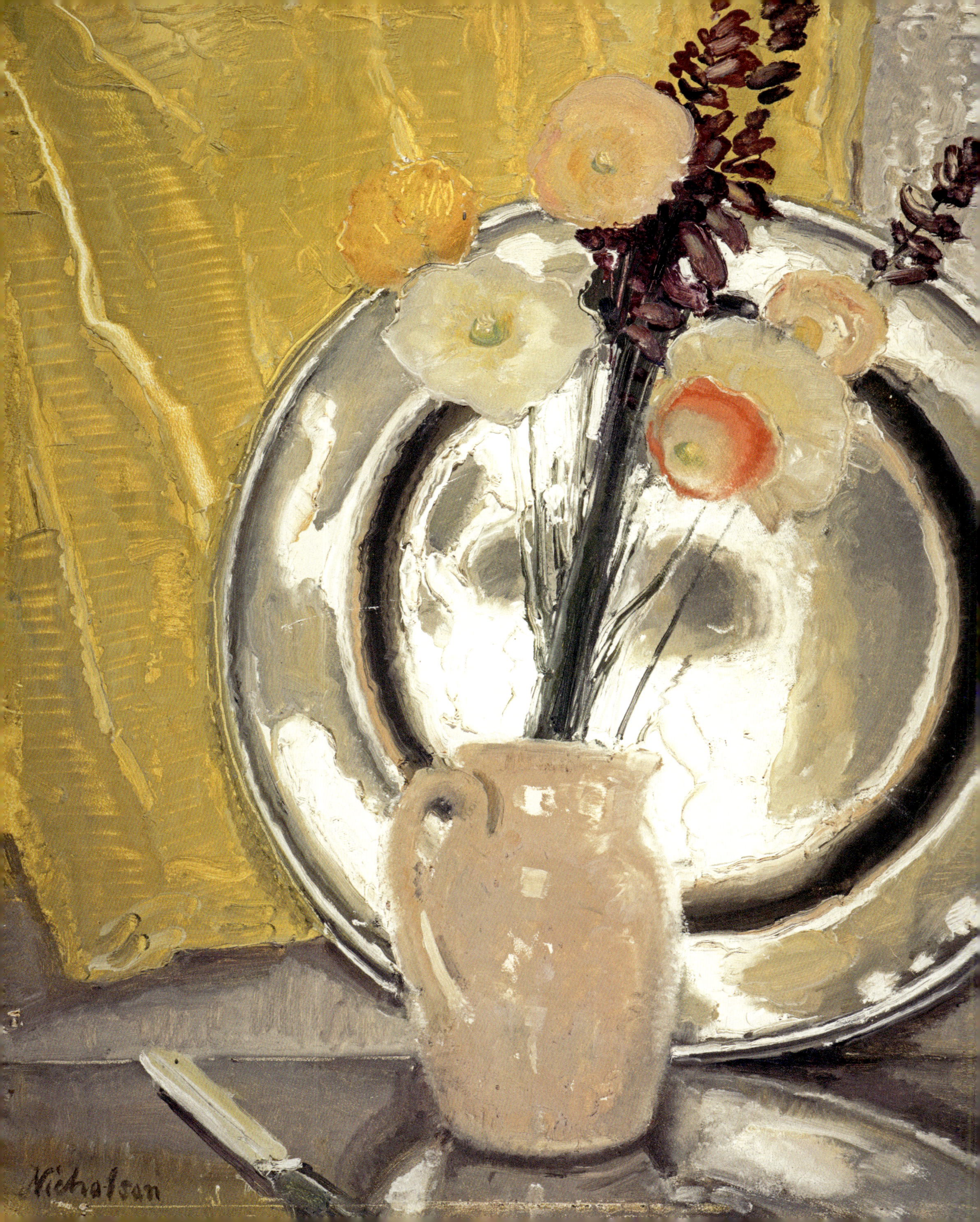
Nicholson

5 NICHOLSON AND BRINGING STILLNESS TO LIFE

MELANIE VANDENBROUCK

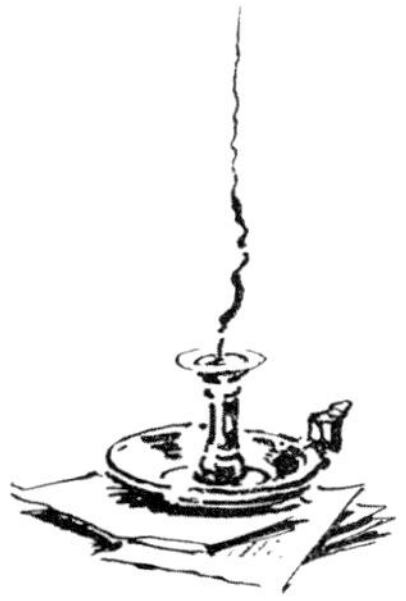

'It is the opinion of certain people who are qualified to judge, that William Nicholson is the greatest master of Still Life of his own or any other age.'[1]

So did the novelist and playwright Marguerite Steen start her biography of William Nicholson, published in 1943. As his late life companion, she may not have been the most objective of writers, yet Nicholson's still lifes retain iconic status to this day. Qualifying this judgement by limiting it to one generation, Ben Nicholson largely acquiesced when he wrote to Steen in 1953:

> In my opinion, Father's work reputation will increase year by year on the basis
> 1. of his still lifes
> 2. of his poetic landscapes
> ... the character studies come into the scheme of things certainly but they are 'local' – and the portraits are even more 'local' – whereas the finest of 1. and 2. above are, in my opinion, universal, and it is this universality which endures and it is this which makes him a finer painter than any other British painter of his generation, except perhaps [Walter] Sickert.[2]

At the time William Nicholson was painting still lifes, the depiction of inanimate objects had long been considered by the British arts establishment, as arbiter of taste, as the very lowest in a hierarchy of genres that placed history painting at its pinnacle, portraiture second, followed by landscape, scenes of everyday life, then animal paintings. The critic Frederick Wedmore commented about how prevalent this prejudice was still in 1918, when he lamented: 'Still Life – I shall not mince matters in the least about it – has been ridiculously neglected by the English public.'[3] Meanwhile, in the early 1900s still life was embraced by British avant-garde circles, whether post-impressionists of the Camden Town and

p.100
87 *Poppies in Pewter*, 1933
Oil on wood, 41.1 x 32.9cm
National Galleries of Scotland. Bequeathed by Dr R.A. Lillie 1977

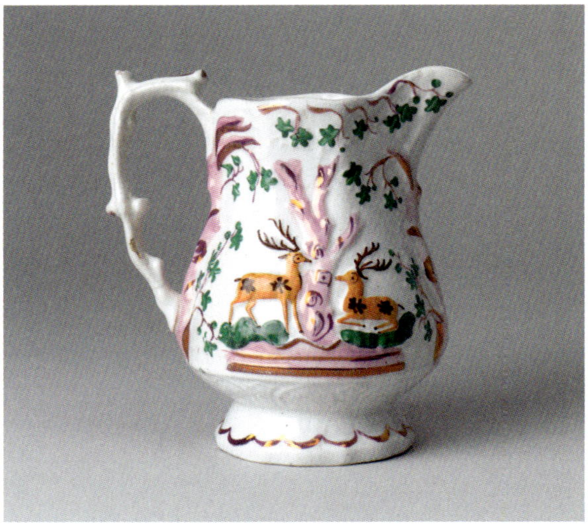

88 BRITISH, 19TH CENTURY
Staffordshire jug, c.1860, belonging to William Nicholson
Ceramic, 16 x 13.5cm
The Courtauld, London (Samuel Courtauld Trust)

Bloomsbury Groups or modernists tending towards abstraction. In his own approach to the genre, Nicholson saw it neither as a lower artistic pursuit nor as a ground for experimentation. And yet still lifes would form a major part of his prolific output, one that went beyond the oft-cited statement that he simply painted 'what was before him'.

It was not until 1907, by which time he had reached artistic maturity, that Nicholson would turn his attention to still life. He was not a complete stranger to the genre: as a teenager, he had dabbled in it with a competent *Still Life Study* (1885), for which he drew a crumpled five pound note (1887; both Newark Town Council Town Hall Museum) as a receipt upon purchase by an early collector, executed in the *trompe l'œil* tradition of the Dutch émigré artist Edwaert Collier (1640–1708), a forerunner of still life in Britain. As a portraitist in the early 1900s, Nicholson revelled in the meticulous and often prominent depiction of feathery hats and crocheted shawls, gloves and sticks, puppets and Staffordshire figures, flower arrangements and tableware. In his 1901 woodcut and oil portraits of W.E. Henley (fig.25) it is the writer's distinctive hat that commands all the attention, lending him an equally genial and louche allure. Steen described it as a 'big, broad-rimmed, crumpled, generous hat that seemed to have absorbed its owner's personality'.[4] With Nicholson, objects indeed acquire character and at times come to stand for their owner, as became the case with the army boots of Gertrude Jekyll (1920; fig.26), executed in daytime, when Jekyll, who 'thought herself unpaintable', was unavailable to sit for her portrait, devoted as she was to her garden.[5] Under Nicholson's brush, they become a spirited metonymic portrait of the gardener. By contrast, *Miss Simpson's Boots*, from the same year (private collection), with its two pairs of white satin lace and red leather elasticated shoes – found items that Nicholson kept in his collection of dressing-up clothes and accessories – creates the imaginary portrait of a fashionable woman-about-town.[6]

Endowed with a character of their own, ceramic- and tableware found their place naturally in family portraits. *The Boy with the Caroline Mug* (1901; Newark College, Lincoln) and *Nancy, the Girl with the Pewter Mug* (1907; private collection) are two examples in which Nicholson lay particular emphasis on containers, their rotundity, reflective sheen and haptic qualities. These objects emphasise rather than hinder the sitters' personalities. Although the Georgian Staffordshire lusterware mug he holds feels uncomfortably outsized, heavy and fragile for his boyish hands, Nicholson's son Ben is focussed on his own thoughts. Nicholson's daughter Nancy looks back at the viewer mischievously, the lid of her solid utilitarian mug slightly ajar, as if made to speak like a puppet – it is said to have belonged to the actor Ellen Terry, with whom the family was staying, thus perhaps explaining Nancy's performative stance.[7] In these portraits, Nicholson may have been indebted to the *bodegones* (everyday kitchen and tavern scenes) of 17th-century Spanish artists, Diego Velázquez chief among them, whom he had first admired when in Paris in the autumn of 1891.

Pots were an important part of Nicholson's studio paraphernalia, as models for his work as much as for stowing paintbrushes. A photograph

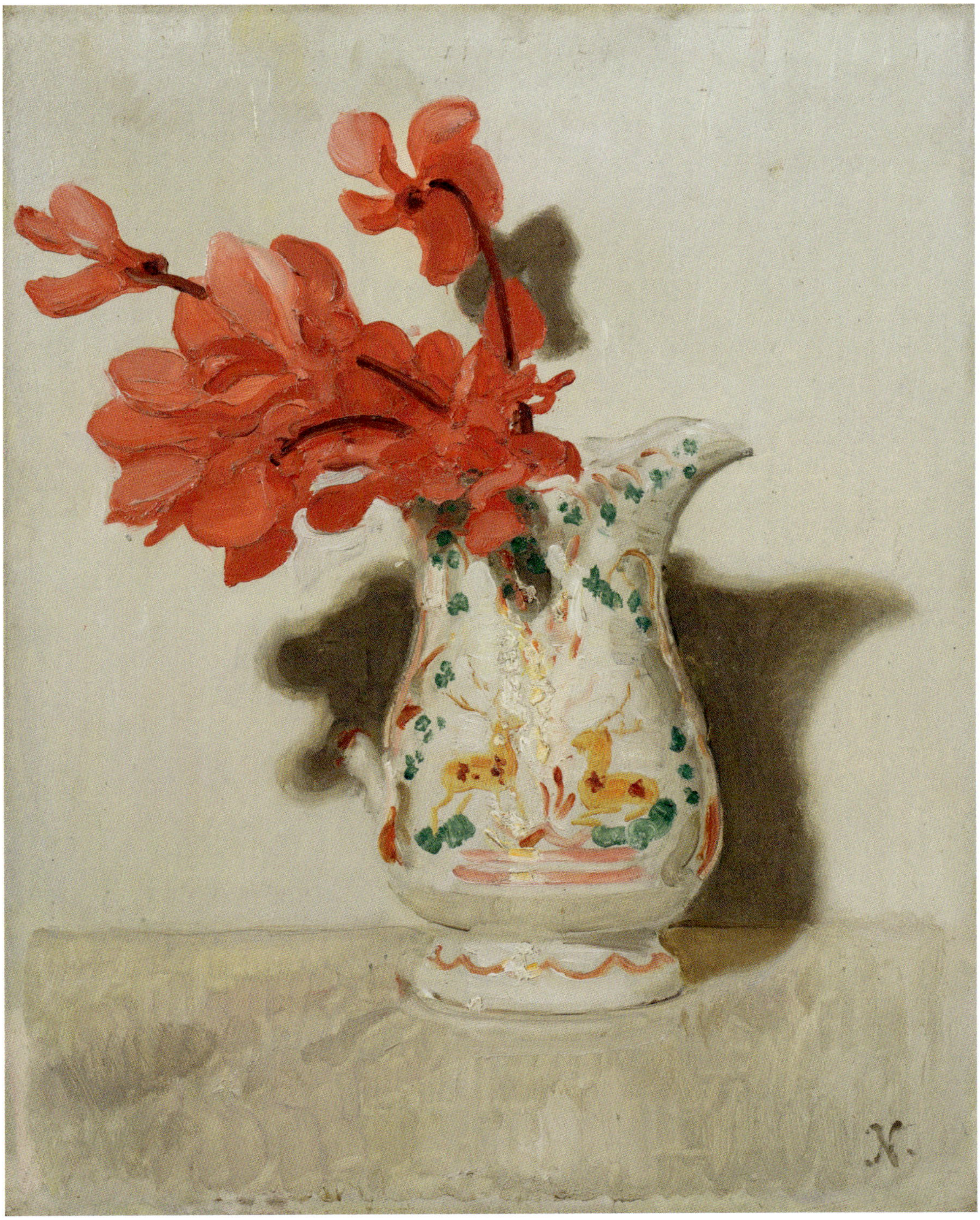

89 *Cyclamen*, 1936
Oil on panel, 39.3 x 31.1cm
The Courtauld, London
(Samuel Courtauld Trust)

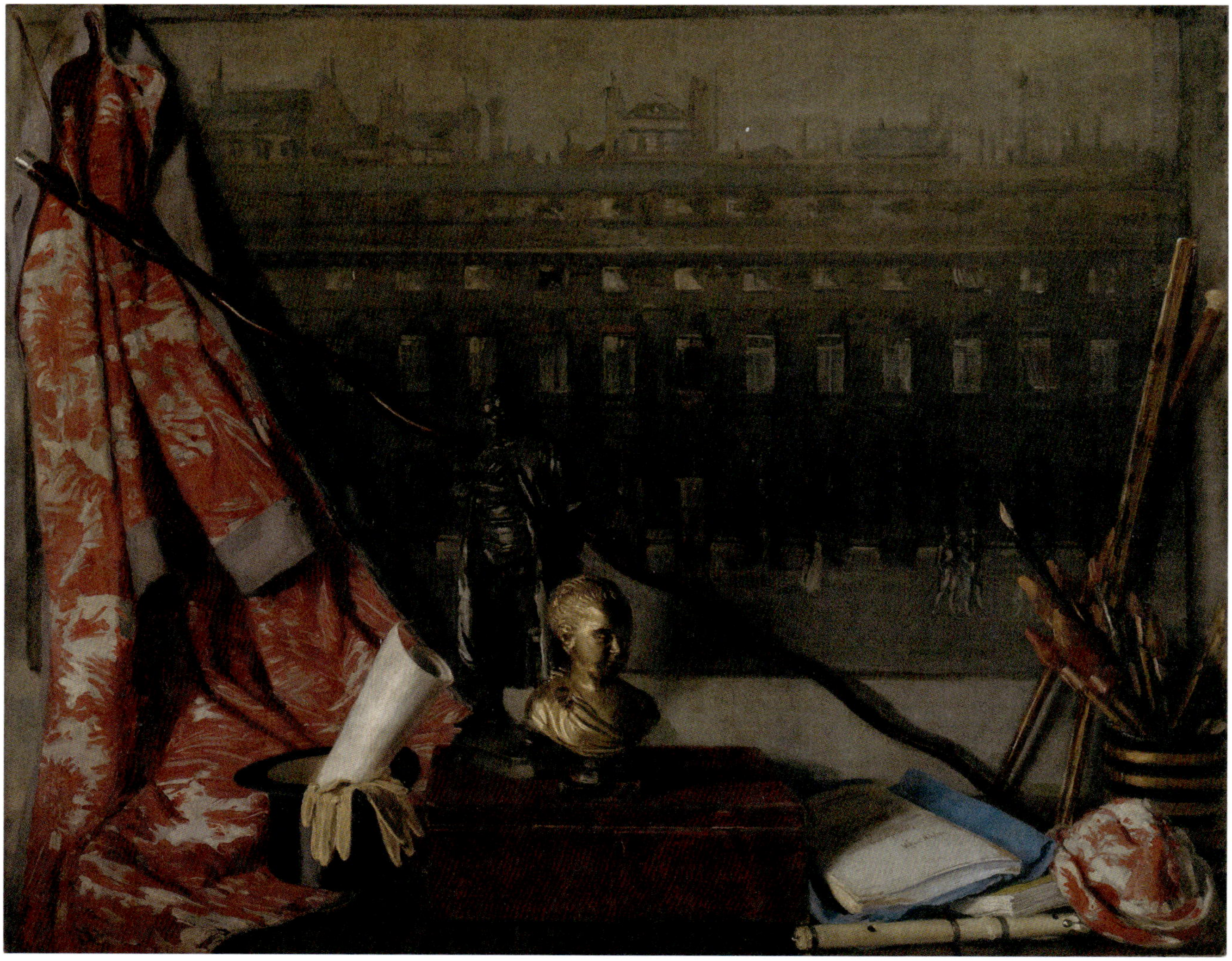

90 *Studio Still Life*, 1914
Oil on canvas, 131.4 x 162.6cm
Tate: Bequeathed by
Edward Knoblock 1945

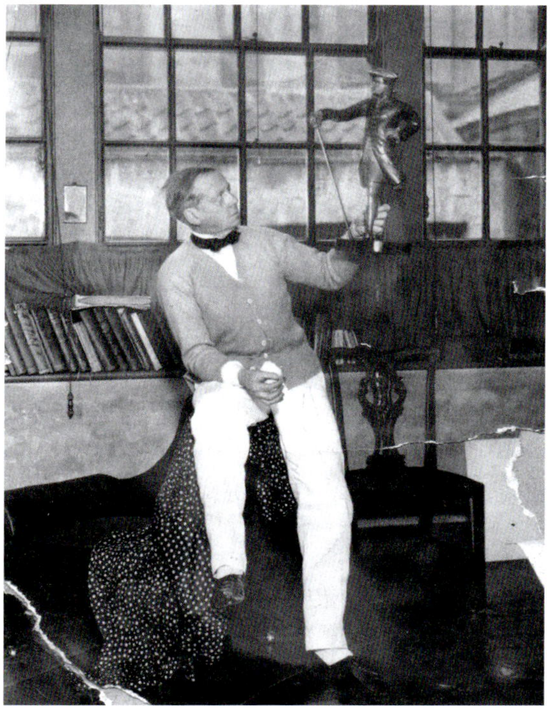

91 MALCOLM ARBUTHNOT (1877–1967)
William Nicholson in Apple Tree Yard holding a wooden figure of a French officer, 1922
Private collection

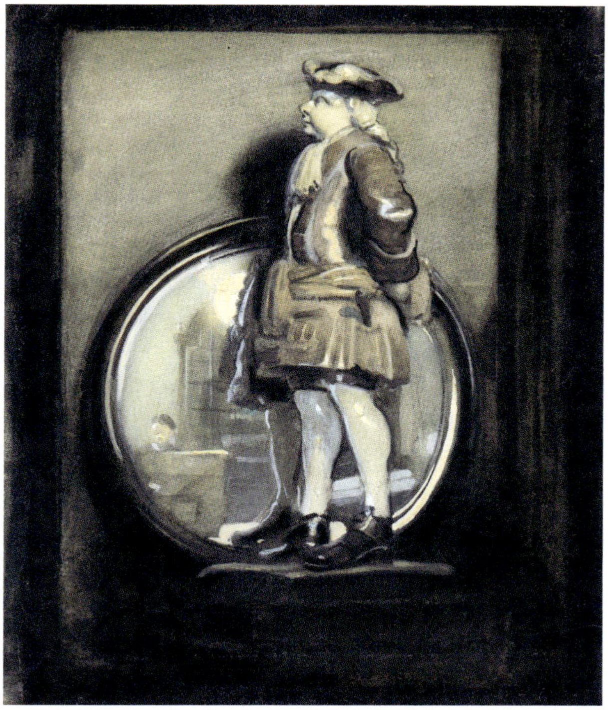

92 *The Convex Mirror*, 1907
Watercolour on paper, 34 x 28cm
Nottingham City Museum & Galleries

by Malcolm Arbuthnot shows the artist, aged 40, standing behind a large, gleaming pot containing a collection of long brushes (fig.51). A delicate Staffordshire jug adorned with a genteel woodland scene 'poses' as a vase for a vibrant sprig of crimson cyclamen (1936; figs.88 and 89) when it was otherwise used for keeping paintbrushes.[8] They are heaped in a striped pot in the ambitious *Studio Still Life* (1914; fig.90), also known as *Chez lui* [At his home], executed for the American playwright and novelist Edward Knoblock. The latter had commissioned Nicholson to create an ambitious decorative scheme for his Parisian home.[9] While Nicholson had set up studio there for the duration of the commission, *Studio Still Life* is more about his patron than it is about the artist's working space. The background is taken up by a painting depicting a view of the Palais Royal as seen from the apartment's windows. The rest of the composition draws a portrait of Knoblock through his interests and sartorial attire: collectibles, such as a bronze statuette, a gilt bust or the wind instruments he hung on his walls; and the *toile de Jouy* gown and cap, the walking stick, top hat and gloves of a dandy. The painter – represented through canvas and paint-brushes – becomes just one of Knoblock's things.

More often though, Nicholson's still lifes include his own objects. At first sight a city scene, the still-life arrangement in *A Young Nobleman Surveys the City* (1910; fig.34) is, in Patricia Reed's words, 'a study in textures and reflective surfaces'.[10] The statuette of a French officer which he kept at home (it is shown in the background of Mabel Pryde's painting of their family home, *The Grange, Rottingdean*, 1911; National Galleries of Scotland) or in the studio (as seen in a photograph at Apple Tree Yard in 1922; fig.91) is artfully placed in front of a glazed cityscape. Nicholson included himself reflected in the glass, at the easel, cigarette dangling from his lips: the artist at work is in dialogue with his subject.[11] He had used a similar approach in an earlier watercolour, *The Convex Mirror* (1907; fig.92), but there the painter remained several steps removed from the statuette (another bewigged and behatted man in 18th-century dress), his gaze on his easel rather than on his subject. In an oil painting with the same title (1917; destroyed), Nicholson used the mirror to depict what Reed called 'perhaps the nearest to a self-portrait in oils that WN produced'.[12] That Nicholson favoured still lifes as a way to represent himself is perhaps telling of the symbolic importance these held in his oeuvre.

The artist's grandson and biographer, Andrew Nicholson, wrote that his still lifes 'grew out of the way he lived', showing 'the objects around him, especially the flowers in vases and jugs'.[13] His daughter-in-law, the artist Winifred Nicholson, recalled seeing in the parlour at Sutton Veny, 'shelves packed with lustre and shimmer of jugs and goblets', and his studio 'so full of things, painter's magic, models of ships, jugs, 18th-century silver, old paper, odds and ends, rubbish, canvas, paints, palettes, and fishermen's glass balls, and more jugs'.[14] He would pass these jugs on to his son Ben, also a painter of still lifes, who later reminisced about the formative role his father's collection, 'the very beautiful striped and spotted jugs and mugs and goblets, and octagonal and hexagonal glass objects', had on his own work.[15] Beyond what might be read as affectionate depictions of treasured possessions, the still lifes are also canny deployments of the elder Nicholson's artistic skill, designed to dazzle, confound and enchant.

Reputedly painted as a wager for his publisher, William Heinemann, *The Lustre Bowl* (1908; fig.100) would establish a formula Nicholson returned to often: focussed on a central object, whether single or accompanied by secondary motifs (here the fan and tassel, in the shadows, are almost hidden from view), on a monochrome, sometimes polished, surface against a dark background, where the subject seems to be light and reflection above all else. While Nicholson had embarked on the pursuit of painting still lifes only the previous year, *The Lustre Bowl* is admirably resolved, with its impeccable composition, chromatic sobriety and deftness of hand: the accents of light, reflected on the inner and outer surfaces of the bowl, achieved with the flick of a brush heavily loaded in white paint. He used the same formula in *The Lustre Bowl with Green Peas* (1911; fig.30), this time with more emphasis on the reflection of the surroundings: the green peapods and white tablecloth on the outer surface of the bowl, the wider room on its interior. It is both empty and containing the space around it, the surrounding shadows charged with drama. Nicholson repeated this sleight of hand with two depictions, *The Silver Casket* and *The Silver Casket and Red Leather Box* (1919 and 1920; figs.98 and 99), showing a tea caddy by the 18th-century silversmith Hester Bateman (1709–1794), whose 'silver masterpieces' Nicholson collected.[16] While the former reflects the blue gloves and jet and vermilion necklaces casually dropped on the tabletop, the latter shows the reflection of a large window alongside Nicholson's own partial and nebulous features, distorted by the rotund shape of the vessel. Intriguingly, an early photograph reveals that the red box on which the 'second' casket rests was originally painted in contrasting diamond patterns. It is unknown why Nicholson altered its appearance so significantly.[17]

These virtuoso exercises harked back to the still-life tradition of the Dutch Golden Age, with their tabletop compositions on undefined backgrounds and illusionistic focus on the distinctive surfaces of things. And yet they eschewed the symbolic essence of that tradition – the moral message about the brevity of life (if perhaps hinted at briefly in such rare examples as *The Lowestoft Bowl* [1911; fig.93], with its shed tulip petal) or the vain pursuit of worldly possessions – as could also be found in

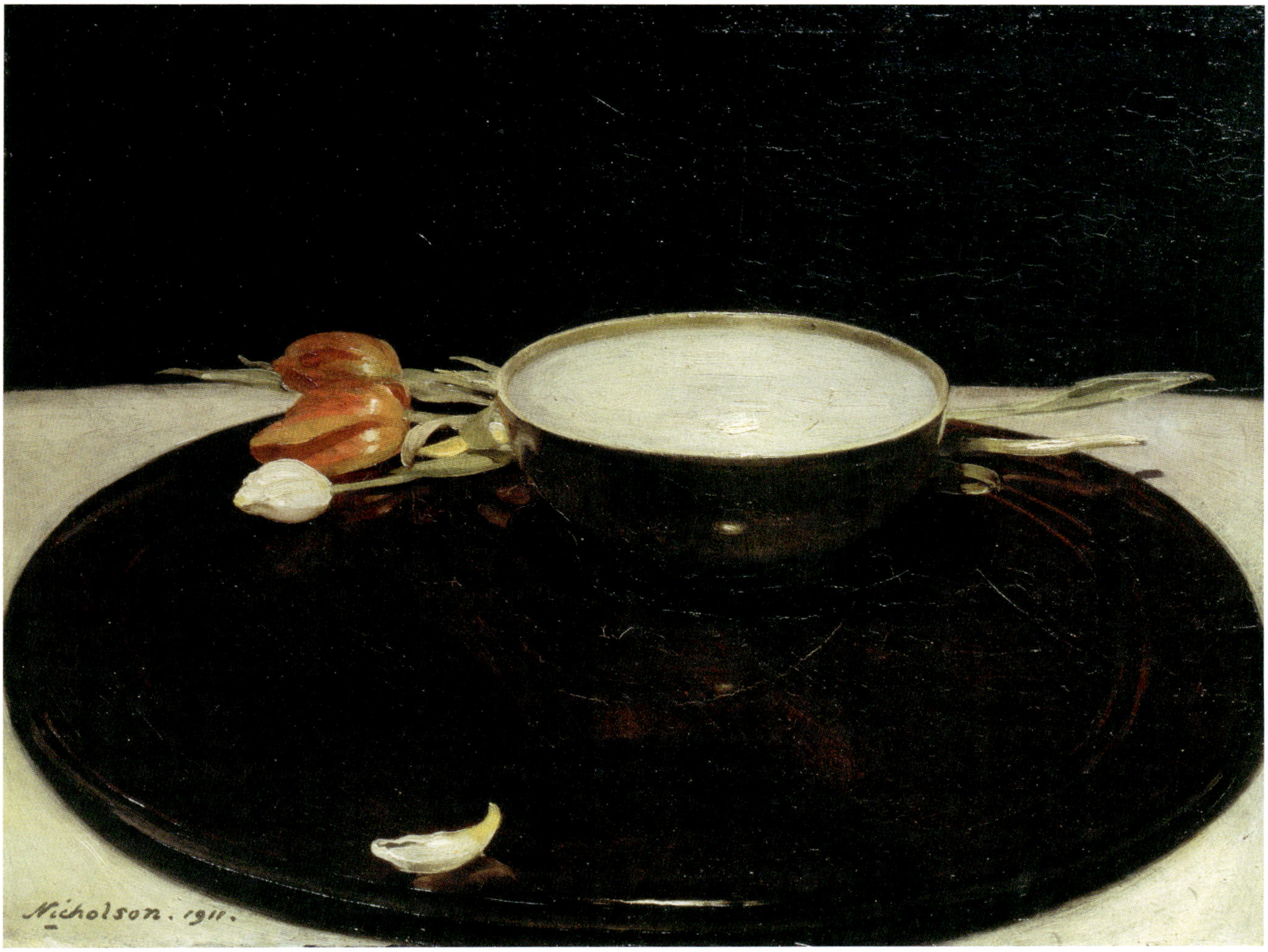

93 *The Lowestoft Bowl*, 1911
Oil on canvas, 47.6 x 61cm
Tate: Presented by the
Contemporary Art Society 1917

the work of the French artist Jean Siméon Chardin (1699–1779), to whom early commentors likened Nicholson's work.[18] The cat licking spilt milk in *The Hundred Jugs* (1915–16; National Museums Liverpool, Walker Art Gallery) certainly nods in Chardin's direction, but there is no moral message here.[19] This bravura – one might say bravado – deployment of still life, which Sanford Schwartz aptly called an 'armada of the modest', was reputedly produced in jest, the result of his son and sometime rival Ben Nicholson's goading his father to fit a hundred jugs in one painting.[20] It also illustrates Nicholson's compulsive collecting of jugs, most of which Reed stated 'he had acquired very cheaply at the Caledonian Road market and in second-hand shops, or from public houses and ironmongers' or, as Steen reminisced, 'wander[ing] round the Lanes [in Brighton] in search of [...] pink lustre'.[21]

While with its large scale and expansive scene *The Hundred Jugs* may feel immersive, Nicholson would soon surpass himself. The decorative scheme he produced for the dining room at Folly Farm, a 17th-century farmhouse enlarged by Edwin Lutyens for Zachary and Rosalie Merton in Sulhamstead, Berkshire (1916–18; destroyed), was a *trompe l'œil* extravaganza of open French windows and tasselled hangings, caged birds, a ceramic cockerel, feathers and paintbrushes, pewter plates and trays, vases, inkpot and quill pens, lamps and more. 'I am completely obsessed with my painting at Folly Farm,' he wrote to Ben on 20 May 1918, 'and it is pretty good my boy. I tell you! All I know of balance, drawing, and decoration, I have put on the walls.'[22] From canvas to walls and beyond, ceramics offered inspiration across his practice; indeed, the cover for the three issues of *The Owl: A Miscellany* (fig.41), featuring the eponymous bird surrounded with owlets, was inspired by a 17th-century Staffordshire slipware dish by Thomas Toft (d.1698) or his family.[23]

Nicholson could be equally punctilious and humorous in some of his depictions: an oft-repeated anecdote has him placing a piece of kipper on the back of a fish painting so its aroma makes the painting more pungently truthful.[24] His later *Sun Fish* (1935; fig.106), its gleaming scales shining in unison with the ice in a light-coloured porcelain dish, has an equal sense of truthfulness, while the background (the plate is resting on a board on the chequered floor of his studio), all angles, contrasts and shadows, creates plays with our senses and perception. Nicholson's fish were not to be found just on tables, plates or indeed floors: in the early 1920s he had been involved in creating illustrations of marine life (figs.107–110) for his friend, the zoologist Edward Boulenger, appointed the first director of the Zoological Society of London's Aquarium in 1923. These came to nothing, but show him experimenting afresh, as they unusually took the form of blueprints, a technique used by architects, which he may have learnt from Lutyens or perhaps his son Kit Nicholson.

More than depictions of individual objects, Nicholson's still lifes are explorations of the relationship between light and darkness, opacity and translucency, absorption and reflection, softness and rigidity and so forth. At times, as in his *Brass Canister* from 1917 (fig.111), which sets a small group of objects as features on a sand-coloured tabletop and background, they have the pared down simplicity of his landscapes, the expansive minimalism of his downland scenes chief among them. Customarily shy of pontificating about art, Nicholson once pronounced, as retold by Robert Nichols, that 'The business of an artist practising realism is "to communicate what in the natural is irresistible to him and what in the act of communication in a particular medium is pleasurable."'[25] That he felt compelled to share what appealed to him and found pleasure in doing so is strikingly demonstrated by his still lifes.

Nicholson's approach to the genre changed after 1919, as a fresh chapter in his life started. That year, he and family friend Edie Stuart Wortley, both recently widowed, married, causing a rift with his son Ben. The daughter of a diamond magnate in South Africa, Edie was independently wealthy, and it may be that the relative financial relief his marriage brought him allowed him to be more experimental with his work.[26] He may also have been inspired by Edie herself, who painted under the name Elizabeth Drury. Be that as it may, his work shifted from dark tones and a concern for verisimilitude to a brighter palette and a looser handling of paint.[27] From late 1924, father and son at last reconciled, his style would also come to be marked by the work of his daughter-in-law Winifred Nicholson, with whom he enjoyed debating about art. A key concern of hers was chromatic harmony and the textural quality of paint. It may be that *Flowers in a Tankard* (1924; private collection) was created in her company, as they were said to have painted the same bouquet of anemones around that time. It shows a vigorous handling of paint, not unlike Winifred's, and a lighter, brighter palette than was customary in his still lifes before then. Winifred recalled discussing 'yellow ochre' with her father-in-law, accents of which punctuate the painting.[28] Perhaps the most experimental in handling is the later *Poppies in Pewter* (1933; fig.87), in which the dazzling colour range is met by the variety of painterly effects, using in turn a palette knife and the wooden tips of variously sized brush handles. Seen also in *Pears* (1938; fig.104), the diagonal of knife handles are used to create depth and draw the eye into the composition – a common device in tabletop still lifes. His 1930s paintings suggest an affinity with the work of the French impressionist Édouard Manet, whom Nicholson admired. Although more likely to depict a brass measure than a gold jug or mug, as it has been various titled, *Gold Jug* (1937; fig.113) is astonishing in its powers of suggestion.[29] The metallic glint of the central object, oozing with light, seems almost liquid. Its effect is rendered most remarkable by the contrast with the almost abstract background loosely sketched in chalk and charcoal with the outlines of a landscape – leading Schwartz to see the painting 'becom[e], in effect, a portrait of a regal entity in a glade', a landscape, portrait and still life all at once.[30] By 1938 this progressive simplification of forms had reached its climax with *Silver* (1938; fig.114), a symphony in silver and whites: tellingly, it was to become one of Ben Nicholson's favourite paintings, for its monochrome brightness verges on abstraction.[31]

Winifred Nicholson astutely observed that 'with his still life he was at ease, and free to express the shine of the scales of the fish on his dish, the shine on the knife, the texture of the crust on the loaf of bread, the glister of the silver teapot, and then his pencil would skip and laugh and he would illustrate with delight his children's books'.[32] In a 1920 painting of a pink 'splash lustre' Sunderland ware goblet set atop a pile of books against a bright yellow wall (fig.94), Nicholson included through an opening (or perhaps mirror) to the right the device of a 'scene within a scene' which Mabel Pryde herself had favoured, perhaps inspired by Velázquez, whose *Christ in the House of Martha and Mary* they both would have seen at the National Gallery in London. In this aperture Nicholson depicted 13-year-old Pamela Bianco, busy writing or drawing. An artist and 'child prodigy', Bianco had been one the contributors to the first issue of *The Owl* in 1919 and she was staying with Edie and Nicholson at Maes-y-Neuadd, Harlech, in the summer of 1920 (fig.95). She was the daughter of children's book author Margery Williams and illustrated her mother's 'The Velveteen Rabbit; or, How Toys Become Real' when it was first published

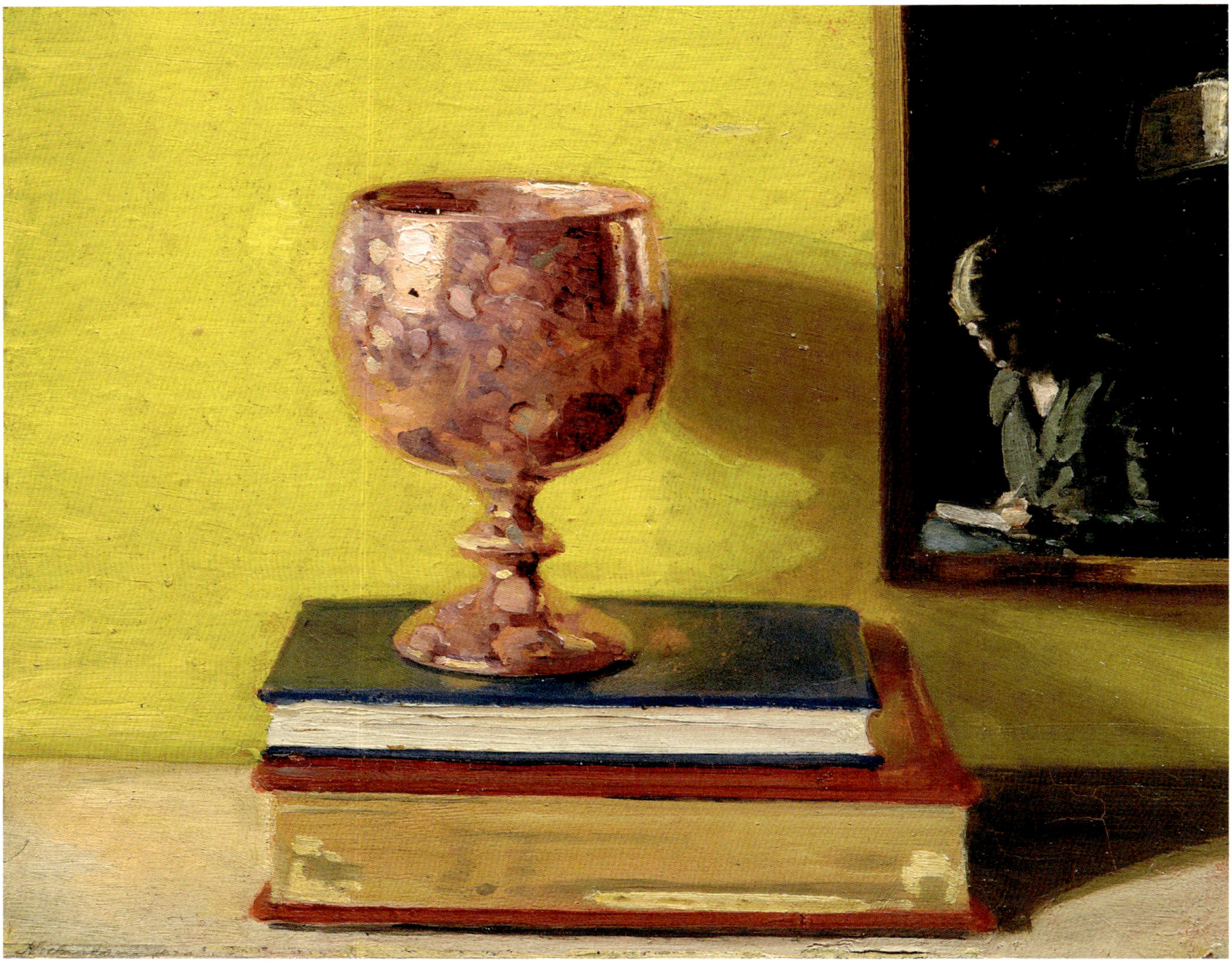

94 *Rose Lustre*, 1920
Oil on panel, 27.5 x 33cm
Private collection, courtesy
Hazlitt Holland-Hibbert

95 William Nicholson and Pamela Bianco in Wales, 1920
Private collection

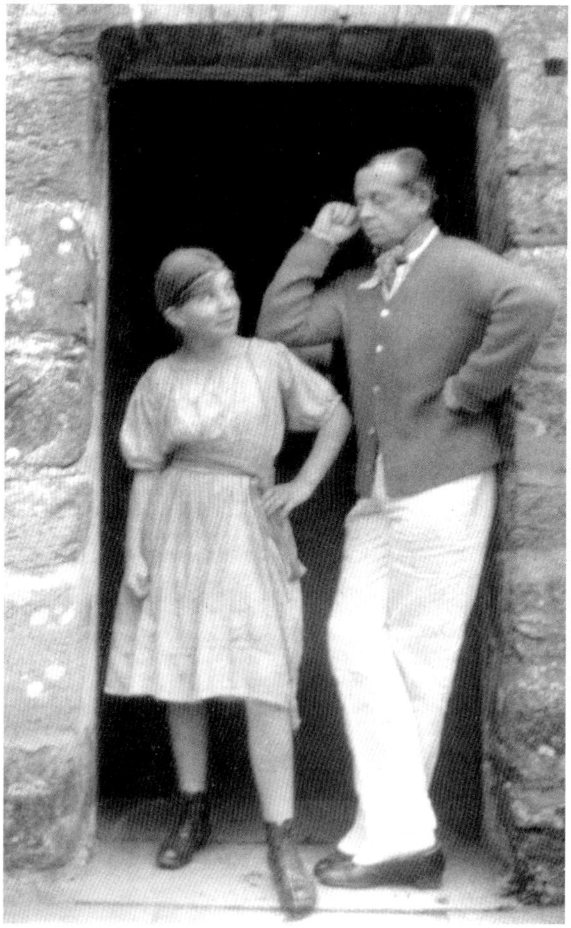

in *Harper's Bazar* in June 1921.[33] Williams also asked Nicholson to illustrate the story for its publication as a book in 1922. His illustrations reveal that, for a man who revelled in depicting inanimate objects, he also excelled at bringing the inanimate to life.

Nicholson first developed his ideas and drawings for *The Velveteen Rabbit* (fig.19) in summer 1921, while holidaying in a farmhouse near Uckfield, Sussex. Andrew Nicholson wrote that the artist's morning routine involved taking 'the children [presumably William and Edie's young daughter, Elizabeth, known as Penny, then about a year old, Nancy's children, Jenny and David, and Edie's children from her first marriage] to find mushrooms and watch the rabbits playing':[34] one of the book's illustrations, *Summer Days* (fig.117), mid-way through the narrative, seems to depict just one of these outings. The story takes young readers through the life of a stuffed rabbit, from his joyful apparition in a little boy's life as a Christmas present, to suffering almost instantaneous neglect, existential doubts and life lessons, reunion with his child owner, happy times as favourite toy, fresh demise, encounter with a fairy and rebirth as a living rabbit. The first illustration shows a spirited bunny (fig.115), its flesh made of sawdust and skin of velveteen, poking out of a Christmas stocking, ears erect and whiskers stiff with anticipation. In *The Skin Horse Tells His Story* (fig.116), a great sense of drama is conveyed: the Rabbit stands on a tower of books to face the horse's head, a floppy doll sitting as a silent witness in the foreground. Beside her, a candle casts strong shadows, but all three faces are bathed in light, evoking a sense of hope. Light envelopes *Spring Time* (fig.97) in a warm glow, that of happy days spent playing in the garden with the Boy, while shadows become ominous in *Anxious Times* (fig.118), as the Rabbit's fate hangs in the balance. A burst of light pierces through darkness with the resplendent figure of the Fairy erupting out of her flower (fig.119), while the final illustration shows the forest floor bursting with rabbits as they welcome their new friend (fig.120). Writing around the same time as Nicholson was completing his designs, Stanley Kennedy North marvelled at the painter's versatility:

> He designs an end-paper like that to *The Velveteen Rabbit* [fig.96], in which hundreds of rabbits are drawn calligraphically without lifting the pen from the paper in a boisterous humour full of

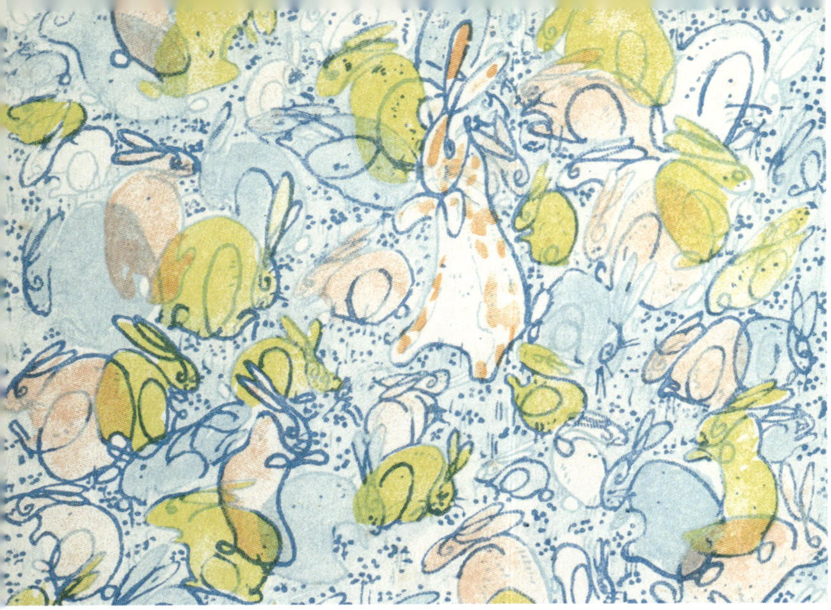

96 Endpapers (detail)
Printer's proof of Margery Williams, *The Velveteen Rabbit*, William Heinemann, London, 1922
Lithograph on paper, 25 x 39cm
Private collection

> surprise. His drawing of cats, horses, cups of tea, ducks, shoes, gloves, hats, anything you like, is a happy diversion of his and he would make a first class uncle for anyone's children, for surprise is the royal road to a child's heart and to that of the best of us who have grown old.[35]

Known as 'The Kid' to his family and friends, Nicholson rejoiced in the company of children, and his books for them reveal both tender observation and understanding. Encouraged by the success of *The Velveteen Rabbit* and inspired by the company of his young daughter, grandchildren and stepchildren, Nicholson undertook to write as well as illustrate children's books of his own. Published by Heinemann in 1926, *Clever Bill* (fig.121) tells of the adventures of a toy Guard soldier in a bearskin hat called Bill Davis (named after Nicholson's friend and sometime collaborator, the poet W.H. Davies), inadvertently forgotten by his loving owner, little Mary, as she hurriedly packs her suitcase to go visit her aunt. Determined not to be left behind, the intrepid toy makes a run for it and sprints through the countryside after Mary's train. In his book Nicholson privileged images over text, the narrative carried by a consummate sense of visual suspense served by brief captions. The plates that narrate Mary's consideration of which toys and accessories she will take on her trip – horse-on-wheels and 'gloves with the thumbs'; the doll Susan and her trumpet; her shoes, miniature teapot and hairbrush; and indeed Bill himself – are fully-fledged still lifes. They also betray Nicholson's familiarity with toys overflowing from the nursery and across home. Susan limply resting on the floor, stitched limbs resting at odd angles, and Bill sat with stiff arms and legs perpendicular to his trunk are poignantly observed. The overstuffed suitcase spilling out its contents could be true reminiscences of many a holiday with children. The book is joyous and tender; playful and loving; made for his own brood as much as for children far and wide. Both this and *The Velveteen Rabbit* are still in print today.

In a letter he sent to his son Ben in 1912, Nicholson annotated a sketch drawing of a bunch of flowers in a jug with the words: 'A still life I am trying to do – all different whites. Rather fun.'[36] He applied the same sense of (serious) fun to his book illustrations as he did to his paintings. In some ways, *The Velveteen Rabbit* could be a metaphor for his art of the still life, not just in the way that representation (as a toy) attempts to reproduce reality (as an animal), but also in their mixed fortunes. Early in the book, the neglected Rabbit reflects on how unextraordinary he feels, compared to other toys: 'The poor little Rabbit was made to feel himself very insignificant and commonplace.'[37] If still life was derided as the lowest genre, it was for the Academy's perception that more skill was required to represent feeling and life than inanimate objects. Yet, as one day the Rabbit asks 'What is REAL?' to his elderly nursery companion, the Skin Horse, the latter replies: 'Real isn't how you are made, ... it's a thing that happens to you. When a child loves you for a long, long time, not just to play with, but REALLY loves you, then you become Real.'[38] This is perhaps where the true value of Nicholson's still lifes resides, for in sharing his pleasure in seeing, depicting and breathing new life into the inanimate, he made the spectacle of everyday objects more enjoyable and altogether more real.

97 *Spring Time*
Study for Margery Williams, *The Velveteen Rabbit*, William Heinemann, London, 1922
Pen, ink and watercolour on paper, 21 x 16.5cm
Private collection

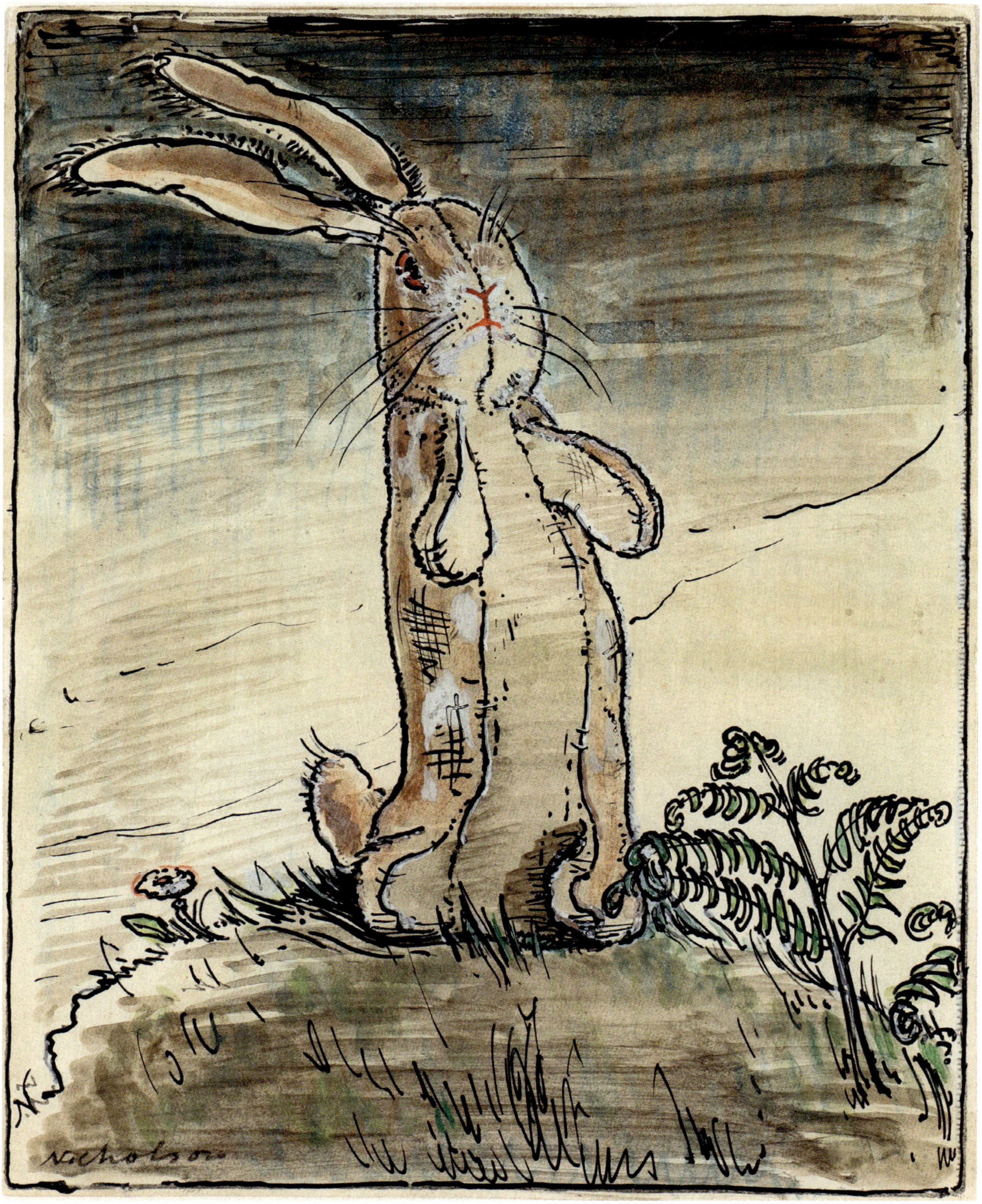

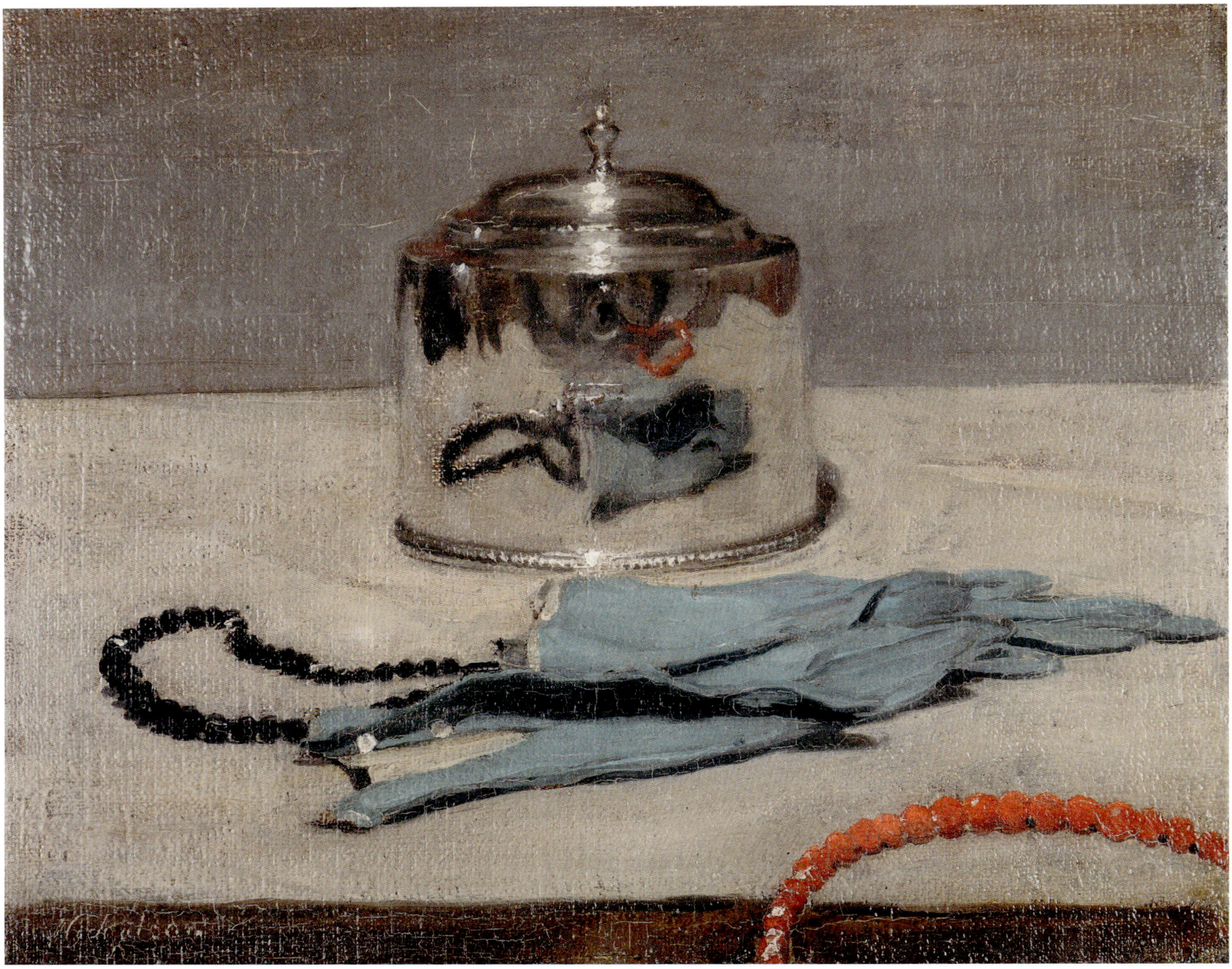

98 *The Silver Casket*, 1919
Oil on canvas, 33 x 40.5cm
Private collection

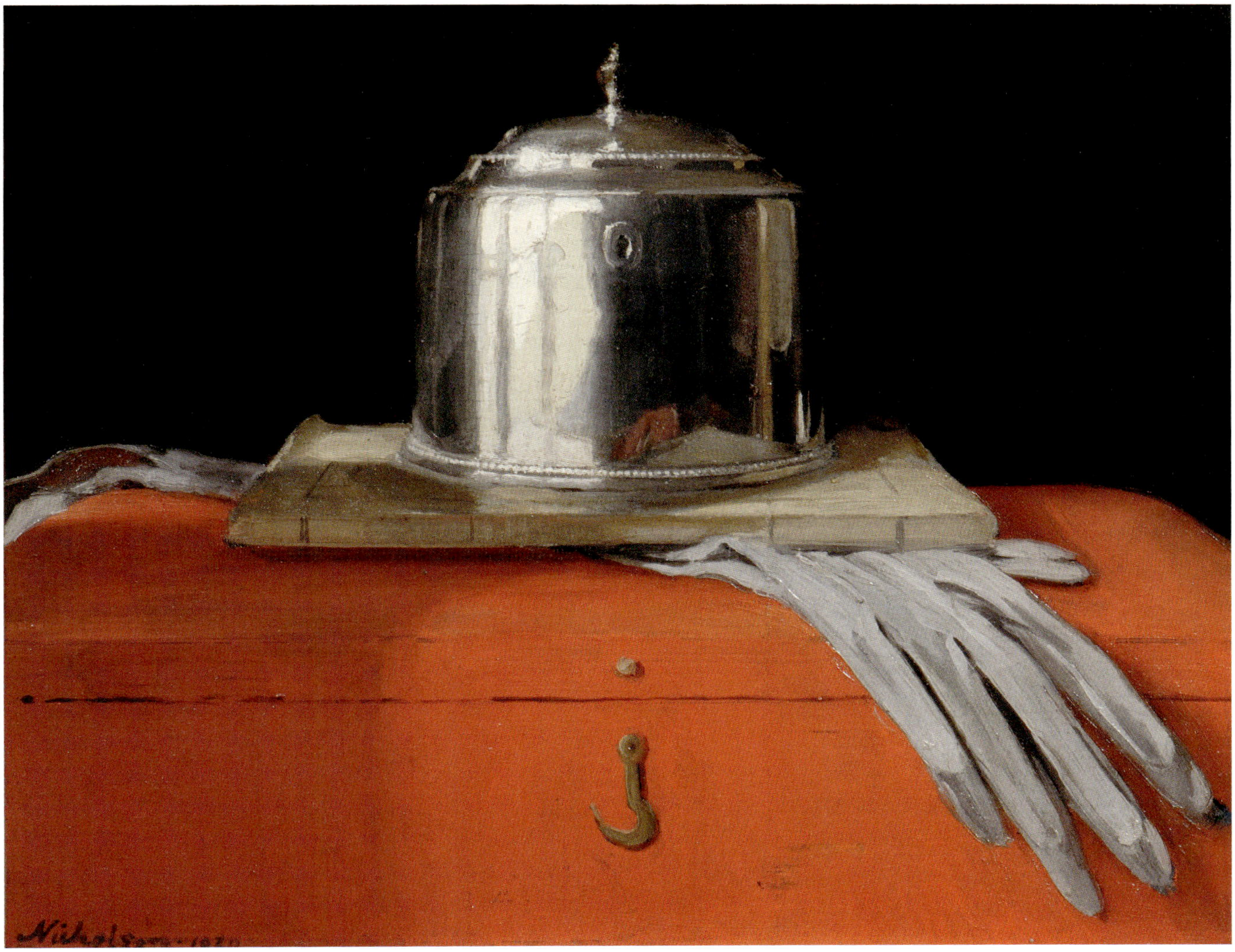

99 *The Silver Casket and Red Leather Box*, 1920
Oil on panel, 33 x 40.5cm
Private collection

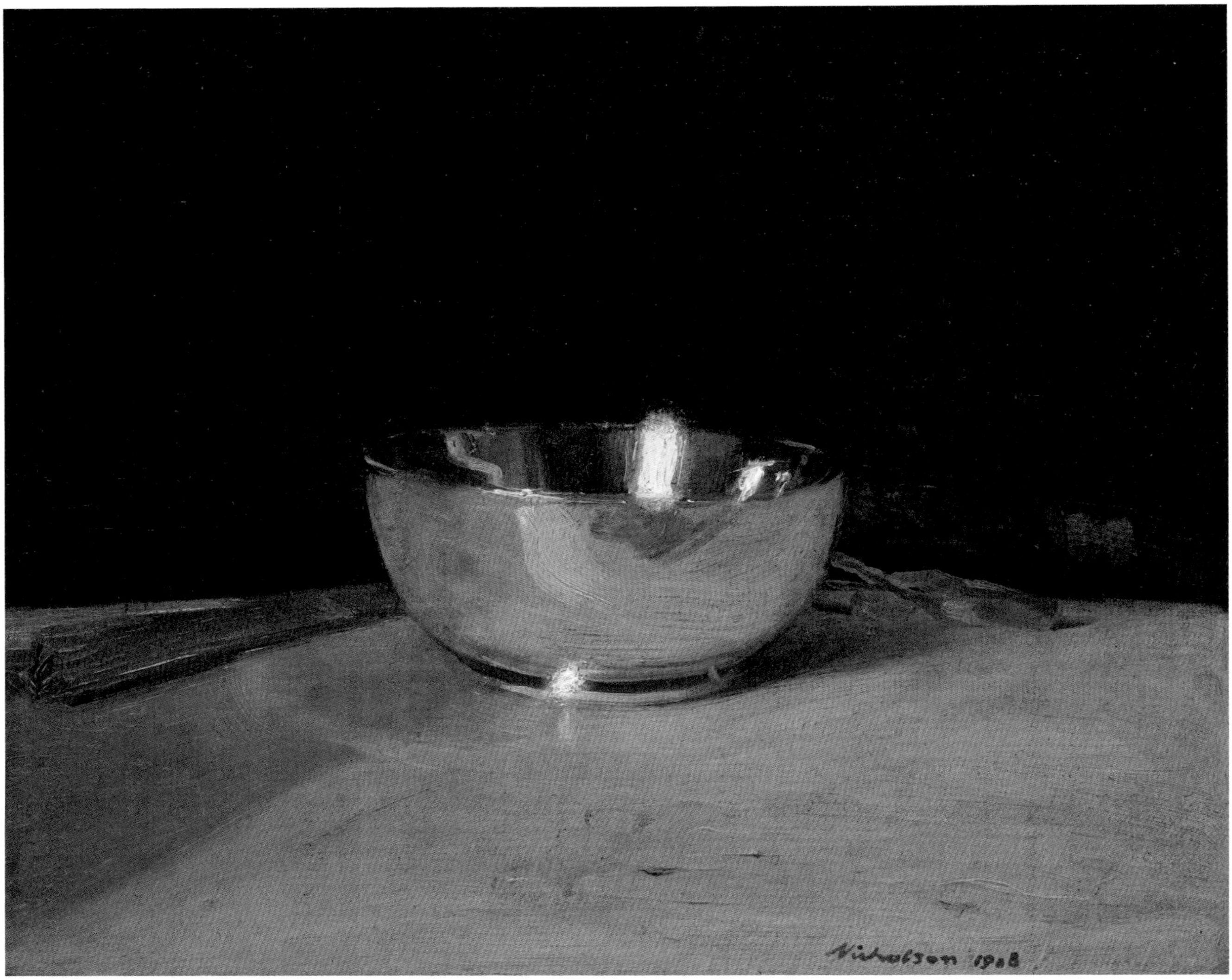

100 *The Lustre Bowl*, 1908
Oil on canvas board, 27.7 x 33cm
Jonathan W Anderson

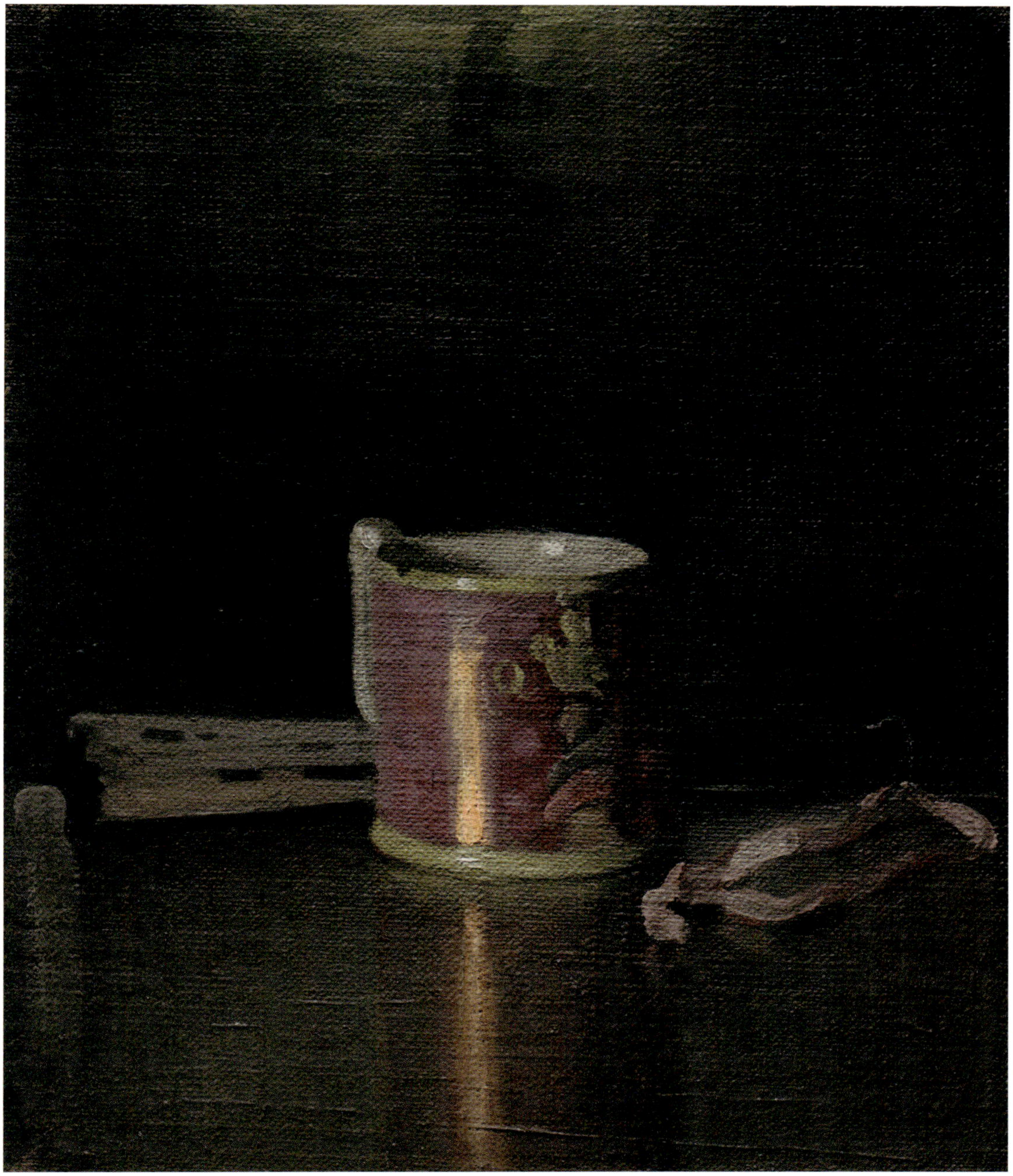

101 *Still Life: Pink Lustre Mug and Fan*, 1909
Oil on canvas laid on panel, 30.5 x 25.5cm
Jonathan W Anderson

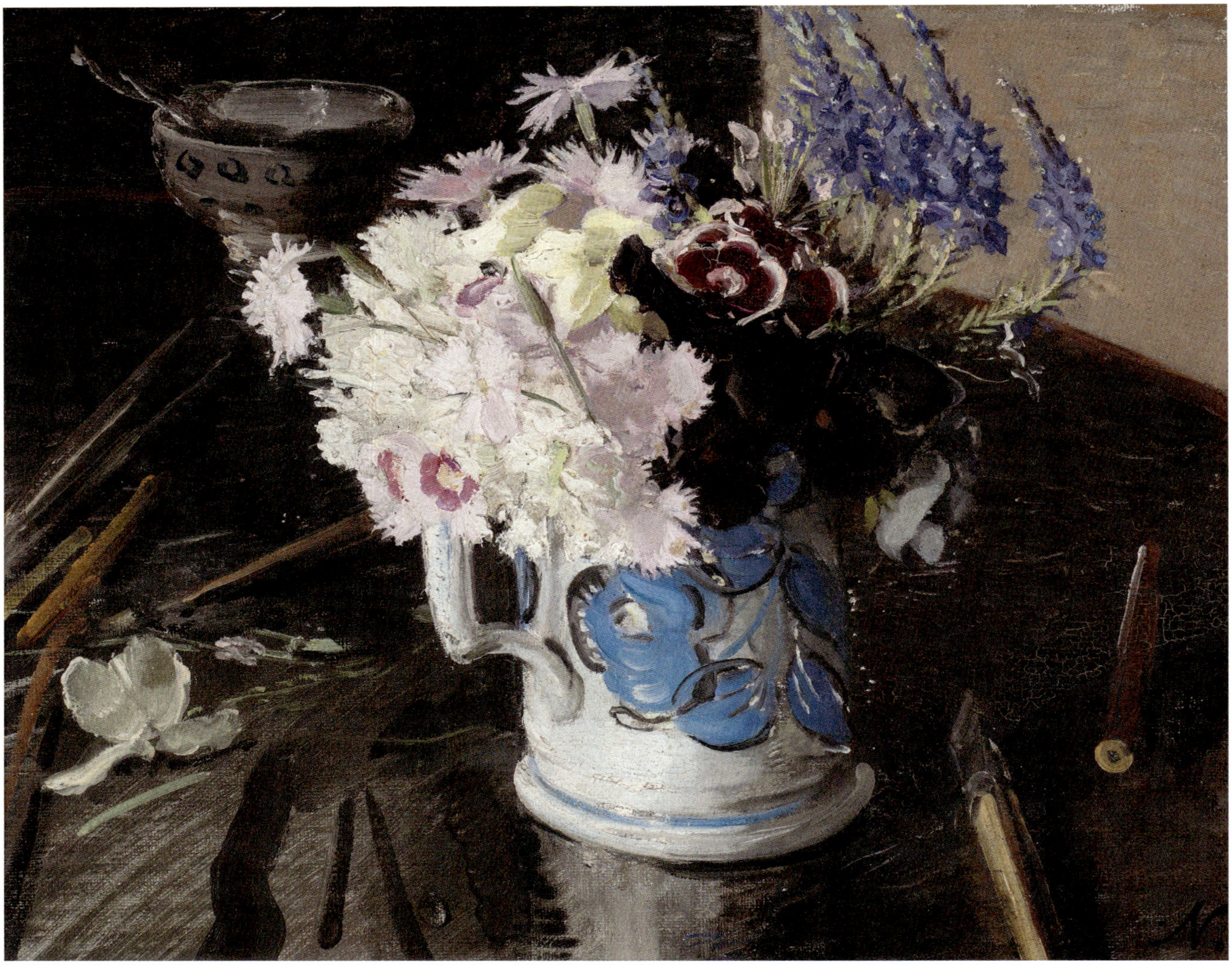

102 *Mixed Flowers in a Mug*, 1929
Oil on canvas, 33 x 40.5cm
Private collection

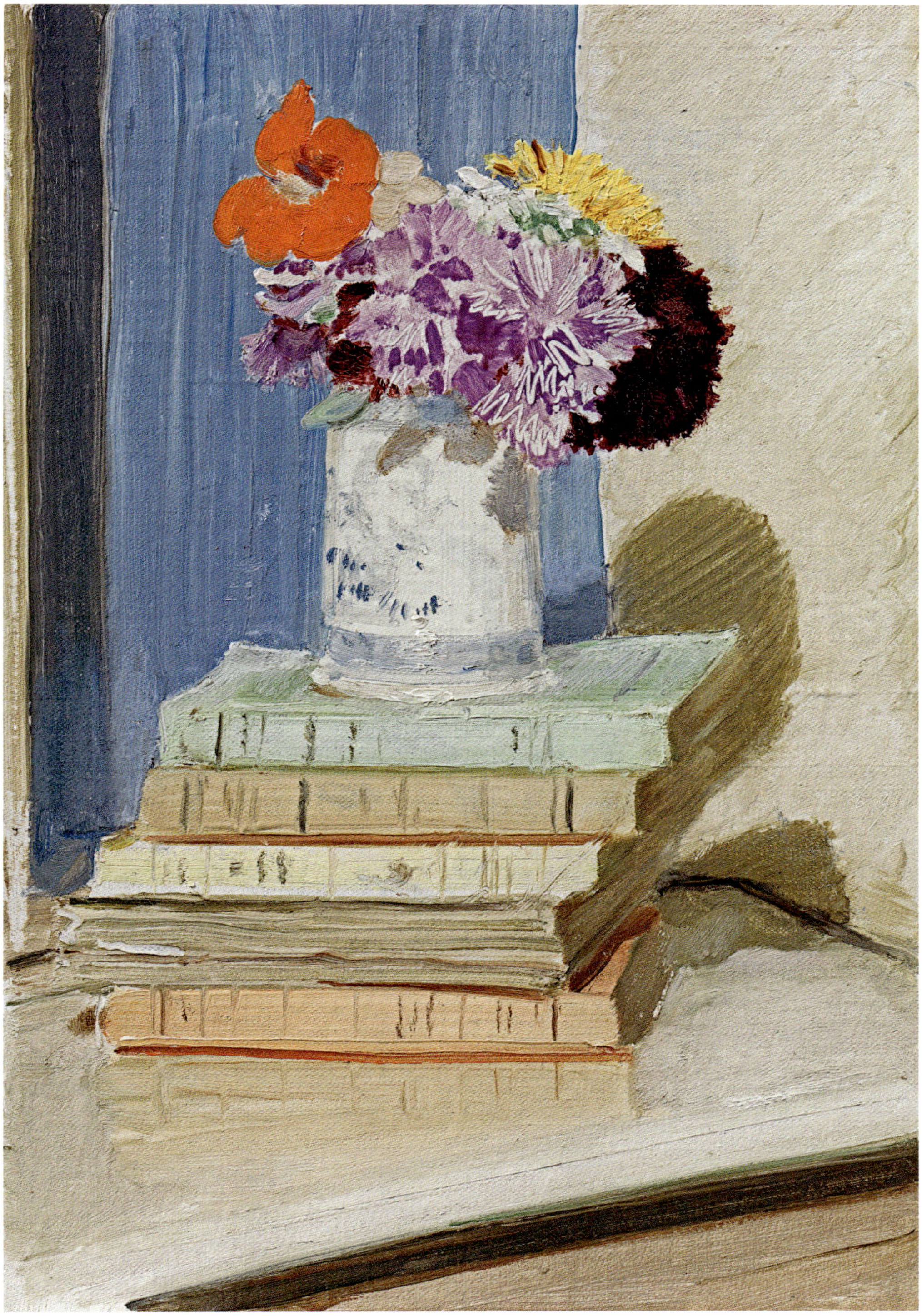

103 *Flowers and Books*
(for Siegfried Sassoon), 1929
Oil on canvas board, 38 x 25.5cm
Private collection

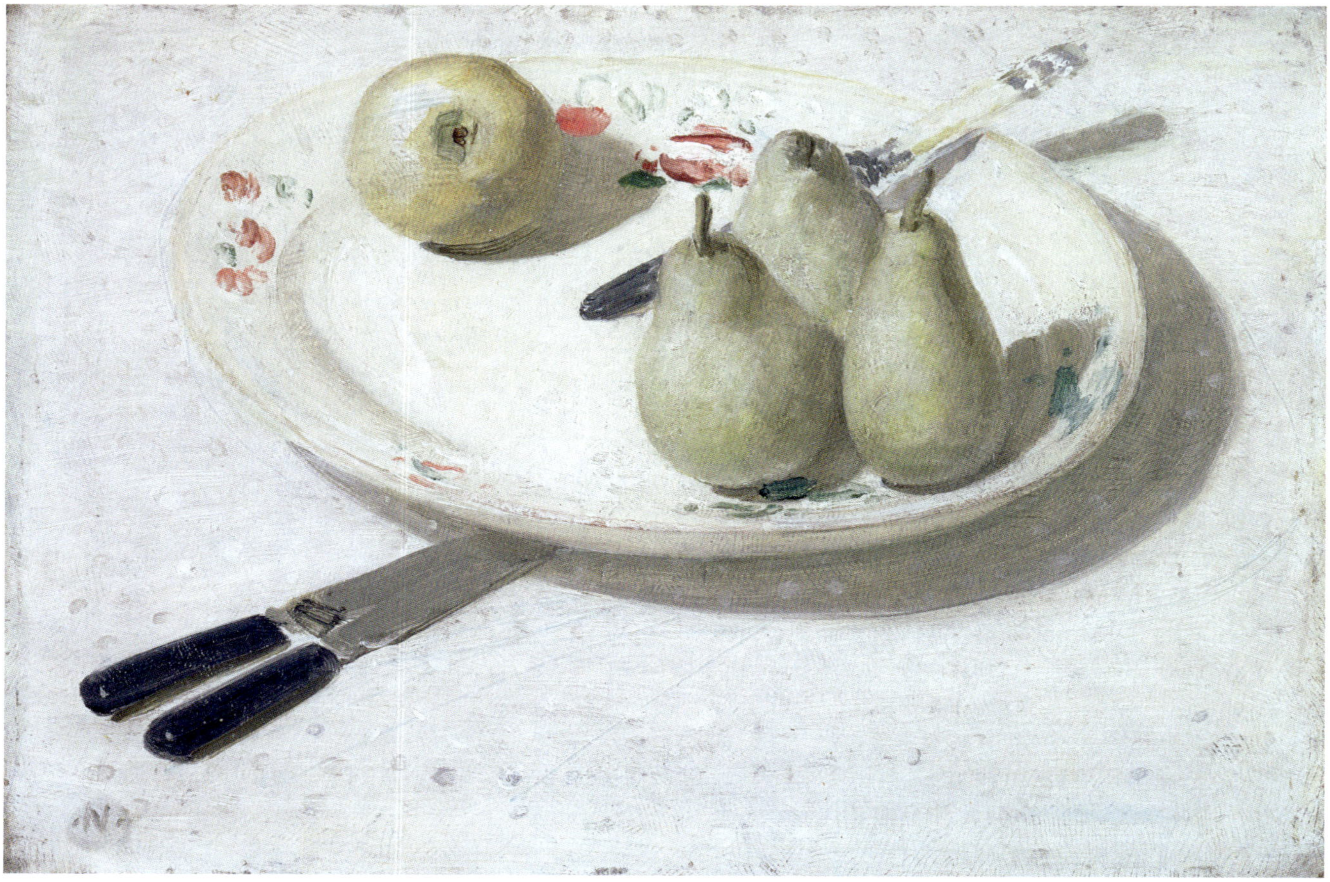

104 *Pears*, 1938
Oil on wood, 31.3 x 43.8cm
Leeds Museums and Galleries
(Leeds Art Gallery), UK

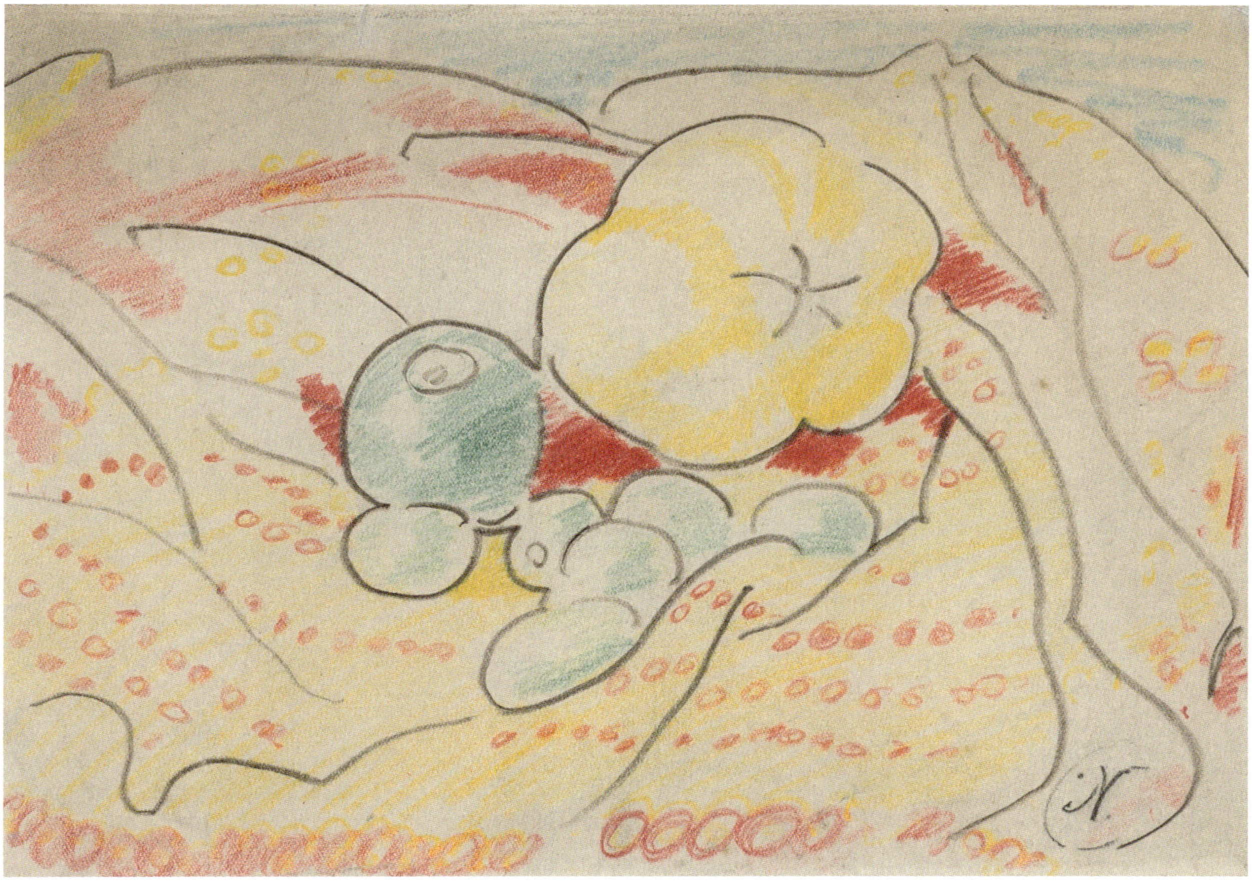

105 *Still Life on a Table*, n.d.
Crayon on paper, 15.2 x 22.9cm
Private collection

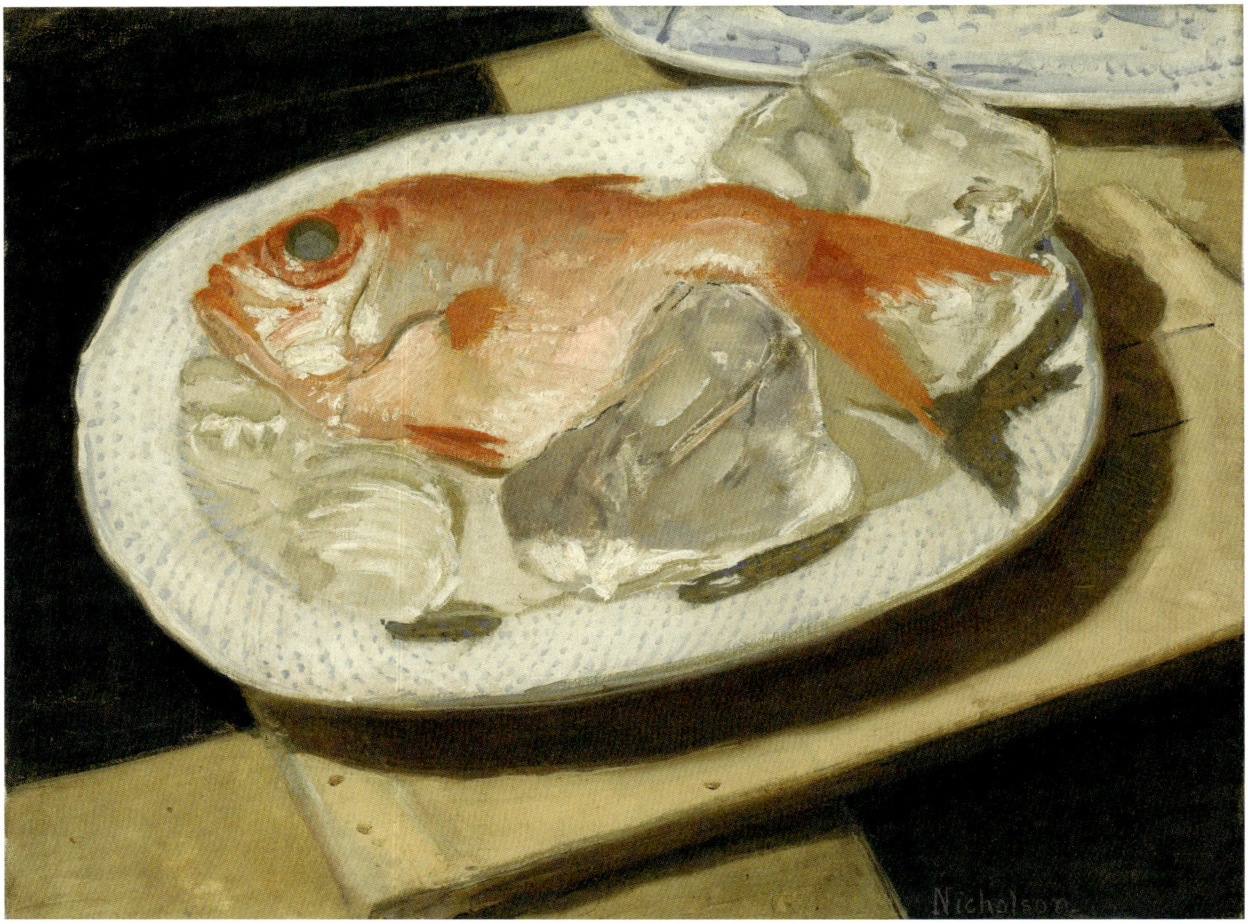

106 *Sun Fish*, 1935
Oil on canvas, 50.8 x 63.5cm
Arts Council Collection,
Southbank Centre, London

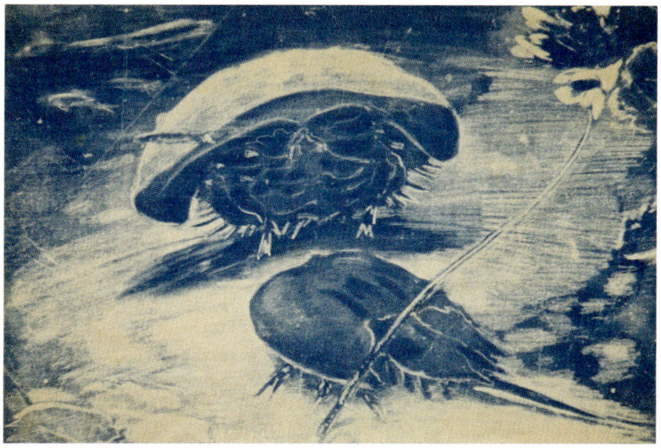
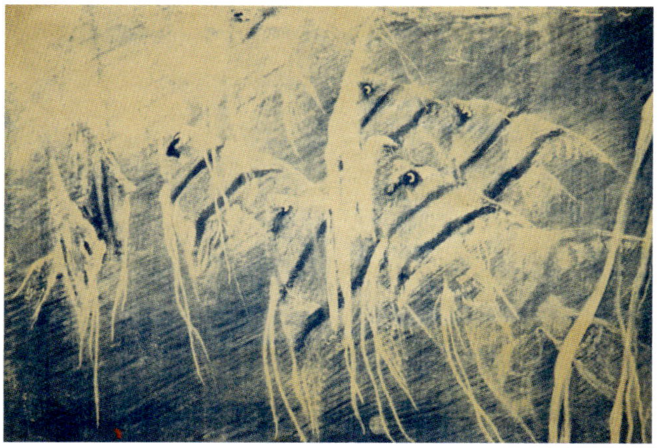
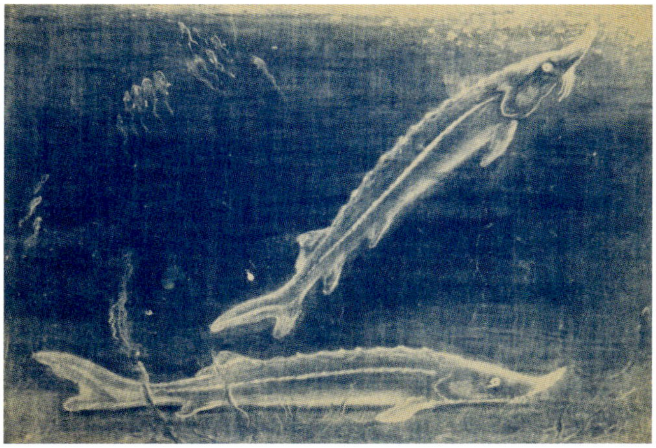
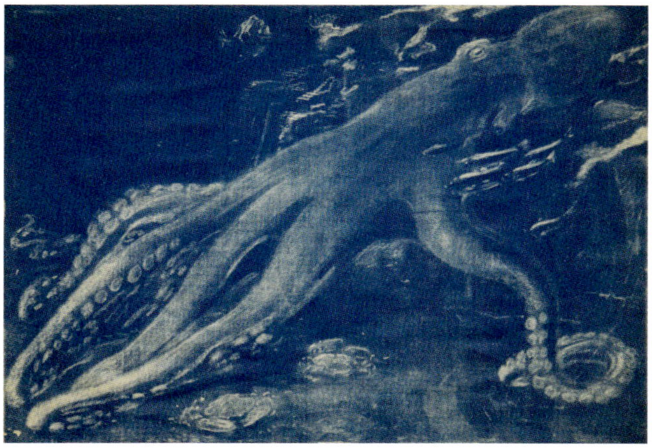

107 *Horseshoe Crab*, c.1923
Blueprint on paper, 19.2 x 27cm
Pallant House Gallery
(On loan from a private collection, 2013)

108 *Sturgeon*, c.1923
Blueprint on paper, 19 x 26.4cm
Pallant House Gallery
(On loan from a private collection, 2013)

109 *Angel Fish*, c.1923
Blueprint on paper, 18.7 x 26.7cm
Pallant House Gallery
(On loan from a private collection, 2013)

110 *Octopus*, c.1923
Blueprint on paper, 19.5 x 26.8cm
Pallant House Gallery
(On loan from a private collection, 2013)

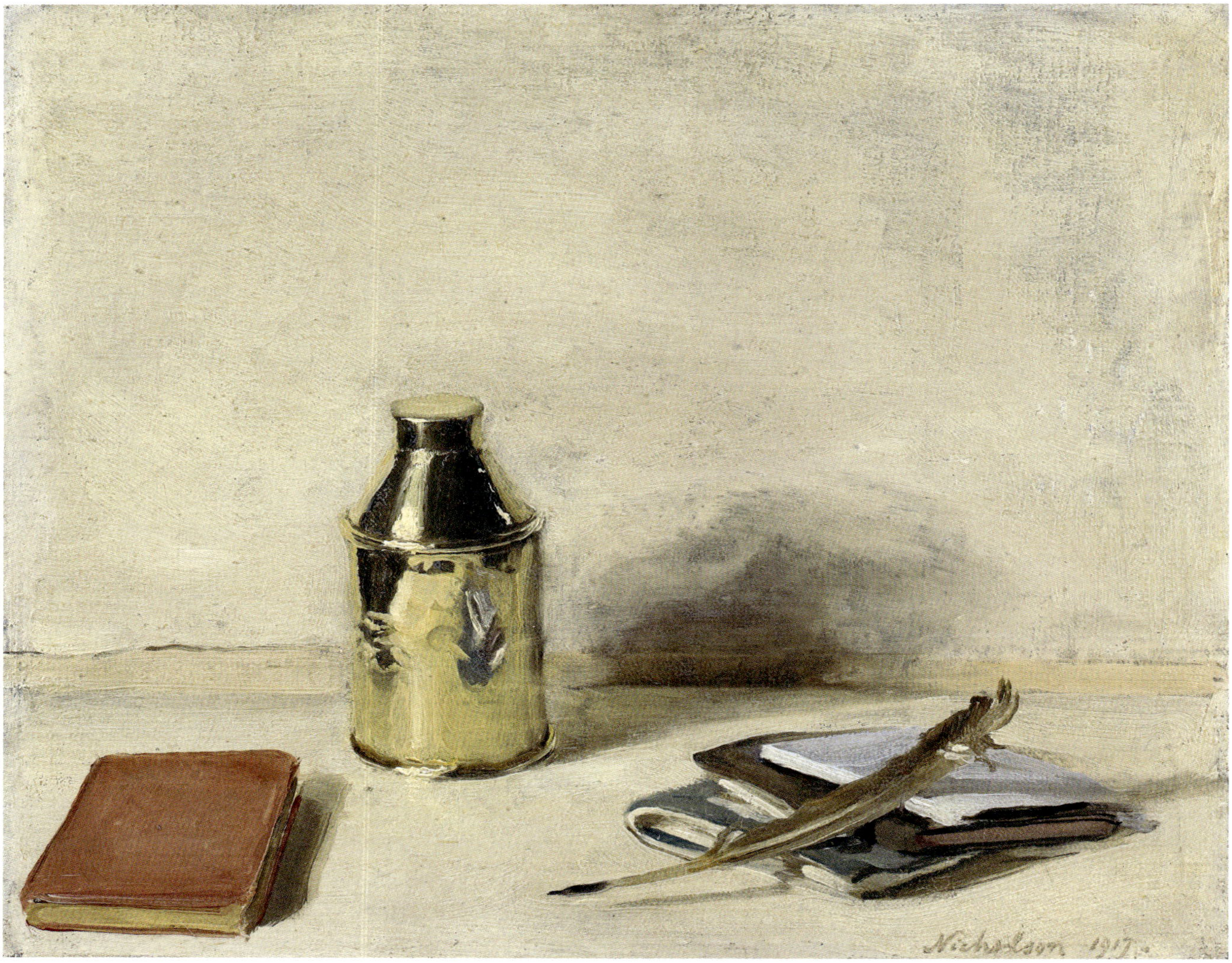

111 *The Brass Canister*, 1917
Oil on canvas board, 33 x 40.6cm
Private collection, courtesy
Patrick Bourne & Co.

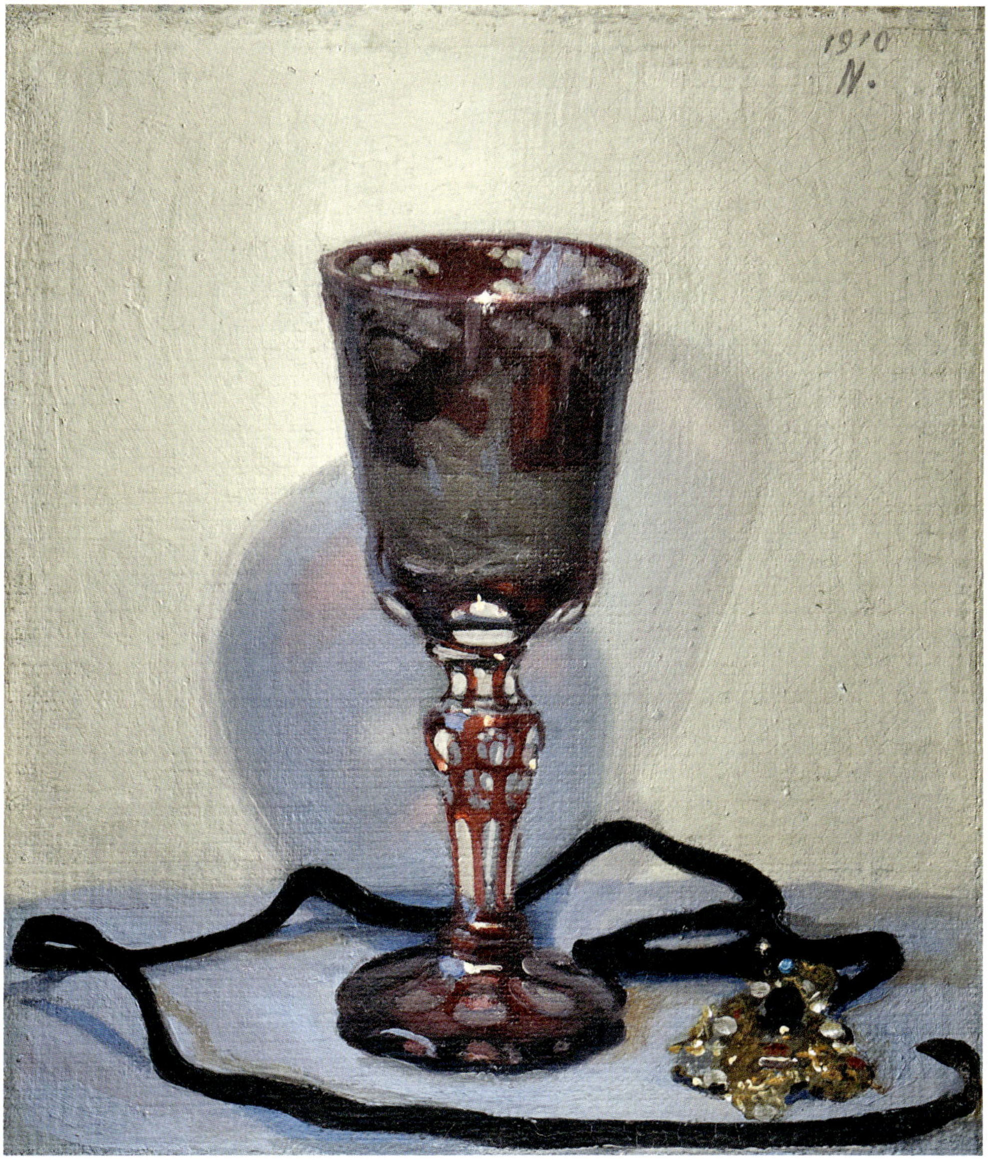

112 *The Ruby Glass*, 1910
Oil on canvas board, 26.3 x 23cm
Private collection

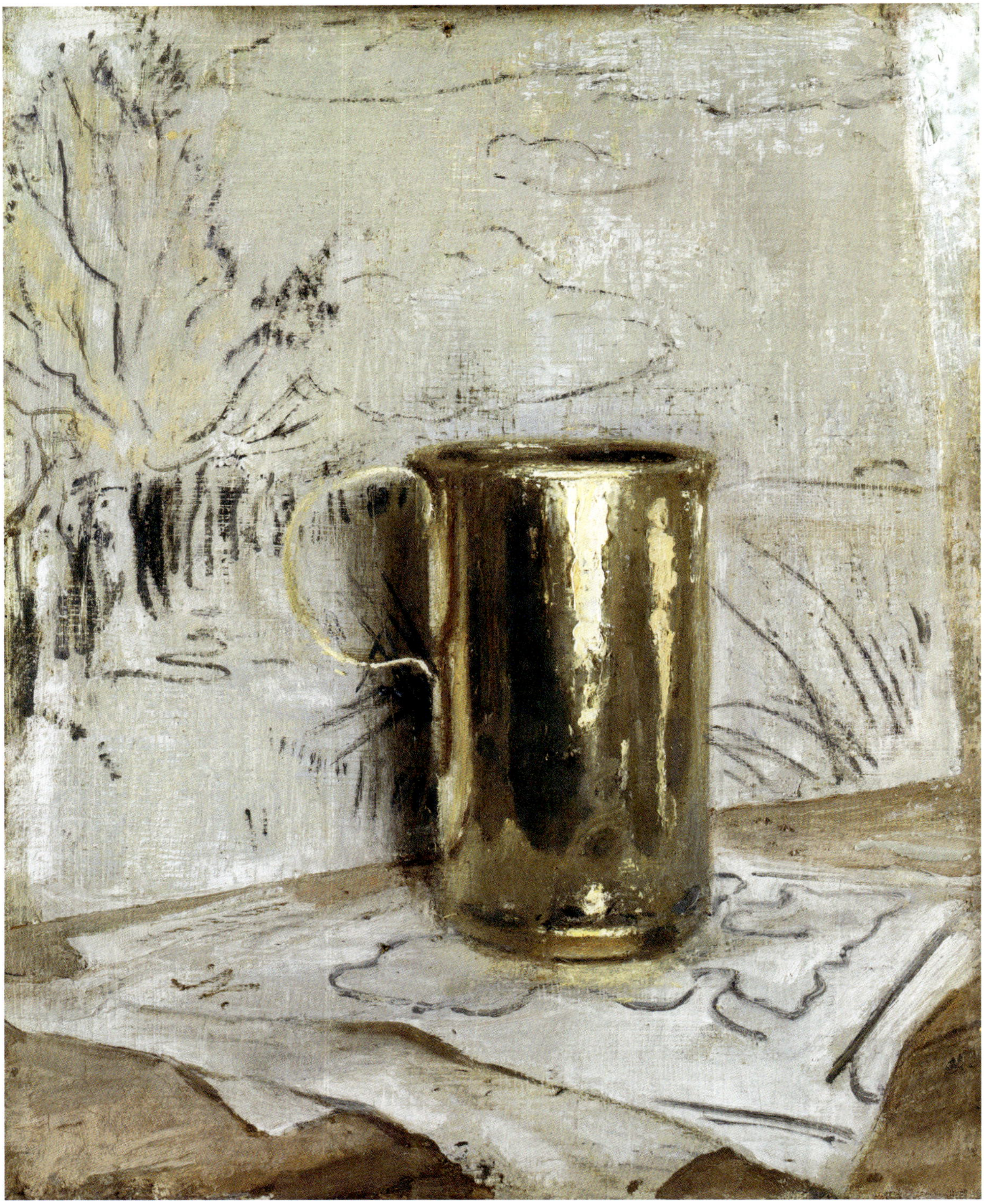

113 *Gold Jug*, 1937
Oil on canvas board, 40.9 x 32.7cm
Lent by His Majesty The King
from the Royal Collection

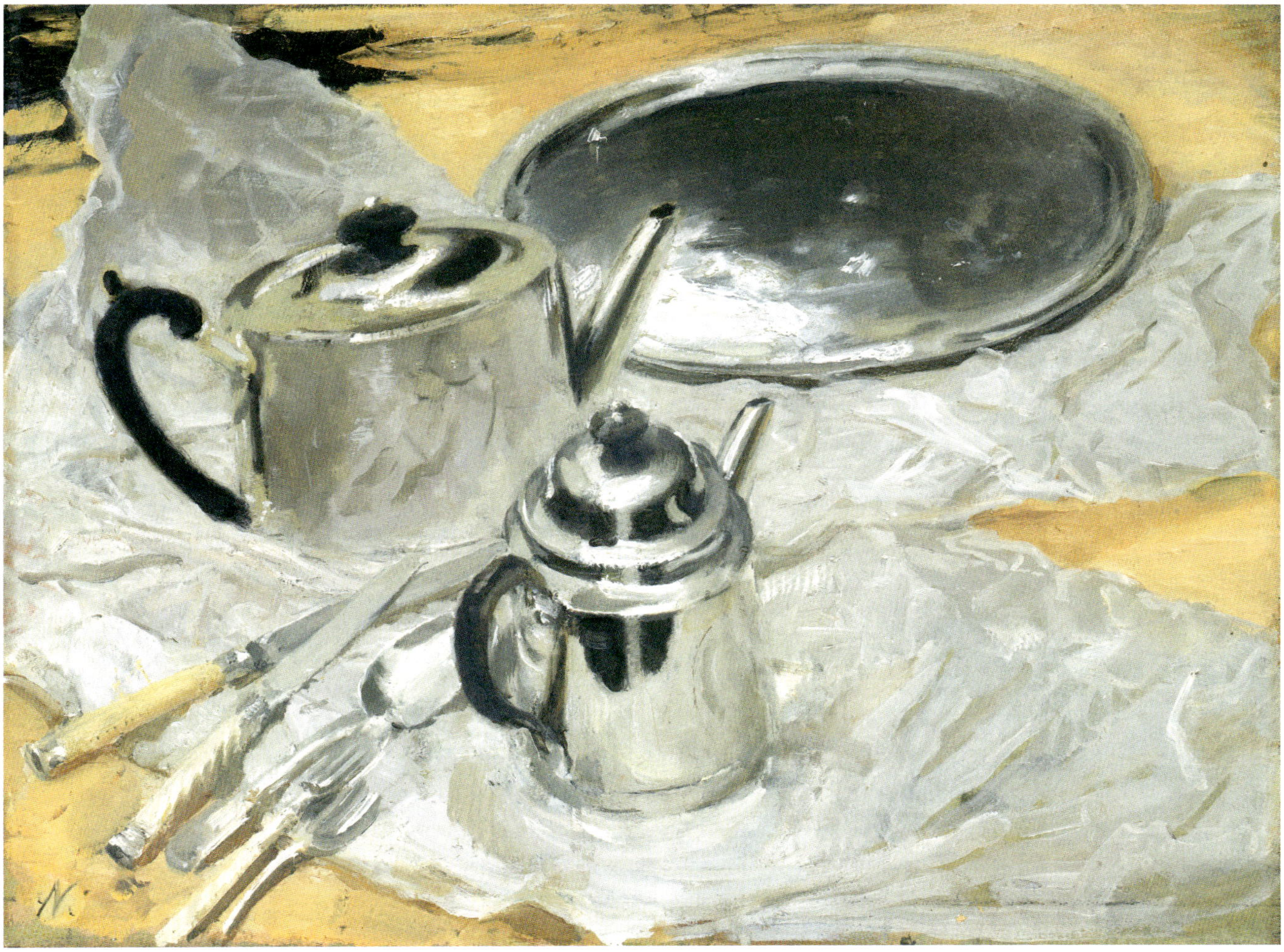

114 *Silver*, 1938
Oil on wood, 43.8 x 57.1cm
Tate: Purchased 1938

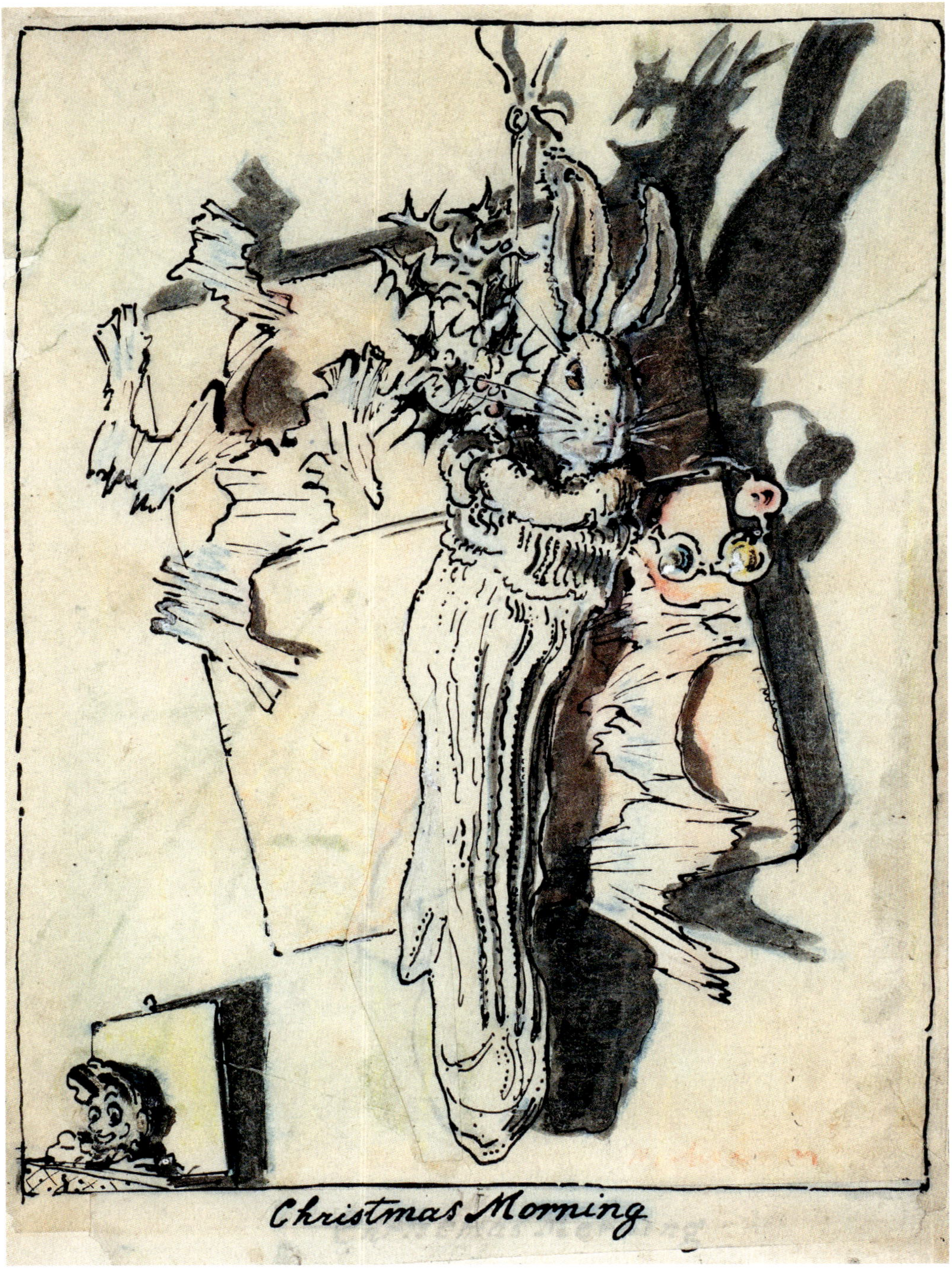

115 *Christmas Morning*
Study for Margery Williams, *The Velveteen Rabbit*,
William Heinemann, London, 1922
Pen, ink and watercolour on paper, 24.5 x 18.5cm
Private collection

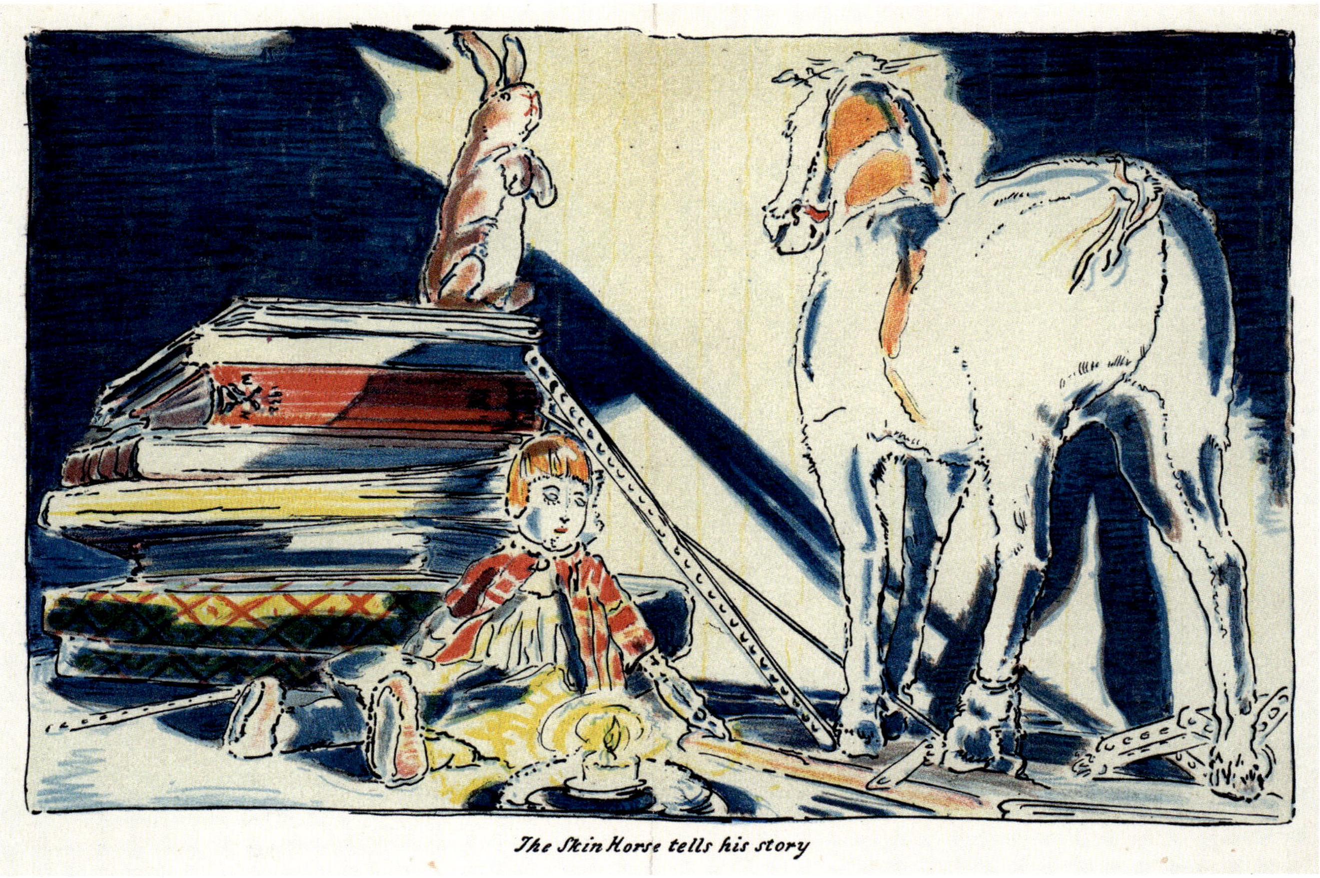

116 *The Skin Horse Tells His Story*
Printer's proof of Margery Williams, *The Velveteen Rabbit*, William Heinemann, London, 1922
Lithograph on paper, 25 x 39cm
Private collection

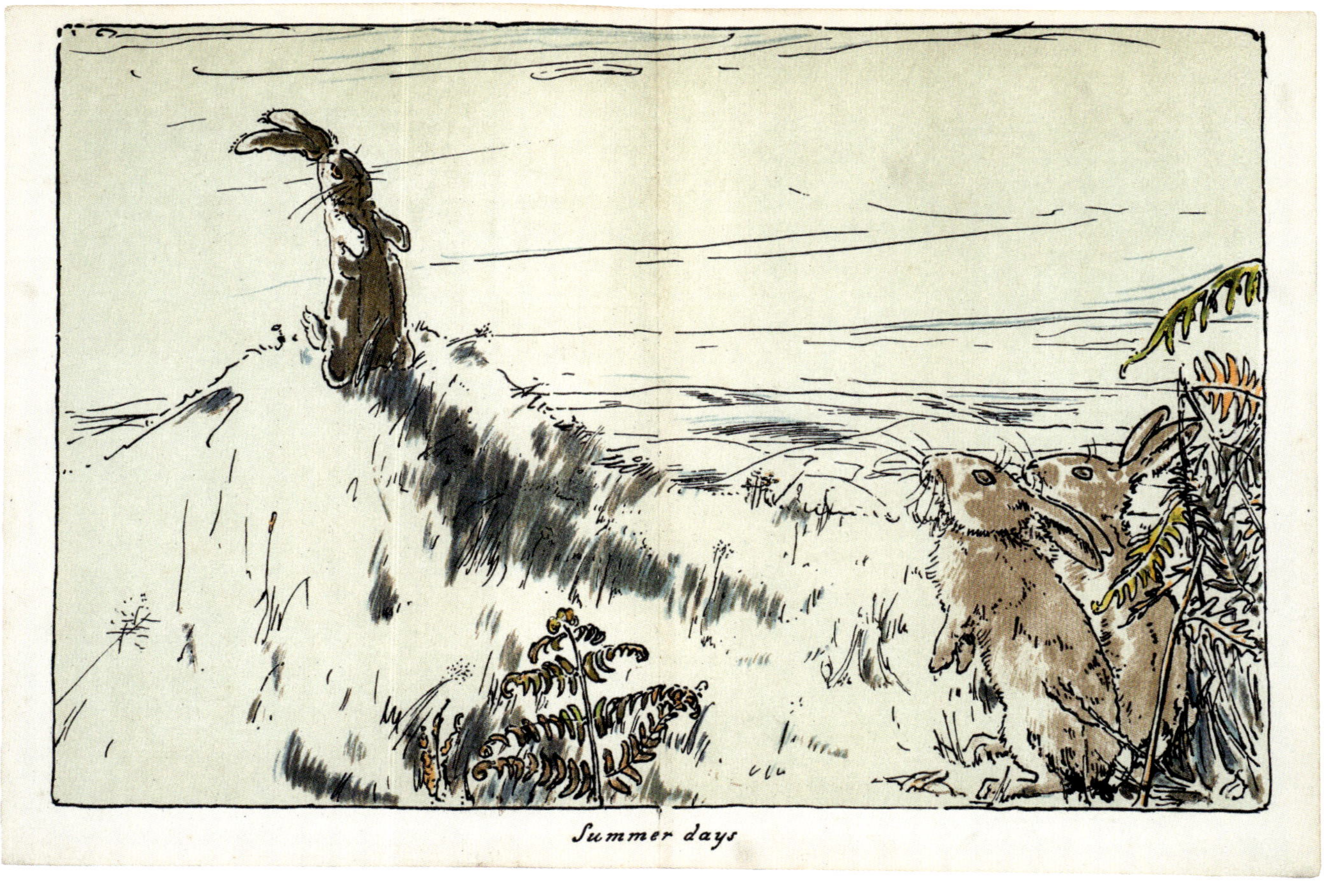

117 *Summer Days*
Printer's proof of Margery Williams, *The Velveteen Rabbit*, William Heinemann, London, 1922
Lithograph on paper, 25 x 39cm
Private collection

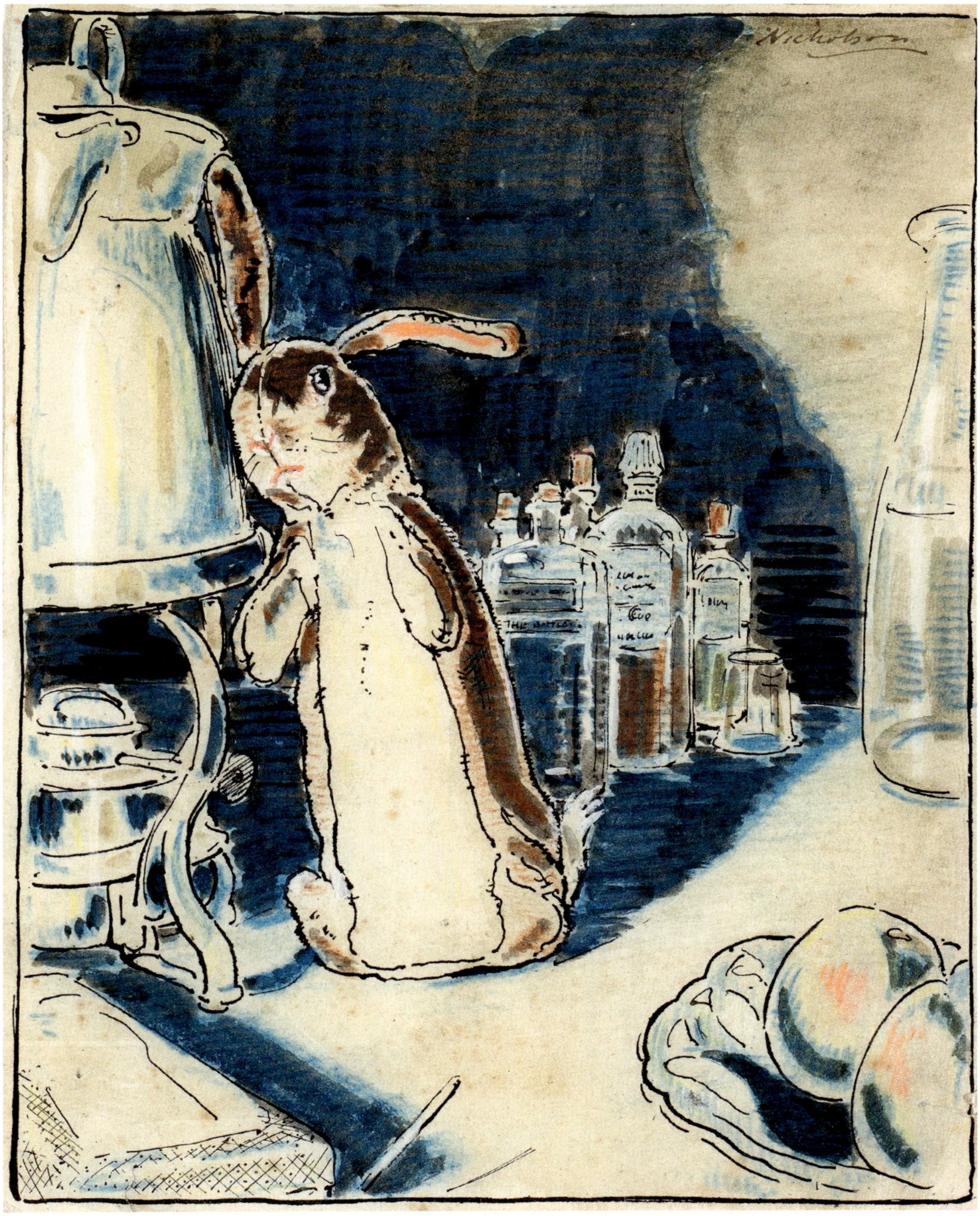

118 *Anxious Times*
Study for Margery Williams, *The Velveteen Rabbit*,
William Heinemann, London, 1922
Pen, ink, watercolour and crayon on paper, 21.5 x 17cm
Private collection

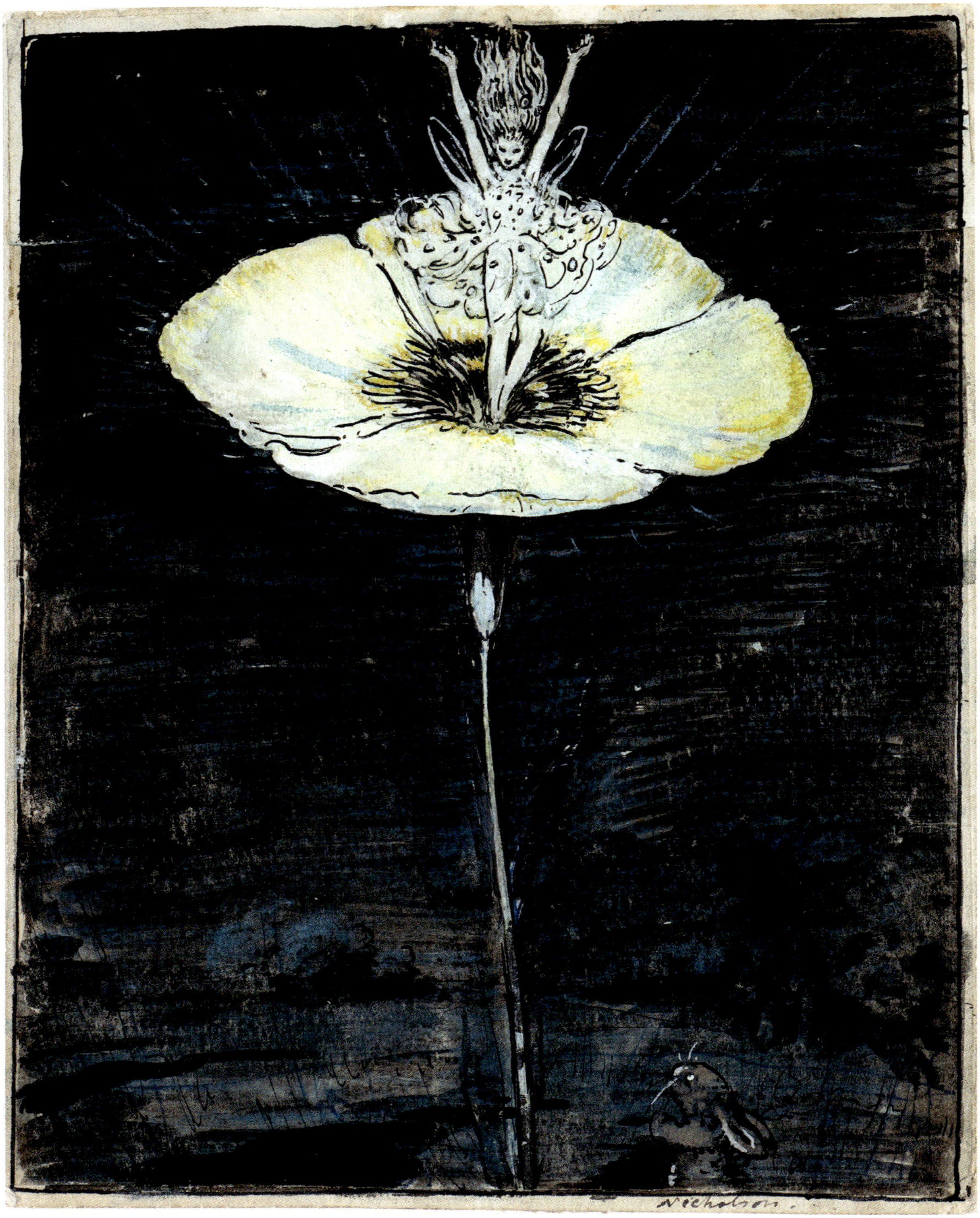

119 *The Fairy Flower*
Study for Margery Williams, *The Velveteen Rabbit*,
William Heinemann, London, 1922
Pen, ink and watercolour on paper, 21.5 x 17cm
Private collection

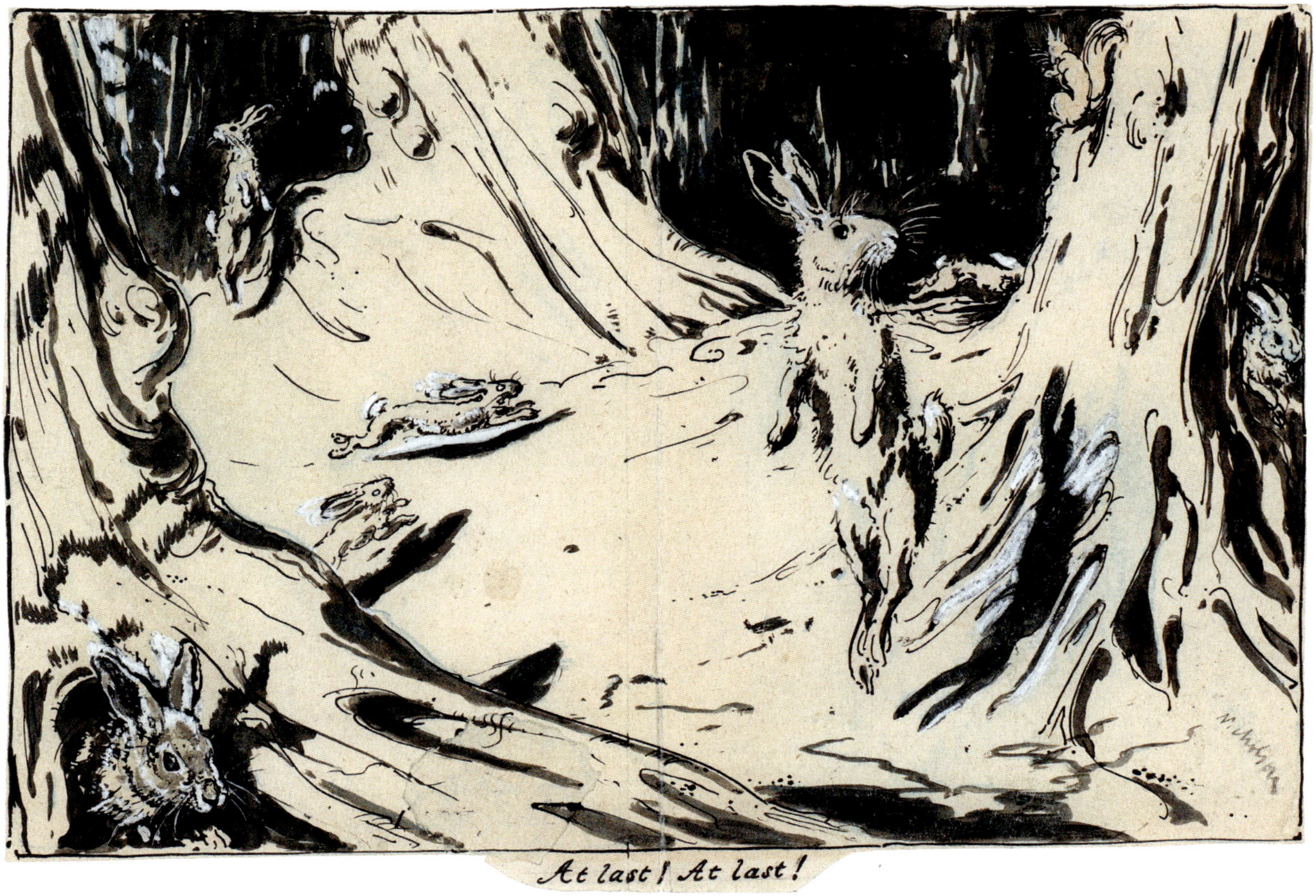

120 *At Last, At Last!*
Study for Margery Williams, *The Velveteen Rabbit*,
William Heinemann, London, 1922
Pen, ink, watercolour and crayon on paper, 24 x 34.5cm
Private collection

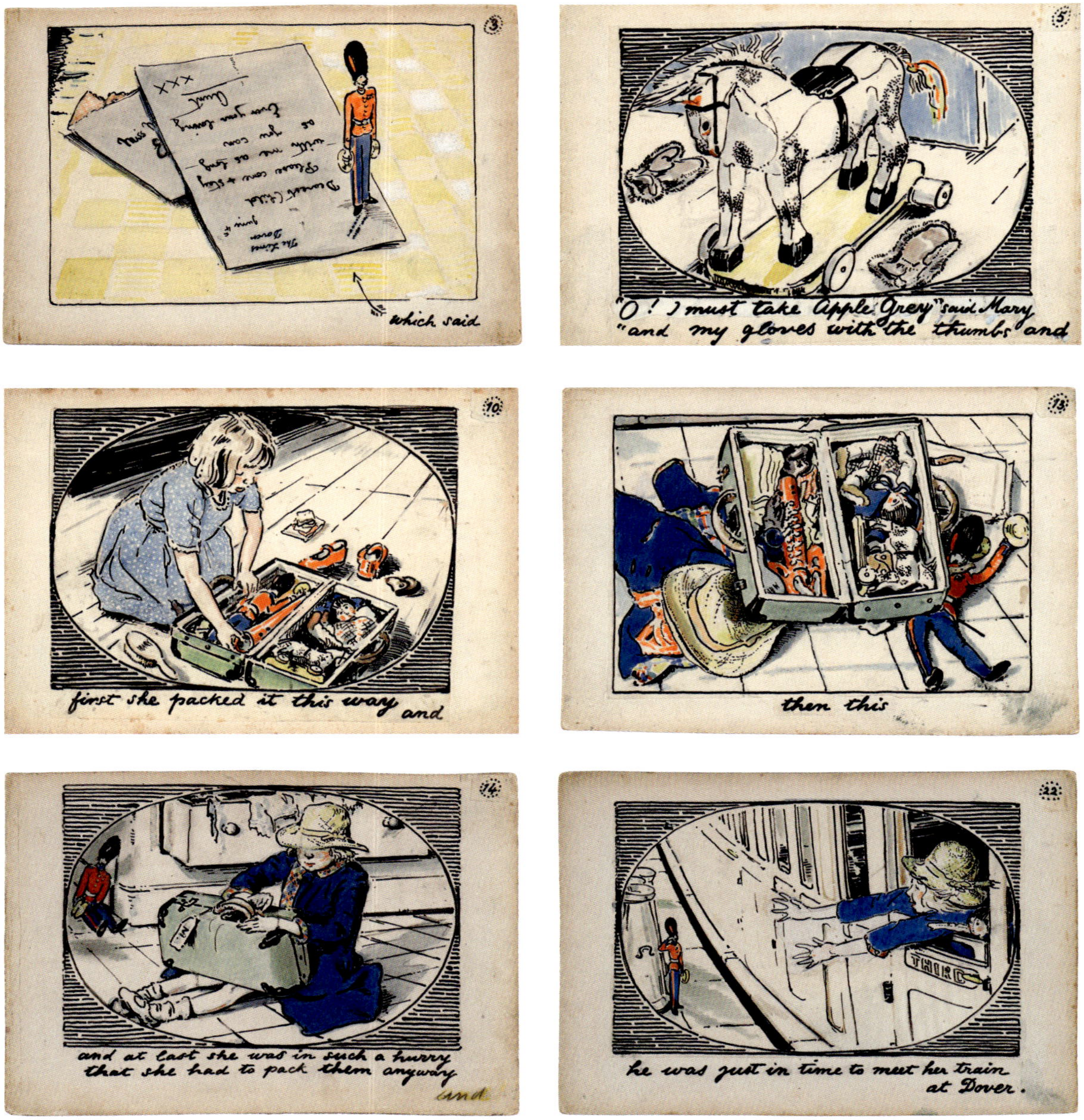

121 Eight sheet designs for *Clever Bill*, 1926
Ink and wash on paper, 14 x 22cm each
Private collection

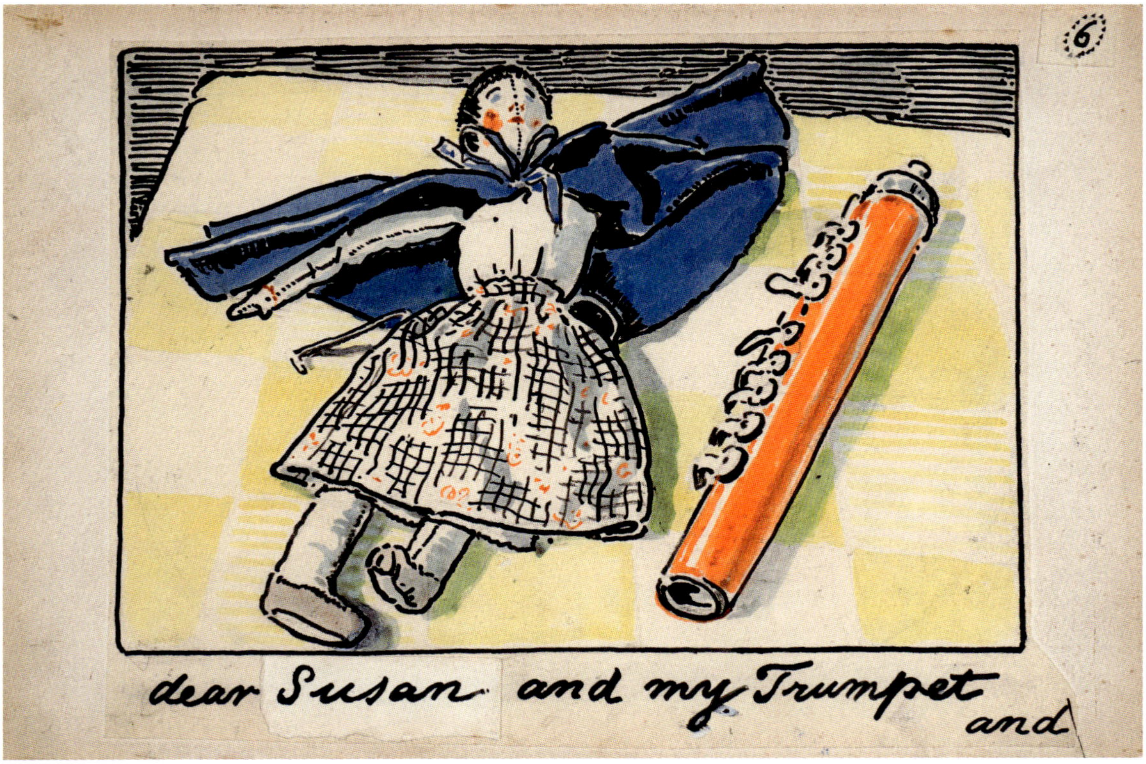
6
dear Susan and my Trumpet
and

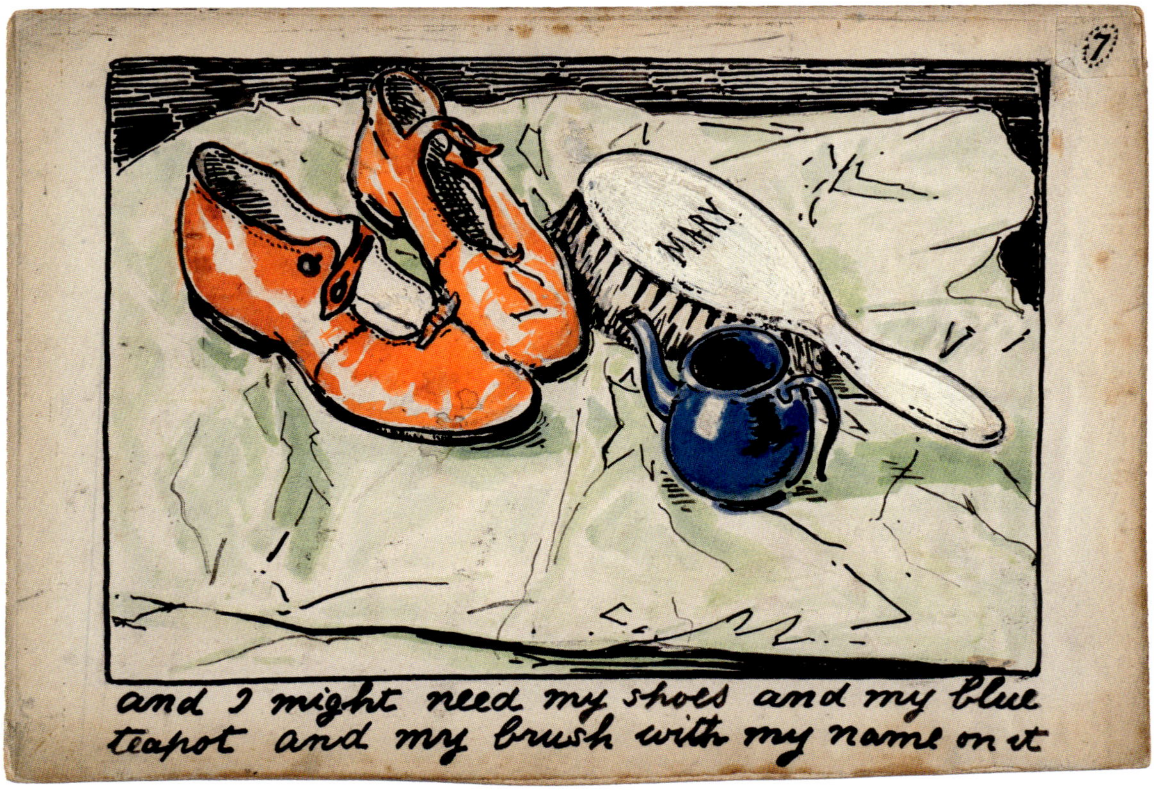
7
MARY
and I might need my shoes and my blue teapot and my brush with my name on it

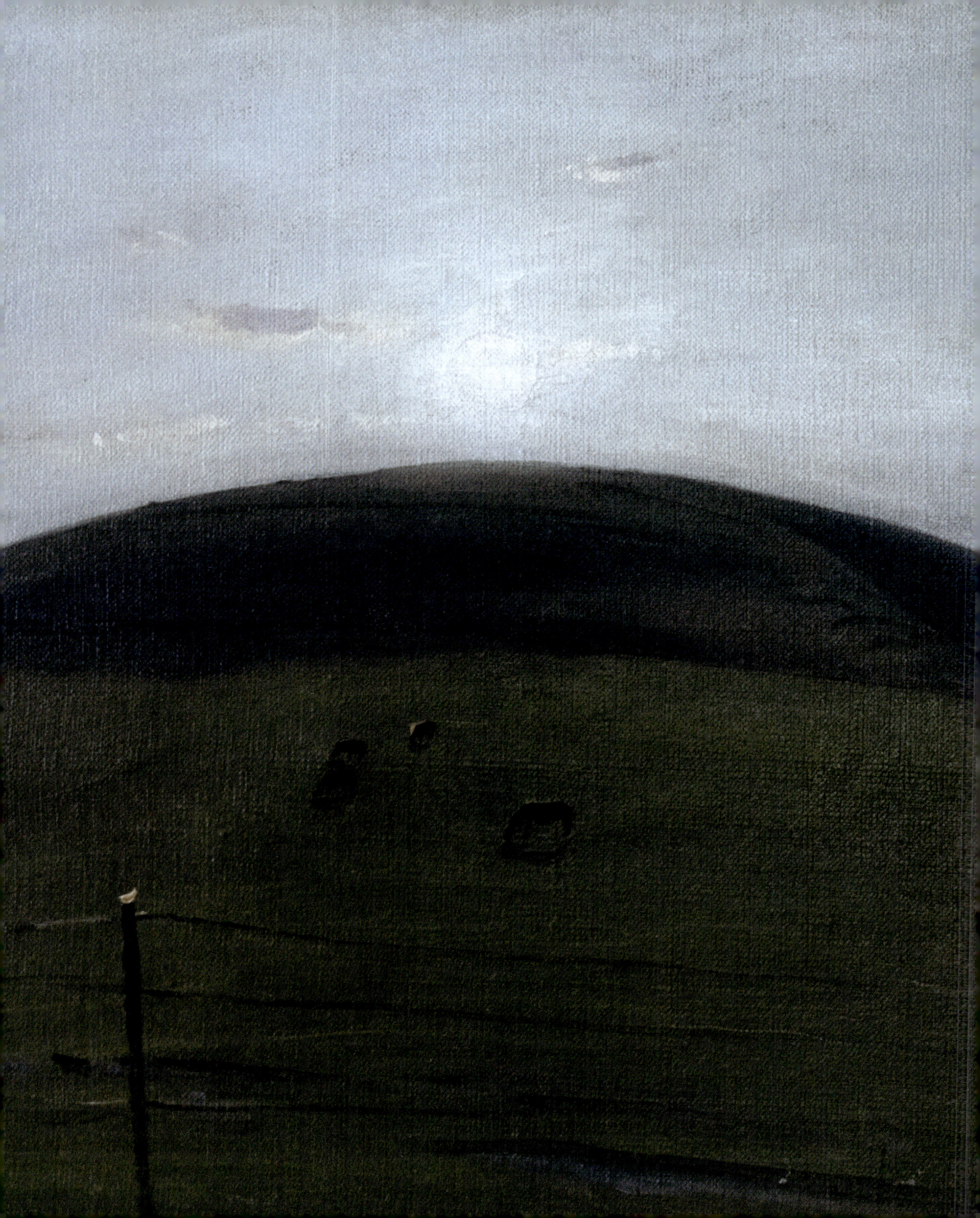

6 'HARMONY OF EYE AND HAND AND SURROUNDINGS': WILLIAM NICHOLSON'S LANDSCAPES AND TOWNSCAPES*

MIRIAM O'CONNOR PERKS

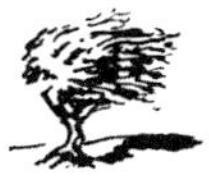

'Rather a good Downs piece I did night before last looking into eye of Sun […] Sun to be looked at only through smothered glass.'[1]

These two small observations were made by William Nicholson to accompany a sketch included in a letter to his son Ben, written in 1912. They most likely refer to a painting now titled *Sunset* (fig.126), which features a view over Mount Pleasant in the Sussex Downs near Rottingdean. The composition is split almost equally between sun and sky, the colour palette is restrained, and the inclusion of the animals grazing on the ridge gives the viewer a sense of the spaciousness of this particular landscape. The pale, hazy sun, as though seen 'through smothered glass' centres our focus. When the painting was first exhibited at the Goupil Gallery in London in 1912, it was shown with the name *Dawn*, but subsequently renamed through reference to the letter quoted above.[2] Nicholson was a great experimenter with the effects of light upon the landscape, particularly at the in-between times of the rise and fall of the sun and with the ways in which shadow can play tricks with our eyes. During the summer of 1919, whilst Nicholson was living in Wales, he was drawn to its ancient features, much like those of the Sussex Downs which he had painted before the First World War. In *Landscape at Harlech* (fig.131), Nicholson's use of bright light and shadow creates a flattened perspective, which plays with our perception of the view. Are we looking across or upwards?

This sense of 'in-betweenness' and the ambiguity behind the title of paintings such as *Sunset* can be seen within Nicholson's oeuvre in a wider sense. Nicholson was an artist who operated both within and without the cultural world and was both 'metropolitan' and 'provincial'. His approach to landscape further rests between two states, that of an almost abstract exploration of the interplay of light, tone and colour, whilst also being resolutely connected to the character of a place – it has been said that Nicholson wanted to know his

p.136 Detail of fig.126

122 *La Place des Papes, Avignon (Le Château, Avignon)*, 1925
Oil on canvas board, 43 x 35.5cm
Private collection

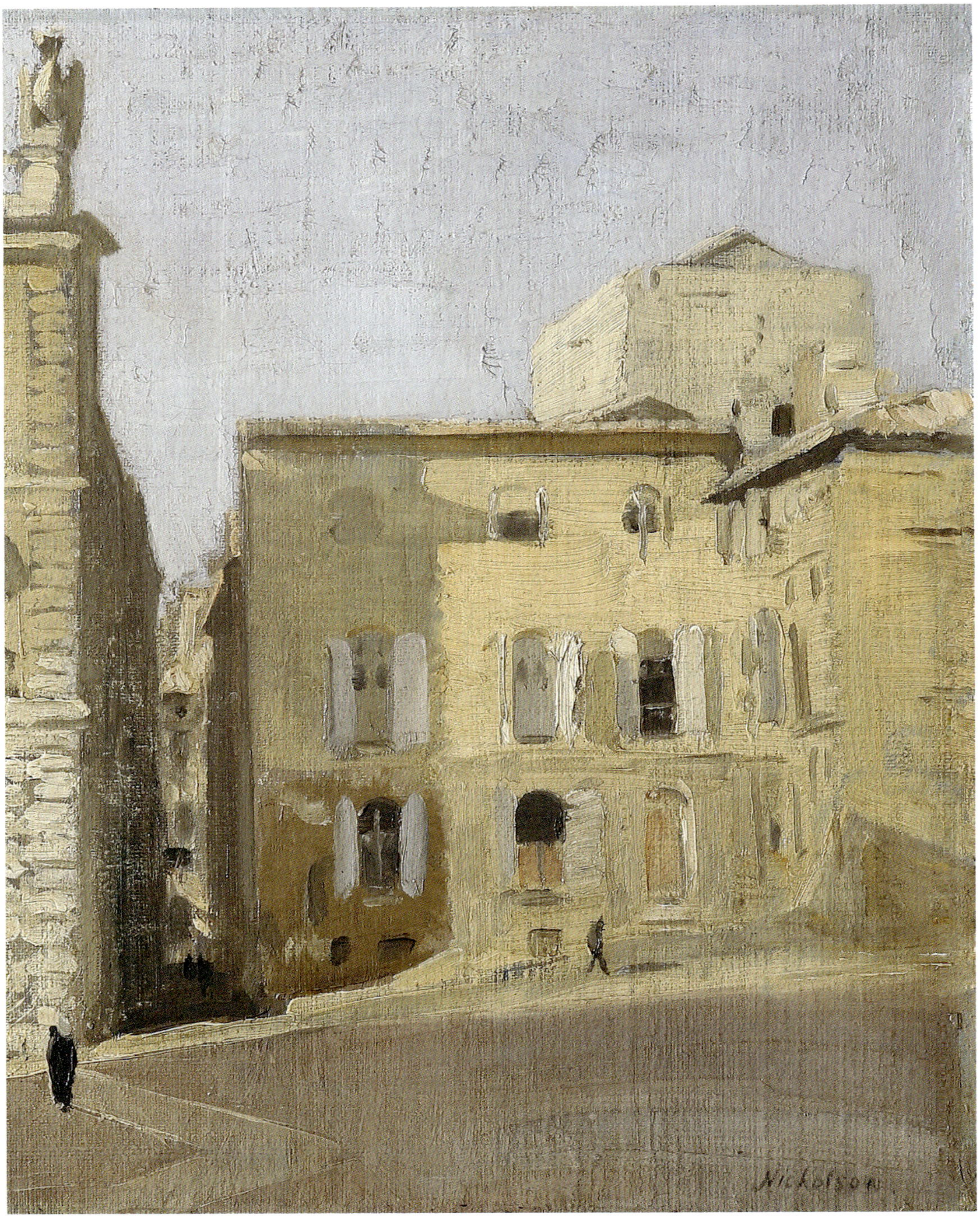

123 *Mending the Nets, Rottingdean*, 1909
Oil on canvas board, 33 x 40.5cm
Private collection

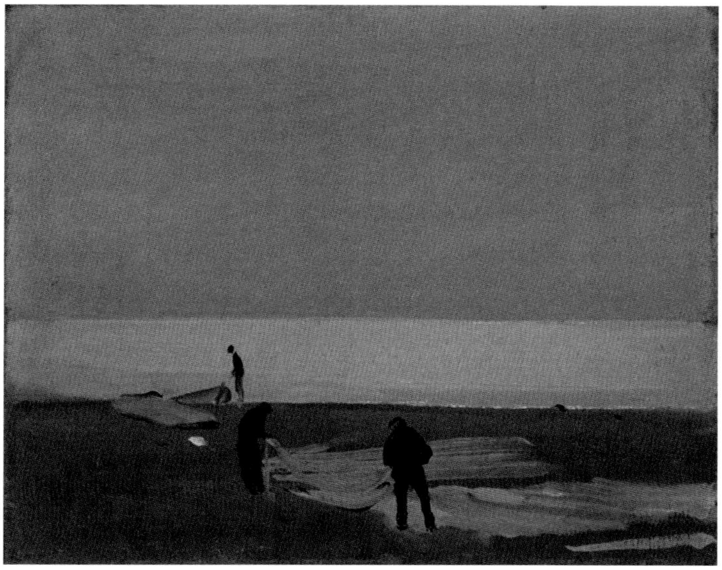

subject as closely as possible, through frequent observation.[3] Chalk downland, in particular in Sussex and Wiltshire, was one of those subjects he knew intimately, although he also travelled widely, creating land- and townscapes from trips to France and the USA in the early 1900s, India during the First World War and South Africa and Spain in the 1930s.

Early on in his career, Nicholson spent time in France, as was to be expected from a young painter. At the end of the 19th century, Dieppe, just across the Channel from Newhaven, was a popular destination for modern painters based in Britain, just as it had been at the beginning of the century, with such artists as Richard Parkes Bonington (1802–1828), J.M.W. Turner (1775–1851) and David Roberts (1796–1864). The fishing town had by then evolved into a busy seaside resort, and for artists such as William Orpen, Walter Sickert, James McNeill Whistler and Jacques-Emile Blanche (1861–1942) both the everyday life of the town and quality of light by the sea became significant sources of inspiration. Nicholson spent summer holidays there in 1903, 1905 and 1907, visiting Orpen in 1903. Whilst many artists concentrated on the leisure scene in Dieppe, Nicholson was drawn to the fishing quarter, Le Pollet, where he made such paintings as *The First Communion* (1907; private collection) and *La Place du Petit Enfer, Dieppe* (1908; private collection), in which he emphasised the claustrophobia of the architecture. His dramatic use of shadow upon the façade of the buildings in this quarter makes them appear almost artificial, perhaps signalling his interest and employment of techniques from the theatre. Significantly, painters in the late 19th century and the early 20th were drawn to painting fishing communities, finding a romance within a way of life seemingly untouched by modern industry.[4] At Dieppe, Nicholson turned his particular gaze to this marginalised sector, within a town increasingly transformed by tourism.

In 1909 Nicholson painted a further scene of fishermen, this time on the south coast of England, in *Mending the Nets, Rottingdean* (fig.123). The anonymous figures and the subject of their labour are in harmony with their surroundings, seemingly unaware of being observed. The calm sky, sea and shingle are practically featureless, approaching a semi-abstract arrangement of subtle tones. Whistler's paintings of Trouville in France (an example being *Harmony in Blue and Silver: Trouville*, 1865; Isabella Stewart Gardner Museum, Boston, MA) have many parallels with Nicholson's coastal scenes. These small-scale paintings by the American artist are made up of horizontal veils of thinly applied paint, suggesting sand, sea and sky, the boundaries amongst these almost dissolving. The inclusion of a small figure serves to bring the composition back from pure abstraction. These works marked a turning point in Whistler's approach, in which the subject became secondary to a formalist exploration of line, tone and colour.

Nicholson was an admirer of Whistler and met him in 1896. This meeting, at which Nicholson was delighted to discover Whistler shared many of the same influences,[5] resulted in one of Nicholson's most significant commissions with the publisher William Heinemann. Whilst Nicholson did not share the same drive to theorise his work that Whistler had, nonetheless his landscape painting shares a similar harmonisation of tone and colour and simplification of form. This is particularly evident in such paintings as *Sea and Sky* (1910; private collection) and, later, *The Coast of Brittany* (1919–20; private collection) – an empty landscape punctuated by the elongated form of Edie, Nicholson's second wife, made whilst they were on honeymoon. As Whistler said of Nicholson's work, 'The art of leaving out is proof of the perfect acquaintance with the art of putting in. Mr. Nicholson states the few essential facts, and makes all else merely accessory.'[6]

Earlier, in 1906, Nicholson had spent the summer with his family in and around Littlehampton, visiting his friend, the writer J.M. Barrie, in the nearby village of Rustington. As well as Barrie, this area of West Sussex attracted other figures from the early 20th-century literary world, including Eleanor Farjeon, D.H. Lawrence and Edward Thomas. That summer was a particularly productive time for Nicholson, when he created many paintings of ships (Littlehampton being an important port for the Baltic timber trade – a subject Nicholson would later abandon due to the difficulty of finding a market for the paintings) and expansive views of the sea and sky. *Near Littlehampton* (fig.124) shows a view of the Clymping Gap – an area of sand dunes running between the River Arun and Littlehampton.[7] Nicholson privileged a vivid blue in this work, interrupted by white clouds scudding across the sky. Whilst the surrounding landscape was one of busy trade – timber mills, breweries, golf courses (as shown in Nicholson's painting, *The Links, Littlehampton*, 1906; private collection) – the Clymping Gap was virtually untouched. It remains today one of the most undeveloped areas along the West Sussex coast – its rare vegetated shingle designating it a Site of Special Scientific Interest and a popular walking route.

Nicholson would return to Sussex in 1909, but this time to the eastern county, in Rottingdean. He purchased the old vicarage, which he renamed The Grange, becoming his summer home and studio until 1915. In her biography of Nicholson, the writer Marguerite Steen wrote: 'Rottingdean of those days was an adorable place, with its duckpond surrounded by the little clutch of mellow houses – the Kiplings', the Burne-Jones's, the Noyeses' and, now, the Nicholsons'; with the beach within easy distance and the downs [*sic*] folded softly behind; a peaceful, paradisiacal sort of place, undiscovered by the vulgarian builder and land agent who has now made that stretch of the English coast hideous.'[8] Here she made reference to both the literary and artistic circles in Rottingdean and presented it as a rural idyll, subsequently ruined by development by the time she wrote the biography in 1943. Writers in the early 20th century, such as Rudyard Kipling and Hilaire Belloc, gave a bucolic interpretation of the Sussex countryside, inventing the idea of an unchanging landscape in opposition to and untouched by contemporary civilisation.[9] Many of Nicholson's paintings of the Downs show a landscape on the cusp of change, due both to a growing population and the tourist trade and to the effects of chalk erosion. Nicholson's painting of a small farmstead nestled within the Downs, *Judd's Farm* (1912; fig.125), stands out, as it is one of the few works he wrote about extensively in print. In an article for *The Artist* in 1934 he wrote: 'The picture represents buildings [...] which stood near Rottingdean, of fond memory, before Peacehaven (which started life as Anzac-on-Sea) poked its nose

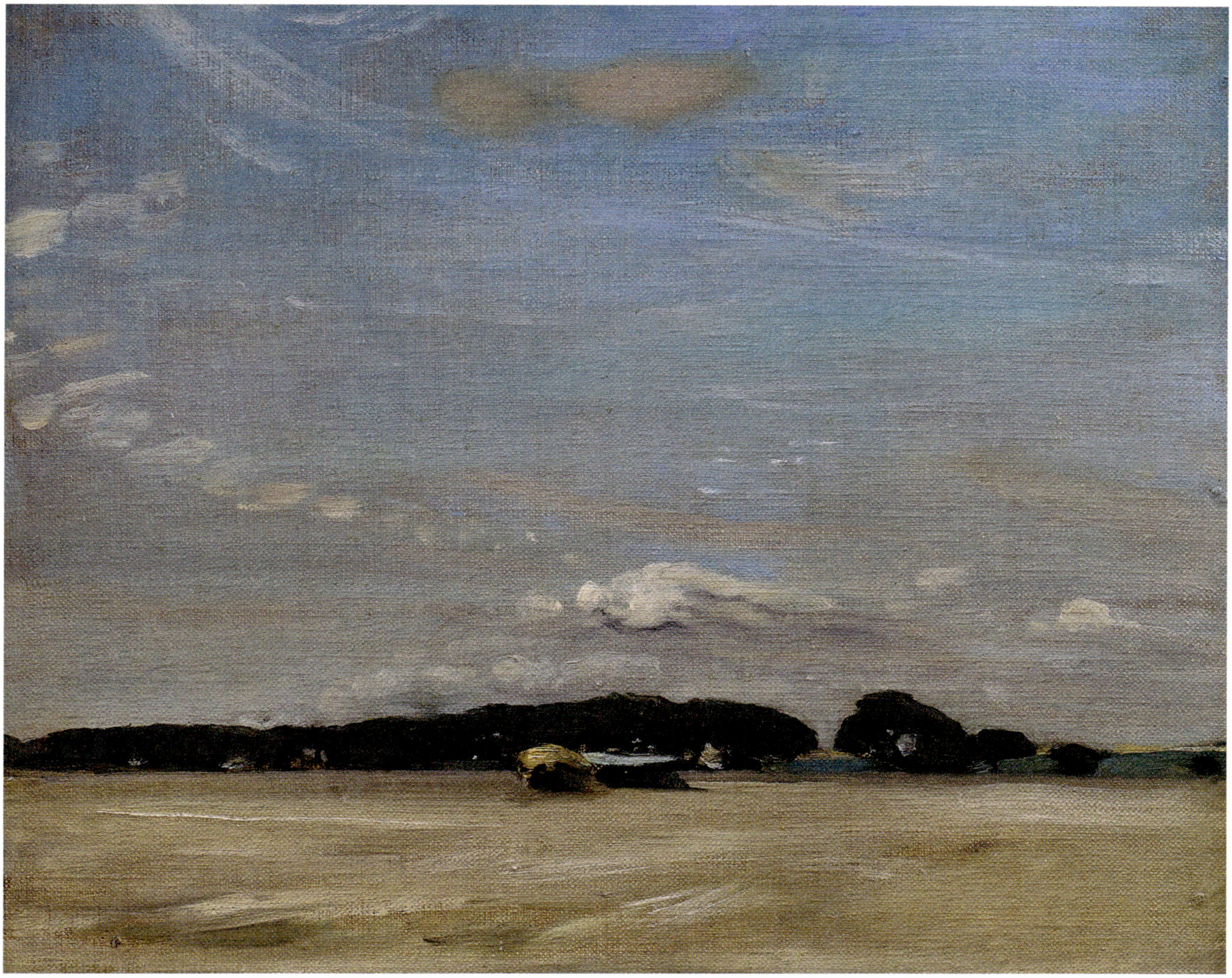

124 *Near Littlehampton*, 1906
Oil on canvas board, 26.5 x 32.5cm
Private collection, courtesy
Patrick Bourne & Co.

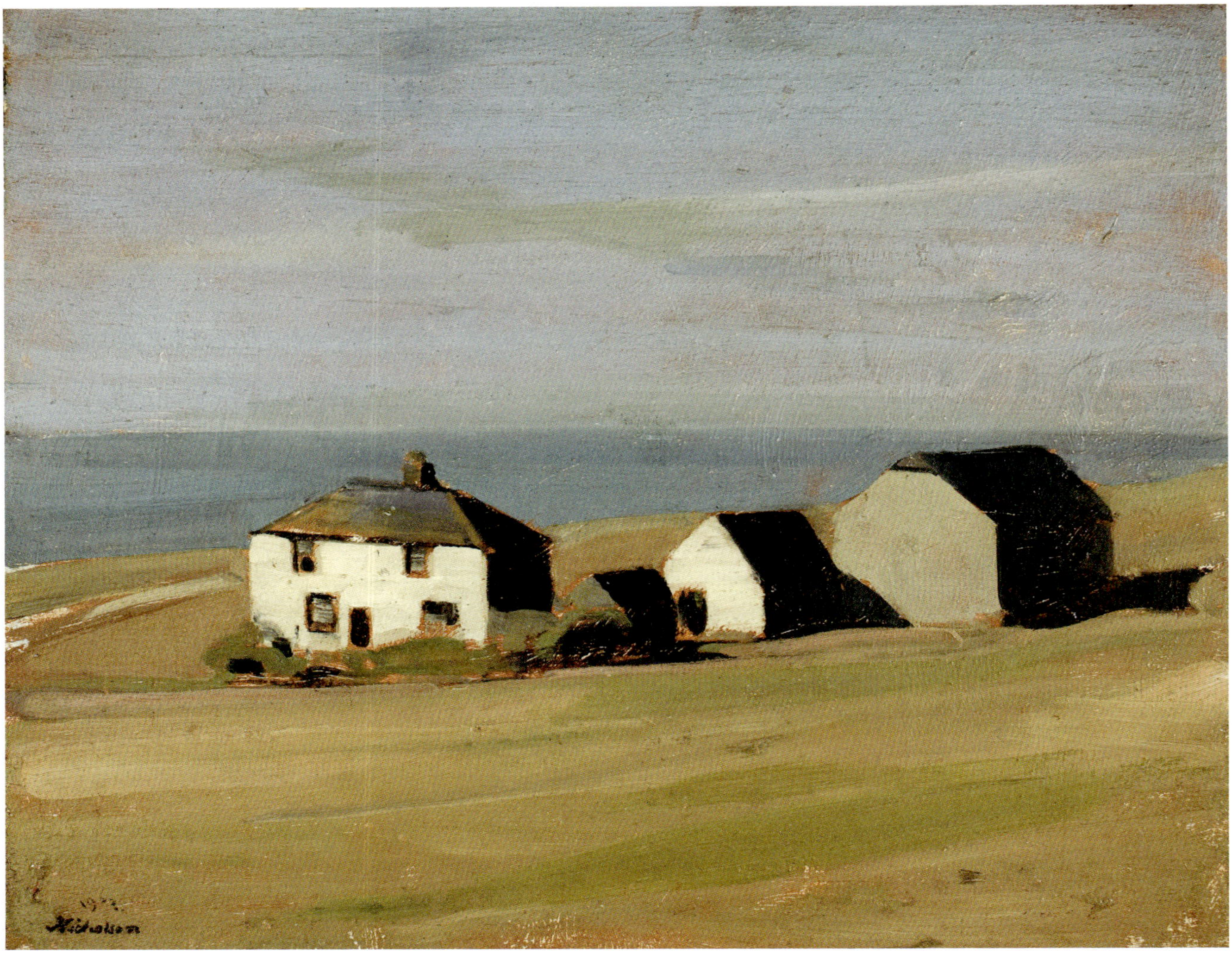

125 *Judd's Farm*, 1912
Oil on panel, 33 x 41cm
Towner Eastbourne. Acquired with the assistance of the MGC/V&A Purchase Grant Fund, National Art Collections Fund and the Friends of the Towner

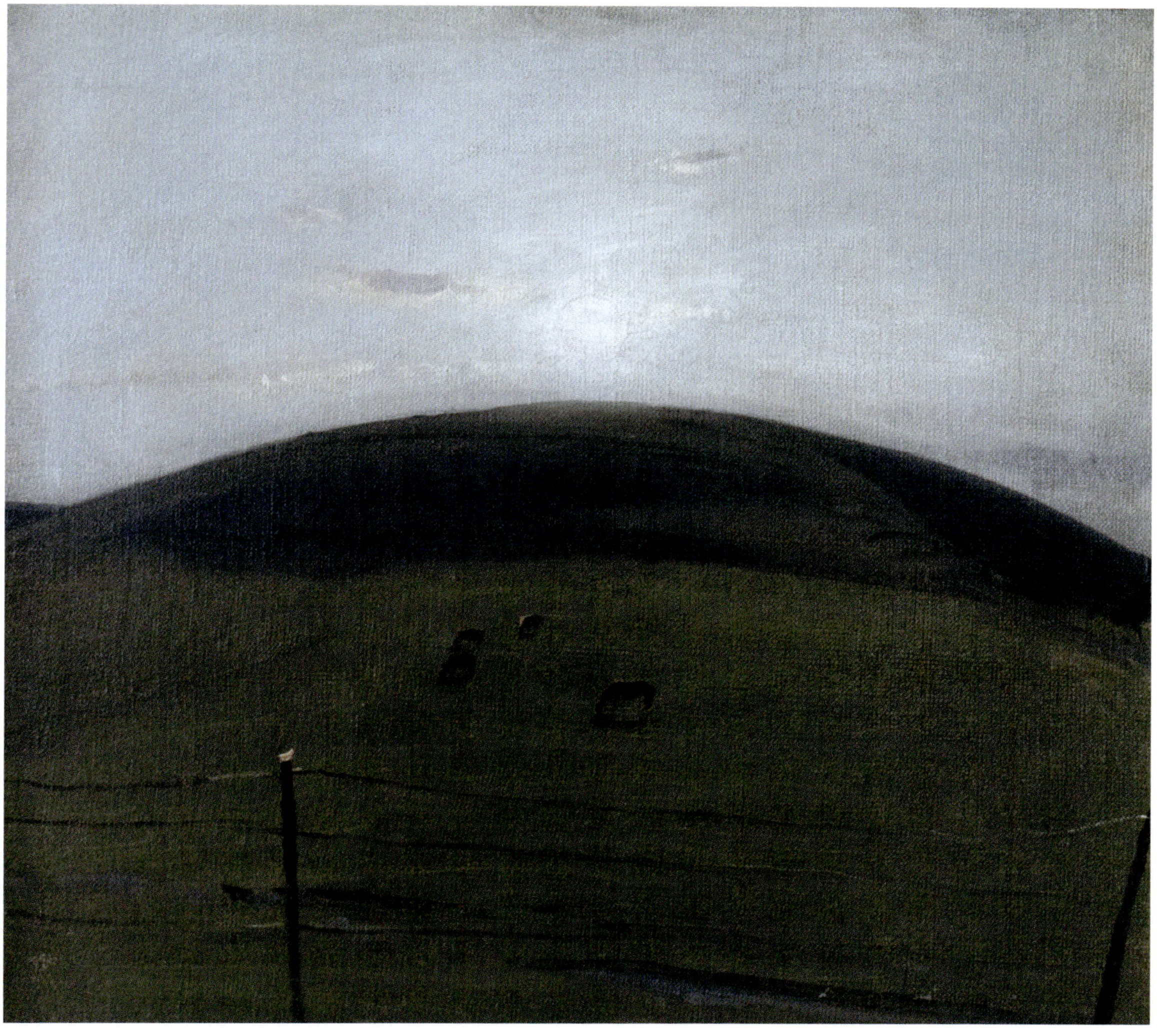

126 *Sunset*, 1912
Oil on canvas, 53.5 x 58.5cm
Private collection

over the white cliffs to smell the emergency exit of the main Brighton drain [...] The colours – few, but inevitable; my subject – so simple that I could finish it in my head before releasing the paint [...] Simplification in tone is a secret of great value, and the difference between colour and tone is of equal importance.'[10] Given the opportunity to reflect and look back, Nicholson highlighted (and deplored) the development of the new seaside town of Peacehaven, when the area was bought in 1915. The aim of the development was to provide affordable plots of land on which to build, for working-class families to relocate away from the city and so benefit from the seaside setting. Nevertheless, this was a contentious development, drawing criticism from such writers as Leonard Woolf and Virginia Woolf, living nearby at Rodmell, who saw its potential to damage the surrounding landscape.[11] These tensions between access to nature and its protection was a growing concern, resulting from a sense of dislocation from the countryside, caused by growing urbanisation during this period.

The late 19th century and the early 20th marked a time when there was a growing demand for access to the land – of which the majority was still (and continues to be) in the ownership of a tiny proportion of the population. The 'right to roam' movement was established in 1876 by the Hayfield and Kinder Scout Ancient Footpaths Association, and the first rambling clubs were established from the 1880s onwards. Nicholson loved walking in the landscape, alone or with family and friends; it provided him with a respite from the bustle of London life. It is significant that he frequently included walkers in his landscapes, most often representations of his own family. The tiny figures who walk along the edge of the *Cliffs at Rottingdean* (1910; fig.129) or stop to rest on the beach beneath them (c.1911; fig.130) give a sense of space within the landscape and draw our attention to their interaction with nature. Indeed, even the scale of the canvas boards, which were of a size that would easily fit into a portable paint box, highlights the fact that these works were made outside, whilst walking and enjoying the landscape, lending a sense of immediacy to the paintings.

The windmill at Rottingdean is an iconic part of the Sussex landscape to this day and was much loved within Nicholson's lifetime. E.V. Lucas, the author of the travelogue *Highways and Byways in Sussex* (1906), an imaginative journey through the county, led a campaign for the preservation of England's windmills in the early 20th century, defending their central role within the countryside.[12] Nicholson's letters were headed with small cartoons of the windmill when written from The Grange, and he would play hide-and-seek with his young son Kit behind the landmark.[13] It is a recurrent subject in his paintings, for example in *The Windmill, Brighton Downs* (1910; fig.32), its black sails just discernible on the tiny fleck on the horizon. In 1923 he painted the windmill when it was under reconstruction. This followed a campaign led by the villagers, in which they raised £400 to rescue the dilapidated building.[14] Whilst in earlier iterations of the mill in Nicholson's paintings the structure is dwarfed by the surrounding rolling hills, in *The Windmill, Rottingdean, under Repair* (1923; private collection) Nicholson almost animated it, instilling dignity to the vulnerable piece of architecture. By returning to the windmill throughout his life, it became a symbol for a sense of continuity within the landscape for Nicholson.

Nicholson decided to sell The Grange when he received a commission to go to India for much of 1915 from the Viceroy of India, Charles Hardinge, 1st Baron Hardinge of Penshurst, to make his portrait to mark his retirement. Nicholson spent half the year there and found painting the portrait challenging, the Viceroy being available only for

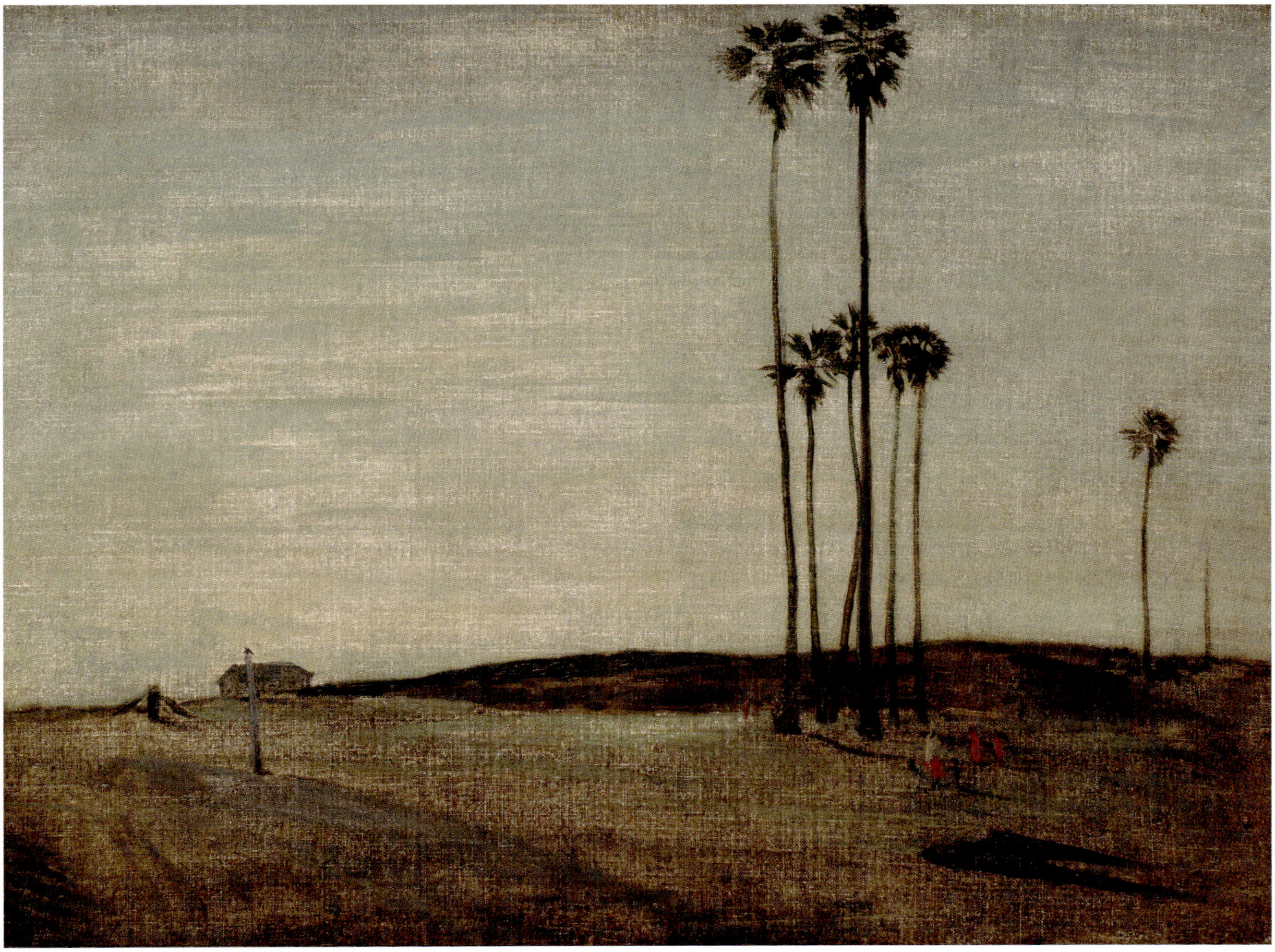

127 *Bombay Landscape*, 1915
Oil on canvas board, 35.5 x 59.5cm
Private collection

sporadic sittings. In her biography of Nicholson, Steen commented that being 'confined within the hidebound circle of viceregal etiquette, the chatter of British society drowning whatever opportunities he might have had of hearing the temple bells, he had not time in which to absorb it, to get beneath its surface.'[15] Despite this, Nicholson painted two atmospheric landscapes (1915; private collection) inspired by his trip to India, of the delta region west of Mumbai (Bombay during British rule). This area was a major gateway for goods and people entering and leaving the city and a strategic location for the British military during the First World War. In Nicholson's composition *Bombay Landscape* (1915; fig.127), however, the scene is emphatically tranquil, made more so by his restricted colour palette, evoking the dim, hazy air of rainfall at dusk. The elongated, thin palm trees resemble the composition of the 17th-century Dutch painting by Meindert Hobbema (1638–1709), *The Avenue at Middelharnis* (1689; National Gallery, London), whose spare composition is defined by twin rows of long slender trees and inspired generations of artists. The avenue as subject was an unusual one and perhaps points to the increasing cultivation of the landscape in the modern era. Like Hobbema, Nicholson played with the viewer's perspective, drawing our eyes up into the sky, a technique he would return to in later landscapes.

Nicholson and Edie moved in 1923 to Sutton Veny in Wiltshire, where again Nicholson made chalk downland his subject, albeit in the west of the country. He wrote to his friend Herbert Ward, 'Edie and I are enjoying our move, at the moment we are full of dust and strawberries.'[16] During this time, Nicholson took on fewer portrait commissions, which allowed him more space to make landscapes. In *Snow in the Horseshoe* (1927; fig.132), Nicholson's mercurial use of white transforms the paint into glistening snow nestled in a bend of the land of the Wiltshire Downs. In an essay celebrating Whistler's use of white, the artist Ian McKeever (b.1946) stated: 'As a colour white is furtive, there but never quite there, either too much or too little [...] In the tube it is this thing named white. Once squeezed out, its substance spread, dispersed into a mere surface, it becomes something else, the pristine feel of a dress, the delicacy that is lace, the glow of light. In the process it has gone from substance to intimation, attribute and atmosphere.'[17] In a painting of the same year, *The Cornfield above Alfriston* (1927; private collection), Nicholson again used white to great effect in conjuring an atmosphere through his rendering of the dramatic sky in thick impasto.

His interest in aerial perspective took a new direction in the early 1930s. In 1932 his son Kit, by then an architect, had taken up gliding and took his father on visits to airfields and on flights. Nicholson's view of South Harting in West Sussex (fig.135) looks down on the copper spire of the parish church of St Mary and St Gabriel, a marker used by the Southdown Gliding Club, which may be how the artist came to know the view. *The Gliders on the Downs* (fig.136) is believed to be a view from Dunstable Downs, looking across the landscape to the gliders of the British Gliding Association. There is evidence to suggest that this painting was inspired by a flight William and Kit had taken together.[18] The viewpoint Nicholson chose gives the viewer the impression of descending from flight, placing us within the action of the painting. Whilst this pastime gave the opportunity for father and son to bond in the 1930s, it eventually became a source of tragedy for the family. In 1948 Kit died in a gliding accident at Samedan, near St Moritz in Switzerland, aged only 43. (Nicholson would survive his son by only a year.)

By the early 1930s there were tensions in William and Edie's marriage, which only worsened during their trip to visit Edie's parents, Sir Lionel

128 *Fish and Sun*, c.1938–9
Pencil on paper, 9 x 12.5cm
Private collection

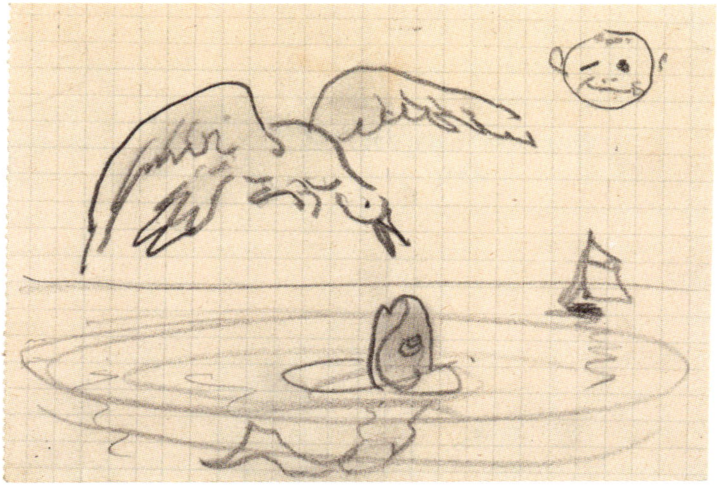

and Lady Phillips, at Vergelegen in South Africa. Nicholson made one landscape whilst working on a commissioned portrait of J.W. Jagger (1931; Iziko South African National Gallery, Cape Town), a British industrialist who had emigrated to South Africa in 1880 and made his fortune as an importer of fabrics. From 1908 to 1909 Jagger was a member of the National Convention, which drafted the South Africa Act, establishing the Union of South Africa, an act which embedded racial segregation through the exclusion of the majority Black African population from political participation. Jagger owned the neighbouring estate to Vergelegen, which looked on to Helderberg Mountain. The long shadows on the mountainside in *The Helderberg* (1931; fig.133) suggest that the view is at sunset, and the rich vegetation and the Lourens River run through the bottom half of the painting. Both the land and climate made it the ideal location in the 17th century for early Dutch colonists, who planted vineyards there, an area which still produces wine today. In a letter to his daughter Elizabeth, Nicholson wrote that painting this view was his favourite part of the whole trip.[19] Nicholson's bright and lively painting of the village of Letterfrack (1931; fig.134) later that year whilst holidaying in Ireland with the family also suggests a happier moment, despite an increasing alienation between him and Edie. These views hint at the ways in which the landscape gave respite to Nicholson during more challenging times.

Painting landscapes continued to provide a sense of solace to Nicholson in the later part of his career. In 1935 he had met and fallen in love with Marguerite Steen, who from then onwards managed both hers and Nicholson's time and finances, allowing the artist more opportunity to paint as he wished. They had met whilst Nicholson was staying with the author, zoologist and instigator of Whipsnade Zoo, Peter Chalmers Mitchell, who had a house near Malaga in Spain. In 1915 Nicholson had already remarked on the beauty of the Spanish landscape, which he saw by sea from the ship taking him to India. Together Nicholson and Steen went on excursions around Malaga, which resulted in a series of landscapes (figs.139 and 141) depicting the range of hills surrounding the city. Nicholson's looser handling of paint and his use of a brighter, more colourful palette, which he used to great effect in Spain, is often attributed to the influence of Winifred Nicholson, his daughter-in-law.[20] He developed these techniques further in a sun-dappled scene from 1937, *A Glade near Midhurst* (fig.138), in the West Sussex countryside. He even went so far as to incorporate the end of his brush, with which he scratched into the surface of the paint. Whilst his painting methods were evolving, nonetheless his subjects endured, as well as his love of the landscape, which so often provided him with an outlet through which to enjoy painting despite the demands of working to commission. As Winifred Nicholson wrote of him in her memoir, 'He was painting the same themes as he had painted in the Edwardian security of pre-First World War, the same themes but an octave higher in key.'[21]

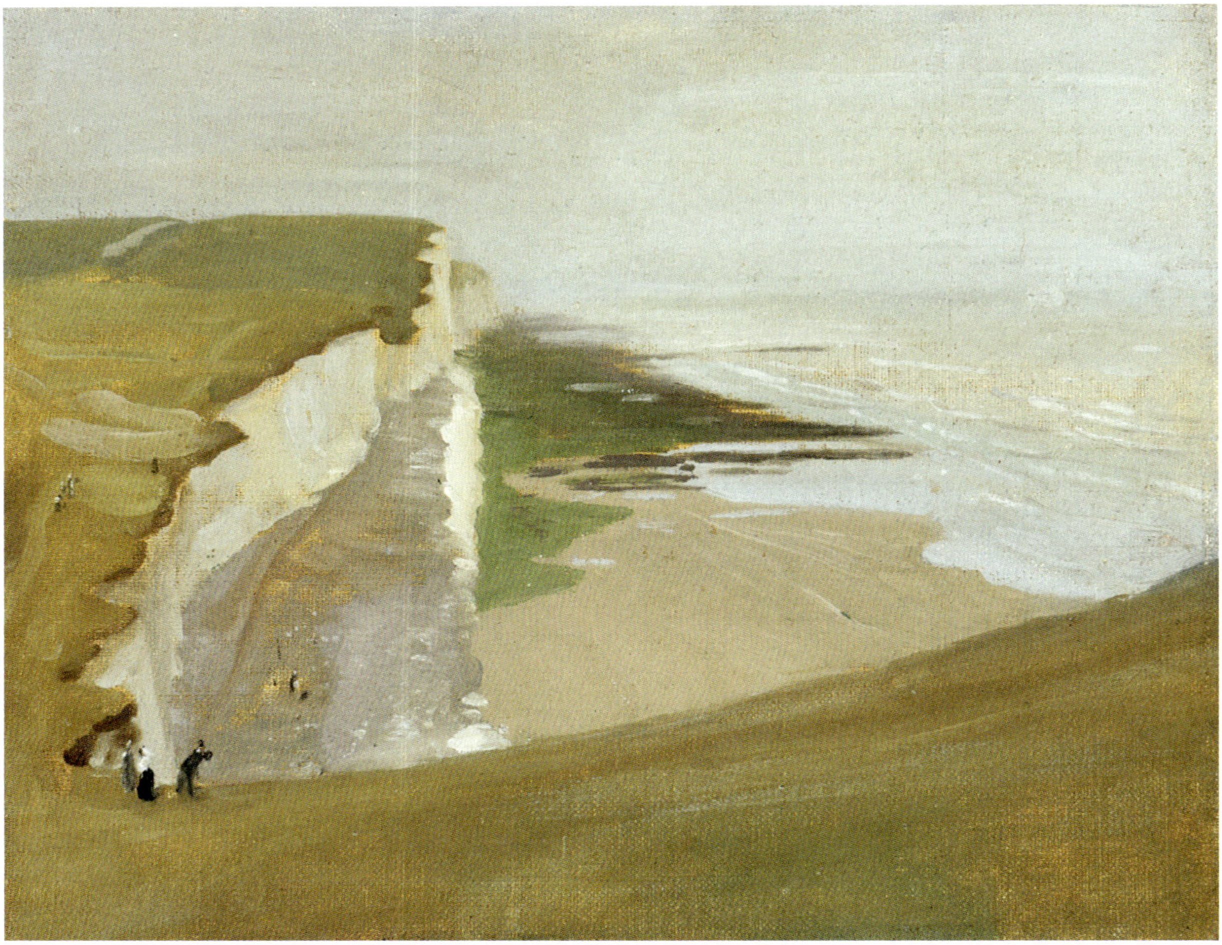

129 *Cliffs at Rottingdean*, 1910
Oil on canvas, 33 x 41.5cm
Southampton City Art Gallery

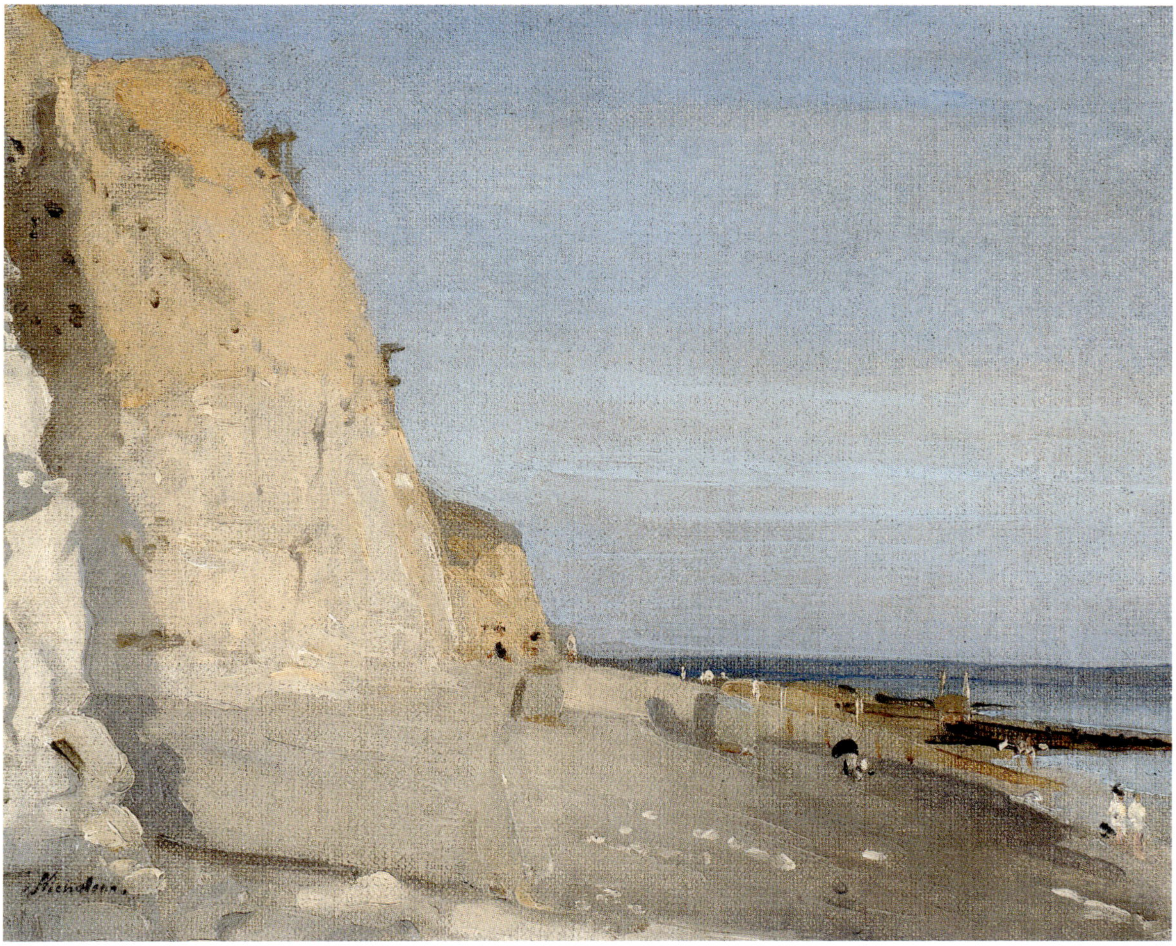

130 *Cliffs at Rottingdean*, c.1911
Oil on canvas board, 32 x 39.5cm
Private collection

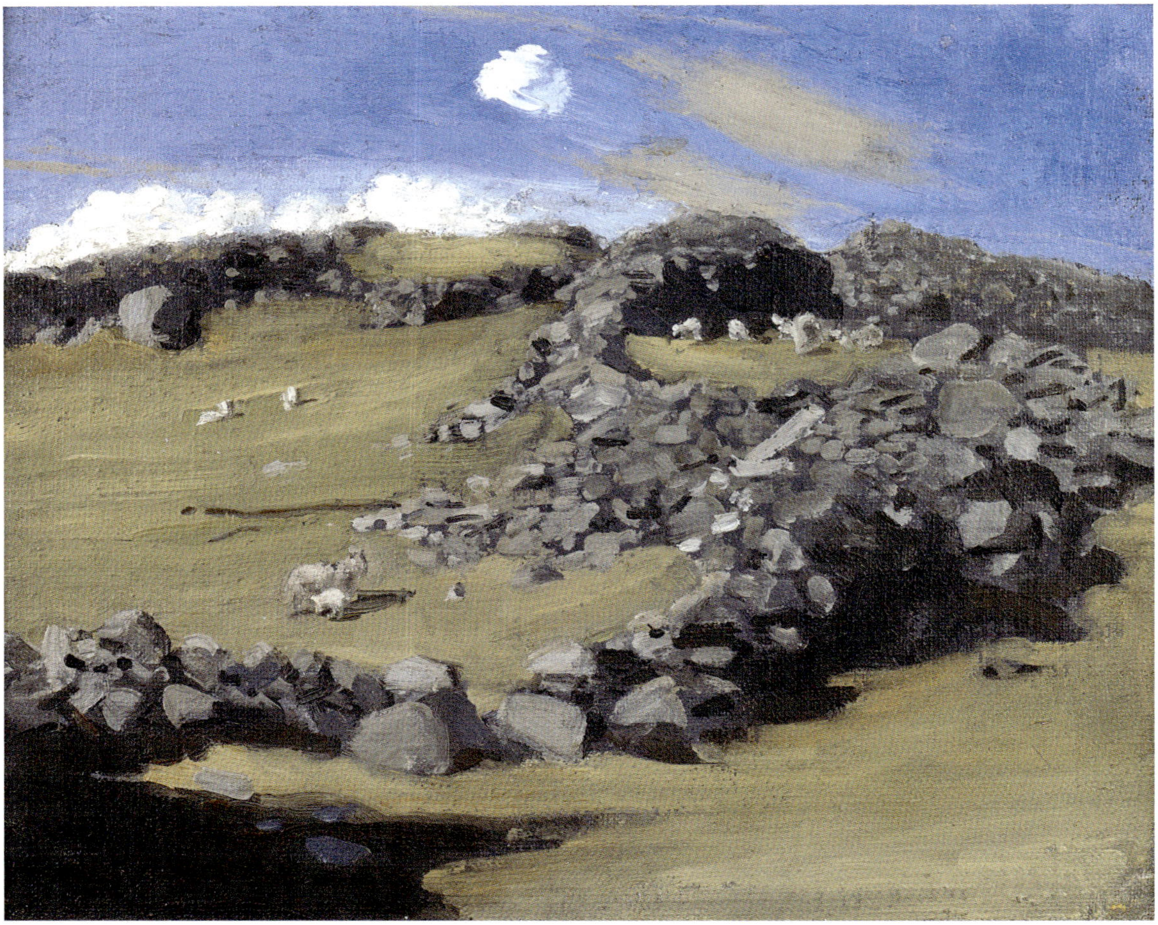

131 *Landscape at Harlech*, 1919
Oil on canvas board, 33 x 40.5cm
Private collection, courtesy
Patrick Bourne & Co.

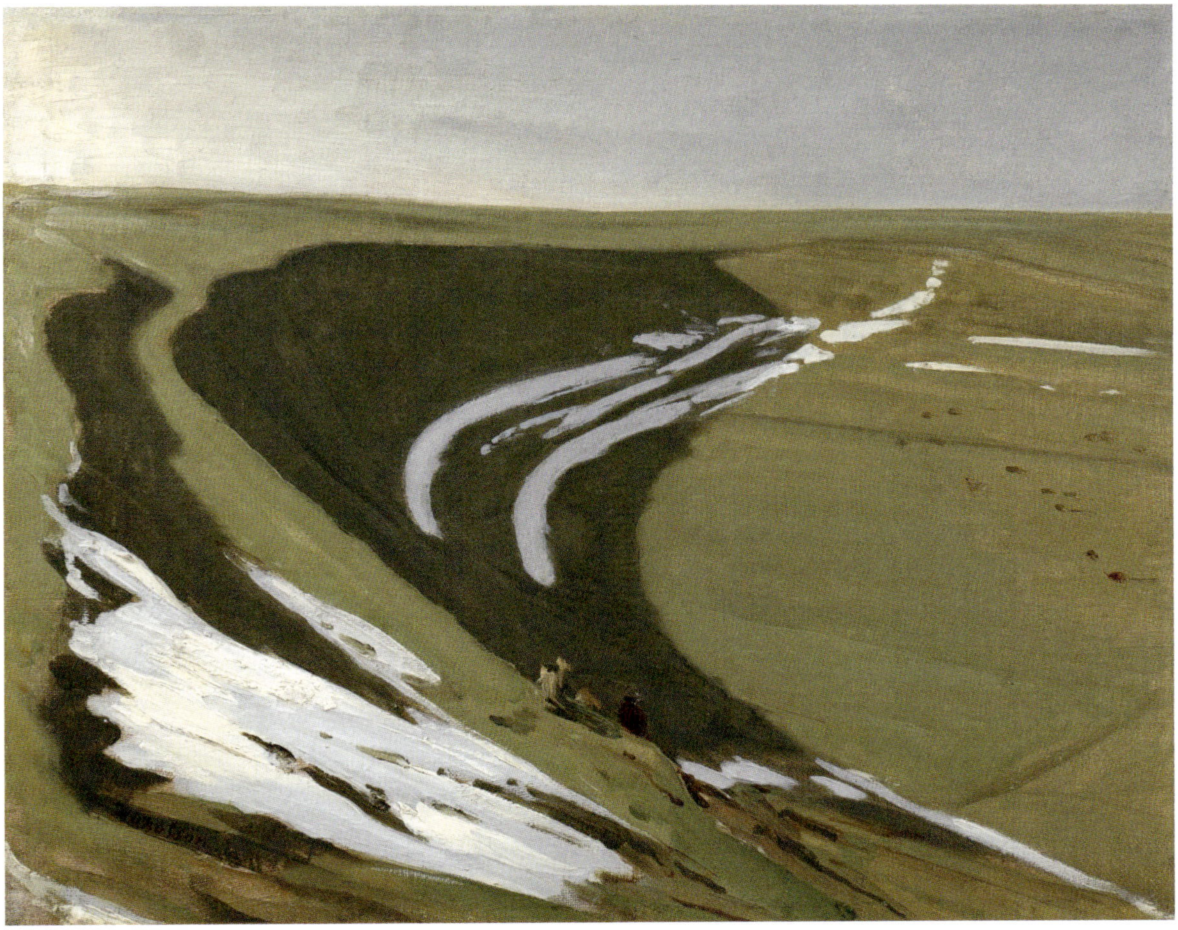

132 *Snow in the Horseshoe*, 1927
Oil on canvas board, 32.5 x 40cm
Private collection, courtesy
Hazlitt Holland-Hibbert

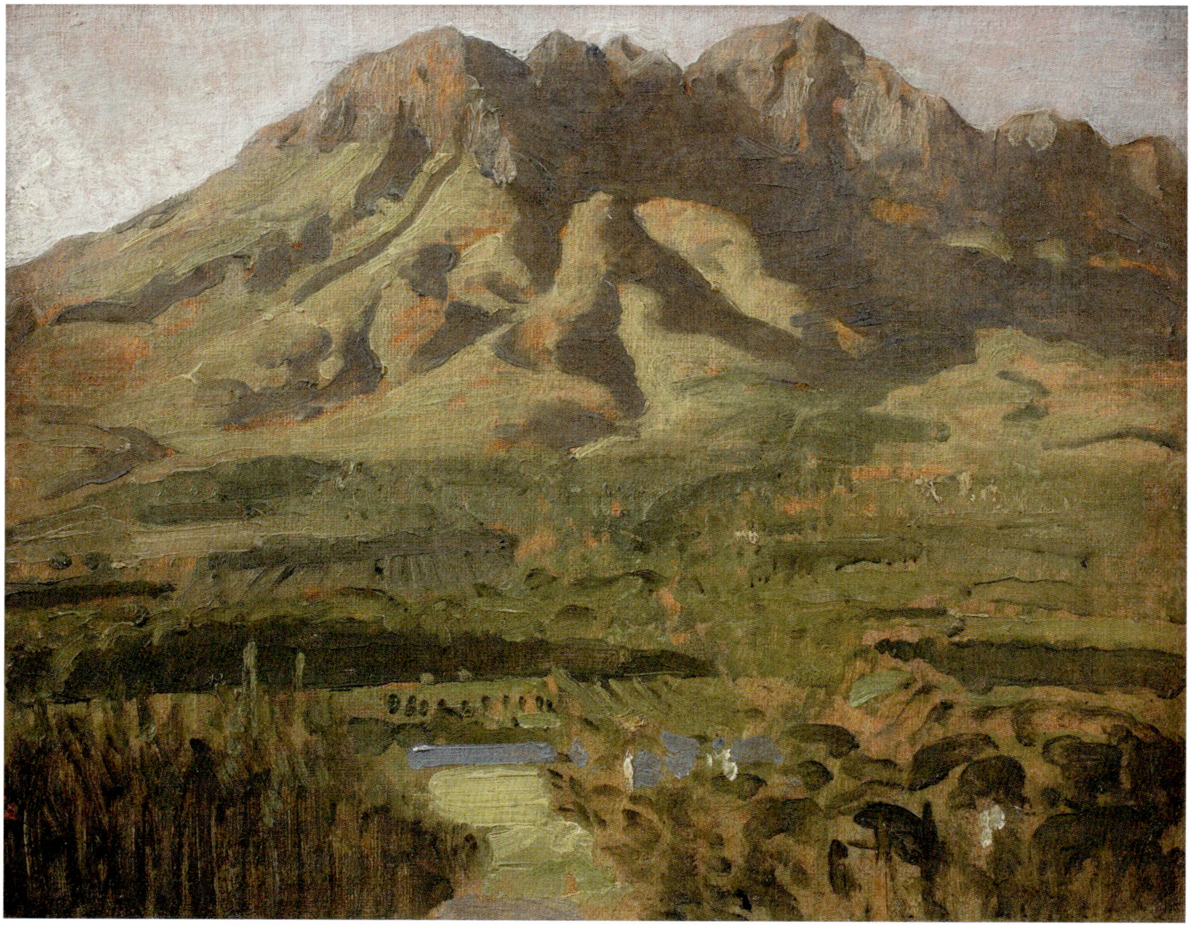

133 *The Helderberg*, 1931
Oil on canvas board, 37 x 44.5cm
Private collection, courtesy
Piano Nobile, London

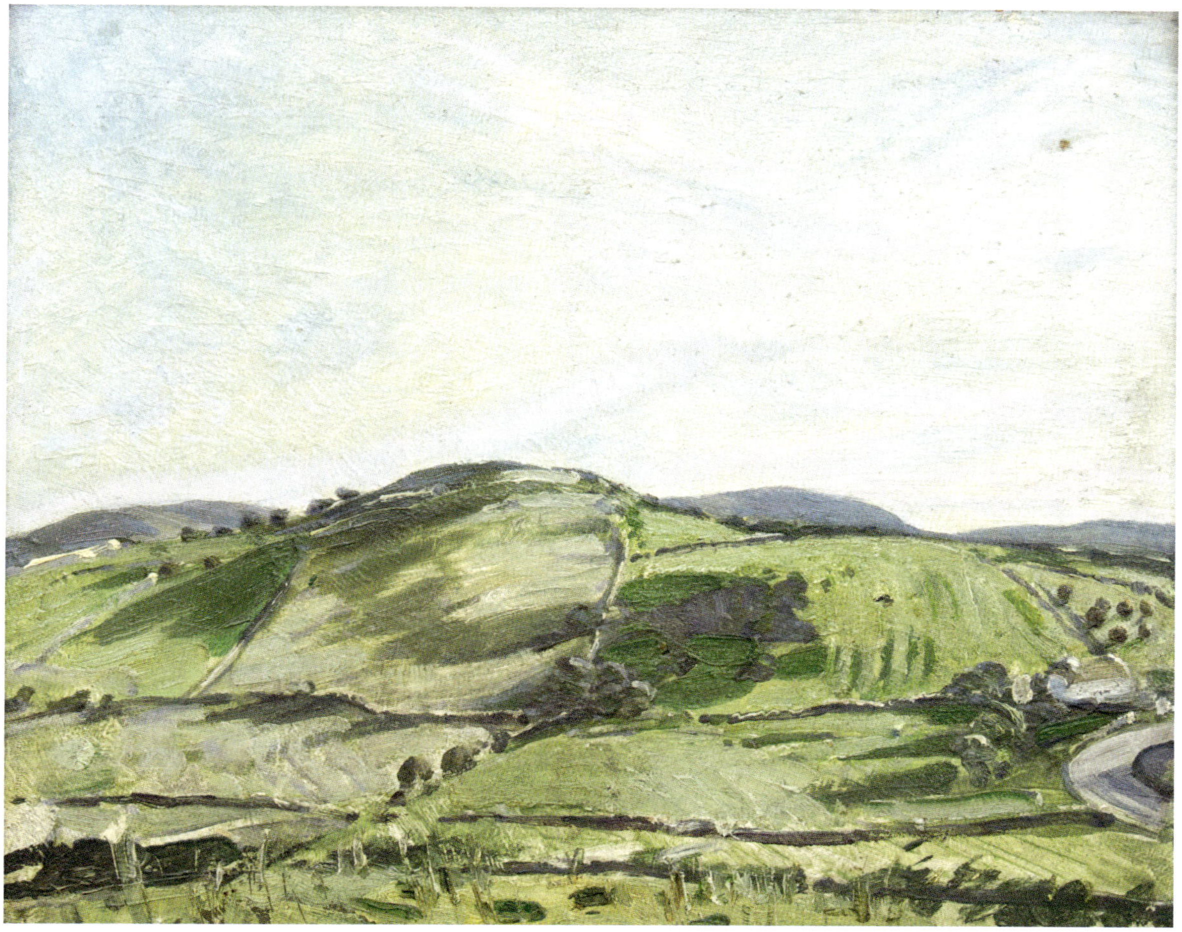

134 *Letterfrack*, 1931
Oil on canvas, 33.1 x 41.2cm
Pallant House Gallery
(On loan from a private collection, 2013)

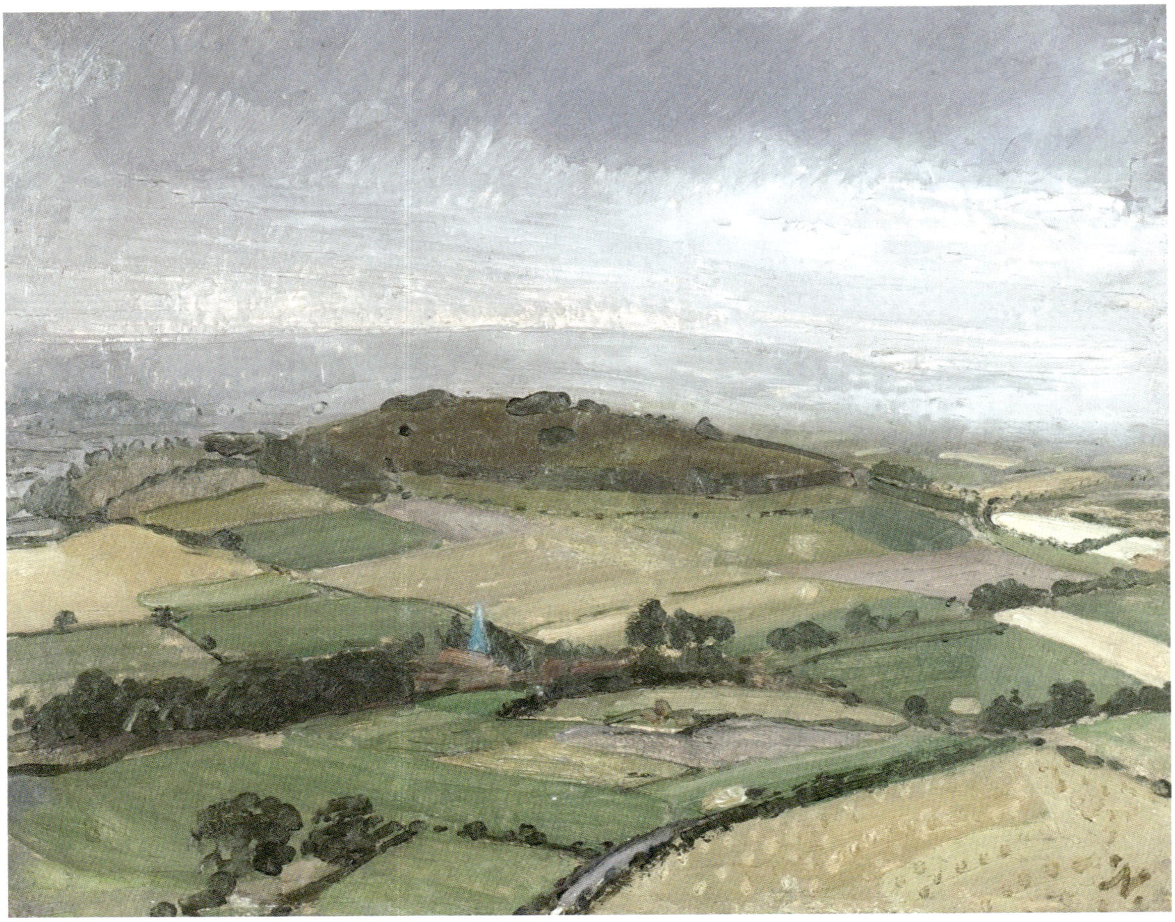

135 *South Harting*, c.1933
Oil on canvas, 33 x 41cm
Private collection

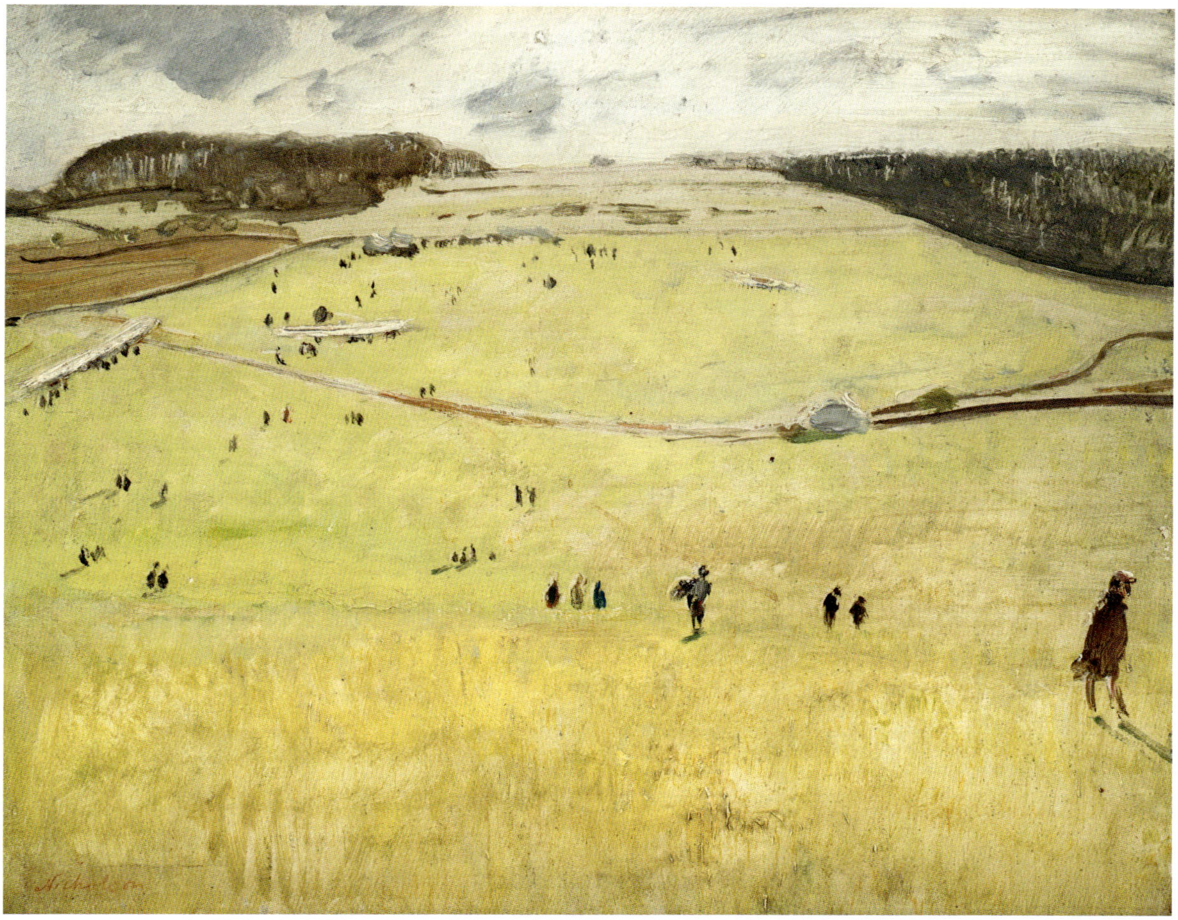

136 *The Gliders on the Downs*, 1932
Oil on panel, 33 x 40.5cm
Lent by The Savile Club, London

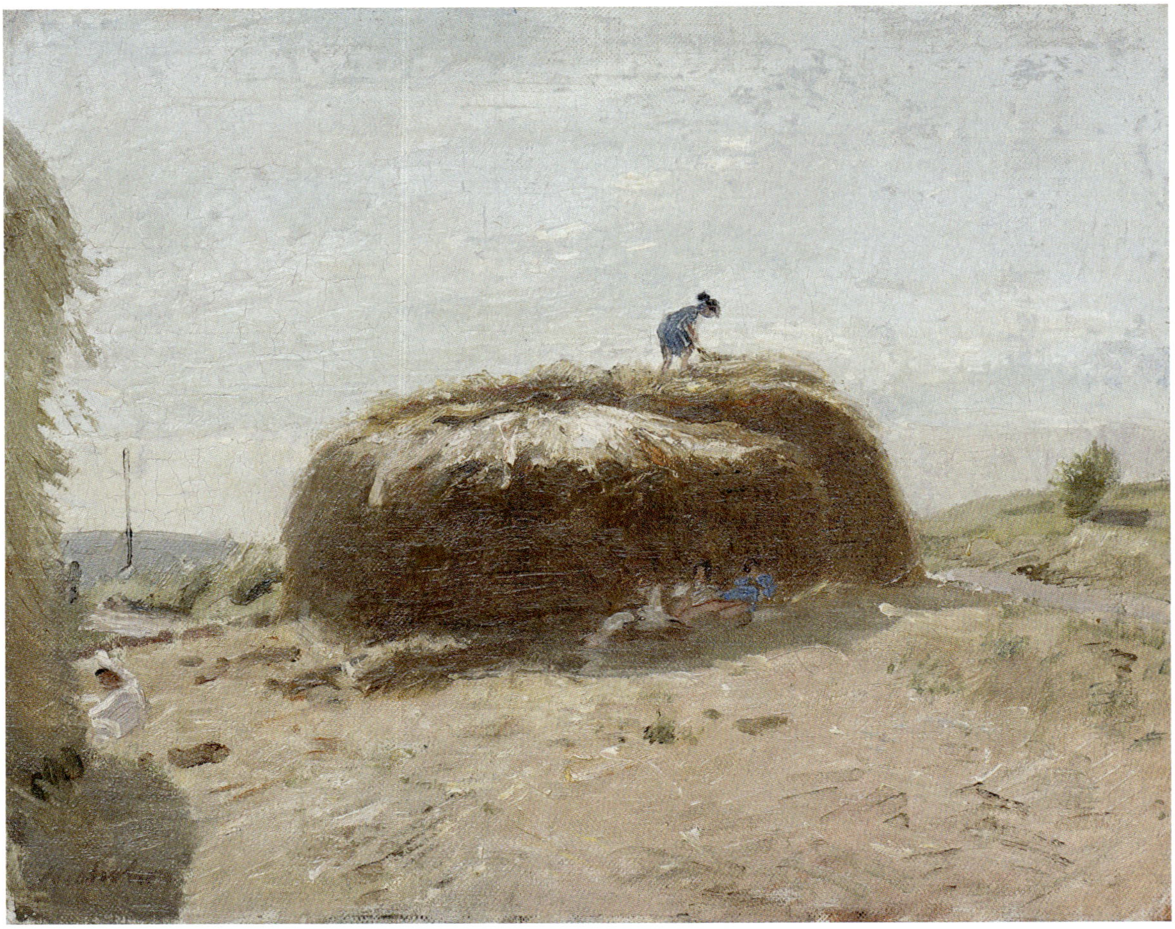

137 *The Picnic*, 1932
Oil on canvas board, 33 x 40.5cm
Estate of Mirabel Cecil

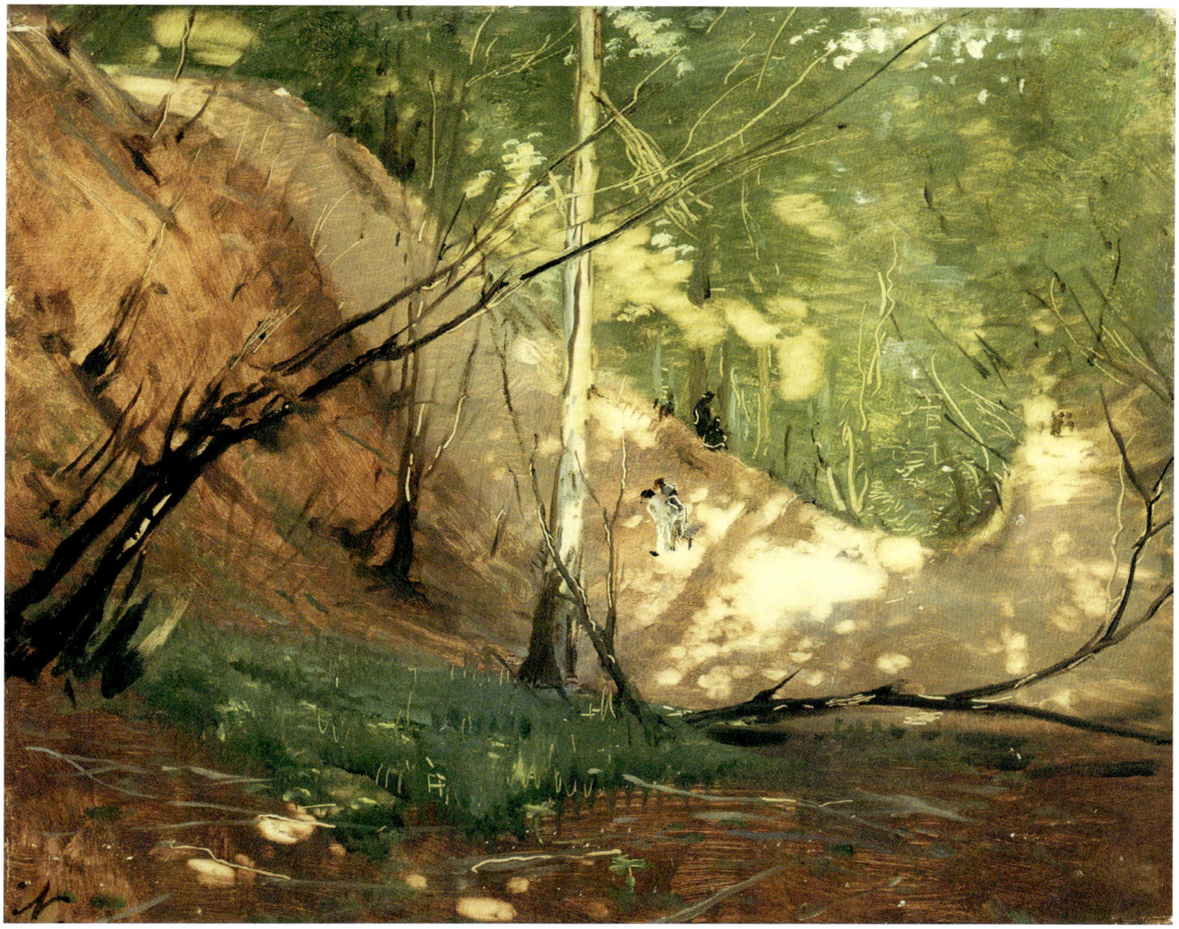

138 *A Glade near Midhurst*, 1937
Oil on wood, 37.8 x 46cm
Southampton City Art Gallery

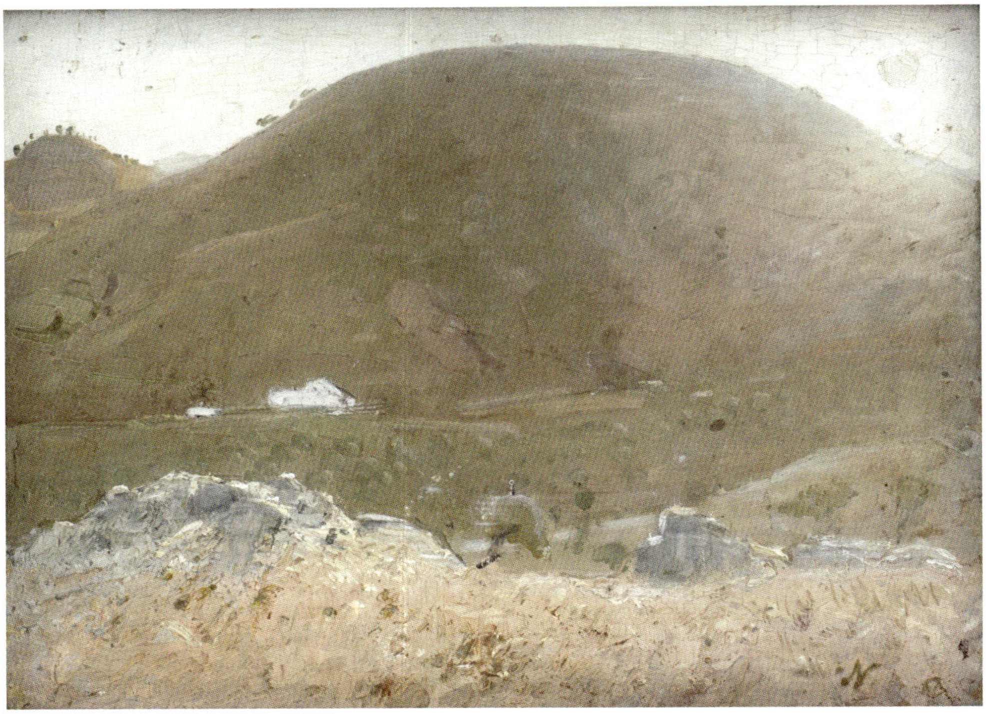

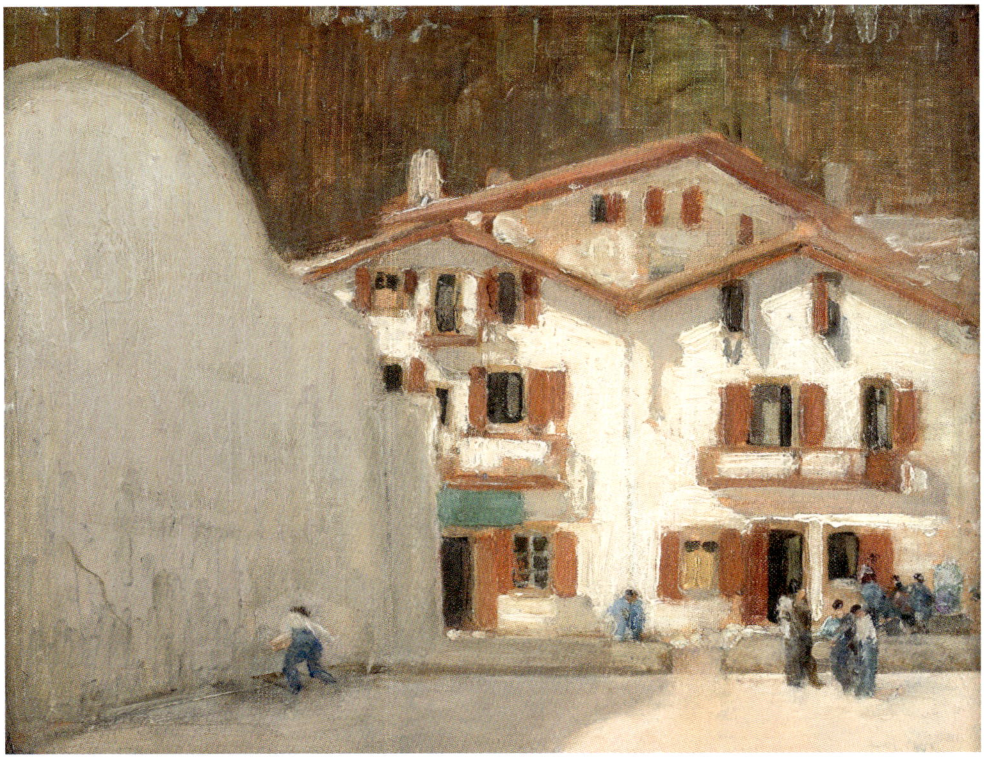

139 *Spanish Hills*, 1935
Oil on wood panel,
29 x 39.5cm
Pallant House Gallery
(On loan from a
private collection)

140 *A Game of Pelota*, 1939
Oil on canvas board,
33 x 40cm
Private collection

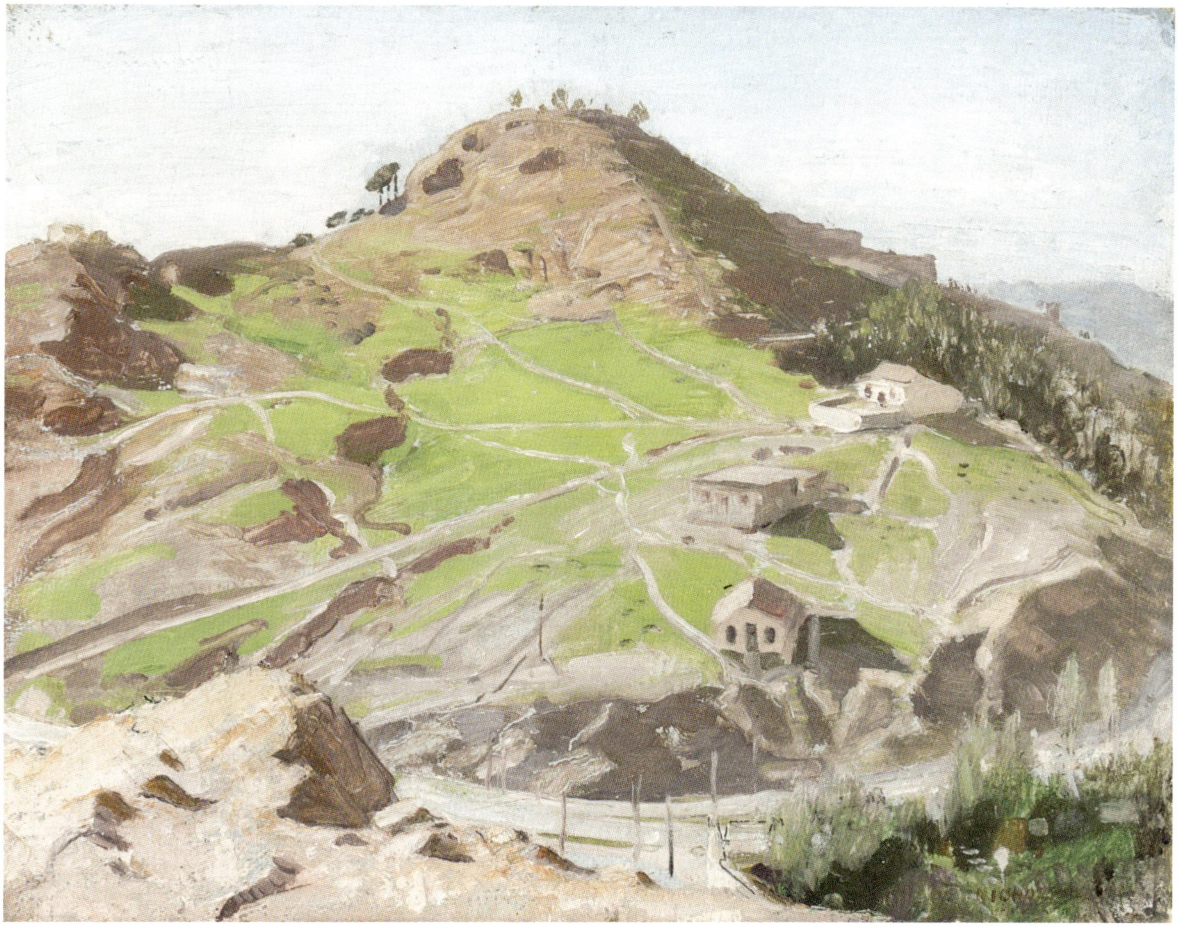

141 *The Castle, Malaga*, 1935
Oil on canvas board, 33 x 41cm
Private collection

WILLIAM NICHOLSON (1872–1949)

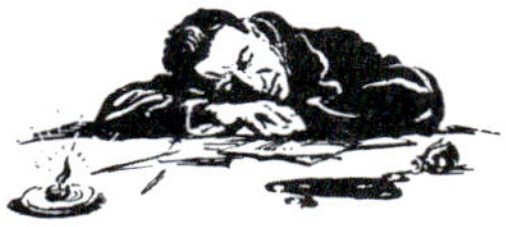

Compiled by Miriam O'Connor Perks from the extensive chronology in Patricia Reed's catalogue raisonné of William Nicholson's oil paintings (2011)

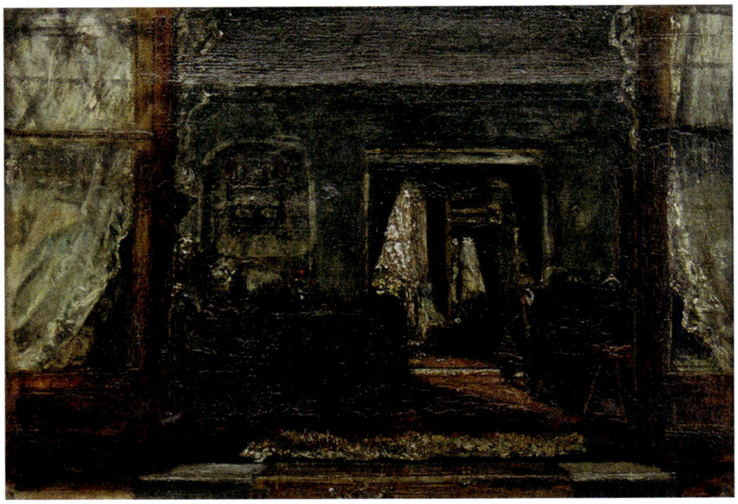

142 *The Family Home*, c.1887
Oil on canvas, 19.5 x 25.5cm
Pallant House Gallery
(On loan from a private collection, 2013)

5 FEBRUARY 1872
William Newzam Prior Nicholson [WN] is born at Newark-on-Trent, Nottinghamshire, to the industrialist William Newzam Nicholson and his second wife, Anne Elizabeth Prior.

1881–7
He is a weekly boarder at Magnus Grammar School, Newark-on-Trent. During this time takes painting lessons from William Cubley, landscape and portrait painter and drawing master. Often stays with his maternal grandparents at Chaucer's House, Woodstock, Oxfordshire.

1888–91
Joins Hubert von Herkomer's art school at Bushey, near Watford, Hertfordshire, where he meets his future wife, Mabel Pryde, and her brother, James Pryde. Leaves the school after disagreeing with its founder.

1891
In the autumn attends the Académie Julian in Paris and makes copies of Diego Velázquez's works at the Louvre.

1892
In London attends a memorable James McNeill Whistler retrospective at the Goupil Gallery and in November exhibits at the New English Art Club.

1893
Marries Mabel Pryde, unbeknownst to their parents. Their first home is at a former public house, The Eight Bells, at Denham, Buckinghamshire. James Pryde soon moves in with them. Through Pryde, he is introduced to Edward Gordon Craig and his mother, Ellen Terry, thereby sealing his relationship with the theatre world.

1894
Begins working with James Pryde as 'J. & W. Beggarstaff', also known as the 'Beggarstaff Brothers'. From this time until 1900, abandons oil painting in favour of posters and woodcuts. On 10 April Benjamin Lauder [Ben] Nicholson, his and Mabel Pryde's first child, is born. In July the first J. & W. Beggarstaff poster, for *Hamlet*, is produced. In October the work of J. & W. Beggarstaff is well-received when first exhibited in the International Artistic Pictorial Poster Exhibition at the Westminster Royal Aquarium in London.

1895
A fertile year for J. & W. Beggarstaff poster production. The Nicholsons move to London at the end of the year.

1896
Meets Max Beerbohm. Makes the woodcut print *Persimmon*, which captures the attention of Whistler, who then introduces him to the publisher William Heinemann. Signs a contract with Heinemann at the end of November to produce *An Alphabet*.

1897
On 23 April his and Mabel Pryde's second son, John Anthony [Tony] Nicholson, is born. His woodcut portrait of Queen Victoria is published in *The New Review*. The family stays in Rottingdean, East Sussex. Works on his woodcut portrait of Rudyard Kipling, who writes verses for WN's *An Almanac of Twelve Sports*, published later that year. *An Alphabet* is published.

1898
The family moves to Chaucer's House. *London Types* is published. Exhibits with the Society of Portrait Painters.

1899
His parents die within three weeks of each other, and he subsequently struggles financially. On 13 September Annie Mary Prydie [Nancy] Nicholson, his and Mabel Pryde's third child, is born. *Twelve Portraits* and *The Square Book of Animals* are published. The final Beggarstaff poster, *Robespierre*, is produced.

1900
Visits New York on a commission for *Harper's Weekly*. Becomes a member of the Savile Club.

1901
Winds down making woodcuts in favour of portrait painting. Begins with paintings of children, family and friends. In May visits W.E. Henley in Worthing, West Sussex, to paint his portrait.

1902
Meets Edwin Lutyens, who would become a lifelong friend, and J.M. Barrie. His second series of *Twelve Portraits* is published.

1903
First solo show at the Stafford Gallery, London, with 23 oil paintings. Visits Paris and holidays in Dieppe, where he would return many times. Whilst in Dieppe, meets William Orpen and his family.

1904
Shares his time between Woodstock and Hampstead, London. Designs his first costume and set designs for the first production of *Peter Pan*. The family holidays in Sussex. On 16 December his and Mabel Pryde's fourth child, Christopher David George [Kit] Nicholson, is born.

1905
Solo show of 12 paintings in Paris. Whilst there, visits the Whistler retrospective at the École des Beaux-Arts. Becomes acquainted with Thomas W. Bacon, who would become his most important patron.

1906
The family moves to 38 Mecklenburgh Square, Bloomsbury, London. Shares a studio with Orpen. Paints landscapes in Sussex.

1907
The Nicholsons holiday in Italy with Beerbohm. Begins to paint still lifes. Commissions Orpen to paint the Nicholson family at 38 Mecklenburgh Square.

1909
Elected a member of the Society of Portrait Painters. Buys the old vicarage in Rottingdean. Chalk downland would prove a long-lasting subject for him.

1910
Paints productively due to increasing financial constraints. Becomes a founding member of the National Portrait Society.

1911
Leaves 38 Mecklenburgh Square in June. Solo show at the Goupil Gallery of 25 oil paintings, his largest exhibition to date.

1912
Through a portrait commission, meets Edith [Edie] Phillips and attends her wedding to Jack Stuart Wortley; the Stuart Wortleys become family friends. Works on his first major decorative scheme for the American playwright and novelist Edward Knoblock in Paris.

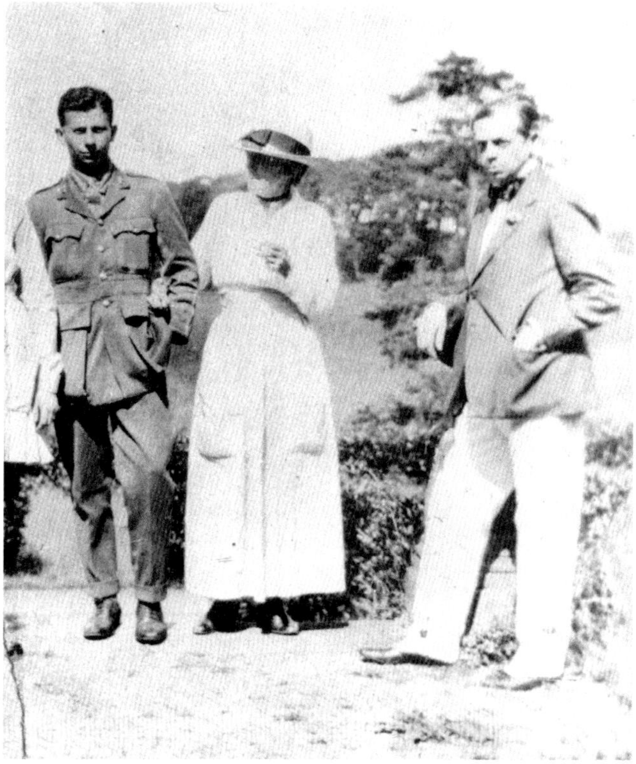

143 ANONYMOUS
Tony Nicholson, Mabel Pryde and William Nicholson, c.1916
Private collection

1913
Emboldened by his commission for Knoblock, paints his first large still lifes and has a particularly productive period living in Paris.

1914
Stays in Rottingdean at the outbreak of the First World War. At the end of the year, travels to India with Lutyens to paint the Viceroy, Charles Hardinge, 1st Baron Hardinge of Penshurst.

1915
Spends time in Delhi, Shimla and Mumbai (Simla and Bombay during British rule), where he makes three portraits, those of Lord Hardinge, his orderly, Duffadar Valayat Shah, and his daughter, Diamond. Also paints landscapes in Mumbai. Travels back to England in July. Mabel Pryde and the children rent a cottage in Harlech, Wales, where Nancy meets Robert Graves.

1916
Secures a commission to paint murals in the dining room at Folly Farm, Sulhamstead, Berkshire, for Zachary and Rosalie Merton, the latter of whom would become a substantial patron. Moves to a studio on Eaton Square, London. His second son, Tony, is called up to fight at the age of 19.

1917
Moves to Apple Tree Yard in London, a former coach house converted by Lutyens, which would be his home and studio until the end of the war. Elected as a member of the Burlington Fine Arts Club. Ben moves to the USA, because of his health. WN receives a commission to paint the Canadian Headquarters staff, his largest work ever.

1918
Solo exhibition of 23 paintings at the Goupil Gallery. Nancy and Robert Graves marry at the beginning of the year. WN is called up to fight, but is declared unfit for service. Mabel dies suddenly of Spanish influenza in July. A month before Armistice is declared, Tony dies from wounds sustained in action.

1919
His first grandchild, Jenny Nicholson, a source of comfort to him, is born. Spends most of his time in Wales, painting still lifes. In a surprising move, he marries the widowed Edie Stuart Wortley in October, causing his estrangement from Ben, who had become close to her. Travels to France with Edie at the end of the year. *The Owl: A Miscellany*, a short-lived review and joint venture with Robert Graves, is published in May and September.

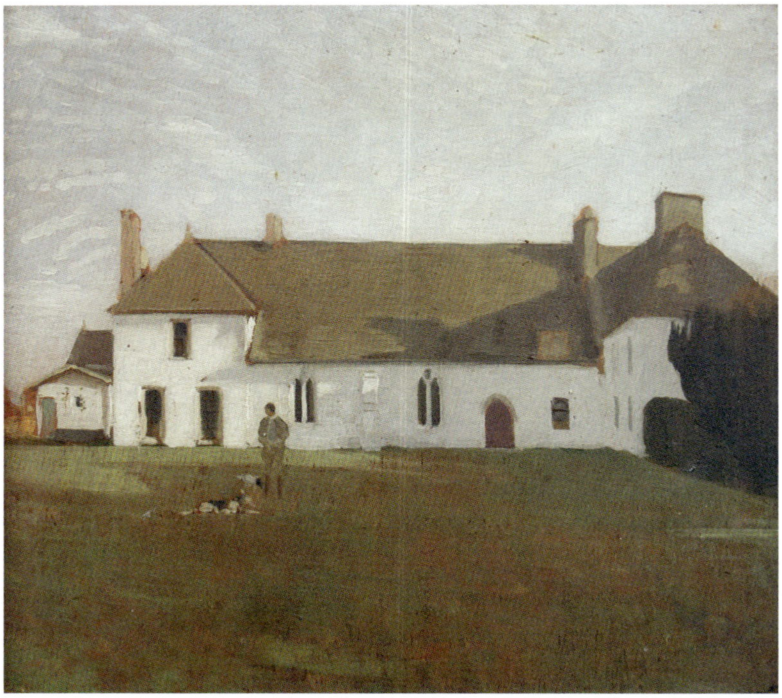

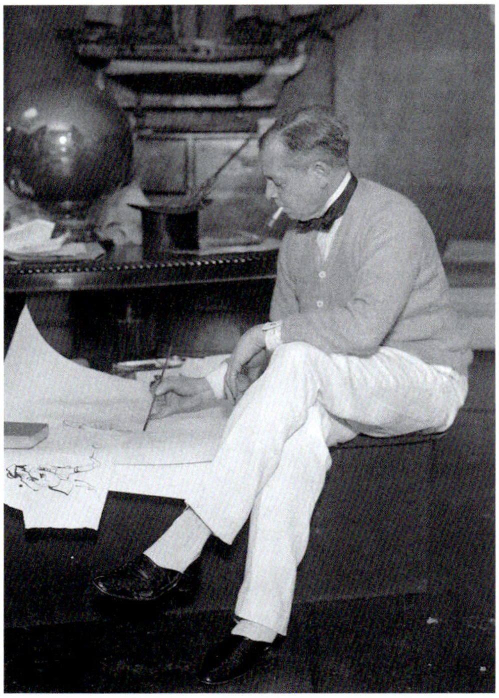

144 *The White House, Sutton Veny (with Kit and Gypsy)*, 1924
Oil on panel, 48 x 53.5cm
Pallant House Gallery
(On loan from a private collection, 2013)

145 ANONYMOUS
William Nicholson, c.1920
National Portrait Gallery, London

1920
Ben and Nancy organise a Mabel Pryde retrospective at the Goupil Gallery. His and Edie's only daughter, Elizabeth, is born in July. They move to North End House in Rottingdean. Secures a commission through Lutyens to paint a portrait of Gertrude Jekyll. Ben marries Winifred Roberts.

1921
Travels with Edie to New York to judge the Carnegie Institute International Art Exhibition in Pittsburgh. Works on illustrations for Margery Williams's *The Velveteen Rabbit* and is invited to provide decorations for Queen Mary's Dolls' House.

1922
Meets Mabel Low, the mother of Diana Low, who would paint a portrait of him, c.1933. Designs the costumes and sets for John Gay's opera *Polly*.

1923
Moves to the White House (originally called the Manor House) in Sutton Veny, Wiltshire. The final issue of *The Owl* is published in November.

1924
Exhibits 21 oil paintings at the Venice Biennale. Reconciles with Ben at Christmas.

1925
In collaboration with Edie, designs costumes for Léonide Massine's ballet *The Rake*, as part of C.B. Cochran's *On with the Dance*, which opens on 30 April. Paints landscapes in Avignon.

1926
Exhibition of 40 paintings at the Seligmann Gallery, New York, which moves on to the Carnegie Institute, Pittsburgh. Works with Edie on costume and set designs for Massine's ballet *The Tub*. Declines an invitation to become a member of the Royal Academy of Arts. Works on decorations for the room to contain Queen Mary's Dolls' House at Windsor Castle (destroyed in 1927). *Clever Bill* is published.

1927
Solo show at the Beaux Arts Gallery, London. Designs costumes and sets for a production of *The Marquise* by Noël Coward. His second child with Edie, William, is born and dies within a month in November.

1928
Works on more portrait commissions than in recent years, including a double portrait of Sidney and Beatrice Webb. Receives a gold medal for his woodcuts in the 'Art Olympics' in Amsterdam. Accompanies Christopher Wood to an art dealer in London in order to promote his work.

1929
Illustrates a new edition of Siegfried Sassoon's *Memoirs of a Fox-Hunting Man*. Solo show at the Beaux Arts Gallery.

1931
Travels to Cape Town, South Africa, to visit Edie's parents; his relationship with Edie is strained. Holidays in Ireland with family and E.Q. Myers, who would marry Kit in December. Ben's marriage to Winifred breaks down, and Ben meets and falls in love with Barbara Hepworth.

1932
Makes several landscapes associated with gliding clubs, following Kit's interest in the sport. His stained glass window in memory of Sir John Horner is presented at St Andrew's church, Mells, Somerset.

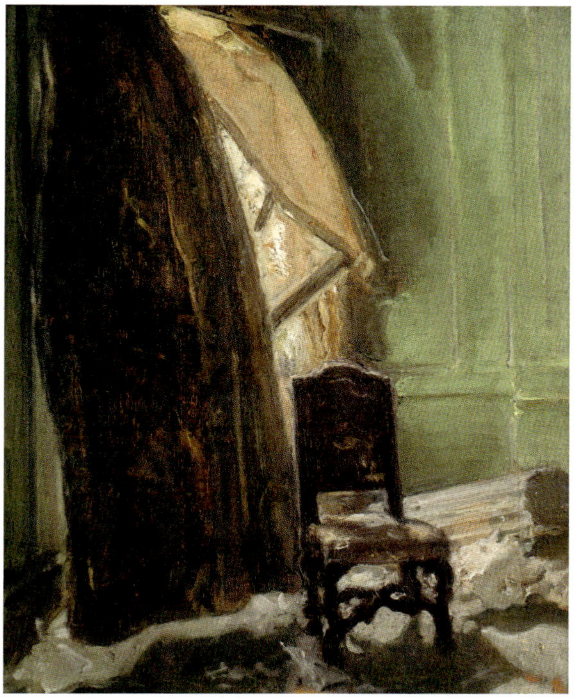

146 *The Legation in the Blitz*, 1941
Oil on canvas, 45 x 36cm
Private collection

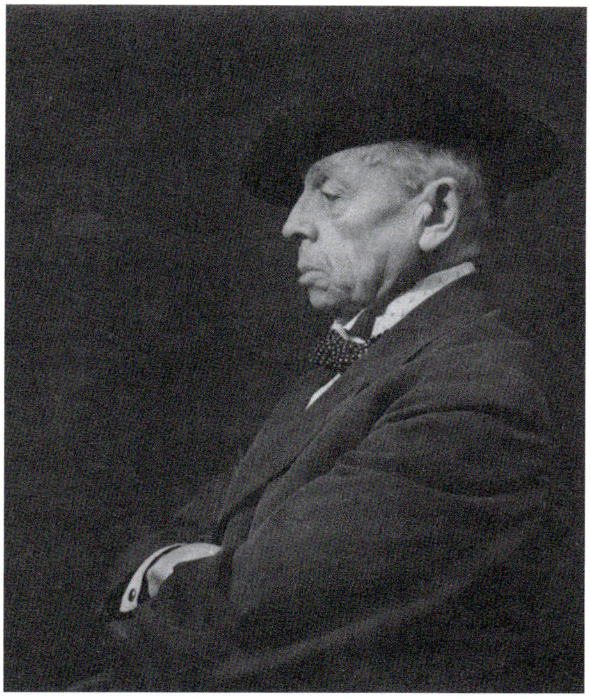

147 A.C. COOPER (1873–1960)
William Nicholson, 1943
National Portrait Gallery, London

1933
Separates from Edie and lives at Apple Tree Yard. Against his wishes, his retrospective at Nottingham Castle opens in March. His largest commercial show to date is held at the Beaux Arts Gallery.

1934
Makes several visits to Chartwell in Kent to give painting lessons to Winston Churchill. Made a Trustee of the Tate Gallery in November. Travels to Spain at the end of the year.

1935
Stays with Peter Chalmers Mitchell in Malaga, where he meets and falls in love with the writer Marguerite Steen.

1936
Receives a knighthood. Solo show at the Leicester Galleries in London. He and Marguerite take a lease on a flat in Hove, East Sussex.

1937
Designs sets for a dramatisation of Steen's novel *Matador*. Makes his first visit to Venice with Steen, where he admires works by Tintoretto. They visit the International Exhibition in Paris on their way back.

1938
Stays in France for much of the year, including sojourns at Toulon and La Rochelle.

1939
Resigns as Trustee of the Tate Gallery. Suffers a stroke whilst staying in La Rochelle and recuperates in Saint-Jean-de-Luz. Joint exhibition with Walter Sickert at the Beaux Arts Gallery. The Second World War is declared in September.

1940
Leaves Apple Tree Yard as the result of a bombing and moves with Steen to Berkshire.

1941
Moves to the Old Rectory, Fenn Ditton, in Cambridge. Works on the dust jacket design for Steen's book *The Sun is My Undoing*.

1942
Joint exhibition with Jack B. Yeats at the National Gallery in London, organised by Lillian Browse. Acts as external examiner for the diploma students at the Royal College of Art in London.

1943
Solo show at the Leicester Galleries. Steen's biography of him is published.

1944–6
In ill health and does little to no painting. Lives in Bruton Street, Mayfair, and later at Little Triton, Blewbury, Berkshire (now Oxfordshire), with Steen.

1947
Arts Council touring exhibition of 47 oil paintings. Stays at the Priory Hospital, Roehampton, London.

1948
Kit dies in a gliding accident in Switzerland. WN leaves the hospital to stay with Steen at Little Triton, Blewbury, until his death.

16 MAY 1949
Dies in Blewbury at the age of 77.

NOTES

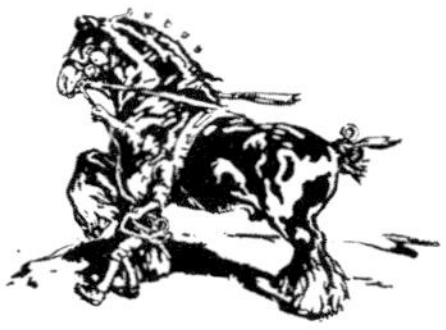

CHAPTER 1

William Nicholson: The Illusionist

Simon Martin

1. William Nicholson (quoting the scientist Michael Faraday's last diary entries) to Harold Sawkins, editor of *The Artist*, 1934; reproduced in Andrew Nicholson (ed.), *William Nicholson, Painter: Paintings, Woodcuts, Writings, Photographs*, Giles de la Mare, London, 1996, p.12.
2. William Nicholson to Harold Sawkins; ibid., p.12.
3. This is not, of course, to directly suggest a correlation with the reading of scopophilia by Sigmund Freud and Jacques Lacan in relation to fetishistic sexuality.
4. Elizabeth Banks, 'A Few Thoughts on Being with My Father, William Nicholson', in Penny Johnson (ed.), *William Nicholson: Landscape and Still Life* (exh. cat.), Towner Art Gallery, Eastbourne, 1995, p.7.
5. Stanley Kennedy North, *William Nicholson*, Contemporary British Artists series, Ernest Benn Ltd, London, 1923, p.9.
6. Unsigned article in *The Times*, March 1967; cited by Sanford Schwartz, *William Nicholson*, Yale University Press for the Paul Mellon Centre, New Haven and London, 2004, p.1.
7. Ibid., p.2.
8. Ibid., p.31.
9. *The Daily Telegraph*, 29 June 1903; cited ibid., p.22.
10. Winifred Nicholson, 'Yellow Ochre – William Nicholson', in Nicholson (ed.), *William Nicholson, Painter*, p.221.
11. See Alan Bowness, *Sir William Nicholson* (exh. cat.), Marlborough Fine Art Ltd, London, 1967, p.[8].
12. Bruce Bernard; quoted by Schwartz, *William Nicholson*, p.13.
13. William Nicholson to Alfred Munnings; quoted by Alan Bowness, in Nicholson (ed.), *William Nicholson, Painter*, p.10.
14. Charles Harrison, *English Art and Modernism, 1900–1939*, 1981; paperback 2nd edition, Yale University Press, New Haven and London, 1994, p.24.
15. Nicholson; quoted in Robert Nichols, *William Nicholson*, Penguin Modern Painters series, Penguin, Harmondsworth, Middlesex, 1948, p.5, and Lillian Browse, *William Nicholson, 1872–1940* (exh. cat.), Browse & Darby, London, 1990, n.p.
16. Nicholson had a further daughter, Liza, later known as Elizabeth Banks, with his second wife, Edie Stuart Wortley.
17. Quoted in Schwartz, *William Nicholson*, p.73.
18. Mabel Pryde apparently disliked the title for locating the family in a particular part of London which later came to be associated with the Bloomsbury Group.
19. Ben Nicholson, 'Memoirs: W.N.', *London Magazine*, June 1967.
20. Quoted by Lilian Browse; in Johnson (ed.), *William Nicholson*, p.13.
21. Ben Nicholson; quoted in *The Sunday Times*, 28 April 1963.
22. Ben Nicholson to Marguerite Steen; quoted in Nicholson (ed.), *William Nicholson, Painter*, p.280 [original emphasis].
23. Alan Bowness, foreword to ibid., p.9.
24. Nicholson, *William Nicholson*, p.18.
25. Schwartz, *William Nicholson*, p.11.
26. Dennis Farr, *English Art, 1870–1940*, Oxford University Press, Oxford, 1978, pp.78–9.
27. In his biography, Schwartz (*William Nicholson*, p.142) revealed that Mabel Pryde had an affair with Edward Gordon Craig, which undoubtedly coloured the way William Nicholson subsequently felt about him, although Nicholson later had a long-standing relationship with Marie Laquelle outside of his marriage to Mabel.
28. Edward Gordon Craig, *Woodcuts and Some Words*, J.M. Dent & Sons, London and Toronto, 1924.
29. Quoted in the entry for 'J. & W. Beggarstaff' in Ian Chilvers (ed.), *The Oxford Dictionary of Art and Artists*, Oxford University Press, Oxford, 2009.
30. Sanford Schwartz, 'The Speck in the Distance, or Rethinking William Nicholson', in Colin Campbell, Merlin James and Patricia Reed, *The Art of William Nicholson: British Painter and Printmaker* (exh. cat.), Royal Academy of Arts, London, 2004, p.15.
31. 'Art Notes', *The Art Journal*, 1895, p.351.
32. Frances Spalding, *British Art Since 1900*, Thames & Hudson, London, 1996, p.11.
33. Colin Campbell, *William Nicholson: The Graphic Work*, Barrie & Jenkins, London, 1992, p.59.
34. Spalding, *British Art*, p.11.
35. Nicholson, *William Nicholson*, p.26.
36. James McNeill Whistler, introductory note in the catalogue of the 'Company of the Butterfly' exhibition of Nicholson's work, 1900; quoted in Campbell, *William Nicholson*, p.246.
37. Nicholson; quoted in Nichols, *William Nicholson*, p.11.
38. William Heinemann, prospectus for *An Alphabet*, London, 1898.
39. Nichols, *William Nicholson*, p.6.
40. See ibid.
41. Quoted in Patricia Reed, *William Nicholson: A Catalogue Raisonné of the Oil Paintings*, Yale University Press, New Haven and London, 2011, p.277.
42. Schwartz, *William Nicholson*, p.128.
43. Frederick Wedmore, 'W.N.', *Art Journal*, July 1909.
44. See Schwartz, 'The Speck in the Distance', p.23.

CHAPTER 2

'Certain congruities of dark cloth, the rigid perfection of his linen': The Self-fashioning of an Artist

Stephen Calloway

1. Friedrich Nietzsche, *Also sprach Zarathustra. Ein Buch für Alle und Keinen*, parts 1–3, Ernst Schmeitzner, Chemnitz, 1883–4; part 4, C.G. Naumann, Leipzig, 1891.
2. Julius Meier-Graefe, *Modern Art*, vol.2, William Heinemann, London, 1908, p.259.
3. Ibid.
4. Phil May is depicted in the style of a Nut in a caricature by 'Spy' [Leslie Ward] published in *Vanity Fair*, 21 February 1895.
5. Coachmen's garb had first been adopted and made fashionable in Regency times by the rowdy 'Corinthians'. Their exploits were celebrated in the once highly popular serial novel by Pierce Egan, *Life in London; or, The Day and Night Scenes of Jerry Hawthorn, Esq., and His Elegant Friend, Corinthian Tom, Accompanied by Bob Logic, the Oxonian, in their Rambles and Sprees through the Metropolis*, printed for Sherwood, Neely, and Jones, London, [1821]. For May's caricature portrait, see *The Studio*, vol.5, September 1895, p.214.
6. Will True, 'Posterdom Caricatures, No.1 Beggarstaff Bros.', *The Poster*, August-September 1898, p.111.

7. Quoted in Duncan Robinson, *William Nicholson: Paintings, Drawings & Prints* (exh. cat.), Fitzwilliam Museum, Cambridge, and other locations, and Arts Council of Great Britain, London, 1980, p.38, cat. no.56.
8. Richard Dighton published his caricature portraits of dandies as a series of single figures, culminating with the group image *The Dandy Club* in 1818; they were later reissued in a collected edition, *Characters at the West End of the Town: Drawn and Etched by Richard Dighton*, Thomas M'Lean, London, 1825.
9. Max Beerbohm, 'Dandies and Dandies', *Vanity*, vol.1, no.4, February 1895, pp.48–9; repr. in *The Works of Max Beerbohm*, John Lane, London, 1899, p.5.
10. Formerly in the collection of Barry Humphries, it was sold at Christie's, 13 February 2025, lot 39; present whereabouts unknown.
11. Quoted in Andrew Nicolson (ed.), *William Nicholson, Painter: Paintings, Woodcuts, Writings, Photographs*, Giles de la Mare, London, 1996, p.106.
12. On Nicholson's stay in Paris for the Knoblock commission, see Stephen Calloway, '"A Special Decoration": William Nicholson and Edward Knoblock', *The Journal of the Decorative Arts Society*, no.10, 1986, pp.18–21.
13. Marguerite Steen, *William Nicholson*, Collins, London, 1943, p.116.
14. W[illiam] H[enry] Davies, *Later Days*, Jonathan Cape, London, 1925, p.185; quoted in Sandford Schwartz, *William Nicholson*, Yale University Press for the Paul Mellon Centre, New Haven and London, 2004, p.244.
15. John had wished to paint his friend, but claimed he could not afford to do so speculatively. To solve the problem, Nicholson 'commissioned' the work, but consistently failed to come up with any payment. In 1933, when the Fitzwilliam Museum indicated a wish to buy the picture for £1000, artist and sitter amiably agreed to pocket £500 each. This impressive, full-length seated portrait was considered by John to be the best thing he had done and it stands as a testament to the friendship that developed between these two quite different men.
16. Augustus John, *Chiaroscuro*, Jonathan Cape, London, 1952, p.79.
17. Ibid.
18. Winifred Nicholson's recollection of a discussion one evening at Sutton Veny, Christmas 1926; quoted in Nicholson (ed.), *William Nicholson, Painter*, pp.220–21.
19. Jane Nicholson, later married to the gallerist John Kasmin, was the daughter of Nicholson's youngest son, Kit, and his wife, the painter and textile designer E.Q. Myers. Though only 11 years old at the time of her grandfather's death, Jane would have been entirely familiar with paints and fabrics in her mother's studio.

CHAPTER 3

Nicholson and Portraiture

Patricia Reed

1. Andrew Nicholson (ed.), *William Nicholson, Painter: Paintings, Woodcuts, Writings, Photographs*, Giles de la Mare, London, 1996, p.211.
2. Colin Campbell, *William Nicholson: The Graphic Work*, Barrie & Jenkins, London, 1992, p.59.
3. James McNeill Whistler's introductory note in the catalogue of the 'Company of the Butterfly' exhibition of Nicholson's work, 1900; see ibid., p.246.
4. [Harold Sawkins], 'William Nicholson', *The Artist*, vol.7, June 1934, pp.102–3.
5. Other works with Russell are *The Morris Dancer* (1902; Southampton City Art Gallery) and *Morris Dancers at Blenheim Gate* (1903; Hill-Stead Museum, Farmington, CT).
6. The other painting with Ben is *Hawking* (1902; private collection); see Patricia Reed, *William Nicholson: A Catalogue Raisonné of the Oil Paintings*, Yale University Press, New Haven and London, 2011, pp.76–7, cat. no.43. The paintings with Nancy are *Nancy* (1901; Ca' Pesaro Galleria Internazionale d'Arte Moderna, Venice) and *La Petite Toilette (Dressing Up)* (1903; untraced); for the latter, see ibid., p.85, cat. no.52.
7. Private collection; see ibid., p.95, cat. no.63.
8. Private collection; see ibid., p.100, cat. no.68.
9. Ruth Draper's humorous monologue 'The Portrait Arrives' is illuminating; available on YouTube in *The Italian Lesson* collection: https://www.youtube.com/watch?v=2xxLGoozIsE.
10. For Ursula Lutyens's recollections of sitting to Nicholson, see Nicholson (ed.), *William Nicholson, Painter*, pp.143–5. For her portrait, see Reed, *William Nicholson*, pp.326–7, cat. no.384.
11. *Morning Post*, 20 January 1911, regarding the portrait of *Arthur Essex Edgeworth Reade* (private collection); see ibid., p.201, cat. no.225.
12. William Nicholson to T.W. Bacon, 26 April 1905, T.W. Bacon Archive, The John Rylands University Library, University of Manchester; quoted in ibid., p.100.
13. William Nicholson to T.W. Bacon, 28 June 1907, T.W. Bacon Archive, The John Rylands University Library, University of Manchester; quoted in ibid., p.119. For the double portrait (private collection), see ibid., p.119, cat. no.103.
14. Undated, illustrated draft letter from William Nicholson to Baron Robert de Rothschild, reproduced in Nicholson (ed.), *William Nicholson, Painter*, p.211. The portrait of *Diane de Rothschild* (private collection) was painted from February to November 1922; see Reed, *William Nicholson*, p.389, cat. no.467.
15. Reed, *William Nicholson*, p.172.
16. Ibid., pp.550–1.
17. English Heritage Blue Plaque: 'Princess Seraphine Astafieva 1876–1934 Russian ballet dancer lived and taught here 1916–1934'.
18. B.M. Collin, *J.P. Hornung: A Family Portrait*, privately printed, London, 1970, introduction unpaginated.
19. For a description, see Marguerite Steen, *William Nicholson*, Collins, London, 1943, pp.127–30. The mews have since been rebuilt.
20. Douglas Sladen, *Twenty Years of My Life*, E.P. Dutton, New York, 1913, p.348.
21. William Nicholson to T.W. Bacon, postmarked 1 December 1910, T.W. Bacon Archive, The John Rylands University Library, University of Manchester [original emphasis].
22. Reed, *William Nicholson*, p.368.
23. As recollected by Mrs Elizabeth Banks, the artist's daughter, in conversation with Patricia Reed, 16 June 1990.
24. Reed, *William Nicholson*, p.277.
25. Ibid., pp.545–7.
26. Percy Lubbock (ed.), *The Diary of Arthur Christopher Benson*, Hutchinson, London, 1931, pp.292, 306.
27. *Arthur Christopher Benson*, Fitzwilliam Museum, Cambridge.
28. Generally considered to be the intellectual founders of the welfare state; see their respective entries in the *Oxford Dictionary of National Biography* online. For this period, see also Barbara Caine, *Destined to be Wives: The Sisters of Beatrice Webb*, Clarendon Press, Oxford, 1988, pp.180–4.
29. London School of Economics Archives, Digital PASSFIELD/1/2/8, 31 March 1928, p.456. Beatrice Webb's diaries are fully digitised and available online: https://archives.lse.ac.uk/records/PASSFIELD/1/2.
30. Ibid., 5 May 1928, p.471.
31. Unfortunately, none of these studies has survived, so it is not known whether this is the composition to which Beatrice Webb was referring.
32. London School of Economics Archives, Digital PASSFIELD/1/2/8, 15 June 1928, p.482.
33. Ibid., 28 September 1928, p.533.

CHAPTER 4
William Nicholson and the Theatre
Jane Pritchard

1. Tower Cottage, Winchelsea, East Sussex, was Ellen Terry's home from 1896 to the early 20th century. The Nicholsons stayed there with her in 1901.
2. National Trust, NT 1117140 (*Becket*); Victoria and Albert Museum, London [hereafter V&A], E.1208–1927 (*Don Quixote*), E.65–1943 (*Robespierre*). All theatres referred to in the text are in London.
3. See National Portrait Gallery, London, NPGX7954, or V&A, S.133:146–2007.
4. The design is reproduced in a Sotheby's catalogue for the sale of *Dance, Theatre, Opera, Music Hall and Film*, New York, 21 November 1984, lot 15, or may be seen online at: https://www.williamnicholson.net/theatre.
5. Information given to Jennifer Aylmer by Mary Lutyens on 15 September 1981. She noted that 'all the scenery except the interior of the "Wendy" house' which was by Nicholson' was by her father and that the Darlings' nursery was based on their family nursery. Signed note in V&A, Theatre & Performance Core Collection, Production Files, Duke of York's Theatre, London, 1904. It is possible that both Nicholson and Lutyens were involved. Nicholson may have been inspired by the Lutyens' nursery, which is what Mary Lutyens remembered so vividly. Sanford Schwartz (*William Nicholson*, Yale University Press for the Paul Mellon Centre, New Haven and London, 2004, p.111) claimed that, 'In 1904 Nicholson had created most of the costumes and been involved with the set designs of the first production of *Peter Pan*.' Schwartz also noted (ibid., p.136) that returning to see the production a few seasons after the premiere, '[Nicholson] found that his contribution had been so transformed that he asked Barrie to take his name off the credits.' For the 1911–12 season all credits for designers, except that for the scene painter Walter Hann, disappeared from the programme.
6. Marguerite Steen, *William Nicholson*, Collins, London, 1943, p.98.
7. Amelia Defries and Maria Pitt Chatham, 'Costume at the Lyric Theatre, Hammersmith – II', in Rupert Mason, George Sheringham and R. Boyd Morrison (eds), *Robes of Thespis: Costume Designs by Modern Artists*, Ernest Benn Ltd, London, 1928, p.84.
8. E.3500 to E.3508–1923. These may be viewed in the V&A Prints and Drawings Study Room.
9. G.E Fussell, 'Notes on Décor: On with the Dance: The Borgia Costumes', *Dancing Times*, June 1925, p.1019.
10. Correspondence from Léonide Massine to William Nicholson in the Howard D. Rothschild collection on Ballets Russes of Serge Diaghilev: Manuscripts and Objects, 1908–1969 (MS THR 414.1; https://hollisarchives.lib.harvard.edu/repositories/24/archival_objects/846204), and the Howard D. Rothschild papers (MS Thr 414.3, [269]; https://hollisarchives.lib.harvard.edu/repositories/24/archival_objects/374889), in the Harvard Theatre Collection, Houghton Library, Harvard University, Cambridge, MA.
11. Press quotations are taken from clippings in the C.B. Cochran Scrapbooks, vol.48, V&A, THM/97.
12. Photographs of Nemchinova in costume are reproduced in the *Illustrated Sporting and Dramatic News*, 8 May 1926, p.370, *The Sketch*, 5 May 1926, p.215, and *Dancing Times*, July 1926, p.345.
13. Unidentified review in V&A, Theatre & Performance Core Collection Production Files, Criterion Theatre, London, 1927.

CHAPTER 5
Nicholson and Bringing Stillness to Life
Melanie Vandenbrouck

1. Marguerite Steen, 'Dedicatory', *William Nicholson*, Collins, London, 1943, p.9.
2. Ben Nicholson to Marguerite Steen; quoted in Andrew Nicholson (ed.), *William Nicholson, Painter: Paintings, Woodcuts, Writings, Photographs*, Giles de la Mare, London, 1996, p.280 [original emphasis].
3. Frederick Wedmore, 'Still Life and Mr. William Nicholson', *The Studio*, vol.LXXIV, no.303, June 1918, pp.2–11.
4. Steen, *William Nicholson*, p.63. Given to Nicholson after Henley's death, it became the focus of an untraced still life, *Henley's Hat* (1917), reproduced in Patricia Reed, *William Nicholson: A Catalogue Raisonné of the Oil Paintings*, Yale University Press, New Haven and London, 2011, p.316, cat. no.371.
5. William Nicholson to Lady Jekyll, Gertrude Jekyll's sister-in-law; quoted in Nicholson (ed.), *William Nicholson, Painter*, p.187.
6. See Reed, *William Nicholson*, p.352, cat. no.414.
7. Ibid., p.124, cat. no.109.
8. *Cyclamen* was gifted to the Courtauld Institute of Art in London by the art dealer and Nicholson scholar Lillian Browse in 1982. Upon Browse's death in 2005, Nicholson's jug, which was in her possession, was also gifted by her executors, together with three paintbrushes Nicholson kept in it.
9. The alternate title was recently discovered by Patricia Reed; email correspondence with the author, 21 July 2025.
10. Reed, *William Nicholson*, p.189, cat. no.209.
11. Sanford Schwartz (*William Nicholson*, Yale University Press for the Paul Mellon Centre, New Haven and London, 2004, p.158) read the background as a mirror into which painting and artist are reflected, which is unlikely, as it would have also reflected the figure. Around that time, Nicholson was painting on glass.
12. See Reed, *William Nicholson*, p.310, cat. no.363.
13. Nicholson (ed.), *William Nicholson, Painter*, p.15.
14. Winifred Nicholson, 'Yellow Ochre – William Nicholson' [1967], in Andrew Nicholson (ed.), *Unknown Colour: Paintings, Letters, Writings by Winifred Nicholson*, Faber & Faber, London 1987, pp.77, 79.
15. John Russell and Vera Russell, 'The Life and Opinions of an English "Modern": Ben Nicholson in Conversation with John and Vera Russell', *The Sunday Times*, 28 April 1963, p.28. See also more generally Louise Weller, *Ben Nicholson: To the Studio* (exh. cat.), Pallant House Gallery, Chichester, 2021.
16. William Nicholson to his friend and patron Ada Pringle, 23 January 1919, in which he mentioned this 'wonderful artist' from whom he has 'four or five of her silver masterpieces'; quoted in Reed, *William Nicholson*, p.358, cat. no.422.
17. See Reed, *William Nicholson*, p.358, cat. no.422, and p.374, cat. no.446.
18. Anonymous reviewer of the 1911 Goupil Gallery exhibition for *The Morning Post*; quoted in Reed, *William Nicholson*, p.213, cat. no.241.
19. For Jean Siméon Chardin's paintings including pilfering moggies, see *The Ray* (1728; Musée du Louvre, Paris) and *Cat with Ray, Oysters, Cruet and Pot* (c.1728; Burrell Collection, Glasgow).
20. Sanford Schwartz in Colin Campbell, Merlin James and Patricia Reed, *The Art of William Nicholson: British Painter and Printmaker* (exh. cat.), Royal Academy of Arts, London, 2004, p.18; Lynton Norbert, *Ben Nicholson*, Phaidon, London, 1993, p.15.
21. Reed, *William Nicholson*, pp.298–9, cat. no.52; Steen, *William Nicholson*, p.184.
22. William Nicholson to Ben Nicholson in Pasadena, CA, sent from Apple Tree Yard, 20 May 1918, Tate Archive, TGA 8717/1/1/1658 [original emphasis].
23. The dish is illustrated in Nicholson (ed.), *William Nicholson, Painter*, p.174.
24. Ibid., p.191; Stanley Kennedy North,

William Nicholson, Contemporary British Artists series, Ernest Benn Ltd, London, 1923, p.16; Nicholson [1967], in Nicholson (ed.), *Unknown Colour*, p.80.

25. Robert Nichols, *William Nicholson*, Penguin Modern Painters series, Penguin, Harmondsworth, Middlesex, 1948, p.8. This notion of pleasure is central to the argument of Luke Farey in 'Pleasure and Table Tops: The Still-life Paintings of William Nicholson, 1900–1920', unpublished MA dissertation, Courtauld Institute of Art, London, 2018.
26. An ever-growing brood of grandchildren and the allowances he paid his children meant that financial worries were never far off, however.
27. See Schwartz, *William Nicholson*, p.196; Reed, *William Nicholson*, p.404.
28. Nicholson [1967], in Nicholson (ed.), *Unknown Colour*, pp.77–80.
29. Reed (*William Nicholson*, p.607, cat. no.812) explained that the title's attribution to 'gold' was most likely the result of correspondence between the artist and the Queen's private secretary, in which the painting is described as a 'picture of a Gold Tankard', at the time when it entered the Royal Collection.
30. Campbell, James and Reed, *The Art of William Nicholson*, p.18; Schwartz, *William Nicholson*, p.234.
31. Nicholson (ed.), *William Nicholson, Painter*, p.282.
32. Nicholson [1967], in Nicholson (ed.), *Unknown Colour*, p.79.
33. Margery Williams, illustrated by Pamela Bianco, 'The Velveteen Rabbit; or, How Toys Become Real', *Harper's Bazar*, June 1921, pp.72–3, 108, 110 [the magazine was *Harper's Bazar* until November 1929, when it became *Harper's Bazaar*].
34. Nicholson (ed.), *William Nicholson, Painter*, p.189.
35. Kennedy North, *William Nicholson*; also quoted in Nicholson (ed.), *William Nicholson, Painter*, p.191.
36. William Nicholson to Ben Nicholson, sent from The Grange, Rottingdean, c. September 1912, Tate Archive, TGA 8717/1/1/1633.
37. Margery Williams, illustrated by William Nicholson, *The Velveteen Rabbit*, William Heinemann, London, 1922, p.3.
38. Ibid.

CHAPTER 6

'Harmony of eye and hand and surroundings': William Nicholson's Landscapes and Townscapes*

Miriam O'Connor Perks

* The quotation in the essay title is from Winifred Nicholson, 'Yellow Ochre – William Nicholson' [1967], in Andrew Nicholson (ed.), *Unknown Colour: Paintings, Letters, Writings by Winifred Nicholson*, Faber & Faber, London, 1987, p.77.

1. William Nicholson to Ben Nicholson, signed 'W.N.' with sketches of a windmill on a hill and an eclipse, 25 April 1912, Tate Archive, TGA 8717/1/1/1631.
2. Patricia Reed, *William Nicholson: A Catalogue Raisonné of the Oil Paintings*, Yale University Press, New Haven and London, 2011, p.229, cat. no.261.
3. Marguerite Steen, *William Nicholson*, Collins, London, 1943, pp.121–2.
4. David Peters Corbett, Ysanne Holt and Fiona Russell (eds), *The Geographies of Englishness: Landscape and the National Past, 1880–1940*, Yale University Press, New Haven and London, 2002, p.xiii.
5. Steen, *William Nicholson*, p.64.
6. James McNeill Whistler's introductory note in the catalogue of the 'Company of the Butterfly' exhibition of Nicholson's work, 1900; quoted in Colin Campbell, *William Nicholson: The Graphic Work*, Barrie & Jenkins, London, 1992, p.246.
7. Also known as Climping; residents prefer the spelling Clymping. See 'Introducing Climping', *Sussex Local Magazine*, n.d., https://sussexlocal.net/sussex-local-magazine-distribution-areas/arundel/climping/.
8. Steen, *William Nicholson*, p.110.
9. Miriam O'Connor Perks, 'Sussex Photographed', in Simon Martin et al., *Sussex Landscape: Chalk, Wood and Water*, Pallant House Gallery, Chichester, 2022, p.85.
10. Letter from William Nicholson in *The Artist*, vol.7, 4 June 1934, p.101; quoted in Reed, *William Nicholson*, p.233, cat. no.267.
11. Julia Winckler, *Fabricating Lureland: A History of the Imagination and Memory of Peacehaven, a Speculative Interwar Garden City Development by the Sea*, De Gruyter Oldenburg, Berlin, 2022.
12. Steen, *William Nicholson*, p.70.
13. William Nicholson to Ben Nicholson, featuring sketches of a windmill and a vase of flowers, c. September 1912, Tate Archive, TGA 8717/1/1/1633.
14. 'The Windmill: A Brief History', *Rottingdean Heritage*, n.d., https://www.rottingdeanheritage.org.uk/history-of-the-windmill/.
15. Steen, *William Nicholson*, p.122.
16. William Nicholson, The Manor, Sutton Veny, Warminster, to Herbert Ward, c. July 1923, Tate Archive, TGA 8623/23.
17. Ian McKeever, 'Whistler's Whites: Creating Presence with a Pared Down Palette', *Royal Academy of Arts*, 5 May 2022, https://www.royalacademy.org.uk/article/whistlers-white-paintings-ra-magazine.
18. Reed, *William Nicholson*, p.521, cat. no.670.
19. Ibid., p.507, no.648.
20. In a letter to Winifred Nicholson of August 1967, Ben Nicholson wrote: 'You both enjoyed each other's *painting jokes* – and he learnt a much lighter scale of painting from you (so did Paul Nash)'; quoted in Nicholson (ed.), *Unknown Colour*, p.182 [original emphasis].
21. Ibid., p.79.

BIBLIOGRAPHY

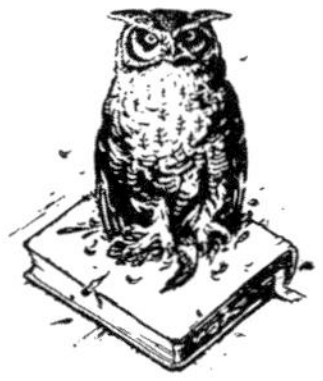

GENERAL WORKS / WORKS ON WILLIAM NICHOLSON

A[lfred] L[ys] Baldry, 'The Paintings of William Nicholson', *The Studio*, 53, June 1909, pp.3–35

Alan Bowness, *Sir William Nicholson* (exh. cat.), Marlborough Fine Art Ltd, London, 1967

Lillian Browse, *William Nicholson*, Rupert Hart-Davis, London, 1956

Lillian Browse, *William Nicholson, 1872–1949: Centenary Exhibition* (exh. cat.), Roland, Browse & Delbanco, London, 1972

Stephen Calloway, '"A Special Decoration": William Nicholson and Edward Knoblock', *The Journal of the Decorative Arts Society*, no.10, 1986, pp.18–21

Colin Campbell, *The Beggarstaff Posters: The Work of James Pryde and William Nicholson*, Barrie & Jenkins, London, 1990

Colin Campbell, *William Nicholson: The Graphic Work*, Barrie & Jenkins, London, 1992

Colin Campbell, Merlin James and Patricia Reed, *The Art of William Nicholson: British Painter and Printmaker* (exh. cat.), Royal Academy of Arts, London, 2004

Kenneth Clark, *Exhibition of Paintings by Sir William Nicholson and Jack B. Yeats* (exh. cat.), National Gallery, London, 1942

Caroline Collier and Julia MacKenzie (eds), *The Dieppe Connection: The Town and Its Artists from Turner to Braque* (exh. cat.), Brighton Museum and Art Gallery, Royal Pavilion, Brighton, and Herbert Press, London, 1992

W[illiam] H[enry] Davies, *Later Days*, Jonathan Cape, London, 1925

Amelia Defries and Maria Pitt Chatham, 'Costume at the Lyric Theatre, Hammersmith – II', in Rupert Mason, George Sheringham and R. Boyd Morrison (eds), *Robes of Thespis: Costume Designs by Modern Artists*, Ernest Benn Ltd, London, 1928, pp.83–9

Luke Farey, 'Pleasure and Table Tops: The Still-life Paintings of William Nicholson, 1900–1920', unpublished MA dissertation, Courtauld Institute of Art, London, 2018

Clement Fothergill Pitman, *William Nicholson: Retrospective Exhibition of Paintings* (exh. cat.), City of Nottingham Museum and Art Gallery, Nottingham Castle, 1933

G.E. Fussell, 'Notes on Décor: On with the Dance: The Borgia Costumes', *Dancing Times*, June 1925, p.1019

Anne Goodchild (ed.), *Dear Winifred: Christopher Wood: Letters to Winifred and Ben Nicholson, 1926–1930*, Sansom & Co., Bristol, 2013

Robert Graves, *Goodbye to All That*, Jonathan Cape, London, 1929; rev. ed., 1957

Charles Harrison, *William and Ben Nicholson: Paintings and Drawings, 1919–1945* (exh. cat.), Browse & Darby, London, 1983

Philip James, *Sir William Nicholson: Paintings, Woodcuts and Lithographs* (exh. cat.), Arts Council of Great Britain, London, 1947

Augustus John, *Chiaroscuro*, Jonathan Cape, London, 1952

Penny Johnson (ed.), *William Nicholson: Landscape and Still Life* (exh. cat.), Towner Art Gallery, Eastbourne, 1995

Stanley Kennedy North, *William Nicholson*, Contemporary British Artists series, Ernest Benn Ltd, London, 1923

Simon Martin et al., *Sussex Landscape: Chalk, Wood and Water*, Pallant House Gallery, Chichester, 2022

Simon Martin et al., *The Shape of Things: Still Life in Britain* (exh. cat.), Pallant House Gallery, Chichester, 2024

Julius Meier-Graefe, *Modern Art*, vol.2, William Heinemann, London, 1908

Robert Nichols, *William Nicholson*, Penguin Modern Painters series, Penguin, Harmondsworth, Middlesex, 1948

Andrew Nicholson (ed.), *Unknown Colour: Paintings, Letters, Writings by Winifred Nicholson*, Faber & Faber, London, 1987

Andrew Nicholson (ed.), *William Nicholson, Painter: Paintings, Woodcuts, Writings, Photographs*, Giles de la Mare, London, 1996

Ben Nicholson, 'Memoirs: William Nicholson', *The London Magazine*, June 1967, pp.69–75

William Nicholson (1872–1949): A Particular Painter (exh. cat.), Browse & Darby, London, 2011

William Nicholson: Paintings (exh. cat.), Paul Kasmin Gallery, New York, 2006

David Peters Corbett, Ysanne Holt and Fiona Russell (eds), *The Geographies of Englishness: Landscape and the National Past, 1880–1940*, Yale University Press, New Haven and London, 2002

Patricia Reed, *William Nicholson: A Catalogue Raisonné of the Oil Paintings*, Yale University Press, New Haven and London, 2011

Duncan Robinson, *William Nicholson: Paintings, Drawings & Prints* (exh. cat.), Fitzwilliam Museum, Cambridge, and other locations, and Arts Council of Great Britain, London, 1980

Sanford Schwartz, *William Nicholson*, Yale University Press for the Paul Mellon Centre, New Haven and London, 2004

Marguerite Steen, *William Nicholson*, Collins, London, 1943

Marguerite Steen, *Looking Glass: An Autobiography*, Longmans, Green & Co. Ltd, London, 1966

Marguerite Steen, *Pier Glass: More Autobiography*, Longmans, Green & Co. Ltd, London, 1968

The Nicholsons (exh. cat.), Crane Kalman, London, 1983

The Nicholsons: A Story of Four People and Their Designs (exh. cat.), York City Art Gallery, York, 1988

Frederick Wedmore, 'Still Life and Mr. William Nicholson', *The Studio*, LXXIV, no.303, June 1918, pp.2–11

Margery Williams, illustrated by Pamela Bianco, 'The Velveteen Rabbit; or, How Toys Become Real', *Harper's Bazar*, June 1921, pp. 72–3, 108, 110

Julia Winckler, *Fabricating Lureland: A History of the Imagination and Memory of Peacehaven, a Speculative Interwar Garden City Development by the Sea*, De Gruyter Oldenburg, Berlin, 2022

SELECTED BOOKS BY AND/OR ILLUSTRATED BY WILLIAM NICHOLSON

W.H. Davies, *The Hour of Magic and Other Poems*, Jonathan Cape, London, 1922

John Gay, *Polly: An Opera*, William Heinemann, London, 1923

Robert Graves, *On English Poetry*, William Heinemann, London, 1922 (cover design)

Robert Graves and William Nicholson (eds), *The Owl: A Miscellany*, no.1, May 1919; no.2, October 1919, both Martin Secker, London; *The Winter Owl*, Cecil Palmer, London, 1923

William Nicholson, *An Alphabet*, William Heinemann, London, 1897 [but dated 1898]

William Nicholson, with 14 quatorzains by W.E. Henley, *London Types*, William Heinemann, London, 1898

William Nicholson, *Twelve Portraits*, William Heinemann, London, 1899; second series, William Heinemann, London, 1902

William Nicholson, *Characters of Romance*, William Heinemann, London, 1900

William Nicholson, *Clever Bill*, William Heinemann, London, 1926

William Nicholson, *The Book of Blokes*, [Faber & Faber, London, 1929]

William Nicholson, *The Pirate Twins*, Faber & Faber, London, [1929]; rev. ed. Andrew Jones Art, London, 2005

William Nicholson and Rudyard Kipling, *An Almanac of Twelve Sports*, William Heinemann, London, 1897 [but dated 1898]

William Nicholson and Arthur Waugh, *The Square Book of Animals*, William Heinemann, London, 1899 [but dated 1900]

Siegfried Sassoon, *Memoirs of a Fox-Hunting Man*, Faber & Faber, London, 1929

David Dwight Wells, *Her Ladyship's Elephant*, William Heinemann, London, 1898 (cover design)

Margery Williams, *The Velveteen Rabbit*, William Heinemann, London, 1922

IMAGE CREDITS

The vignettes used throughout this book and the design of the endpapers are from: *The Hour of Magic and Other Poems* by W.H. Davies, Jonathan Cape, London, 1922, private collection; and *Memoirs of a Fox-Hunting Man* by Siegfried Sassoon, Faber and Gwyer, London, 1929, private collection.

p.122 © Arts Council Collection, Southbank Centre, London; pp.63, 96, 97 © Jonathan Banks; p.138 Image courtesy of Bonhams; pp.121, 147, 153, bottom 158 photographs by Trevor Burrows for Pallant House Gallery; pp.39, 116, 117 © Christie's Images, Ltd; pp.43, 102, 103 © The Courtauld, London (Samuel Courtauld Trust); pp.6, 10 Images courtesy of Daniel Katz Gallery; p.80 Image courtesy of The Fine Art Society; pp.45, 61 © The Fitzwilliam Museum, University of Cambridge; front cover, pp.110, 115, 151 Images courtesy of Hazlitt Holland-Hibbert; pp. top 37, 38, 42, 68, 72, 156 photographs by Tim Higgins for Pallant House Gallery; pp.27, 40 photographs by Barney Hindle for Pallant House Gallery; pp.65, 114 photographs by Keiko Ikeuchi for Pallant House Gallery; p.73 © ING UK Art Collection; p.159 Image courtesy of Jenna Burlingham Gallery; p.120 © Leeds Museums and Galleries, UK/Bridgeman Images; p.13 photograph by Colin Mills; p.77 © London School of Economics and Political Science; p.33 © Modern Art Press; pp.35, 50, 57, 79, 100 © National Galleries of Scotland; pp.12, 31, 78 © National Portrait Gallery, London; pp.34, bottom 37, 66, 105 © Nottingham City Museums & Galleries/Bridgeman Images; back cover, p.41 Images courtesy of Osborne Samuel Gallery, London; pp.44, 87, 123, top 158, 160, 162 © Pallant House Gallery; pp.124, 141, 150 Images courtesy of Patrick Bourne & Co.; pp.81, 152 Images courtesy of Piano Nobile, London; pp.2, 18–20, 22–4, 26, 46–9, 55, 56, 63, 70, 82, 86, 90–98, 112, 113, 118, 128–35, 145, 149, 155, 163 photographs by Justin Piperger for Pallant House Gallery; p.125 © Private collection/Bridgeman Images; pp.69, 119 Images courtesy of Richard Green Gallery, London; pp.71, 136, 143 photographs by Simon Roberts for Pallant House Gallery; pp.8, 126 © Royal Collection Enterprises Limited 2025 | Royal Collection Trust; pp.148, 157 © Southampton City Art Gallery; pp.28, 30, 104, 107, 127 © photo: Tate; p.142 © Towner Eastbourne; pp.84, 85, 91 © Victoria and Albert Museum, London; p.64 © Wolverhampton Art Gallery, © Estate of Diana Low

LIST OF EXHIBITED WORKS

HESTER BATEMAN (1709–1794)
Tea caddy, c.1780, belonging to
William Nicholson
Silver, 15cm high
Private collection

J. & W. BEGGARSTAFF
Hamlet, 1894
Stencil on brown paper, 180 x 75cm
Victoria and Albert Museum, London

BRITISH, 19TH CENTURY
Staffordshire jug, c.1860, belonging to
William Nicholson
Ceramic, 16 x 13.5cm
The Courtauld, London (Samuel
Courtauld Trust)

IVAN WILKIE BROOKS (?) (1891–1952)
William Nicholson and Ben Nicholson, c.1916
Ink and wash on paper, 30.8 x 20.3cm
Lent by the National Portrait Gallery, London.
Given by an anonymous donor, 1996

ELIZABETH DRURY [EDIE NICHOLSON]
(1890–1958)
William Nicholson, 1921
Oil on board, 46 x 37.5cm
Private collection

WILLIAM NICHOLSON (1872–1949)
The Family Home, c.1887
Oil on canvas, 19.5 x 25.5cm
Pallant House Gallery
(On loan from a private collection, 2013)

Lady in Yellow, 1893
Oil on canvas, 72.5 x 62cm
Private collection

An Alphabet, 1897
Hand-coloured woodcuts
on paper, 24.6 x 19.8cm each
UK Government Art Collection

Bookplate for William Heinemann, 1897
Woodcut on paper, 7 x 7cm
Private collection

James McNeill Whistler, 1897
Lithograph on paper from the
original woodblock, 24.5 x 22.5cm
Pallant House Gallery
(Muriel Wilson Bequest, 2019)

Cover design for *Her Ladyship's Elephant* by
David Dwight Wells, William Heinemann,
London, 1898
Book, 19.7 x 12.7cm
Private collection

London Types, 1898
Colour woodcuts on paper, 25.5 x 23cm each
Private collection

H.M. The Queen
From *Twelve Portraits*, William Heinemann,
London, 1899
Colour woodcut on paper, 24.2 x 23cm
Private collection

Rudyard Kipling
From *Twelve Portraits*, William Heinemann,
London, 1899
Colour woodcut on paper, 24.2 x 23cm
Private collection

Sarah Bernhardt
From *Twelve Portraits*, William Heinemann,
London, 1899
Colour woodcut on paper, 24.2 x 23cm
Private collection

Sir Henry Irving
From *Twelve Portraits*, William Heinemann,
London, 1899
Colour woodcut on paper, 24.2 x 23cm
Private collection

W.E. [William Ewart] *Gladstone*
From *Twelve Portraits*, William Heinemann,
London, 1899
Colour woodcut on paper, 24.2 x 23cm
Private collection

William Nicholson and Arthur Waugh,
The Square Book of Animals, William
Heinemann, London, 1899 [but dated 1900]
Book, 28 x 29cm
Private collection

Woodblock for *Cockerel*
From William Nicholson and Arthur
Waugh, *The Square Book of Animals*, William
Heinemann, London, 1899 [but dated 1900]
Woodblock, 12.5 x 12.5cm
Private collection

Bookplate for William Ernest Henley, 1900
Woodcut on paper, 7.5 x 7.5cm
Private collection

*Ben Nicholson as a Child of Six or
Seven Years*, 1901
Oil on canvas, 89 x 71.3cm
Private collection

Edward Russell Dancing the Morris, 1901
Oil on canvas, 52 x 24.3cm
ING UK Art Collection

Portrait of a Man of Letters: W.E. Henley, 1901
Oil on canvas, 37.5 x 29.8cm
Tate: Bequeathed by Mrs W.E. Henley 1925

Rosy of Winchelsea, 1901
Oil on panel, 26.5 x 20.5cm
Estate of Mirabel Cecil

*Chairing the Feathers: The Eynsham Morris at
the Gates of Blenheim Palace*, 1902
Oil on canvas, 114 x 92cm
English Folk Dance and Song Society

La Petite Marchande (The Little Shopkeeper), 1902
Oil on canvas, 114.5 x 90cm
Estate of Mirabel Cecil

Portrait of Nancy Nicholson beside a Table, 1902
Pencil and ink on paper, 30.5 x 21.6cm
Estate of Mirabel Cecil

Sir Max Beerbohm, c.1902
Oil on canvas, 51 x 42.5cm
Lent by the National Portrait Gallery, London.
Bequeathed by Gertrude Kinnell (née Cass), 1953

Sir James Matthew Barrie, 1904
Oil on canvas, 58.4 x 52.7cm
National Galleries of Scotland.
Purchased with Art Fund support 1943

Ellen Terry Jubilee scroll, 1906
Lithograph on paper, 16.2 x 149.5cm
Private collection

Near Littlehampton, 1906
Oil on canvas board, 26.5 x 32.5cm
Private collection, courtesy
Patrick Bourne & Co.

The Convex Mirror, 1907
Watercolour on paper, 34 x 28cm
Nottingham City Museums and Galleries (Nottingham Castle)

The Lustre Bowl, 1908
Oil on canvas board, 27.7 x 33cm
Jonathan W Anderson

Mending the Nets, Rottingdean, 1909
Oil on canvas board, 33 x 40.5cm
Private collection

Still Life: Pink Lustre Mug and Fan, 1909
Oil on canvas laid on panel, 30.5 x 25.5cm
Jonathan W Anderson

A Young Nobleman Surveys the City, 1910
Oil on canvas board, 34 x 27.6cm
Private collection

Cliffs at Rottingdean, 1910
Oil on canvas, 33 x 41.5cm
Southampton City Art Gallery

Nancy in a Feather Hat (The Artist's Daughter), 1910
Oil on canvas, 75 x 62.2cm
Richard Green Gallery, London

The Grey Shawl, 1910
Oil on canvas, 90 x 70cm
Private collection, courtesy Piano Nobile, London

The Ruby Glass, 1910
Oil on canvas board, 26.3 x 23cm
Private collection

The Windmill, Brighton Downs (Brighton Downs, Rottingdean), 1910
Oil on canvas, 33 x 40.6cm
Nottingham City Museums and Galleries (Nottingham Castle)

The Lowestoft Bowl, 1911
Oil on canvas, 47.6 x 61cm
Tate: Presented by the Contemporary Art Society 1917

The Lustre Bowl with Green Peas, 1911
Oil on canvas, 55 x 60cm
National Galleries of Scotland. Bequeathed by Sir Alexander Maitland with life interest to Colonel Peter Dunphie. Presented by Colonel Dunphie 1997

Cliffs at Rottingdean, c.1911
Oil on canvas board, 32 x 39.5cm
Private collection

Judd's Farm, 1912
Oil on panel, 33 x 41cm
Towner Eastbourne. Acquired with the assistance of the MGC/V&A Purchase Grant Fund, National Art Collections Fund and the Friends of the Towner

Sunset, 1912
Oil on canvas, 53.5 x 58.5cm
Private collection

The Vale of Health, Hampstead, 1912
Oil on canvas, 60.5 x 55cm
Estate of Mirabel Cecil

Jennie as Infanta, 1913
Oil on canvas, 58.5 x 55cm
Eric and Rosayn Anderson, courtesy The Fine Art Society

Miss Wish Wynne, Actress, in the Character of Janet Cannot for the Play The Great Adventure, 1913
Oil on canvas, 59.1 x 54.3cm
Nottingham City Museums and Galleries (Nottingham Castle)

Sybil Hart-Davis, 1913
Oil on canvas, 86.5 x 63.5cm
Private collection

Studio Still Life, 1914
Oil on canvas, 131.4 x 162.6cm
Tate: Bequeathed by Edward Knoblock 1945

Bombay Landscape, 1915
Oil on canvas board, 35.5 x 59.5cm
Private collection

The Viceroy's Orderly (Duffadar Valayat Shah), 1915
Oil on canvas, 198.1 x 99.1cm
Nottingham City Museums and Galleries (Nottingham Castle)

A View of the Shop from Chelsea, 1916
Ink on paper, 47 x 29cm
Private collection

A Soldier of the 1914–18 War, 1917
Oil on canvas, 89 x 85cm
Private collection

The Brass Canister, 1917
Oil on canvas board, 33 x 40.6cm
Private collection, courtesy Patrick Bourne & Co.

The End of War, 1917
Lithograph on paper, 43 x 58cm
Pallant House Gallery (Purchased 2024)

Armistice Night, 1918
Oil on canvas, 54 x 59.1cm
The Fitzwilliam Museum, University of Cambridge

Edie Nicholson's dress, 1918
Ink on glazed cotton with blue silk trim
Private collection

Lady in Grey, 1918
Oil on canvas laid on board, 100.5 x 66.5cm
Private collection, courtesy Osborne Samuel Gallery, London

Landscape at Harlech, 1919
Oil on canvas board, 33 x 40.5cm
Private collection, courtesy Patrick Bourne & Co.

Cover design for *The Owl: A Miscellany*, no.1, edited by Robert Graves and William Nicholson, Martin Secker, London, May 1919
Journal, 32 x 26cm
Private collection

The Silver Casket, 1919
Oil on canvas, 33 x 40.5cm
Private collection

Gertrude Jekyll, 1920
Oil on canvas, 76.5 x 77.5cm
Lent by the National Portrait Gallery, London. Given by wish of Sir Edwin Lutyens, 1947

Miss Jekyll's Gardening Boots, 1920
Oil on wood, 32.4 x 40cm
Tate: Presented by Lady Emily Lutyens 1944

Rose Lustre, 1920
Oil on panel, 27.5 x 33cm
Private collection, courtesy Hazlitt Holland-Hibbert

The Silver Casket and Red Leather Box, 1920
Oil on panel, 33 x 40.5cm
Private collection

Sport on the SS Cedric, 1921
Oil on canvas board, 58.5 x 40.5cm
Estate of Mirabel Cecil

Costume design of a pirate for *Polly* by John Gay, 1922
Watercolour on paper, 25.5 x 15cm
Pallant House Gallery (On loan from a private collection, 2013)

Cover design for *On English Poetry* by Robert Graves, William Heinemann, London, 1922
Book, 20 x 13cm
Private collection

Cover design and illustrations for Margery Williams, *The Velveteen Rabbit*, first edition, William Heinemann, London, 1922, inscribed by William Nicholson: *For Penny Nicholson from The Velveteen Rabbit and from Father who drew him*, 1922
Book, 24 x 19cm
Private collection

Anxious Times
Study for Margery Williams, *The Velveteen Rabbit*, William Heinemann, London, 1922
Pen, ink, watercolour and crayon on paper, 21.5 x 17cm
Private collection

At Last, At Last!
Study for Margery Williams, *The Velveteen Rabbit*, William Heinemann, London, 1922
Pen, ink, watercolour and crayon on paper, 24 x 34.5cm
Private collection

Christmas Morning
Study for Margery Williams, *The Velveteen Rabbit*, William Heinemann, London, 1922
Pen, ink and watercolour on paper, 24.5 x 18.5cm
Private collection

Spring Time
Study for Margery Williams, *The Velveteen Rabbit*, William Heinemann, London, 1922
Pen, ink and watercolour on paper, 21 x 16.5cm
Private collection

The Fairy Flower
Study for Margery Williams, *The Velveteen Rabbit*, William Heinemann, London, 1922
Pen, ink and watercolour on paper, 21.5 x 17cm
Private collection

The Skin Horse Tells His Story
Printer's proof of Margery Williams, *The Velveteen Rabbit*, William Heinemann, London, 1922
Lithograph on paper, 25 x 39cm
Private collection

Endpapers
Printer's proof of Margery Williams, *The Velveteen Rabbit*, William Heinemann, London, 1922
Lithograph on paper, 25 x 39cm
Private collection

Designs for *The Hour of Magic and Other Poems* by W.H. Davies, Jonathan Cape, London, 1922
Book, 23 x 15cm
Private collection

Illustration of 'Mrs Trapes' for *Polly* by John Gay, William Heinemann, London, 1923
Colour plate, 26.7 x 20.3cm
Private collection

Cover design for *The Winter Owl*, edited by Robert Graves and William Nicholson, Cecil Palmer, London, 1923
Journal, 32 x 26cm
Private collection

Angel Fish, c.1923
Blueprint on paper, 18.7 x 26.7cm
Pallant House Gallery
(On loan from a private collection, 2013)

Horseshoe Crab, c.1923
Blueprint on paper, 19.2 x 27cm
Pallant House Gallery
(On loan from a private collection, 2013)

Octopus, c.1923
Blueprint on paper, 19.5 x 26.8cm
Pallant House Gallery
(On loan from a private collection, 2013)

Sturgeon, c.1923
Blueprint on paper, 19 x 26.4cm
Pallant House Gallery
(On loan from a private collection, 2013)

The White House, Sutton Veny (with Kit and Gypsy), 1924
Oil on panel, 48 x 53.5cm
Pallant House Gallery
(On loan from a private collection, 2013)

Costume design of 'The Cat' for *The Rake*, 1925
Performed in C.B. Cochran's 1925 revues *On with the Dance* and *Still Dancing*
Pencil and crayon on paper, 25.2 x 19.1cm
Private collection

Costume design of 'The Cock' for *The Rake*, 1925
Performed in C.B. Cochran's 1925 revues *On with the Dance* and *Still Dancing*
Pen and watercolour on paper, 41 x 25cm
Private collection

Costume design of 'The Rake' for *The Rake*, 1925
Performed in C.B. Cochran's 1925 revues *On with the Dance* and *Still Dancing*
Pen and watercolour on paper, 40.8 x 24.8cm
Private collection

La Place des Papes, Avignon (Le Château, Avignon), 1925
Oil on canvas board, 43 x 35.5cm
Private collection

Clever Bill, first edition, William Heinemann, London, 1926
Book, 18 x 25cm
Private collection

Clever Bill, 1926
Poster, 58 x 43.5cm
Private collection

Ten sheet designs for *Clever Bill*, 1926
Ink and wash on paper, 14 x 22cm each
Private collection

Costume design of 'Esteban' for *The Marquise* by Noël Coward, 1927
Pen and watercolour on paper, 40.8 x 24.8cm
Private collection

Costume design of 'The Marquise' for *The Marquise* by Noël Coward, 1927
Pen and watercolour on paper, 40.8 x 24.8cm
Private collection

Snow in the Horseshoe, 1927
Oil on canvas board, 32.5 x 40cm
Private collection, courtesy Hazlitt Holland-Hibbert

Sidney and Beatrice Webb, 1928
Oil on canvas, 134.5 x 174cm
London School of Economics and Political Science

Cover design for *Memoirs of a Fox-Hunting Man* by Siegfried Sassoon, Faber and Gwyer, London, 1929
Book, 23 x 16cm
Private collection

Flowers and Books (for Siegfried Sassoon), 1929
Oil on canvas board, 38 x 25.5cm
Private collection

Mixed Flowers in a Mug, 1929
Oil on canvas, 33 x 40.5cm
Private collection

The Book of Blokes, first edition, [Faber & Faber, London, 1929]
Book, 18.8 x 13cm
Private collection

Glove Letter, c.1920s
Ink and wash on paper, 32 x 23cm
Private collection

The Twelve Days of Christmas (days 1–7), c.1920s
Pen and watercolour on paper, 14 x 22cm each
Private collection

Letterfrack, 1931
Oil on canvas, 33.1 x 41.2cm
Pallant House Gallery
(On loan from a private collection, 2013)

The Helderberg, 1931
Oil on canvas board, 37 x 44.5cm
Private collection, courtesy Piano Nobile, London

The Gliders on the Downs, 1932
Oil on panel, 33 x 40.5cm
Lent by The Savile Club, London

The Picnic, 1932
Oil on canvas board, 33 x 40.5cm
Estate of Mirabel Cecil

Diana Low, 1933
Oil on canvas, 61 x 56cm
Private collection

Poppies in Pewter, 1933
Oil on wood, 41.1 x 32.9cm
National Galleries of Scotland.
Bequeathed by Dr R.A. Lillie 1977

South Harting, c.1933
Oil on canvas, 33 x 41cm
Private collection

Spanish Hills, 1935
Oil on wood panel, 29 x 39.5cm
Pallant House Gallery
(On loan from a private collection)

Sun Fish, 1935
Oil on canvas, 50.8 x 63.5cm
Arts Council Collection, Southbank Centre, London

The Castle, Malaga, 1935
Oil on canvas board, 33 x 41cm
Private collection

Cyclamen, 1936
Oil on panel, 39.3 x 31.1cm
The Courtauld, London (Samuel Courtauld Trust)

A Glade near Midhurst, 1937
Oil on wood, 37.8 x 46cm
Southampton City Art Gallery

Gold Jug, 1937
Oil on canvas board, 40.9 x 32.7cm
Lent by His Majesty The King from the Royal Collection

Waiting for the Heraclea, 1937
Oil on panel, 33 x 40cm
Private collection. On long term loan to The Courtauld Gallery, London

Pears, 1938
Oil on wood, 31.3 x 43.8cm
Leeds Museums and Galleries
(Leeds Art Gallery), UK

Silver, 1938
Oil on wood, 43.8 x 57.1cm
Tate: Purchased 1938

Fish and Sun, c.1938–9
Pencil on paper, 9 x 12.5cm
Private collection

A Game of Pelota, 1939
Oil on canvas board, 33 x 40cm
Private collection

The Legation in the Blitz, 1941
Oil on canvas, 45 x 36cm
Private collection

Still Life on a Table, n.d.
Crayon on paper, 15.2 x 22.9cm
Private collection

WILLIAM NICHOLSON (1872–1949) AND ELIZABETH DRURY [EDIE NICHOLSON] (1890–1958)
Costume design of 'The Husband' for *The Tub*, 1926
Performed in C.B. Cochran's 1926 revue
Pen and watercolour on paper, 28.7 x 17.8cm
Private collection

Costume design of 'The Wife' for *The Tub*, 1926
Performed in C.B. Cochran's 1926 revue
Pen and watercolour on paper, 28.8 x 19cm
Private collection

WILLIAM ORPEN (1878–1931)
A Bloomsbury Family, 1907
Oil on canvas, 86.5 x 91.5cm
National Galleries of Scotland. Presented by the Scottish Modern Arts Association 1964

JAMES PRYDE (1866–1941)
Portrait of William Nicholson, 1901
Lithographic reproduction on paper of a hand-coloured woodcut published in *The Studio*, 21 x 14cm
Private collection

MABEL PRYDE NICHOLSON (1871–1918)
Portrait of William Nicholson, 1911
Oil on canvas, 91.5 x 81.5cm
Private collection

ACKNOWLEDGEMENTS

We are grateful to the authors Stephen Calloway, Simon Martin, Miriam O'Connor Perks, Jane Pritchard, Patricia Reed and Melanie Vandenbrouck for their contributions to this book. Trevor Burrows, Tim Higgins, Barney Hindle, Keiko Ikeuchi, Justin Piperger and Simon Roberts shot new photography. This volume was elegantly designed by Adrian Hunt; copy edited, proofread and indexed by Alexandra Pel; and its production managed by Harriet Olsen at Eiderdown Books. We also extend our thanks to Mark Eastment and his colleagues at Yale University Press.

An exhibition of this scope and ambition is dependent on a huge number of individuals, mentioned individually below unless they chose to remain anonymous. We thank all the museums and public collections and their staff who have facilitated loans, the private collectors, and the auction houses and commercial galleries which assisted in locating works. We are also grateful to the Arts Council England Government Indemnity Scheme, which enables us to borrow such valuable works.

The following individuals facilitated loans from public collections (plus many others behind the scenes):
Paula Cooper and Alona Pardo at the Arts Council Collection; Hannah Kauffman, Chloe Le Tissier, Ernst Vegelin van Claerbergen and Barnaby Wright at the Courtauld; Tiffany Hore at the English Folk Dance and Song Society; Ellie Saggers and Luke Syson at the Fitzwilliam Museum, University of Cambridge; Olivia Christophers and Eliza Gluckman at the Government Art Collection; Christine Bradley, David Hopes and Sarah Murray at Leeds Museums and Galleries; Lisa McQuillan at the London School of Economics and Political Science; Jacqueline Austin, Patrick Elliott and Anne Lyden at the National Galleries of Scotland; Rosie Broadley, Claire Greenaway, Michelle Jones, Sarah Moulden and Victoria Siddall at the National Portrait Gallery; Louise Dunning at Nottingham City Museums and Galleries; Tim Knox and Madeleine Whicheloe at The Royal Collection Trust; Benedict Hall, Dan Matthews and Rebecca Moisan at Southampton City Art Gallery; Maria Balshaw, Thomas Kennedy and Olivia Maguire at Tate; Joe Hill and Karen Taylor at Towner Eastbourne and Leona Bowman; Zorian Clayton, Lucy Gray, Tristram Hunt and Valerie Kohler-Regel at the Victoria and Albert Museum, London.

In addition, the following individuals and commercial art galleries who assisted in relation to artworks in the exhibition:
Tom Edwards at Abbott & Holder; John Austin at Austin Desmond; Ingram Reid at Bonhams; Sian Philips at Bridgeman Images; Charles Bradstock at Browse & Darby; Nathan Barker and Jenna Burlingham at Jenna Burlingham Gallery; Samantha Moreno and Alice Murray at Christie's; Tom Davies and Sam Wadham at Daniel Katz Gallery; Emily Walsh at The Fine Art Society; Anna Fleming; James Holland-Hibbert and Olivia Patteson-Knight at Hazlitt Holland-Hibbert; Clara Harrow at ING Bank; Robin Cawdron-Stewart at Offer Waterman; Matthew Bradbury at Osborne Samuel; Robin Start at The Park Gallery; Cordelia Bourne and Patrick Bourne at Patrick Bourne & Co.; Selina Fischer and Robert Travers at Piano Nobile; Patricia Reed; Rachel Boyd Hall and Richard Green at Richard Green Gallery; Julian Malone-Lee at The Savile Club.

The following private collectors, and all other lenders who wish to remain anonymous:
Eric and Rosalyn Anderson; Jonathan W Anderson; The Estate of Mirabel Cecil; The Savile Club, London.

The exhibition was conceived by Director Simon Martin with the help of Curatorial Assistant Zef Ahmed, Curator Miriam O'Connor Perks and Chief Curator Melanie Vandenbrouck. Registrars Eleanor Chant and Paulina Shearing handled all the loans logistics and installation arrangements in all their complexity and variety. Led by Nick Benham, our team of art handlers ensured that the works were installed in the most professional manner. Head of Collections Sarah Norris prepared the collection works for display, while Librarian Jane Holt helped with many reference queries. We are also grateful to Sarah Deere and Sharon Hambly, who worked on the conservation and framing of works; to Jonathan and Jacqueline Gestetner, who funded this work; and to Janet Brough for assisting in checking the condition of all objects upon arrival. David Wynn worked on the exhibition's design. The press, marketing and interpretation for the exhibition were managed by Liv Seater and Pallant House Gallery, with Lauren Hare, Rosanna Hawksley, Yasmin Hyder and Zab Oliver at Rees & Co. We are also grateful to our Development team, Sam East, Reuben Tendler and Tess Viljoen, and to our Chief Operating Officer, Sarah Songhurst. Finally, we thank the wider team of staff and volunteers at Pallant House Gallery for their support during this season of exhibitions.

INDEX

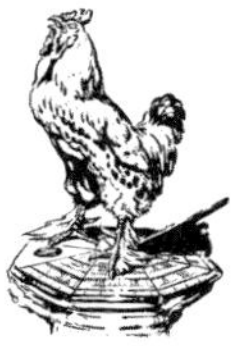

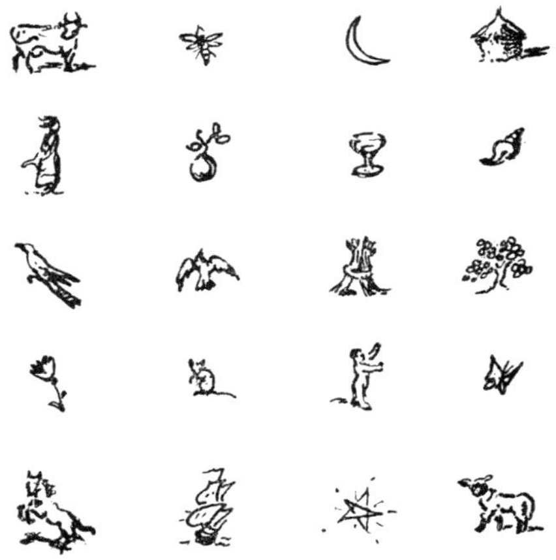

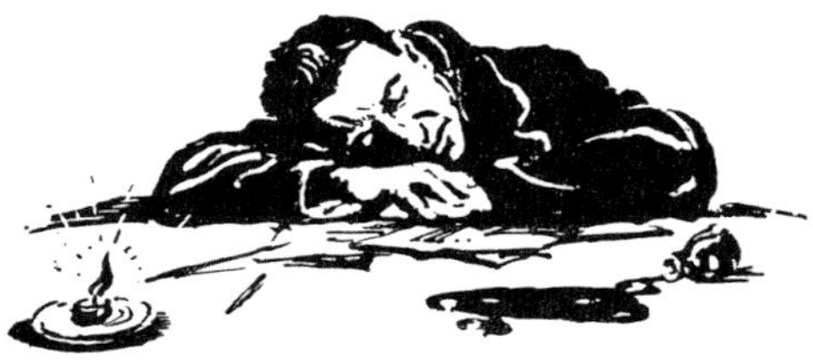